MW00653858

The Mahler Family Letters

Edited, translated, and annotated by Stephen McClatchie

OXFORD
UNIVERSITY PRESS
2006

OXFORD
UNIVERSITY PRESS

Oxford University Press, Inc., publishes works that further
Oxford University's objective of excellence
in research, scholarship, and education.

Oxford New York
Auckland Cape Town Dar es Salaam Hong Kong Karachi
Kuala Lumpur Madrid Melbourne Mexico City Nairobi
New Delhi Shanghai Taipei Toronto

With offices in
Argentina Austria Brazil Chile Czech Republic France Greece
Guatemala Hungary Italy Japan Poland Portugal Singapore
South Korea Switzerland Thailand Turkey Ukraine Vietnam

Published by Oxford University Press, Inc.
198 Madison Avenue, New York, New York 10016

www.oup.com

Library of Congress Cataloging-in-Publication Data
Mahler, Gustav, 1860–1911
[Correspondence. English. Selections]
The Mahler family letters / Stephen McClatchie
p. cm.
Includes index.
ISBN-13 978-0-19-514065-1
ISBN 0-19-514065-6
1. Mahler, Gustav, 1860–1911—Correspondence.
2. Composers—Austria—Correspondence. 3. Mahler family—
Correspondence. I. McClatchie, Stephen, 1965– II. Title.
ML410.M23A413 2005
780'.92'2—dc22 2004021483

3 5 7 9 8 6 4

Printed in the United States of America
on acid-free paper

To
Henry-Louis de La Grange
and
Alfred and Maria Rosé, in memoriam

Preface

In 1983, Mrs. Maria Rosé donated the core of the Mahler-Rosé Collection to the Music Library at the University of Western Ontario in London, Ontario, Canada. In addition to musical manuscripts, memorabilia, and letters to her father-in-law, violinist Arnold Rosé (who was married to Mahler's sister Justine), from leading composers and musicians, the donation included more than 500 unpublished letters from Gustav Mahler to his parents and siblings.[1] The majority of these letters were written before the fall of 1894 and document such things as Mahler's burgeoning career as a conductor and composer, his parents' illnesses and death, and the numerous trials and tribulations of his siblings Alois, Justine, Otto, and Emma. In the fall of 1894, the character of the letters changes when Justine and Emma begin living with Mahler in Hamburg and, later, Vienna, thus obviating the need to communicate by letter about quotidian matters. Instead, the later letters are written when Mahler is away from home, conducting his works or otherwise engaged. At this point, then, the coverage becomes markedly less thorough.

Many passages from these letters will not be totally unfamiliar to Mahler scholars. In the 1950s, Henry-Louis de La Grange travelled several times to London, Ontario, to stay with Alfred and Maria Rosé and read the letters. He then paraphrased or used translated excerpts as the basis for his account of Mahler's earliest years and his family relationships. Mahler scholars can only be grateful to the Rosés for their generosity in sharing these documents with him at the time. Nevertheless, when I began to work with the letters, it soon became clear that Rosé had allowed La Grange to see only about half of the letters. It is difficult to determine on what basis—if any—his choices were made, as many of the letters used by La Grange are critical of Justine (who was, of course, Alfred's mother), and many of the letters that Rosé did not show to him are completely innocuous.

In addition to all of the letters in the Mahler-Rosé Collection, this edition includes a number of other family letters. Several letters from Mahler to his parents and sister Justine were sold by Alfred Rosé during his lifetime. In most instances, he kept a photocopy of the letter; in one or two cases, however, I have had to rely on transcriptions made by La Grange. The letters to Emma Mahler were sold by her son Ernst Rosé at auction by Sotheby's in 1984 and are now

1. For an overview of the entire collection, see Stephen McClatchie, "The Gustav Mahler–Alfred Rosé Collection at the University of Western Ontario," *Notes* 52 (December 1995): 385–406.

dispersed. Fortunately, La Grange's transcriptions of these letters are also in the Bibliothèque Musicale Gustav Mahler. Copies of fourteen letters to Mahler from his parents and several of his siblings are found in the typescript of Alma Mahler's memoirs at the University of Pennsylvania. All but one of these letters were first published in translation in *Selected Letters of Gustav Mahler*, and are included here in my own translation with the permission of the University of Pennsylvania;[2] the German edition of this volume is their first publication in the original language. Finally, the Mahler-Rosé Collection contains several unpublished letters from Mahler to close family friends; I have included these in my notes to the family letters. (Admittedly, a number of the family letters are of staggering unimportance—letter 545 particularly comes to mind. As these are, without exception, short and few in number, they have been included in the interest of completeness.)

Mahler seldom dated his letters to his family. Once or twice he went through phases when he dated letters, once even admonishing his sister to always date *her* letters; unfortunately, some of his dates are demonstrably incorrect—even as much as a year off. As few envelopes have survived, a significant challenge has been to establish dates for the letters. Many may be dated on the basis of a performance mentioned in the letters.[3] Occasionally Justine wrote a date across the top of a letter. In such cases, I have indicated this in the annotations and noted whether or not I have followed her suggestion (the reliability of these dates varies greatly). Many letters have dates in pencil by Alfred Rosé. For the most part, I have ignored these, as they are often incorrect. Although many of the letters are mentioned in Henry-Louis de La Grange's monumental biography of Mahler, as already mentioned Alfred Rosé did not show him all of the letters in the 1950s. Consequently, he made some understandable errors in dating the letters that he did use (these errors are generally not noted in my annotations).

When the letters were donated to the University of Western Ontario, they were in twenty-one manila envelopes, likely as they had been stored in the vault of the Bank of Montreal downtown. While the arrangement of the letters was not chronological, there were nevertheless pockets of chronology; at times, this helped me to determine, for example, that a letter belongs to the Budapest years as opposed to the Hamburg years. (The first element of the shelfmark for each letter refers to the envelope, thus E3-MJ-113 is a letter to Justine from the third envelope; the last number is the unique accession number for each item.) I have also examined the paper (type and watermark) used in each letter. In a few

2. *Selected Letters of Gustav Mahler*, the original edition selected by Alma Mahler, enlarged and edited with new introduction, illustrations, and notes by Knud Martner and translated by Eithne Wilkins, Ernst Kaiser, and Bill Hopkins (New York: Farrar Straus Giroux, 1979), pp. 375–84.

3. Information about Mahler's conducting activities is found in Zoltan Roman, *Gustav Mahler and Hungary* (Budapest: Akadémiai Kiadó, 1991); and Bernd Schabbing, *Gustav Mahler als Konzert- und Operndirigent in Hamburg* (Berlin: Ernst Kuhn, 2002); the database of Hofoper rehearsals and performances is found on the Internationale Gustav Mahler Gesellschaft Web site, www.gustav-mahler.org; and also see Knud Martner, *Gustav Mahler im Konzertsaal: Eine Dokumentation seiner Konzerttätigkeit 1870–1911* (Copenhagen: Knud Martner, 1985).

instances, based on the use of a type of paper found only between two years, I have been able to assign a likely date.

In assigning dates to the letters, I have relied on the type of evidence described above, as well as the internal evidence of the letters themselves. I have also read many hundreds of unpublished letters from Mahler in search of references connected to the family letters, often with great success. As a result, there are only a few letters that cannot be dated with reasonable certainty; these undated letters are found at the end of each chapter.

Where possible, the letters have been transcribed from the originals. For those letters not in the Mahler-Rosé Collection, I have made every effort to locate photocopies of the originals. In some instances, as noted above, I have relied on transcriptions made by Henry-Louis de La Grange. The early family letters survive only in Alma Mahler's typescript. These letters have been newly translated in an effort to maintain stylistic conformity (although I did consult the published translation); likewise for the four letters to Justine published in *Gustav Mahler Unbekannte Briefe*.[4] In my translation, I have generally used the titles for works which are most familiar to English-speaking readers, thus *Don Giovanni* instead of *Don Juan*. Mahler frequently uses the Italian expression *Vederemo* (We will see), which I have left untranslated. In this volume, Mahler's emphases have been rendered in italics; words and phrases that he underlines twice are italicized and underlined.

Most of Mahler's frequent enclosures (reviews, letters, etc.) are lost, although some letters that were sent to Justine for her autograph collection do survive in the Mahler-Rosé Collection. In most instances, they are included in the annotations. For individuals mentioned more than once or twice, I have provided brief biographical notes, which may be found in the appendix. To assist the reader, I have prefaced each section with a chronology outlining significant events in the lives of Mahler and his family members; for the most part, these chronologies reflect the events surrounding the letters in this volume (and thus are much less detailed after 1902, when there are many fewer family letters). They are not to be read as an exhaustive chronology of that period of Mahler's life.

One final aspect of the letters is worth mentioning here. While Mahler usually addressed his letters either to his parents or to Justine, he fully expected that they would be read by other family members as well as friends. Thus, one occasionally finds a comment directed specifically to Justine in a letter to his parents, or an aside to Natalie Bauer-Lechner in a letter to Justine.

The letters in the Mahler-Rosé Collection are published with the kind permission of Marina Mahler and the University of Western Ontario Library System. The letters will appear in the original German (and a translation of the rest of this volume) next year with the Weidle Verlag, Bonn. I am grateful to Stefan Weidle and Helmut Brenner for their helpful comments and suggestions, some of which are reflected in this volume. The Social Sciences and Humanities

4. Ed. Herta Blaukopf (Vienna: Paul Zsolnay, 1983).

Research Council of Canada provided support for this project in the form of a Postdoctoral Fellowship (1994–1996) and a Standard Research Grant (1997–2000). For transcription and translation assistance, I am grateful to Astrid Heyer, Bruce Plouffe, and Barbara Reul and to Herta Blaukopf, Rita Steindl, and the late Emmy Hauswirth of the Internationale Gustav Mahler Gesellschaft. Zoltan Roman kindly shared his expertise on matters Hungarian, and Jerry Bruck generously offered copies of two letters to Emma Mahler from his collection. I also wish to thank Mary Beth Payne, formerly of Oxford University Press, and her successor, Kim Robinson, for their support and encouragement.

This project has taken far longer to complete than I could ever have imagined. Five individuals have played particular roles in seeing it through. I wish to thank Henry-Louis de La Grange for his hospitality in Paris during my visit to the Bibliothèque Musicale Gustav Mahler and for so generously sharing material with me. His support has been crucial to this edition, and I am honoured that he has allowed me to dedicate it to him, in part. In Vienna, my friends Morten and Doris Solvik not only put me up on my first visit to the city, they also were very helpful in many other ways—deciphering Austrianisms not being the least of these. Stephen Hefling read the entire manuscript and provided many helpful comments and suggestions; he also generously shared his transcriptions of Mahler's letters to Anna von Mildenburg. Finally, my friend and colleague Lisa Philpott, reference librarian in the Music Library at the University of Western Ontario, answered innumerable questions and made what probably seemed like endless numbers of trips into the Mahler-Rosé Room to check minor details in the collection. Her kindness and unfailing good humour means a lot to me.

And, as always, Peter was there every step of the way.

Contents

Abbreviations

BGA	*Ein Glück ohne Ruh': Die Briefe Gustav Mahlers an Alma*. Edited and annotated by Henry-Louis de La Grange and Günther Weiß. Berlin: Siedler Verlag, 1995.
BWB	Bruno Walter. *Briefe 1894–1962*. Edited by Lotte Walter Lindt. Frankfurt-am-Main: Fischer, 1969.
GMB²	*Gustav Mahler Briefe*. 2d ed. Edited by Herta Blaukopf. Vienna: Paul Zsolnay, 1996. (This is an additional revision of the 1983 expansion and revision of the first edition of GMB, originally published in 1924 by Alma Mahler-Werfel.)
HLG	Henry-Louis de La Grange. *Gustav Mahler: Chronique d'une Vie*. 3 vols. Paris: Fayard, 1979–1984.
HLGE	Henry-Louis de La Grange. *Gustav Mahler*. Oxford and New York: Oxford University Press, 1995–. (This is a revised English translation of HLG. To date, volumes 2 and 3 of a projected four volumes have been issued: *Vienna: The Years of Challenge (1897–1904)* and *Vienna: Triumph and Disillusion (1904–1907)*. I have not used the original English version of volume 1, published by Doubleday in 1979.)
MSB	*Gustav Mahler–Richard Strauss Briefwechsel 1888–1911*. Edited by Herta Blaukopf. Munich: Piper, 1980.
NBL	*Gustav Mahler in den Erinnerungen von Natalie Bauer-Lechner*. Revised and expanded version, edited by Herbert Killian, with notes by Knud Martner. Hamburg: Karl Dieter Wagner, 1984.
Selected Letters	*Selected Letters of Gustav Mahler*. The original edition selected by Alma Mahler, enlarged and edited with new Introduction, Illustrations, and Notes by Knud Martner. Translated by Eithne Wilkins, Ernst Kaiser, and Bill Hopkins. New York: Farrar Straus Giroux, 1979.

The Mahler Family Letters

Introduction
Gustav Mahler and His Family

Gustav Mahler's letters to his family are almost entirely unknown, yet they form the largest and probably most important single source of information about all aspects of his life before the mid-1890s: his personality; his relationships with his family and several close friends; his first positions in Kassel, Prague, Leipzig, Budapest, and Hamburg; and several of his earliest compositions. They also document significant later events such as his campaign to be named director of the Vienna Hofoper,[1] his conducting tours throughout Europe, and his courtship of Alma Schindler. Many of these things will emerge from the letters themselves (or from the annotations), but several elements are worth exploring at the outset, as they do not emerge as clearly from the individual letters, or because the letters themselves do not tell the entire story. First, it will be useful to introduce Mahler's family and provide a brief sketch of each of Mahler's siblings. Second, in addition to the family members, there are several other individuals worthy of commentary with regard to the roles that they played in Mahler's life: his friend Natalie Bauer-Lechner; his lover Anna von Mildenburg; and his wife, Alma. Our understanding of Mahler's relationships with the first and last, in particular, is significantly changed by these letters.

It is largely to Mahler's sister Justine that we owe the survival of more than 500 letters to her, his parents, and several of their siblings. Beginning in the mid-1880s, when she was sixteen or seventeen, Justine carefully preserved his letters to her, as well as other letters that came into her possession. None of Mahler's earlier letters to his family have survived.

By this time, only six of Bernhard and Marie Mahler's fourteen children were still living: Leopoldine, Gustav, Alois, Justine, Otto, and Emma. Both Bernhard and Marie were often unwell, and many of the first letters concern visits to doctors and suggested treatments. Bernhard seems to have suffered from a heart ailment, from which he eventually died on 18 February 1889. Marie, while doubtless also worn out by the rigours of childbearing, had asthma. She died on 11 October 1889, predeceased by her eldest surviving daughter, Leopoldine (b. 1863), on 27 September. Gustav's earliest surviving letter to his parents concerns his surprise about Leopoldine's engagement to businessman Ludwig

1. For a discussion of this, see Stephen McClatchie, "Gustav Mahler's Vienna Campaign: Unpublished Letters from the Gustav Mahler–Alfred Rosé Collection," *Studies in Music from the University of Western Ontario*, forthcoming.

Quittner (letter 5), with whom she subsequently had two children. In August 1889, Leopoldine fell ill with severe headaches, which Gustav mistakenly suggested were related to her nerves (letter 82) but which probably were manifesting a brain tumour.

After his mother's death, Gustav sent Emma to Vienna to join Otto (a student at the Conservatory) with their friends Friedrich and Uda Löhr, and had Justine come to him in Budapest. Toward the end of 1889, he described the family situation in a letter to his former director in Leipzig, Max Staegemann:

> A younger sister and brother I am having educated in Vienna, and another [brother] (somewhat older) is now in the military. My [other] sister is very ailing. She literally destroyed her nerves through the terrible physical exertions at my parents' sickbeds and all the violent emotions associated with it.[2]

After her brother, Justine (1868–1938) is the dominant presence in this volume. In an unpublished passage from her memoirs, family friend Natalie Bauer-Lechner describes Justine's character in terms amply confirmed by the family letters:

> Justi, who looked after the Mahler siblings and household, at once won all of my interest and sympathy. She was not equal to the office that fell upon her so early—she herself first needed the guidance and education that she and the others (there were 13 [*sic*] children in all) had *never* had the benefit of, owing to the poorest and most neglected economic circumstances out of which they came. Her very weakened health (which Justi had acquired from three years of devoted care for her seriously ill parents)—her youth, and her (Gustav-like) impetuous, passionate, and far-from systematic [*pädagogisches*] nature did not make her well suited as a mentor for Otto and Emma.[3]

She did indeed have to assume many responsibilities at an early age: first, caring for her ill parents, and then assuming primary responsibility for her younger siblings, Otto and Emma. Undoubtedly, she had lots to learn about managing money and running a household and not infrequently chafed in her quasi-maternal role, but Alma Mahler's portrayal of her in *Erinnerungen und Briefe* as duplicitous and scatter-brained is both unfair and exaggerated.[4] Much later, however, Justine herself recognised how much she had been educated by Gustav (see letter 510). The passage from Natalie's memoirs quoted above concludes with a description of Mahler's siblings' education—or lack thereof:

> A fanatical Catholic governess for Emma, who came to her from God knows where, and the supervision and instruction provided for by the

2. Erich H. Mueller von Asow, "Ein ungedruckter Brief Mahlers," *Österreichische Musikzeitschrift* 12 (1957): 63–64.

3. "Mahleriana," Bibliothèque Musicale Gustav Mahler.

4. Alma Mahler, *Gustav Mahler: Memories and Letters*, 4th ed., trans. Basil Creighton, ed. Donald Mitchell and Knud Martner (London: Cardinal, 1990), pp. 9–14, 36, 55–56, 143–44.

> good Löhrs (who lived in the same house and to whom G. had attached the siblings) did not improve the confusion: since, on the one hand, without absolute authority nothing could be done at all, and on the other, Löhr's idealism, and the impracticality . . . of this good and admirable man, was yet another misfortune for our wild Mahler pack—for whom only the most practical, realistic, and often even the most brutal treatment would have been suitable. Everything possible in terms of unusual and expensive instruction was undertaken, but showed no results. Otto neither completed secondary school [*Gymnasium*] nor did he finish the Conservatory, as outstandingly musically talented as he was. Indeed, he couldn't manage the preparation for the one-year voluntary recruit examination (which any idiot can do) [even] with the most expensive teachers, which G. engaged for him! The same went for the girls, as a supplement of their defective Iglau education: a lot was begun, without ever leading to anything.

Although Mahler initially intended to move his family to Budapest with him in late 1889, in the end, Justine, Otto, and Emma rented an apartment in Vienna on the Breitegasse—a fact for which posterity can only be grateful, as it necessitated regular communication by letter on Mahler's part. Throughout the Budapest and early Hamburg years, Mahler wrote Justine hundreds of times during the operatic season; during the summers, however, they were generally together, unless Mahler was off on a bicycling or walking tour, or other solitary trip. In the autumn of 1894, however, Justine and Emma moved to Hamburg and the character of the letters changed. Justine continued to keep house for her brother in Hamburg and then Vienna until they both married in March 1902.

Justine's conversion to Christianity illustrates her closeness to her brother. In early December 1896, she wrote to her friend Ernestine Löhr:[5]

> We are all still taking instruction, and yesterday the priest said that we'll probably be finished by the middle of February. Emma and I are doing it only to make the matter easier for Gustav; it relates to the position at the Vienna Opera (secret). . . . The first priest asked why we were doing it; I didn't have the heart to tell him that it was out of conviction, and he didn't seem to have any great desire [to do it], so I went to another one—coincidentally an Austrian, very liberal, and such a nice fellow that we have invited him to dine next week. The whole business seems as if I were acting in the theatre, since I do not believe a word and could

5. Ernestine Löhr (1863–1942?) was the sister of Mahler's close friend Friedrich; in fact, the Mahlers were close to the entire family (see appendix). The Mahler-Rosé Collection contains typewritten copies of seventy-six letters from Justine to Ernestine written between April 1893 and July 1900 (a copy of one additional letter is in the Bibliothèque Musicale Gustav Mahler). It is unclear when these copies were made, although since they have what appears to be Justine's handwriting on them, it must have been before her death in August 1938. As these letters come largely from the period after September 1895 when the family correspondence is less informative about personal matters, they provide invaluable context for, and illumination of, the family letters.

immediately refute everything he is saying; I am learning the subject like a poem in a foreign language.[6]

On 23 February 1897, Mahler's conversion took place in the Hamburg Kleine Michaeliskirche. It seems likely that Justine and Emma were baptised on the same day, since Justine commented to Ernestine that "we don't want to let G[ustav] jump into it on his own."[7] Despite Justine's apparent lack of conviction in her conversion, the Mahler family letters make it clear that certain aspects of Christianity had long been part of their lives: the Mahler family had celebrated Christmas, at least insofar as exchanging gifts and decorating a Christmas tree, since the 1880s.

Mahler's eldest surviving sibling was his brother Alois (1867–1931). No photograph of him survives, and very little is known about much of his life. While his parents were living, it appears that he assisted his father with the business and may have inherited it, or a portion of it, after their deaths (all of the Mahler siblings had an inheritance). In the fall of 1889, Alois was drafted into the army, and he served in a regiment based in Brünn.[8] He seems to have served less than his full three years, however, as he was looking for work in early 1892. Natalie Bauer-Lechner describes Alois as the "worst" of the siblings: "Moreover, in addition, the worst of them came from a distance—Alois, who had served his 3 years in Brünn as a private in the military and continually assaulted her [Justi] and G. with troubles and demands of the most unprecedented sort."[9] Her judgement is amply illustrated by the family letters, which frequently attest to Alois's unreliability and even dishonesty.

Mahler made efforts to find Alois a position in the business world, but ultimately decided to let him go his own way (see letter 326). At first, having changed his name to Hans Christian, he lived in Vienna and worked as a chief accountant (*Oberbuchhalter*); at times, he lived together with Otto. In December 1894, Justine wrote to Ernestine that she never heard from Alois other than when he needed money; in July 1895, she asked her not to tell him that she was coming to Vienna. After the mid-1890s, he is never mentioned in the letters to Justine.[10] In 1910, Alois emigrated to the United States, and, as Susan Filler has discovered, died in Chicago on 14 April 1931.[11]

Mahler's brother Otto (1873–1895) was a musician. At the age of fifteen he was admitted to the Conservatory of the Gesellschaft der Musikfreunde,

6. Justine Mahler to Ernestine Löhr, 2–3 December 1896.

7. Justine Mahler to Ernestine Löhr, 18 February 1897.

8. Letter 81 indicates that he expected to be drafted during the next six weeks.

9. "Mahleriana," Bibliothèque Musicale Gustav Mahler.

10. In a letter to Alma of 29 January 1904 (BGA 61), Mahler mentions that he encountered Alois at the Westbahnhof in Vienna—seemingly for the first time in a very long time—and was afraid that they would have to travel together or even share a sleeping car.

11. Susan M. Filler, "The Missing Mahler: Alois (Hans) in Chicago," in *Neue Mahleriana: Essays in Honour of Henry-Louis de La Grange on His Seventieth Birthday*, ed. Günther Weiß (Berne: Peter Lang, 1997), pp. 39–45.

but left of his own volition in early 1892;[12] Justine and Natalie Bauer-Lechner kept the news from Gustav, who was furious. Since only a single letter of Otto's survives in the Mahler-Rosé Collection (letter 81), and not much more in other collections, Justine's comments in her letters to Ernestine about Otto's lazy character are all the more valuable and corroborate Mahler's own comments in his letters to Justine. These sources reveal Mahler's efforts in 1894 to find a suitable position for Otto. Posts in neither Bremen nor Leipzig were successful, and by the end of 1894 the situation was becoming desperate. By early 1895, Justine was hearing "unpleasant [*unerquickliches*]" news: "[Otto] is becoming alarmingly thin; in the course of this, I can't help thinking of Hans Rott, and there one can't do anything."[13] On 6 February 1895, Otto Mahler shot himself in Nina Hoffmann's flat in Vienna. Gustav's reaction is not recorded in any of his letters. Fortunately, Justine communicated frequently with Ernestine during this period; she soon wrote that she had awaited the news daily; only the day before Gustav had asked her to "spare [him] all agitation now" because he was "too tired," and then the news came: "What has happened to Gustav, you will appreciate," she wrote to Ernestine, and commented that it was good that he was so busy.[14] Later she wrote rather eloquently to Ernestine:

> The *photograph* has been in my possession since yesterday. It is so lifelike that one hears him speak—I cannot imagine that I will never again be able to hear him speak. The thought it can no longer be undone is so awful. Today I showed the photograph to Gustav, but now I am sorry because he became so terribly sad. . . . Spring has come with a vengeance, but it fills me with melancholy. The life that I have before me seems so unbearably long. . . . I never ever wished that there would be a meeting again after death, not even when my mother died; now I do. I always have the feeling that he was not serious about dying, and can say to you that if he had had the fortune to have had different people around him—people who would not have taken his desire to die seriously—it could not have happened, it also would not have happened. I certainly know how it really looked inside him the last time he was here in Hamburg; you already have his letters from then. I can still hear him telling me "if I don't shoot myself now, it would be like blackmail!" And I talked him out of it, so that he went to Vienna and lived there for 3 months; in Nina's first letter [she wrote that] "he has now given up certain thoughts." Alois's proximity, to a large degree, contributed to the catastrophe, but he is certainly limited [*beschränkt*]; one can't tell him anything. I long with my whole heart to

12. The annual yearbook of the Conservatory for 1891–1892 indicates that Otto left the school on 27 April 1892 (*Jahresbericht über das Conservatorium für Musik und darstellende Kunst . . . für das Schuljahr 1891–1892* [Vienna: Verlag des Conservatoriums der Gesellschaft der Musikfreunde in Wien, 1892]). For Otto's studies at the Conservatory, see Elisabeth Maier, "Ein Bruckner-Schüler namens Mahler," *Nachrichten zur Mahler-Forschung* 49 (Fall 2003): 16–23.

13. Justine Mahler to Ernestine Löhr, 8?–9 and 16–17 January 1895.

14. Justine Mahler to Ernestine Löhr, early February 1895.

> be able to say: "the Lord hath given, the Lord hath taken away, the name of the Lord be praised!"[15]

A trunk containing Otto's effects, including his compositions and, perhaps, Mahler's letters to him, was destroyed when a bomb hit Alma Mahler's house towards the end of the Second World War; according to Alma, Mahler had been afraid to open it.

The youngest Mahler, Emma (1875–1933), is rather more of a cipher. She and Gustav were not close, and Justine, too, seems to have shared her brother's difficulties with Emma, complaining often about her laziness and self-centeredness. After moving to Hamburg with Justine in the fall of 1894, Emma fell in love with Bruno Walter, who had joined the Stadttheater in the 1894–1895 season;[16] in September 1895, Justine wrote to Ernestine:

> He was engaged here last year as chorus director, and this year advanced to conductor. I was there this week when he conducted—I cannot tell you how I felt as I sat there. G. says that he will be a highly significant conductor. Emma is infatuated with him, and while he has a lot of "regard" and "respect" for me, he seems to care more for Emma.[17]

Justine makes similar comments in other letters to Ernestine throughout 1895 and 1896 (by which time Walter had left Hamburg). At this point, it is unclear what happened, but by 1898 all had changed. That year, Walter met his future wife, Elsa, in Riga, and Emma married cellist Eduard Rosé (1859–1943) on 25 August. Emma was clearly not over Walter, however, as Justine intimated to Ernestine on 16 July 1898:

> I am staying here with Emma until the 4th, since in the meantime Schlesinger [Walter] is going to Vienna with G's piano score and I do not want her to see him; she doesn't know that he is coming, otherwise I probably couldn't keep her here.[18]

15. Justine Mahler to Ernestine Löhr, 21–22 February 1895.

16. An unpublished passage from Natalie Bauer-Lechner's memoirs (Bibliothèque Musicale Gustav Mahler) about Walter's impending departure from Hamburg in 1896 provides an additional layer of significance to the Mahler-Walter relationship:

> "We are losing the only one," Justi said to me, "with whom one can associate spiritually and humanly, and of whom one can be glad in one's heart. Heaven sent him to us last year in deliverance as a replacement for Otto, whom he resembles a little bit both in his appearance and in his colossal natural musical ability. In him we have realised all the splendid and considerable hopes that we had vainly placed in Otto; I can still not see him today without painful joy."

17. Justine Mahler to Ernestine Löhr, 13 September 1895.

18. Justine Mahler to Ernestine Löhr, 16 July 1898. There are two unpublished letters from Gustav to Walter from late July 1898 in the Bruno Walter Papers at the New York Public Library for the Performing Arts. In one, Gustav writes that Justine had already indicated to Walter why a visit that August was not advisable (fol. 347/iv). In the other, Mahler says that he will be back in Vienna on 1 August and arranges to meet Walter in his office; however "my sisters will follow already on Wednesday, and this means (as sorry as I am for it) that you ought not to be in Vienna any longer—for reasons of which you are aware" (fol. 350/iii.).

Immediately after their marriage, Emma and Eduard Rosé moved to the United States, where Eduard was engaged by the Boston Symphony Orchestra. Emma was unhappy there, however, so the Rosés returned to Europe in August 1900. Through Mahler's intercession, Eduard was engaged as *Konzertmeister* (concertmaster) and cello soloist in Weimar, where they spent the rest of their married life. Eduard ultimately fell victim to the Nazis, was deported, and died in Theresienstadt in 1943.[19] Their two children, Ernst (1900–1987)—born in the United States—and Wolfgang (1902–1977), both emigrated to the United States.

There is no question that Mahler's siblings caused him many anxious moments. The unpublished passage from Natalie's memoirs cited above concludes with an apt summary of the situation as it appeared to a close family friend:

> To manage these 3 [Alois, Otto, Emma], it would have required an all-powerful paternal authority—which might itself not have sufficed in the face of the almost pathological stubbornness and disobedience—indeed, even stupidity [*Ausgebundenheit*]—of these little Mahlers. It was like they were possessed by an evil spirit. These were not manageable circumstances from the outset, which continually brought on only the worst consequences—in spite of all of Gustav's endless care and far-too noble and lenient goodness, and Justi's trouble and best intentions.[20]

Mahler's close friend and confidante Natalie Bauer-Lechner (1858–1921) is a rather significant presence in the letters in this volume. She was quite intimate with Mahler and his family, almost from the very beginning of their renewed acquaintance in 1890 (Mahler had first met Natalie while attending the Conservatory, of which she was an alumna). Beginning with the summer of 1892, Natalie spent every summer with Mahler and his family and faithfully recorded her impressions and conversations with Mahler, which were subsequently published after her death.[21] She often accompanied Justine on house-hunting trips (by bicycle) and generally arrived for holidays earlier and left later than Mahler so that she could help Justine with household chores. Natalie also frequently travelled with Justine apart from Mahler: she spent time with her in Merano during the winter of 1892–1893 and in Italy the following winter. In addition, in his letters to Justine, Mahler frequently sends his greetings to Natalie, occasionally asking Justine to let her read the entire letter.

Natalie, however, clearly desired more than friendship from Mahler, and many passages in the family letters indicate that he was not interested, and

19. For more on Eduard, see Bernhard Post, "Eduard Rosé: Ein Musikerschicksal im Spannungsfeld zwischen europäischer Kultur und deutscher Provinz," *Mainzer Zeitschrift* 96–97 (2001–2002): 417–35.

20. "Mahleriana," Bibliothèque Musicale Gustav Mahler.

21. Natalie's *Erinnerungen an Gustav Mahler* first appeared in 1923; NBL is an enlarged edition published by her great-nephew in 1984, but portions still remain unpublished.

Although Natalie's memoirs contain nothing about the summer of 1894, Justine's letters to Ernestine make it clear that she did spend some time at Steinbach, although perhaps not while Mahler was there (see note 2 to letter 380).

told her so. She was extremely jealous of Mahler's relationship with Anna von Mildenburg, although he discussed it with her openly (see below). The letters also reveal that, on numerous occasions, he was irritated by her constant meddling as well as her browbeating of him. As an example of the latter, consider the following letter to Mahler:

> What do you do then *after* the opera? Please don't sit too long in the restaurant afterwards. It would be better to have your ham sandwich and then a little something else in the *theatre*, as in Hamburg. Going to bed late and eating late at night ruins your nerves and your health—especially drinking lots of coffee! Sleep your fill in the *morning* as well and do not neglect your siesta every afternoon: you do have to save up for the summer and your hut [*Häuschen*]—*that* is the one and only thing that matters, right?[22]

Given Natalie's romantic hopes, she naturally also had the obvious motivation of keeping Mahler at home and away from other women.

Despite their occasional crises, Mahler did value her friendship and worried when he thought that he might have hurt her (see, for example, letters 349 and 381). It must be admitted, however, that there was something rather perverse in Mahler's treatment of Natalie: he clearly knew what she wanted and in some senses he indulged her hopes, yet he was not prepared to marry her. And this treatment went on for about a decade.

One extended story is worth telling, as it is difficult to piece together from the letters themselves: the crisis of the second half of 1901, which led to the dissolution of Natalie's friendship with Mahler. In Alma Mahler's account, it is tied up with Gustav's discovery of the liaison between Justine and Arnold Rosé.[23] There are two intertwined issues, as reported (and mediated) by Alma.[24] The first involves Mahler's alleged anger at Justine's "treachery": her romantic attachment to violinist Arnold Rosé (1863–1946). According to Alma, Natalie and Justine had made a pact to facilitate each other's liaisons, but Natalie ultimately betrayed the news to Gustav. The second issue revolves around Natalie's renewed attempt to persuade Mahler to marry her. Alma alluded to this somewhat opaquely in her *Erinnerungen und Briefe*, but was more candid in the unpublished version of these memoirs:

> It was autumn 1901. Mahler had gone back to Vienna after the holidays. Justine was supposed to put the Maiernigg house in order with the help of their "friend" [Natalie] and follow after him. Frau Bauer Lechner, however, couldn't bear the distance and <ordered> ~~had~~ a telegram

22. Unpublished letter of 5 August 1897 (Bibliothèque Musicale Gustav Mahler).

23. Alma Mahler, *Memories and Letters*, pp. 12–14.

24. Alma Mahler, *Memories and Letters*, pp. 12–14. See also HLGE II, pp. 578–79. Alma's assertions about her sister-in-law in her published books are not particularly reliable, as they had come to dislike each other when these were written. (Traces of this later tension are visible in several of the later letters in this volume; see letters 529, 561, and 566.)

~~sent~~ <from Vienna> that her mother was dying in order to have a well-founded reason to give Justine for going to Vienna.—Meanwhile Frau Bauer had left no stone unturned in Vienna trying to prevail upon Mahler. She fell around his neck and tried to embrace him, but he repulsed her. She became even more insistent and finally there was an exchange that [later] was a *catch phrase* in the Mahler house.

Bauer: Marry me, for God's sake.
Mahler: No.
Bauer: Why not?
Mahler: I can't love you, I can only love a beautiful woman.
Bauer: But I *am* beautiful. I am beautiful. Just ask [Henriette] Mankiewicz. (She was a kitschy painter.)

Frau Bauer Lechner suffered greatly from this rebuff, but soon comforted herself with a painter, Schl . . . , and strongly flaunted this liaison. Mahler, who was completely indifferent towards her as a woman, was annoyed about this and said to me: well—she could at least have waited until the year of mourning was over.[25]

New information from the family letters serves to refocus the situation somewhat. Natalie's *Erinnerungen* reports that the summer of 1901 was a time of particular closeness between her and Gustav; as a token of their "time of closest mutual harmony [*besten Übereinstimmung*]" that summer, Mahler gave her the preliminary materials of his most recent *Lieder.*[26] Likewise, Mahler's letters from the summer of 1901 often mention Arnold Rosé in a friendly fashion, as they had for several years. If the news of Rosé's relationship with Justine did indeed emerge during this period, it does not seem to have floored Mahler, for there is no trace of any conflict in the family letters. The surviving documents do not make it possible to ascertain when Mahler was first aware of his sister's liaison—letters 508–510 from December 1901 make it clear that by then, at least, it was out in the open—but they do not record any estrangement whatsoever; rather to the contrary. At one point he even told Justine that people were gossiping about the two of them, just as they did about him and Natalie (letter 494).

The letters from early September 1901 suggest two possible interpretations, between which it is difficult to choose. Either Justine and Arnold were underhandedly concealing their relationship from Mahler by attempting to discredit Natalie's hints about it—in this scenario, Justine diverted Mahler by accusing Natalie that she was trying to drive a wedge between them by making up stories. Or, Justine and Arnold had had enough of Natalie's machinations—the supposed "pact" allowing her frequent access to Mahler—and were trying to warn him about it.

25. "Ein Leben mit Gustav Mahler" (Bibliothèque Musicale Gustav Mahler); a copy of this passage can be found in the Musiksammlung, Österreichische Nationalbibliothek, F 102 Vondenhoff 1/1413.

26. NBL, p. 195.

Regardless of the situation with Justine and Rosé, it is clear that Natalie renewed her pursuit of Mahler in the late summer of 1901. The urgent telegram calling her back to Vienna, which Alma Mahler uncharitably assumed was a fake, may in fact have been real (see letters 492 and 502). Still, at some point a confrontation between the two did take place, into which Justine was drawn (see letter 503). It is noteworthy that even at this difficult moment, Mahler was capable of seeing the good in Natalie; he was concerned that Justine would allow her grudge against Natalie to fester and reminded his sister that they all must continue to get along with each other. Again, Mahler did not wish to hurt Natalie. Despite his optimistic hope that the matter was settled, it was not: less than a week later, Mahler was obliged to tell Natalie the "unvarnished truth" (*ungeschminckte Wahrheit*): that he did not love her (letter 505). At this point, Natalie vanishes from the family letters, although the final break with Mahler did not occur until after his engagement to Alma Schindler that December.

The arrival of soprano Anna von Mildenburg (1872–1947) in Hamburg for the 1895–1896 season is not reflected in Mahler's letters, since he, Justine, and Emma were all living together at the time. She is first mentioned in a letter of 7 October 1895 in which Justine tells Ernestine that "according to Gustav [Anna was] a talent, the like of which has not been seen for years."[27] Justine's letters to her friend show that Anna was a frequent visitor to the Mahler home that fall. In early November, after Gustav had walked Anna home one night, Justine and Gustav talked until the early hours; although she does not say so specifically, she implies that the talk was about his feelings for Anna. Moreover, unpublished letters from Mahler to Anna indicate that they had already taken the acquaintance to the next step, friendship, by late November, as they were now using the familiar *Du*.[28]

Later letters to Ernestine make it clear that Justine was fully apprised of the nature of their relationship, and she traces its ups and downs—real or imagined on her part—in her letters to Ernestine. By September 1896, Justine herself had become quite good friends with Anna, only she did not want Natalie to know about it, since "she would immediately become unnecessarily jealous, and because of that her behaviour towards G[ustav] would become unnatural and there would be unpleasant scenes again."[29] She also admitted to Ernestine that, because of Gustav's relationship with Anna, "I have come to terms with the fact that I am no longer the nearest to G[ustav]'s heart."[30] Her admiration for Anna's talent was considerable, although typically it was reflected through Mahler himself, who—to Justine at least—had shaped her as an artist and a human being. Justine's letters to Ernestine suggest that, contrary to Alma's later

27. Justine Mahler to Ernestine Löhr, 7 October 1895.

28. Mahler's letters to Mildenburg are found in the Theatersammlung of the Österreiche Nationalbibliothek; approximately 126 of them are unpublished. I am grateful to Stephen Hefling for sharing his transcriptions of these letters with me.

29. Justine Mahler to Ernestine Löhr, 12 September 1896.

30. Justine Mahler to Ernestine Löhr, 5 November 1896.

portrayal, Mahler's relationship with Mildenburg must have been common knowledge, at least in Hamburg; their mutual Hamburg friend Adele Marcus, apparently, was "dying of jealousy."[31]

In March 1902, Mahler married the young, beautiful, and talented Alma Schindler (1879–1964). Alma occupies a lesser place in the family letters (which are many fewer in number after 1901) than does Natalie or Anna. The letters do offer a new perspective on their courtship, however, as they include four letters from Justine to Gustav written during the crucial month of December 1901; Justine, always acutely conscious of her brother's place in history, must have kept copies of them (Mahler's replies make it clear that the letters were actually sent). When read in conjunction with Gustav's letters to Justine, as well as the unexpurgated edition of his correspondence with Alma and her contemporary diaries, we are able to form a more rounded perspective on the events of that December.[32]

Much has been written about Alma and her relationship with Gustav.[33] Before Henry-Louis de La Grange's pioneering work, our view of the Mahler marriage was largely shaped by Alma herself, in works written many years after the fact. Her biography of Mahler and her autobiography are fascinating and frustrating monuments of self-aggrandisement and self-justification.[34] Both are riddled with errors, distortions, and self-serving depictions of events; the 1995 edition of Mahler's letters to Alma (BGA) shows just how much Alma suppressed in her partial publication of the correspondence in the biography. Alma was anxious to portray her marriage in a certain light for posterity, possibly to alleviate her guilt over her betrayal of Gustav with Walter Gropius in the summer of 1910—thus, her insistence on certain myths about Mahler's character, principally relating to his emotional and sexual life before meeting her. Alma's image of Mahler as neurotic, ascetic, sexually inexperienced, and in thrall to his family allowed her to depict herself as his saviour.

Such myths, however—as well as many other things in the books—are contradicted by sources in her own hand, such as her diaries and unpublished drafts

31. Justine Mahler to Ernestine Löhr, 5 November 1896. In the same letter she wrote that Anna "is a true Viennese girl, rather frivolous, but very unassuming this year and interested in us too."

32. BGA; and Alma Mahler-Werfel, *Tagebuch-Suiten 1898–1902*, ed. Antony Beaumont and Susanne Rode-Breymann (Frankfurt-am-Main: Fischer, 1997).

33. In addition to HLG II and HLGE II, see the introduction to Alma Mahler, *Memories and Letters*; Karen Monson, *Alma Mahler: Muse to Genius* (Boston: Houghton Mifflin, 1983); and Françoise Giroud, *Alma Mahler; or, The Art of Being Loved*, trans. R. M. Stock (Oxford: Oxford University Press, 1991). See also Stuart Feder, "Before Alma: Gustav Mahler and 'Das Ewig-Weibliche'," in *Mahler Studies*, ed. Stephen E. Hefling (Cambridge: Cambridge University Press, 1997), pp. 78–109; and Stuart Feder, *Gustav Mahler: A Life in Crisis* (New Haven, Conn.: Yale University Press, 2004).

34. Alma Mahler, *Memories and Letters* (first appeared in 1940 as *Gustav Mahler: Erinnerungen und Briefe*). The autobiography was first published in a shortened English version as *And the Bridge Is Love*, trans. E. B. Ashton (New York: Harcourt, Brace, 1958) before appearing in the original German as *Mein Leben* (Frankfurt am Main: Fischer, 1960).

35. See Mahler-Werfel, *Tagebuch-Suiten*. Copies of her book drafts may be consulted at the Bibliothèque Musicale Gustav Mahler. To take one example, Gustav's letters to Anna, as well as many comments in letters from Justine to Ernestine Löhr, make it clear that this affair was widely known and, in

of her books, as well as letters by others.[35] As part of her campaign of disinformation, Alma destroyed all of her own letters to Gustav, thus robbing us of half of the correspondence. Her contemporary diary entries, however, as well as Gustav's responses to her (lost) letters in his, function as something of a palimpsest of her own missing letters to him, in terms of character at least.[36] Given her need to shape events according to her version of the truth, it is surprising that she did not destroy these self-incriminating items; for that, at least, we can be grateful to her.

Stuart Feder has written extensively about the psychological impact of the haemorrhage Mahler suffered in February 1901.[37] In his estimation, this near-death experience marked a significant caesura in Mahler's creative and personal life. It was followed in rather short order by his resignation from the Vienna Philharmonic; his shift from the *Wunderhorn*-influenced world of his first symphonies to the Fifth Symphony and Rückert settings begun that summer; the crisis with his confidante and hopeless admirer Natalie Bauer-Lechner in September 1901; and, possibly, the surprise of Justine's liaison with Arnold Rosé. According to Feder, the newly acquired consciousness of his own mortality also prepared Mahler psychologically to marry, to seek both the stability and continuity of a wife and children. And this marriage, of course, provoked further breaks: with Natalie, with most of his former friends, and with the domestic life he had shared with his sister.

In most accounts of the marriage, at least those by Mahlerians, it is Alma's character that comes most into question. Her published diary stops in early 1902, although selected entries until 1906 are found in the autobiography. Taken as a whole, these entries do reveal considerable self-awareness on her part: she often acknowledged what she called her other, vain (or "bad") self and struggled valiantly to overcome it. Although many of the published entries are critical of Gustav and the marriage, they do seem to have been written largely to let off steam, especially after arguments. For Alma, the role of Frau *Direktorin* was not an easy one to play; she disliked her other role as wife and mother and resented the loss of the intellectual life she had enjoyed before marriage. She certainly did rebel against her husband's domination, and it is striking to note that all of her subsequent affairs and marriages were with younger men; she too was looking for someone to dominate. Her friend Max Burckhard warned her before she married Gustav that it was wrong to join two such personalities—joining fire with water.[38] In this he was certainly right, but psychologist Stuart

---

all likelihood, fully physical, despite Alma's assertions in her published works. In fact, Alma herself called Gustav a flirt in her diary in November 1901, mentioning that he had had affairs with many singers, including Mildenburg.

36. Although from a later period (1910–1911), Alma's letters to Gropius clearly expose her lies and deceits about their affair in her published works; Gropius resisted her importunate demands to return her letters to him. These fascinating letters play a central role in Reginald R. Isaacs, *Walter Gropius: Der Mensch und sein Werk*, 2 vols. (Berlin: Mann, 1983–1984).

37. See above, note 33.

38. Mahler-Werfel, *Tagebuch-Suiten*, 747 (22 December 1901).

Feder has also written persuasively that Alma may have taken some masochistic pleasure in self-effacement, at least during her marriage with Gustav; the trait is not much in evidence after his death.

But, in assessing the marriage, to focus solely on Alma's character and her flaws is both unkind and unfair: Gustav was at least as self-centred as she was, if not more so, as well as brutally honest and direct. These facets of his personality are seen throughout his letters, particularly in those contained in this volume.[39] There is no question that he was not an easy man to live with: Alma's diary and biography also record his obliviousness to the people around him and her continual embarrassment at his absent-mindedness.[40]

In Feder's estimation, the balance of power in the relationship shifted noticeably after the three crises of 1907: the death of their daughter Maria; the diagnosis of Gustav's heart ailment; and his decision to leave the Court Opera. The final crisis came in the summer of 1910: while undertaking a cure at Tobelbad, Alma met and fell in love with the young architect Walter Gropius. Alma's published account of the mis-addressed letter, sent by Gropius to Gustav instead of Alma, and the subsequent meeting of the three in Toblach appears to be broadly correct.[41] Although Alma chose to stay with Gustav, he was now terrified of losing her. His letters to Alma of the period are almost embarrassingly abject and fervent, and he displayed his love of Alma publicly in the dedication of the Eighth Symphony and by facilitating the publication of some of her *Lieder*. It was in this state of mind that Gustav sought out Sigmund Freud in Leiden in August 1910.

The Mahler marriage, of course, ended badly. Alma's affair with Walter Gropius continued, and in fact was facilitated by Alma's own mother, Anna Moll, with whom Gustav was extremely close. How much he knew of these events will never be known, for, as far as we can tell, he did not confide in anyone about the problems in his marriage.

Many other aspects of Mahler's life, personality, and career emerge in his letters to his family. In terms of his personality, these letters reveal not only his love, care, and concern for his family, but also his irritability, sarcasm, and need for control.[42] They show the excitement of the young Mahler at his growing fame

39. After the terrible dinner with Alma in January 1902, Siegfried Lipiner wrote to Gustav that "[a]t heart, you don't consider anyone a person; we're all just *objects* to you. For no reason at all, you throw people away—you usually pick them up again—but not always." He also referred to Gustav's "inimitable coldness and irony." See HLGE III, p. 596.

40. See, in particular, the diary excerpts in *Mein Leben*.

41. Alma Mahler, *Memories and Letters*, pp. 172–75.

42. Mahler was not above lying to his family: for example, in early 1894 he hid the terms of his contract renewal in Hamburg from Emma because he did not want to bring her to Hamburg with Justine. There are other times in the letters where he and Justine agree not to tell Alois, Otto, or Emma certain things. As with all letters, a certain caution needs to be exercised in assessing Mahler's letters to his family and close friends. Letters are speech acts in and of themselves, written to convey a particular image or view of the world.

as a conductor and, eventually, as a composer and document his interactions with other significant figures such as Brahms, Bruckner, Bülow, and Richard Strauss. Without a doubt, these letters are the most significant source for Mahler's early career and for understanding—at least to a point—something of his relationships with his family and particularly close friends.

The Early Years
Vienna, Kassel, Prague, Leipzig

Chronology

1860 *7 July*: GM born in Kalischt (Kalište) to Bernhard and Marie (née Herrmann) Mahler.
23 October: Mahler family moves to Iglau (Jihlava).

1863 *18 May*: birth of Leopoldine Mahler.

1867 *6 October*: birth of Alois Mahler.

1868 *15 December*: birth of Justine Mahler.

1873 *18 June*: birth of Otto Mahler.

1875 *10 September*: GM enters the Conservatory of the Gesellschaft der Musikfreunde in Vienna.
19 October: birth of Emma Mahler.

1876 Earliest surviving piece composed: first movement of a piano quartet.

1877 *September*: GM obtains his *Matura* (*Gymnasium* diploma leading to university education) and enrolls at the Universität Wien.

1878 *18 March*: GM completes the text of *Das klagende Lied*.
2 July: GM completes his studies at the Conservatory.
Summer: GM's four-hand piano arrangement of Bruckner's Third Symphony is published by Rättig (made with the assistance of Rudolf Krzyzanowski, although his name does not appear on the title page).

1880 *19 and 27 February, 5 March*: completes three of five songs dedicated to Josephine Poisl (the manuscript forms part of the Gustav Mahler–Alfred Rosé Collection).
June, July, and *August*: GM employed conducting operettas at the theatre in Bad Hall. This was his first conducting position.
November: *Das klagende Lied* complete.

1881 *3 September*: first conductor at the Landschaftliches Theatre in Laibach (Ljubljana).
15 December: *Das klagende Lied* fails to win the Beethoven Prize.

1882 *2 April*: Laibach Landestheater closes, leaving GM without employment.

1883 *10 January–17 March*: conductor at the Königliche Städtische Theatre in Olmütz (Olomuoc).
13 February: Richard Wagner dies in Venice.
July: GM's first visit to Bayreuth (*Parsifal*).

21 August: *Königlicher Musik- und Chordirektor* at Königliches Theatre in Kassel.

1884 *4 May*: Leopoldine Mahler marries Ludwig Quittner.
23 June: premiere of *tableaux vivants* after Scheffel's *Der Trompeter von Säkkingen* with incidental music by GM (lost, although the tune of a serenade was subsequently employed in the *Blumine* movement of the original version of the First Symphony).
December: *Lieder eines fahrenden Gesellen*.

1885 *16 March*: GM engaged as conductor at the Leipzig Neues Stadt-Theater as of July 1886.
27 April: GM released from his contract in Kassel at his request.
End June: GM leaves Kassel for Prague and Iglau.
1 August: conductor at the Königliche Deutsche Landestheater in Prague (debut: Cherubini, *Die Wasserträger*, 17 August).

1886 *15 July*: the season, and GM's contract, ends in Prague.
1 August: GM takes up his duties in Leipzig (debut: *Lohengrin*, 3 August).

1887 *Spring/Summer*: begins work on completion of Carl Maria von Weber's *Die drei Pintos*.
September–October: completes the score of *Die drei Pintos*.
13 October: first meeting with Richard Strauss.

1888 *20 January*: premiere of *Die drei Pintos* in Leipzig, conducted by GM.
February–March: composition of First Symphony.
17 May: after conflicts with Staegemann, GM's resignation is accepted.
June–August: composes *Todtenfeier* and completes the score of the First Symphony.

Letters

1 *To Uncle Joseph and Aunt Barbara Fleischberger*[1]

Vienna, 17th September [1876 or 1877][2]

My dears,

This time I have to apologise doubly: first, for not writing for so long, and second, for it being my fault that Frank's letter, which was already finished before your letter, dear uncle, arrived, and which only awaited my note, did not go off earlier. It is almost a luxurious feeling if one can intend to do something but can put it off again until the next day. You should have heard our conversations, which went, daily:

"Have you written to Ledetsch yet?"
"No, nor you!"
"Tomorrow we really have to write."
"Certainly! As soon as you've written, tell me."

And so on, without end. Finally, I managed to pull myself together, and finally you have that which was long awaited!—Incidentally, in the last two weeks I really have not had any time, literally. I couldn't even write to Iglau once.

I have very little news that would interest you, apart from the fact that it seems that one of my compositions will be performed at a Conservatory concert (thus creating a lot of work for me). I have enough lessons, and: "we are also getting along well with Gustav Frank!" What more could I ask? If any of you are coming to Vienna this year, we would be most pleased to have you as guests.

It is probably also interesting that I am now more or less standing on my own two feet, i.e. that, apart from this month, my parents do not have to send me a single kreutzer more. What is J[osef] Stransky[3] doing? Please say hello to him from me.

Greetings to everyone.

Your devoted nephew,
Gustav Mahler

SHELFMARK: E6-MF-320
NOTES

[1] This letter was written jointly with Mahler's cousin Gustav Frank (1859–1923); both address themselves to their uncle and aunt in Ledetsch. Frank's portion is not included.

[2] According to HLG I, pp. 57–58.

[3] Josef Stransky (1872–1936), Czech conductor; in 1911, he was Mahler's successor at the New York Philharmonic.

2 *From Leopoldine Mahler to Gustav*

[Iglau, Christmas 1880]

Dear Gustav!
You can imagine how excitedly we received your Christmas presents. On behalf of everyone, I want to thank you for them. Dear mother would have gladly written you herself, but she has a headache. We are all already looking forward to your visit at the end of January. You can prolong it as long as you like, then? Have you already spoken to G[ustav] Frank? At his request, we recently sent him your address. Apropos, I must announce the most recent event in our family to you. Albert Mahler[1] has become engaged to Frl. Sofie Adler, sister of Gottlieb.[2] I recently told you that the rumour spread that Frau Adler's husband was insane. The situation is this, you see: he had a stroke at the coffeehouse and he began to suffer from a mental illness under which he continues to labour; according to the physicians, no recovery is possible for him. Frl. Stella[3] probably doesn't like us anymore, because she hardly ever visits anymore, and it would be too pushy of me if I went to visit her without having been invited.

Best wishes, and "here's to the New Year."

Your sister Leopoldine

Write to us soon!

SOURCE: Alma Mahler, "Ein Leben mit Gustav Mahler" (unpublished manuscript in the Bibliothèque Musicale Gustav Mahler); not in *Selected Letters*

NOTES

[1] First cousin, married in 1881.

[2] Physicist Gottlieb Adler (1860–1893) attended the Universität Wien at the same time as Mahler.

[3] Unidentified; nickname for Sophie.

3 *From Marie Mahler to Gustav*

Postcard
[Iglau, 14 November 1882]

Dear Gustav!
We are *all* well. You must have already got my letter today. I only ask you not to laugh at my worries and *take my advice*. Dear Father is quite well. Just don't worry. There is nothing new with us. May everything turn out according to the wish

of your faithful mother
Marie

Iglau 14.11.1882

SOURCE: Alma Mahler, "Ein Leben mit Gustav Mahler" (unpublished manuscript in the Bibliothèque Musicale Gustav Mahler); *Selected Letters* S1

4 *From Marie Mahler to Gustav*

Iglau, 15.12.1882

Dear Gustav!
We received your dear letter, and I am now replying to let you know that it would be our opinion that you would do better if you came home by the excursion train instead of staying in Vienna, since this year the Christmas holidays last for four days and you will certainly not be able to give lessons, and will have to live off available cash, and that would certainly cost you more than the journey to Iglau. You need not bring any luggage, of course. If necessary, I will help you out with laundry, although if you have any torn socks or shirts, you can bring them with you in the coach in your travel bag and the journey will cost you next to nothing. Then you can stay at home for a few days, and we can discuss everything in detail. The children and both of us are looking forward to seeing you, so this will be best, since it is too tiring for me to travel during the winter.—Will you write us right away if you are coming? And when? so that I can heat your room. I will also be able to properly finish quarrelling with you about those things that I really cannot in letters. Why these endless changes of apartment? I don't believe that there can be a single person apart from you who changes his apartment every 2 weeks. Will you end up changing your apartment every time

you change your underclothes? And in the end won't you find yourself without any underclothes or clothes? For as I know you, you will forget something in each place—and will continue to move until you have nothing left. Am I not right? However, I will leave the rest to discuss in person. Enough for today. One more thing: if you come home, bring me another bottle of *French brandy*.

Fond farewell; best wishes from us all.

Your faithful mother
Marie

Otto and Emma were very pleased with your letters. Emma writes to you several times a day; in fact, when she is home from school, she devotes herself exclusively to you. We would appreciate it very much if you would also look up Uncle Hermann before you came home. Also, I have given G[ustav] Frank your previous address, so if you have moved again, he will naturally not be able to find you, and so you must look him up. We wrote to him at the Academy of Fine Arts.

SOURCE: Alma Mahler, "Ein Leben mit Gustav Mahler" (unpublished manuscript in the Bibliothèque Musicale Gustav Mahler); *Selected Letters* S2
NOTE
[1] According to *Selected Letters*, p. 377, Mahler's father's brother Hermann Mahler.

5 *To Parents*

[c. 1884]

Dear Mother and Father,
I am flabbergasted. Poldi [Leopoldine] is engaged?[1] To whom? When? How? Wouldn't you like to tell me these little details sometime or other? I would at least like to learn, after the fact, something about those things for which there was no time *previously*. I am too furious to write any more, and I await *prompt* news!

Ever yours,
Gustav

P.S. No answer came to my last letter!

SHELFMARK: E2-MF-76
NOTE
[1] According to Henry-Louis de La Grange (unpublished chronology), Leopoldine married Ludwig Quittner in Vienna on 4 May 1884.

6 *To Justine*

Kassel, 26 April 1885

Dearest Justi,
You probably will not expect special thanks for finally remembering that I exist.—I cannot even spare you the reproach that your messages and news turned out to be rather sparse. Why do you express yourself so sparingly? What

sort of emotional agitation were you writing about? Now sit down sometime and write to me how you live and what you think about.—

I have heard nothing more from Poldi for months; they also seem to be angry with me.

You will certainly know that I have asked for my release here as of 1 July,[1] and also that it seems that I will probably spend next winter in Vienna, since my engagement in Leipzig does not begin until June 1886. So I will likely again be in Iglau now and then. What are our siblings up to? I never hear anything from them, and you know how important this is to me, don't you?

I myself am greatly indebted to Herr Schneck for receiving you in such a friendly manner. Give him my most courteous greetings—also to his wife, whom I do not know. If he comes to Leipzig sometime, hopefully he will take advantage of my hospitality too.

Today I write you only a little bit, because I am very busy. Once you've written me a really detailed letter, I'll do the same for you.

Very best wishes
from your brother
Gustav

Shelfmark: S1-MJ-728
Note

[1] On 20 April 1885, Mahler asked the *Intendant* of the Königliche Schauspiele, Adolph Freiherr von und zu Gilsa (1838–1910), for the third time to be released from his contract; his request was granted on 27 April 1885. See Hans Joachim Schaefer, *Gustav Mahler in Kassel* (Bärenreiter, 1982), p. 49.

7 *To Justine*

Cassel, 9 May 1885

Dear Justi,
I received both of your letters, and am pleased that you have at least started to get healthy again. What you write me about household circumstances is very distressing. I feel confident that you will behave like a sensible girl—as your letters already suggest—and above all will never forget the consideration you owe to your parents, on one hand, and to your siblings on the other.—Now you must take my place at home.—So, what do you have to tell me?! You always start so very mysteriously, but then never seem to have the courage to come out with it. Just be completely open with me, that is best.—If you have done something wrong, then it is my business to tell you so, and you can then put up with a little dressing-down. If I had had such an adviser by my side, as you have with me, I would have been spared a lot of frustration and grief. If perhaps at home I am unable to answer as I might like to, no doubt an opportunity will arise when I can at least *hint at* what I think.

What your friend wrote you about *Basel* is not true. It was possible, mind you, but I have now made another decision for next year.[1] You'll soon hear about it.

You certainly shouldn't worry yourselves about reviews at all.—It is just as if Emma were to give her judgement about a performance. Moreover, I have already quarrelled with the critics here, and whenever they can, they grumble about me—which, by the way, does not touch me at all, and lowers me in the eyes of the public even less.

If Frau Poldi has become so proud, then she herself must bear the consequences. I remember, though, that at the time she sent me a few brief words of congratulation about my engagement in Leipzig. Perhaps she is waiting for a letter thanking her for it.

Give my regards to your kind hosts, and the very best wishes from your brother

Gustav

Write me soon, and in detail.

SHELFMARK: S1-MJ-729
NOTE

[1] On 1 August 1885 Mahler began a one-year contract as second conductor (*zweite Kapellmeister*) at the Königliche Deutsche Landestheater in Prague; see Vladimír Lébl, "Gustav Mahler als Kapellmeister des Deutschen Landestheaters in Prag," *Hudební veda* 12 (1975): 351–71.

8 *To Parents*

[Prague, 7 July 1885][1]

Dear Mother and Father,
I arrive tomorrow, Wednesday, on the same train that Father usually takes—the one that leaves here at 10:30.

If the weather is nice, please meet me at the station with a landau—but *only* if it is nice out, otherwise I'll go on foot.

Best wishes
from
Gustav

SHELFMARK: E2-MF-70
NOTE

[1] Mahler arrived in Iglau on Wednesday, 8 July, after having spent a few days in Prague.

9 *To Parents*

[Prague, end August 1885]

Dear Mother and Father,
The enclosed card[1] will give you the best idea of the state of things—On Saturday I am probably conducting *Tannhäuser* (without rehearsal) because Seidl has to leave early that morning.—I am rehearsing *Don Giovanni* (the aristocrat of operas) and *Trompeter von Säkkingen* (a premiere).[2]—

You would hardly believe what a tremendous amount of work I have to get through. I have to newly stage [*einrichten*] both works.—I *really* hardly have time to eat or sleep.

Write me soon, won't you, because I am very concerned that I have had no news for so long. What are Poldi and Justi doing? Why don't they write me?—

Best wishes from
Gustav

Write at once!

SHELFMARK: E2-MF-51
NOTES
[1] Not extant.
[2] *Tannhäuser* was performed on Saturday, 22 August; the repertory list in Lébl, "Gustav Mahler als Kapellmeister des Deutschen Landestheaters in Prag," does not list the conductor. Seidl's last appearance was actually *Die fliegende Holländer* on Wednesday, 26 August. Mahler conducted the premiere of *Don Giovanni* on 6 September (see next letter) and *Der Trompeter von Säkkingen* on 12 September.

10 *To Parents*

Prague, 6 September 1885

Dear Mother and Father,
Only today have I had the time and leisure to write you a few lines. Dear Toni[1] will now have told you how things are going for me here; in addition, I can set down that it exceeds all my previous expectations. The orchestra, choir, soloists, and director treat me with greatest respect, and if nothing goes amiss, I can say that, with this step this year, I have come *much* farther. This advance means more than all the others put together. Tonight I conduct *Don Giovanni*, and it is a sign of Neumann's particular confidence that he hands over to me just this opera, because it is of great significance for Prague since Mozart composed it specifically for Prague, and he himself rehearsed and conducted it here. The citizens of Prague especially make the greatest demands. The newspapers—mainly the *Tagblatt*—will probably tear me to pieces, for I predict now that they will all cry "Oh! Oh! 'Tradition' has gone to the devil!" With this word, one means in fact the long-standing habit—or rather, rut—of performing a work on a stage. I have been concerned with none of this, and tonight I will calmly follow *my own* path.

By the way, now is the time when we could enjoy being together if you wanted to come and visit here. I await you <u>*as soon as possible*</u>! Mother dear, you must come and spend a few days with Toni. You can all go to the theatre together in the evening. She really is a good soul and is touchingly attentive to me, as is her entire family. She even sent me a whole lot of *cream-cheese tarts* [*Kolatschen*] recently.

If you come, don't forget to bring my photographs with you—I need them very much. The letter to Feld[2] came to my house all right, but when I read it over again, I realised how *fruitless* it would be, and that Ludwig would only awaken a *vain* hope. If Feld were in Vienna, I would have sent it to him anyway, but I am afraid that, in his optimism, he would travel straight to Budapest, and toss money away unnecessarily. This *certainly would not do*. With the *best* of intentions, I am not now in any position to help him *materially*. But rest assured, dear Poldi, I am thinking about it, and as soon as an *opportunity* presents itself, I will do *everything* in my power. I herewith invite you to come and visit me for a few weeks if the *time* arises that you need a *rest*. Perhaps we'll think of something together then. Write me soon.[3]

What is *Justi* doing, and why does she not write me?

And what about *Alois* and *Otto*? So many fingers—and none are to be stirred!

Best wishes to you all
from Gustav

Now I'm off to the theatre.

SHELFMARK: E13-MF-538
NOTES

[1] Unknown, but apparently a family friend living in Prague.

[2] Apparently the father of Jenny Perrin-Feld, former owner of the 1893 manuscript of the First Symphony; see HLG I, pp. 93–94, n. 19; 153; and 966. A letter from her son to Alfred Rosé, dated 2 July 1968, sheds further light on this friendship:

> As a young girl, my Hungarian-born mother, Jenny Feld, and her sister and brother lived in Vienna around 1880 for the sake of their education. The siblings' musical talents were overseen by a young Conservatory student named Gustav Mahler, who was taken in as a member of the family, as happened then. The good friendship lasted, despite the varying course of their lives. The family moved to Budapest and then, lo-and-behold, Mahler went to Budapest and the old friendship resumed—all the more since he brought his sister Justi, your mother, with him. A close friendship joined the two until my mother married my father, an American, in 1892. It continued via correspondence, first in Italy and eventually, in 1894, in Belgium. I think that I remember that your mother accompanied your brother to Hamburg; at any rate, he came to Brussels a few times and even spent a few days with us. In 1901 we moved to Vienna and the old friendship with your mother resumed. (Gustav Mahler–Alfred Rosé Collection)

[3] Although E13-MF-538 ends here, unsigned, a short fragment found with E19-MJ-653 almost certainly forms the conclusion and is appended here.

II *To Parents*

[Prague, October 1885]

Dear Mother and Father,

I am sending you 10 fl. right away, dear Mother, and promise to send the other 10 fl. next month.

I now have more to do here than before. *Meistersinger* on the 25th will really be something.

When will one of you come and visit me? Can't you come, dear mother? It might be a nice rest if you were here for a week. You could stay with Toni, and you would have all the care that you need—she is really an extremely nice person. Mind you, I get around to visiting her only rarely.

But why do you write so little?

I generally associate with Hellmann[1] from Iglau—we always lunch together.

From Cassel I hear that life isn't a bed of roses for my successor.[2] I am still much spoken about. In the meantime, I ask you to write me right away and tell me that this letter has arrived.

With best wishes,
Your
Gustav

Shelfmark: E2-MF-52
Notes

[1] Unknown.

[2] According to *Gustav Mahler in Kassel*, p. 53, Mahler's successor was twenty-eight-year-old Franz Beier, "an active, experienced musician."

12 *To Parents*

[Prague, November 1885]

Dear Mother and Father,
Today I can give you the welcome news that Director Neumann has begun negotiations regarding the extension of my contract.[1] Since we are both sharp fellows, the matter may take some time.—In the meantime, I am rehearsing and conducting "Meistersinger," "Rheingold," "Walküre," and "Tristan" here, and my career has taken a great upturn.[2]—As you can see, everything has turned out better than we might have hoped.—I will not accept *less* than 250 fl. a month and also have requested a month off each year, which he will probably give me.

Anyway, I will now begin to earn money. When now you come to see me sometime, you should have more enjoyment.

How are you feeling, dear mother? And all the others? Thank dear Justi for her letter, which I will answer sometime when I have a chance.

Write me again soon!
Best wishes from your
Gustav

I am moving into private quarters on 15 November.

Shelfmark: E17-MF-627
Notes

[1] These negotiations came to naught, as Mahler was unable to free himself from his commitment to the Leipzig Neues Stadt-Theater (see his letter of 3 December to Fritz Löhr, GMB[2] 42).

[2] Mahler conducted the Prague premieres of *Das Rheingold* and *Die Walküre* on 19 and 20 December 1885. His colleague Ludwig Slansky gave the Prague premiere of *Tristan und Isolde* on 30 April 1886; Mahler conducted it for the first time in Hamburg, on 18 May 1891.

13 *To Parents*

[Prague, early December 1885]

Dear Mother and Father,
Just a few lines!
I've just been in bed again for a few days because of my damned haemorrhoids.[1] Because of them, the Nibelungen have had to be postponed again.—At any rate, I still hope to put them on this month. Then I hope to have some time. Maybe I'll come and visit on the way through.

Today was my first rehearsal back.

Best wishes from your
Gustav

How are things with you?

Write soon!

SHELFMARK: E2-MF-53
NOTE

[1] This is the first of many references in the letters to Mahler's various ills and infirmities. The chapter "Der kranke Mahler—eine pathographische Skizze," in Jens Malte Fischer, *Gustav Mahler: Der fremde Vertraute* (Vienna: Paul Zsolnay, 2003), pp. 394–408, gives an excellent overview of Mahler's health. See also Susan M. Filler, "Mahlers Krankheiten in der Medizinischen Literatur," *Nachrichten zur Mahler-Forschung* 23 (1990): 7–13.

14 *To Parents*

[Prague, 1885–1886]

Dear Mother and Father,
Since I am very busy, I can only be quick.—Tomorrow Neumann comes back from Berlin. Only then can I conclude how I will arrange my itinerary. At the same time, I am sending you some clippings that you may not have yet read.

By the way, there were notices of varying lengths in all the Viennese papers.

Write soon. Best wishes

from your
Gustav

[written across the top of the letter:] There were also articles in all the Berlin papers!

SHELFMARK: E2-MF-69

15 *From Marie Mahler to Gustav*

B. MAHLER, IGLAU
MAKER OF LIQUEURS, RUM, ROSOGLIO, PUNCH, ESSENCES, AND VINEGAR

Iglau, 3.3.1886

My dear Gustav!
At your father's request, I am asking you to go to Uncle Weiner[1] as soon as you receive this letter, and to console him on the sudden death of your aunt. At such a misfortune, all quarrels and enmity cease. Please convey deepest sympathy to your uncle from us as well. We are all well. We read Director Neumann's letter in the Bohemia.[2] Did he write it to you, or simply send it to the paper? Write us about everything soon, and in detail.

Please, dear Gustav, *once again*, go right away. Fond farewell, and best wishes from your faithful mother

Marie

Dr. Freund visits us often, and I am awfully glad about this, since the talk is mostly about Gustav, of course. He is perhaps the best of your friends, apart from us.

SOURCE: Alma Mahler, "Ein Leben mit Gustav Mahler" (unpublished manuscript in the Bibliothèque Musicale Gustav Mahler); *Selected Letters* S3

NOTES

[1] This was an uncle on Mahler's mother's side.

[2] 1 March 1886. The rather flattering letter appeared after he and Mahler had had a violent disagreement about the ballet in Gounod's *Faust*.

16 *From Bernhard Mahler to Gustav*

Karlsbad, 6.5.86

Dear Gustav!
I will get straight to the point, since I have a lot of correspondence here.

Although there has been no further trace of sugar since my third day here, until today I have had severe *inflammation of the kidneys* and my cure has been hindered a lot by the bad weather.

Since my arrival, my way of living is that apart from when I go out to eat at midday, I hardly ever leave my room and at night am already in bed by 7:30. Accordingly, it is quite impossible to meet anyone, for it will not occur to anyone to come to me in my room. So there is nothing else to be done other than to be patient and comfort myself with the thought that there are others here who are even worse off.

With best wishes,
your father
B. Mahler

SOURCE: Alma Mahler, "Ein Leben mit Gustav Mahler" (unpublished manuscript in the Bibliothèque Musicale Gustav Mahler); *Selected Letters* S4

17 *From Justine to Gustav*

Iglau, 9 May [1886]

Dear Gustav!
I have been meaning to write you for ages, but with the best will in the world, it has not been possible since we have been continually busy with home redecorating since your departure. Did you write to dear father already? He wrote us that his condition is highly satisfactory, however he did suffer a lot with the bad weather. You hardly write to us anymore. Do you have a lot to do? There is certainly no new opera in prospect now, so you will be able to recuperate a little bit. I am already really looking forward to July when you will be at home again. Your visit will compensate me for many deprivations I have had to impose on myself. I have only been out walking twice since dear father has been away, since dear mother was prevented from going with me by painful feet and too much work. Yesterday we had a letter from dear Leopoldine. She complains a lot that you have never replied to any of the letters that she has written you. If you wanted, you could congratulate her on her birthday on the 18th of this month, since she has never failed to do so on yours, and you cannot imagine how much that would please her. I will close for today with my best wishes.

Your faithful
Sister

SOURCE: Alma Mahler, "Ein Leben mit Gustav Mahler" (unpublished manuscript in the Bibliothèque Musicale Gustav Mahler); *Selected Letters* S5

18 *From Marie Mahler to Gustav*

Iglau, 31.5.86

Dear Gustav!
Only today am I able to send you a few lines. Dear father has been home since Tuesday and is feeling quite well, God be praised. Only he still has to take things very easy and above all avoid anger and agitation—which is hard to do in a business. But we are pleased with him, and the doctor holds out the best for him.

Incidentally, there is nothing at all of note to report. How are things with you, dear Gustav. Will you be coming home in July, then? I am writing now with great reluctance and so will close with best wishes and kisses to you from all of us—

Your
faithful mother
Marie

SOURCE: Alma Mahler, "Ein Leben mit Gustav Mahler" (unpublished manuscript in the Bibliothèque Musicale Gustav Mahler); *Selected Letters* S6

19 *To Justine*

[Prague, early June 1886]

Dear Justi,
From your letter I take it that you all don't know what to make of each other. Forever and ever the same misery! I want to say a few, brief words to you.

Tolerate everything, and everything that is to come, and know that you still have a long future before you, one that will teach you to bear happiness and suffering. Be considerate to father, who is odd just now, like all sick people, and because of that often lets himself be brought to actions that he later regrets.

Above all, though, see to it that you make things as easy for mother as possible; watch that she looks after herself properly, and do not pour oil on the fire where there is a squabble.

By the way, what are these hints of "your own troubles" etc. in your letters? What's the trouble, then? *Simply confide in me*, and write me what is wrong. Maybe I will have some advice.

Mother must come here anyhow and consult Dr. Pribram,[1] so that we might perhaps discover what is wrong with her, and how she can get better.

In any case, write me about everything soon—and also *about yourself*. You do know that in me you do not just have a brother, but also a friend.

[unsigned]

Shelfmark: E18-MJ-638
Note

[1] Dr. Alfred Pribram (1841–1912) from Prague is also mentioned in several letters from March 1889.

20 *From Justine to Gustav*

B. MAHLER, IGLAU
MAKER OF LIQUEURS, RUM, ROSOGLIO, PUNCH, ESSENCES, AND VINEGAR

Iglau, 4 June 1886

Dear Gustav!
Your letter pleased me very much, and I have acted in the way that you advised. I am taking care, to the best of my ability, to get back on good terms with father. Often I succeed for a little while, then once again I make mistakes (in his view) and the good is again undone. Dear mother's health was much better while father was not in Iglau. I think that her journey to Prague to see Dr. Pribram is gradually being forgotten about. You could bring it back to mind in a letter so that we will know what mother should do. She is now drinking Marienbad water, but it does not seem to suit her. We should turn to the matter energetically. And now I will tell you about myself. The marriage brokers and all kinds of old women are now beginning to come to the house, and it

upsets me greatly that my future is supposed to be decided by such people. I feel within myself that it would cost me a great effort of self-control to marry such a man, and yet that really will be my fate, for ideals are never attained, and whatever one wishes for most never happens, so I cannot take any comfort at all in my future. Do not be angry that I tell you everything. If you hadn't permitted it, I certainly would not have done so. It is already easier for me that I have told you, and I am convinced that you will not laugh at me, but will sympathise with my feelings.

Farewell, and best wishes and kisses from

your faithful Sister

SOURCE: Alma Mahler, "Ein Leben mit Gustav Mahler" (unpublished manuscript in the Bibliothèque Musicale Gustav Mahler); *Selected Letters* S7

21 *From Leopoldine to Gustav*

Vienna, 8.6.1886

Dear Gustav!

I delayed answering your letter in order to send you a photograph of Annie[1] which we have just had done; the picture is ready today, so I am doing this. I have only good news of us to report. We are all very well, and our Annie is coming along splendidly and is a very good and loveable child. Ludwig gets on very well with his boss and, as for me, I now feel very fortunate and happy. In your last letter you asked me what sort of prospects we have for the immediate future. I must admit candidly that I don't properly understand this question. Did you perhaps think that Ludwig wants to change his job? I can only tell you that nothing is further from his mind than a change of job. As I already said, he gets on very well with his boss, and only recently received proof of his good will and satisfaction by being presented with 100 fl. for a yearly pass on the tramway. And Ludwig himself is so delighted and enthusiastic about his boss as rarely any man is about another. Now, about my visit home, I still do not know anything definite. Ludwig is going to Hungary and Transylvania in the middle of August and will be away 3–4 weeks; possibly I'll use this time for a summer holiday. Ludwig never goes to Prague on his travels, only Hungary, Transylvania, and Moravia.

As I only still have to thank you warmly for your birthday greetings, I remain, with best wishes

Your sister Leopoldine

Do you know already that Minna Frank is married? My address: L. Qu. Meidling, near Vienna, Hufelandgasse 10, 2nd floor.

SOURCE: Alma Mahler, "Ein Leben mit Gustav Mahler" (unpublished manuscript in the Bibliothèque Musicale Gustav Mahler); *Selected Letters* S8

NOTE

[1] Leopoldine's first child, Anna, was born on 4 November 1885.

22 *From Marie Mahler to Gustav*

B. MAHLER, IGLAU
MAKER OF LIQUEURS, RUM, ROSOGLIO, PUNCH, ESSENCES, AND VINEGAR

Iglau, 10.6.1886

Dear Gustav!
I still cannot tell you the exact day of my arrival, but I hope to come in two weeks. By then we think that dear father will be able to travel. Right now he needs as much rest as possible. He is not even supposed to walk around the room too much as long as the swelling is on his feet. At any rate, I am not sure right now whether it might not be better for us to go to Vienna to see Bamberger.[1] Father really doesn't know whether he is being treated properly, so I do not know what I should do. I do not dare make the trip on my own. Anyway, let me know what you think would be best, and whether you will still be conducting something in Prague. I would really like to see you conduct sometime—is that not a very reasonable wish?

It will be quite impossible for me to come to Leipzig. But try *at any rate* to come home for a few days. We *all* look forward to seeing you. Best wishes and kisses from us *all*.

Your faithful mother
Marie

The letter from Leipzig *will follow immediately*.

SOURCE: Alma Mahler, "Ein Leben mit Gustav Mahler" (unpublished manuscript in the Bibliothèque Musicale Gustav Mahler); *Selected Letters* S9
NOTE
[1] Dr. Heinrich von Bamberger (1822–1888).

23 *From Justine to Gustav*

Iglau, 16.6.86

Dear Gustav!
We received your letter today, and I am very glad that you will be coming home for some time. Dear mother's trip came to naught, as usual. She had another violent attack, and so does not dare. Later, perhaps, she will go with dear father to Vienna to see Prof. Bamberger. Dear father will certainly go in order to consult about his health. He already feels so well that they tested him again today, and we all can attest to the improvement—however, he is still often very irksome. Did you already receive the picture of Annie? Don't you think that she looks strikingly like our mother? Poldi is coming here with her for a few days in August because Ludwig is going on a trip to Transylvania. This week Babi Tausig was here from Vienna and told us a lot of nice things about Poldi.

She feels very happy and things are now going very well for her. On Sunday Tini Krauss and Fanni Kellner have weddings. Yesterday Doctor Adler Gottlieb[1] from Vienna visited us and sends you his greetings. My health is now very good. Doctor Schwarz prescribed pills for me which have worked remarkably effectively. Everyone is amazed at how well I have been looking for the last three weeks. Dear father just told me that he is not going to see the Professor in Vienna since you will be coming home so soon[2] and will be able to arrange it so that you can take dear mother to Prague or Vienna. She has to consult a professor, since she does not dare to go for walks, and that is really her best medicine.

Farewell, and greetings from

Your faithful Sister Justine

SOURCE: Alma Mahler, "Ein Leben mit Gustav Mahler" (unpublished manuscript in the Bibliothèque Musicale Gustav Mahler); *Selected Letters* S11

NOTES

[1] Gottlieb Adler's sister, Sofie, was married to Mahler's cousin Albert; see letter 2.

[2] After leaving Prague shortly after the end of the season on 15 July 1886, Mahler spent several days in Iglau before taking up his new position in Leipzig.

24 *From Marie to Gustav*

Iglau, 16.6.1886

My dear Gustav!

Apparently it is written in the stars that I am not to see you conduct in Prague—for although I would very much have liked to see it, it is absolutely out of the question. I cannot risk the journey after having had another violent asthma attack last Friday. Now I need another long period of as much rest as possible and cannot expose myself to the journey to Prague. I am *very* glad that you, dear son, will be coming home for a while, and hopefully we will have some happy days with you here. Dear father is very much looking forward to seeing you too. Your presence will do him good. He needs the distraction very much, as his feet are still swollen. Nevertheless, all in all, he is feeling *better.* As far as your room is concerned, you do know what our apartment is like. We will do all we can to try to make you comfortable here. In any case, will you let me know exactly when you are coming?

Bring home *all* your old things and clothes—perhaps I can use something from them (for the children). Meanwhile, best wishes and kisses from me, and from dear Father too.

Your faithful
mother
Marie

SOURCE: Alma Mahler, "Ein Leben mit Gustav Mahler" (unpublished manuscript in the Bibliothèque Musicale Gustav Mahler); *Selected Letters* S10

25 *From Justine and Marie to Gustav*

Iglau, 5 July 1886

Dear Gustav!
Warmest best wishes for your birthday. We hoped that you would have been able to spend it in our midst, but fate has decreed otherwise and robbed us of this great pleasure. I think it had to be like that: because I was madly looking forward to seeing you, and when I look forward to something too much, it does not happen. Dear mother baked you a birthday cake and I embroidered a bookmark for you, but we will not send them along because the delay won't make it worthwhile. Yesterday dear father went to Vienna to see Professor Bamberger and Dr. Schwarz went with him. Dear mother has been quite well for several days. Dear father bought a one-horse carriage and we have gone out twice. That does her a lot of good as she cannot walk because the country is mountainous all around us and she is not supposed to climb hills. It's just too bad that Alois is already going away with the wagon tomorrow. Let us know exactly when you are coming and dear mother will utilise it to come and meet you, otherwise she would not take a wagon. Otto is now playing the Beethoven sonata that you did with Camilla Ott at the concert.[1] He is making good progress. Emma is also beginning to learn piano this week. The music that I couldn't find, dear father had locked it away in the book armoire.

Good-bye until soon, then.

Your faithful sister
Justine

Dear Gustav!
Accept my warmest wishes as well on your birthday. I am very much looking forward to seeing you. Warmest greetings from

your faithful mother
Marie

SOURCE: Alma Mahler, "Ein Leben mit Gustav Mahler" (unpublished manuscript in the Bibliothèque Musicale Gustav Mahler); *Selected Letters* S12

NOTE

[1] Beethoven's Sonata in A Major for violin and piano, "Kreutzer," op. 47. According to HLG I, p. 168, the violinist's name was Mila von Ottenfeld. The concert took place in Iglau, 11 August 1883.

26 *From Justine to Gustav*

Iglau 14.7.86

Dear Brother!
Today I am sending you the latest greetings from Iglau. We received your card and, in case you can't come on Friday, intend to meet your train on Saturday, as Friday and Saturday would be too expensive. Also, on Friday Alois comes home from his trip. I will put off telling you everything else until we meet. Our parents have both been in better health, thank God. We are all very much looking

forward to seeing you—it's just too bad that you'll only be home for such a short time. Dear mother already weeps when she thinks that you are going to Leipzig; she always thought that she would come to see you while you were in Prague. However, it is not possible for her, since she cannot risk any trips. Dr. Schwarz did not allow her to go with dear father to Vienna to see the professor, and she cannot bear the cure he has prescribed for her. For her, calmness has been the main requirement throughout her illness. The doctor has examined her and cannot find anything wrong organically, it is all just nerves. Dear father is entirely reconciled with Ludwig and Poldi. She is very happy, but they are both upset that you have not answered any of their letters, even when they sent you the picture of Annie. He now earns 180 fl. a month on average, and they can live very well on that. Poldi even puts something aside every time, which he doesn't know about. It is not yet certain that she will come in the summer, as he is probably not going on the trip and therefore she would rather stay in Vienna with him.

Farewell for today, then, with warmest wishes

from Justine

Until we meet!

SOURCE: Alma Mahler, "Ein Leben mit Gustav Mahler" (unpublished manuscript in the Bibliothèque Musicale Gustav Mahler); *Selected Letters* S13

27 *To Justine*

[Leipzig, late August 1886]

Dear Justi,

In haste I am sending you a few lines to relieve your anxiety! So far, my position is very agreeable, which bodes very well. We will probably perform the Nibelungen next year. If so, it will be divided between Nikisch and me. My orchestra is really one of the *best* in the world, and you would be pleased if you saw how much they respect me. I was recently invited to the first concert master's (Petri)[1] and we got on so well that I was there until *4 o'clock* in the morning.—It never occurs to anyone here to draw comparisons between Nikisch and me—from the outset they have recognised my equal rights and independence.

In the next while I will send you a very good review of Freischütz and Hugenotten from the "Nachricht."[2] At Thiemer's I subscribed to the Leipziger Tageblatt for you, since it is the most important newspaper here. There is always a lot in it, especially important reviews. I'll send you the most noteworthy ones from time to time.

Today I am calling on Staegemann for the first time. He is tremendously obliging towards me.

It is a little different here than it was with Neumann. Almost daily I reserve two seats for my landlady—and she always takes the *balcony* without further ado (the *best* seats here). By the way, she is a very nice old woman, who really mothers me and provides me with all the comforts I could imagine.

I have to eat at the inn, usually around 2:00, and then I almost always go home and rest a while.

By the way, the Leipzig air seems to do me good—I feel very well.

Best wishes to you all
from your
Gustav

Write soon!

SHELFMARK: S1-MJ-730

NOTES

[1] Henri Petri (1856–1914) was a student of Joachim and the father of pianist Egon Petri.

[2] As *Der Freischütz* was performed on 20 August and *Les Huguenots* on 22 August, this letter must have been written shortly after the 22d. (In HLG I there is a photograph of an annotated review of the *Freischütz* performance from the *Leipziger Zeitung* [photographs, p. 16].)

28 *To Justine*

[Leipzig, early October 1886]

Dear Justine,

I received the letter that dear mother started on the 23rd and that you continued on the 29th with the note that she has been unwell since then.—If you think that this comforts me—as your own words suggest—at least you show yourself to be a st . . . thoughtful person.[1] However, I would now like you to finish off your letter right away and give me a detailed report about our dear parents' health.

Did you receive the *letter to Poldi* and forward it to her? I would like to know that too! I will gladly subscribe all of you to the Leipziger Nachrichten. In every regard things are excellent with me.

Yesterday I received a direct engagement offer from Neumann. He offers me a salary of 3000 fl. He might even agree to 4000 fl.! This is interesting, is it not! At any rate, everyone in Prague is supposed to be sighing for me. The enclosed advertisement from a Bavarian newspaper was sent to me by Fritz Löwi [Löhr].—He also wonders, dear father, when you are finally coming to Vienna?[2] He says he has already arranged everything.

Send news *right away*! Gather your thoughts together a bit too.

Best wishes to *everybody*
Gustav

There certainly is a temple here too!

SHELFMARK: E18-MJ-629

NOTES

[1] Mahler separates the first letter from the rest of the word (*denkendes*) with a large space, perhaps implying *dummes* (stupid).

[2] Mahler had asked Fritz Löhr to arrange a medical consultation for his father in Vienna; see GMB[2] 53 and 54.

29 *To Parents*

[Leipzig, October 1886]

Dear Mother and Father,
Yesterday I received a letter from Fritz Löwi [Löhr]. I am happy that your expedition, dear father, turned out so well.—As I see it, it simply comes back to what the doctor in Prague said that time.—Send me the test results regularly.

I am amazed that you hardly ever write me!

Yesterday Šubert,[1] the director of the Bohemian National Theatre, visited me—and he is only stopping here for one day, so you can see what sort of reputation I have in Prague.

I am remarkably well here, and hope to establish a significant position here over time.

What are you all up to? Until you are more recovered, dear father, you could make a small jaunt and drop in here some time, and perhaps take along dear mother. You would be amazed what a beautiful theatre there is here! It is much more significant than the one in Prague. Nevertheless I do miss it a little, because for the first time I actually had a really important position—which I certainly could not say of Kassel.

Give *Freund* and Brosch[2] my greetings, and *write soon, won't you!*

Best wishes to all,
Gustav

Shelfmark: S1-MF-761
Notes

[1] Frantisek A. Šubert (1849–1915), director of the National Theatre in Prague between 1883 and 1900.

[2] Iglau pianist Johannes Brosch was one of Mahler's teachers.

30 *To Parents*

[Leipzig, January 1887]

Dear Mother and Father,
Although I have had almost no rehearsals lately and have lazed about continually, I was still at home so little that I didn't get around to writing. Also, I wanted to go out because my room is so cold and dark that I hate staying in it.

I enclose a very important letter from the Intendant in Cassel.[1] You must certainly know that such a Prussian Baron and Intendant is very proud, and seldom condescends to write at all himself. You can just imagine how surprised I was to receive this answer right away to my New Year's card.

There is almost nothing new here. *Kraus* from Iglau was here, and I sent him along with a few little things for the children. Did he deliver them?

Why do you almost never write? Are you all healthy?

Anyhow, I am moving on 1 Feb.[2] It is so cold here in my room that I have to end this letter so that I can get out of here.

Best wishes to you all
from
Gustav

SHELFMARK: E2-MF-74
NOTES

[1] On 26 December 1886, Mahler wrote to von Gilsa for a recommendation for a position in Karlsruhe in case Nikisch did not leave Leipzig as he hoped. This letter and von Gilsa's positive reply of 28 December are published in *Gustav Mahler in Kassel*, pp. 92–93.

[2] Gustav Adolfstraße 12. (On the basis of this letter, GMB²60 can probably be dated 2 February 1887.)

31 *To Parents*

[Leipzig, 15 April 1887]

Dear Mother and Father,
To my great distress, dear father, this time it is not possible to obtain the saccharin for you as quickly, and I must put you off for a while. As you know, it is not yet in the formulary and only through the personal patronage of the inventor himself was I able to obtain a small dose that time. Mind you, he said to me then that the supply should last for at least a year—that is why I was so amazed when I heard from Justi that you had already finished it. Naturally I will now move heaven and earth, and hope to send you more as soon as possible.[1]

What is up with my plan? Have you already thought about it? Don't think that I am merely dreaming—I am thinking quite seriously of bringing it to fruition. As soon as you decide, I will rent an apartment in a nice little place near Leipzig, where such things are certainly cheaper.

I enclose a review from the other paper. Please read it carefully from beginning to end so that you see that my position here improves from day to day.

I am off now to [rehearse] Siegfried,[2] which I finally hope to bring off at the beginning of May.

As soon as I have the saccharin, I will send it immediately.

Best wishes from
Gustav

I am now off to the premiere of "The Tales of Hoffmann"—(I am conducting major operas almost every day.)

[across the top of the letter:] I received these stamps [*Marken*] in a letter.[3]

SHELFMARK: E17-MF-625
NOTES

[1] In 1886, one of the inventors of saccharin, Constantin Fahlberg (1850–1910), established the saccharin plant Fahlberg, List & Co. in Salbke-Westerhüsen a. d. Elbe.

[2] The premiere took place 13 May 1887.

[3] Lost.

32 *To Parents*

THE MANAGEMENT [*REGIE*] OF THE
LEIPZIG STATE THEATRE

[Leipzig, 30 April 1887]

Dear Mother and Father,
With Siegfried, I have a tremendous amount to do right now.—Justi told me about your plan, and of course you can count on me for everything.

The question is, dear mother, whether it is not simply a matter of getting you into healthy air and to living peacefully in quiet distraction. In this case, my suggestion would be best, wouldn't it? Consider it carefully and let me know! Next I'll send you some nice reviews from the out-of-town newspapers (I don't have them at hand right now). Here too the press is already very friendly towards me.

Yesterday was Fidelio;—after the big overture I had a storm of applause that lasted a minute, just like in Prague.[1] I have won the public over.

Siegfried will be the crowning touch.

Very best wishes, and write soon.

your
Gustav

Shelfmark: E2-MF-56
Note

[1] 29 April 1887. Mahler's comment about the "big overture" certainly suggests the *Leonore* Overture No. 3, which at the time was commonly played before act II. This remained Mahler's practice until the famous Roller production in Vienna in 1904 when it was inserted between the scenes in the second act.

33 *To Parents*

[Leipzig, 13 May 1887]

Dear Mother and Father,
Tonight is the premiere of *Siegfried*. Before the dress rehearsal, the director, Staegemann, made a very flattering speech about me in front of the entire cast and orchestra. He emphasised my great contribution and at the end stressed that he will do everything in his power "to keep such an extraordinary talent at the Leipzig theatre." Nikisch, who ought to have come two weeks ago, then asked for another short extension of his leave since it is so *painful* for him to be at the Leipzig premiere of Siegfried and see someone else conducting it.—As you see, I have already achieved a great deal—more than anyone else in Leipzig has ever achieved in such a short time. The press and the public have changed their tune.

When the reviews appear, I will send them to you right away.

I am at Staegemann's almost more than I am at my own house. I eat with them at every opportunity and am just like one of their children.

Write soon! When do you leave, father?

Best wishes from your
Gustav

In the greatest of haste!

SHELFMARK: E13-MF-539

34 *To Parents*

[Leipzig, 23 May 1887]

Dear Mother and Father,
Why do you never write? Is dear father in Karlsbad already? Were you at the doctor's in Prague, and what did he say.—You will know from the newspaper that Nikisch has already returned.[1]—I am really now his equal.—Enclosed are some reviews, from which you'll see how those who used to be my bitterest opponents write about me now.

My relationship with Staegemann is still as close as it always has been. I eat there almost every Sunday and holiday, and overall I have a standing invitation there. They do not get along with Nikisch, and would be happy if he rather submitted his resignation.—I will have my holiday at the beginning of July, since there is a Wagner cycle before then. Please, write me, won't you? Even a few words. With best wishes from

your Gustav

Now I'm off to "William Tell"!

SHELFMARK: E2-MF-79
NOTE
[1] Nikisch's first appearance was on 22 May in *Die Meistersinger.*

35 *To Parents*

THE DIRECTORATE [*DIREKTION*] OF THE
LEIPZIG STATE THEATRE

[Leipzig, early June 1887]

Dear Mother and Father,
Why do I never get any news? I literally do not know where you are! My holiday begins on 15 July and lasts until around 6 August (about 3 weeks). Of course I'll just come to wherever you are.

It doesn't seem like a bad idea at all to go to Retz, or at least to that area.[1] It is certainly healthy and invigorating there, and that is what you need most.

I will be extraordinarily happy to see you all again.

Everything is going excellently for me here, touch wood. My relationship with my director is such a warm and friendly one that, because of this, of course, my position is a very dominant one. Even if Nikisch still gets to conduct the majority of the so-called "significant operas" because of his seniority (which, by the way, will soon have an end too), it is still evident that my influence on things is stronger than his. If nothing intervenes, sooner or later I will have to be regarded as the *first* [conductor]. In this case, this triumph over a Nikisch carries ten times more weight than one over a Slansky[2] in Prague.—The following Wagner operas have been definitely assigned to me: *Rienzi*, *Flieg. Holländer*, *Lohengrin* and *Siegfried*.—and next season I get *Meistersinger* too.[3]

I now have very lovely contact with several families that are friends of Staegemann.

Since the people in Leipzig are so tremendously hospitable, I eat at friends' houses almost more than at the inn. Since Nikisch is now rehearsing Götterdämmerung,[4] I have almost nothing to do and go to the country every afternoon.

Write soon—above all, how you are all feeling!

Best wishes to everybody
from your
Gustav

Shelfmark: E17-MF-626
Notes

[1] Between Vienna and Iglau.

[2] Ludwig Slansky (1838–1905), first conductor (*erster Kapellmeister*) in Prague.

[3] Mahler conducted these works, as well as *Tannhäuser*, during the Wagner cycle (24 June–10 July) that concluded the 1886–1887 season.

[4] The premiere of *Götterdämmerung* under Nikisch took place on 17 June.

36 *To Parents*

Reichenhall, 28 July 87.

Dear Mother and Father,
I have been here for two days and have already made a few excursions (to Lake Tum). I will not be going up onto Mount Watzmann,[1] because I am pushing off again tomorrow evening and heading to Innsbruck and the surrounding area to meet up with both Krzyzanowskis. In Vienna, I received a four-page letter from Staegemann. Among other things, he tells me that they haven't yet gone anywhere. I also had a note from Frau von Weber. From Innsbruck, I am off to Lake Starnberg, where I will be staying until the end of my vacation.

I did find the jacket in the suitcase. I didn't notice it at first.

I was two days with the Löwis in Perchtoldsdorf. They send their greetings to everybody. They all were amazed at how well I look. How is your health, both of you?

For now, best wishes. I will write again from Starnberg. Hopefully there I will have a letter from you again—use this address:

Dr. Heinrich Krzyzanowski in Starnberg bei München

your
Gustav

Shelfmark: E2-MF-57
Note

[1] Near Berchtesgaden.

37 *To Parents*

[Postmark: Leipzig, 7 September 1887]
[Arrival postmark: Iglau, 9.9.87]

Dear Mother and Father,
I am consistently lucky in my work. A few days ago my former intendant from Cassel was here. I was invited to Staegemann's with him and also played "Pintos" to a large assembly.[1] *Gilsa* was completely bowled over and immediately took on the opera for Cassel. Tomorrow I am conducting "Die Loreley."[2] Of course, under these circumstances I must be terribly diligent. Luckily everything has been going well right from the outset, and my work is making unbelievable progress. Best wishes from

Gustav

How are you all? Write soon!

Shelfmark: E2-MFp-58
Notes

[1] According to HLG I, p. 257, this private hearing of Mahler's completion of Carl Maria von Weber's unfinished opera *Die drei Pintos* took place on 28 August.

[2] Opera by Max Bruch.

38 *To Parents*

[Leipzig, end September 1887][1]

Dear Mother and Father,
This time I have to make very special reference to my diligence. In the last week, I completed *two acts* of the score [*in Partitur fertig gestellt*].[2] If all goes well, the whole opera will be ready for publication by the end of the month. Everywhere I receive the greatest respect.

You may have been surprised by the 2nd shipment of saccharin (you received it, right?) The *inventor* himself sent it to me. You don't need to ration it any longer—you can use as much as you like. I can send you a new dose any time.

At the theatre, I am rehearsing Spohr's opera, Jessonda.[3]

Write soon how things are with you.

Best wishes from
Gustav

Shelfmark: E2-MF-72
Notes

[1] Dated on basis of the next letter (4 October), announcing the completion of the score (*Partitur*).

[2] Of *Die drei Pintos*.

[3] *Jessonda* was not performed until 4 December.

39 *To Parents*

[Postmark: Leipzig, 4 October 1887][1]
[Arrival postmark: Iglau, 5.10.87]

Dear Mother and Father,
Just completed the score. It's already at the copyist's. As soon as the parts are ready, it will go into rehearsal. The premiere is scheduled for *December*. You can just imagine how much work it was. Everything surpassed all expectations.

Best wishes from Gustav.

SHELFMARK: E2-MFp-59
NOTE
[1] Erroneously dated 8 October in HLG I, p. 258.

40 *To Parents*

[Leipzig, November 1887]

Dear Mother and Father,
I am now mired in work. The materials for the performance of the opera must be made quickly. Everyday I get offers from publishers and intendants. Top people from all over Germany have already announced that they are coming to the first performance.

There is also a lot about it in the Paris and London newspapers, and it seems that the work will also be performed there. At the theatre, I am rehearsing this work next, and then Meistersinger.[1]

I hope to be able to come to Iglau for a few days at Christmas.

Write again soon, won't you!

I sent Malek 30 marks and ordered another suit from him.

Best wishes to you all
from
Gustav

SHELFMARK: E2-MF-75
NOTE
[1] Not performed until 10 February 1888.

41 *To Parents*

[Leipzig, second week November 1887]

Dear Mother and Father,
This month, once again, I have a lot planned. First: Tannhäuser Sunday,[1] and Cosima Wagner has announced that she will be at the performance.—A week after that, I conduct the first performance of Spohr's "Jessonda,"[2] and at the end of the month, there is a big Wagner concert at the theatre, in which I am conducting "Parsifal."[3]

Then, rehearsals for "Die 3 Pintos" begin immediately. Director Staegemann himself will stage it.

All of the intendants and important musicians have already announced that they will be at the first performance.

Write again soon, won't you. Is Freund back in Iglau?

Best wishes
from
Gustav

SHELFMARK: E2-MF-73
NOTES

[1] 13 November.

[2] Delayed until 4 December.

[3] 30 November. Mahler conducted the final scenes of the first and third acts of *Parsifal*, and Nikisch conducted the *Wesendonck Lieder*, Symphony in C, and *Eine Faust Ouverture*.

42 *To Parents*

THE DIRECTORATE OF THE
LEIPZIG STATE THEATRE

[Leipzig, end November 1887]

Dear Mother and Father,

The rehearsals for the Wagner concert are now in progress. As I'm sure that I wrote you, I am conducting the second part: "Parsifal." Two days after that is the premiere of Jessonda, under my direction.[1]

Then the "3 Pintos" rehearsals begin immediately.

So, as you see, a very eventful month.

A publisher has already offered 20 000 marks for the piano-vocal and full scores, but we do not want to hand them over just yet.[2] 10 000 of it will be mine. The most important revenue will be from the theatre royalties, which—if we're lucky—could easily be 4 or 5 times as much.

So I am not coming home for Christmas. Instead, I have to use the time to rehearse the opera. The premiere is scheduled for 20 January.

Tomorrow I am off to Berlin, where I will play "Pintos" to a large and select group—among whom Count *Hochberg*[3] will probably be found.

Perhaps I'll also go to Vienna for a few days in December to confer with Jahn and Hanslick.

Have you received the saccharin yet, dear father?

You can send me your Christmas list—hopefully, I will now play the rich uncle from America.

Write soon, won't you.

Best wishes
from your
Gustav

Source

Letter sold by Alfred Rosé. Transcribed from a photocopy in the Mahler-Rosé Collection.

Notes

[1] *Jessonda* was postponed until 4 December.

[2] C. F. Kahnt, Leipzig.

[3] Graf Botho von Hochberg (1843–1926), Berlin *Intendant*.

43 *To Parents*

[Leipzig, end November 1887]

Dear Mother and Father,
Today I received dear Justi's letter. You must not blame me for writing so little. You really could hardly believe how much I have to do.

The opera is to be readied for publication and to be rehearsed by the cast.—

So, the first 10 000 marks have been earned. I get them on the day of the premiere, *20* January. Of course I will telegraph you right away about how it went.

The photograph is very good and pleases me very much.

The piano-vocal score should appear in the New Year, and I will send a copy to you immediately.

Write again soon.

Best wishes to you all
from
Gustav

Shelfmark: E2-MF-60

44 *To Parents*[1]

[Leipzig, end December 1887]

Dear Mother and Father,
Today, briefly, best wishes for a Happy New Year, and above all for *health*—I now hope to be able to take care of the *other* myself from now on.

Mr. Stanton,[2] the director of the German Opera in New York, has just announced that he is coming over for the performance and wants to acquire the opera for America.—Well, he can bring a tidy sack of dollars with him.

On Christmas Eve I was at Webers' first, and then with them at Staegemanns'. I received so many presents from everybody that I can hardly list them all to you. Among many other things from the Webers, a large gold medallion, 2 dozen fine handkerchiefs, silk scarves, etc. From Staegemann, a large clock with an alarm, a typewriter [*Briefmaschiene*][3] etc. etc.—masses of Christmas baking [*weihnachtsstrizeln*]—books, photographs with stands, wallets etc. From Webers, a little desk with embroidery on it—the latter from Frau von Weber.

Pintos is being diligently rehearsed in the theatre.—Everyone is taking pride in it, which is not usually the case here. I have just written a new entr'acte, which is one of the best things in the opera.

Beforehand, though, no one must know what is mine and what is Weber's, otherwise the critics would have an "easy time" of it! I don't yet have the *money*, but if you need something *at present*, I could easily borrow 1000 marks and send it to you immediately.

Let me know about it.

Best wishes
from
Gustav

Write soon!

SHELFMARK: E2-MF-55
NOTES

[1] First published by Hans Holländer, "Gustav Mahler vollendet eine Oper von Carl Maria von Weber," *Neue Zeitschrift für Musik* 116, no. 12 (1955); reprinted in GMB[2] 64. I have corrected some errors in transcription and restored the original emphases and paragraph divisions.

[2] Edmund C. Stanton, director of New York Metropolitan Opera, 1885–1891.

[3] Unclear. There are no typewritten letters from Mahler from this or any other period in his life.

45 *To Parents*[1]

[Leipzig, 22 January 1888]

Dear Mother and Father,
In great haste, just a brief report! Everything went magnificently. The cheering was frenzied. Today the house is again sold out.[2] Don't be surprised if my contribution is somewhat minimised by the newspapers. For "business considerations," it must be kept secret for now what is mine and what is Weber's. This much I can already tell you, that two of the most successful numbers, which the newspapers everywhere mention especially (No. 1: Student chorus, and the Ballad of Kater Mansor), are by *me*, as well as many other things.—*All* this must be kept *secret*, however, until the opera is performed everywhere. For now it means the less the prestige, the more the money! That is how it will be until all is revealed. In any case, from this day on I am a man of *world renown*.

Kapellmeister Levi[3] from Bayreuth was there too, and terribly enthusiastic about me. He also told me that Cosima Wagner wrote him a four-page letter about me.

By the way, I got masses of wreaths—among which there was one from Director Staegemann and his wife with a wonderful dedication. The 10 000 marks from the publisher were already deposited for me in the Reichsbank. Imagine: Weber and his wife didn't want to give me the money at all, but took it to the bank themselves and gave me the deposit receipt, because they were afraid that I would squander it away. Now come the royalties, the amount of which one cannot estimate with certainty because it depends on the number of locales and performances the opera is given.

So, at the moment I have the above amount at my disposal—or, rather, not at my disposal, but have the deposit receipt for it.

I am going now to conduct *Pintos* again. When it is performed in Vienna, you must go and hear it.[4] I'll write in more detail soon.

Best wishes
from
Gustav

Write immediately how things are with you all.

SHELFMARK: E13-MF-540

NOTES

[1] First published in Holländer (see above), then GMB[2] 68.

[2] The premiere of Mahler's completion of Carl Maria von Weber's *Die drei Pintos* took place on 20 January. It was performed again on 22 January and thirteen more times that season (twice conducted by Nikisch).

[3] Hermann Levi (1839–1900), *Hofkapellmeister* in Leipzig.

[4] The Vienna premiere took place on 18 January 1889.

46 *To Parents*[1]

[Leipzig, 29 January 1888]

Dear Mother and Father,

Unfortunately, I still cannot get away from here. Today is Pintos again (sold out for the third time). It really seems to have drawing power. Tuesday and Friday it's on again. Naturally, I have to stay here, but I hope to be able to come home for at least a week at Easter. I recently reckoned up with Weber. With the money and the proceeds in general, I plan to proceed *as follows*. Now I get 10 000 marks. 1000 marks go to pay my debts. 1000 marks I am sending immediately to you. 8000 marks I am investing, and will let the royalties etc. grow until there is a sum of 30–40 000 marks—which hopefully will be the case over a year.

This capital ought to be a *secure income* for you, then, so that you can give up your business and live however and wherever you like. When I come home, I will talk with you about the administration of the capital, dear father. I myself will live on my salary, just like before, and since I no longer have any debts, I can get by splendidly—especially since I will get 4000 marks starting in July. I cut off the first coupons on 1 March. Of course, I will send them to you immediately. Hopefully you all agree with my plans.

Write me about it soon!

I am conducting Meistersinger next week!

Best wishes from your
Gustav

SHELFMARK: E13-MF-541

NOTE

[1] Handwritten copy of the original letter, with "Originalbrief an Mrs. Lanier in New York geschenkt" on the back in Justine Rosé's hand. Whereabouts of the original unknown.

47 *To Parents*

THE DIRECTORATE OF THE
LEIPZIG STATE THEATRE

[Leipzig, early February 1888]

Dear Mother and Father,
I enclose 1000 marks in Reich bonds. It is worth more than 1000 marks because you must also get the interest. Have it worked out properly for yourselves.

I have invested the other 8000 marks similarly, and gave up the main certificate at the deposit office.

At the same time, I am sending you a handbill and a *libretto.*[1]

You must be very careful with the libretto, though. It is no *ordinary* libretto. Only a few copies are in existence and it is printed *as a manuscript*. If it came into unauthorized hands, we could lose a lot of money on it. So take care of it. When I come home, I will tell you how it all fits together.

The piano-vocal score is still not published—as soon as it appears, I'll send it to you immediately.

Best wishes
from your
Gustav

Let me know if everything arrives safely.

SHELFMARK: E2-MF-63
NOTE
[1] Neither survives in the Mahler-Rosé Collection.

48 *To Parents*

[Leipzig, February 1888][1]

Dear Mother and Father,
I am quite astounded that you write me, dear mother, that you have not had a letter from me in two months. *Certainly* some must have gone astray.

Today I am invited to Staegemann's for dinner.

We have received offers from America, England, and Paris. As well, articles about me have already appeared in the papers there. Also in *Dutch* ones.

I have become a celebrity overnight, and not just in Germany either, but in the whole world.

I am very happy that you are feeling better again, dear mother. From the outset, I thought that this to-ing and fro-ing over the summer would not pass by without consequences for you.

Now, thank heavens, it is over. If only spring were here again.

By then, I hope to be a capitalist already. I am certainly counting on 50 000 marks.

Best wishes to everyone
from
Gustav

SHELFMARK: E2-MF-61
NOTE

[1] On the basis of the contents, the letter seems to have been written after the premiere of *Die drei Pintos*, despite the first sentence.

49 *To Parents*

THE MANAGEMENT OF THE
LEIPZIG STATE THEATRE

[Leipzig, February 1888]

Dear Mother and Father,
I just received your letter, dear mother, and I am really astounded about a few words.—

I see now that I was not exactly understood by you all.—Fine! First of all, let me tell you this: above all, I do not want to hold back the money for *me*, but it is my firm intention that the money is *not* put into the shop—"*You are certainly enough for me*," as you said, but no shop in the world is secure enough for you and me!

Simply put, I *want* the money to stay together for the time being, until it has increased (if it increases at all). *By no* means should it be split up.

Come on now, is it not enough if I tell you that I have not spent a penny of it on myself—nor will I.

And I certainly don't even have it with me; it's in an *office*.

I only sent you the 1000 marks so that you could afford a few little *luxuries*—I *intended* that every penny be used for your *pleasure*. Regarding the shop, I've told you again and again that if you want to keep it for Alois, I agree completely. But *you both* must free yourselves of it and come to live, in peace and contentment, *with me* here in Leipzig, or wherever you prefer, and be free of these agonizing worries in your old age. You will thank me for it eventually.

However that might appear to you, I actually understand this better now. Once again, I tell you: as soon as the idea grows on you, then let business be business and come to me, or if you don't want to do that, then I will do everything possible for you so that you can live completely without care.

All this only briefly, because I have a rehearsal. Dear mother, I hope that you do not find me insensitive anymore, because I count on your understanding.

Above all, you must not imagine that this is such a simple calculation—now I have to have capital *at hand* in order to be prepared for business purposes—(for example, to have performance material made, pay agents etc.). This lasts for months and years before such a thing bears fruit—that is, unless one does as the others and sells one's birthright for a mess of pottage. Then, admittedly, one is free of all work.

Best wishes from
your
Gustav

Write soon!

SHELFMARK: E13-MF-542

50 *To Parents*

THE MANAGEMENT OF THE
LEIPZIG STATE THEATRE

[Leipzig, 14 or 21 February 1888]

Dear parents!
There is a particular reason—which ought not to [surprise][1] you—why you haven't heard from me for so long: namely, I am working again on a new composition, a *large* symphony that I would like to have finished over the course of next month.[2]—Because I am so hard at it again, I have not got around to writing you even once. I use every free moment.

Tonight is a performance of Pintos.[3] The King and Queen of Saxony are coming—the King is especially interested. Yesterday he made a nice joke (to General Tschirschky): "Now I am curious what is *painted* [*gemalt*] and what is *woven* [*gewebt*] in Pintos."[4]—I will write you straight away about how it all turns out.

I am just sending the piano-vocal score,[5] also some newspapers.

I am very happy that you are all feeling better. Once the symphony is finished, I shall come home. Right now, I must take advantage of the favourable current—that's why I am working so hard.

Best wishes to you all. Write again soon.

Emma writes beautifully? She must already be a big girl! When I find time some time, I will *answer* her.

Best wishes
from your
Gustav

SHELFMARK: E2-MF-64
NOTES

[1] The word is obscured by a hole in the paper.

[2] First Symphony.

[3] *Pintos* was performed on 14 and 21 February. It is unclear which performance was attended by King Albert I of Saxony (1828–1902; reigned 1873–1902) and his queen.

[4] The pun is based on the composers' surnames: Mahler/*malen* (to paint) and Weber/*weben* (to weave).

[5] Does not survive in the Mahler-Rosé Collection.

51 *To Parents*

[Leipzig, 15 or 22 February 1888][1]

Dear Mother and Father,
A quick report about last evening. Everything went well. The King invited me up to his box after the second act and talked to me in the most *amiable* way. He talked only with me for the entire intermission. Then, just as the act ought to have started, the Queen came up and spoke to me. So I had to remain, and this lasted for maybe 10 minutes, during which time the entire audience had to wait. She knew that I was from *Iglau*, and told me that she often passed through, and that a new railroad to Meseritsch is being built, which I didn't even know. She also asked if my parents lived in Iglau, and I told her that I would tell you about [her question], and that you would be very pleased. The King, who is extraordinarily knowledgeable about music himself, ~~thanked~~ asked me about several numbers, and who they were by. And of these, those that he liked best were by me. He and those present were quite amazed. You would be amazed what affable people they are. It is easier to talk with them than with the mayor of Iglau. We chatted together like we had known each other forever.

It is quite a special honour that the *Queen* came to me as well—one that only rarely happens even to the aristocracy, because generally men are addressed *only* by the King, and ladies *only* by the Queen. As well, I seem to have made a favourable impression upon her, since she talked a lot about me with General Tsch[irschky] at the reception afterwards.

The King also said to me that he is already very much looking forward to the performance in Dresden.[2]

Their Majesties stayed until the *final curtain*.

The Duke of Coburg-Gotha is coming to the next performance.

Best wishes
from your
Gustav

Write me right away that you received this letter.

SHELFMARK: E17-MF-624
NOTES

[1] See note 3 to letter 50.

[2] The premiere of *Die drei Pintos* in Dresden took place on 10 May 1888.

52 *To Parents*

[Leipzig, March 1888]

Dear Mother and Father,
Just a few lines so that you won't worry.

I am working hard at my piece,[1] and still hope to have the final copy [*Reinpartitur*] finished this month—the middle of next month at the latest. Then I'll laze about. Anyhow, I will also come home for a few days.—This ought to be the second half of *April*, then.

Recently I got an offer from the Stadttheater in Frankfurt-am-Main: first Kapellmeister in place of *Dessoff*.[2]—I asked for 10 000 marks a year and two months holiday. If this is granted, I will leave here for there in the next few months. Dessoff has been ill for ages and will soon be pensioned off. Write soon.

Best wishes
from your
Gustav

SHELFMARK: E2-MJ-54
NOTES

[1] First Symphony.

[2] (Felix) Otto Dessoff (1835–1892), German conductor, active in Vienna (1860–1875), Karlsruhe (1875–1881), and Frankfurt (1881–1888?).

53 *To Mother*

THE DIRECTORATE OF THE
LEIPZIG STATE THEATRE

[Leipzig, 1 March 1888]

Dear Mother,

Today, above all, warmest birthday congratulations.[1] I hope that you all are *quite* well today! I am *quite busy* right now, that is why I write so *seldom*. Before my new piece is finished, I will not rest, but afterwards, I will relax a bit, and hope to come to Iglau for at least a week then. Perhaps it will already have got that far by May. I will be very happy to see you this time—I really have taken a big step forward again, haven't I?

Tonight is the tenth performance of Pintos. The Duke of Coburg-Gotha is coming to the performance. The opera will be performed in Hamburg next (still in March), and then in Munich on 5 April, and then in Dresden later in the month. The other theatres will probably put it on in the fall because that is the main season.[2]

This Dr. Heinrich Braun[3]—the one who sent you a telegram—is a friend of mine from *Vienna*. He is the brother-in-law of Albert Spiegler, who specifically came to the Leipzig premiere and brought me a beautiful laurel wreath "from the Viennese friends."

How are you both feeling? Let me know right away!

The day before yesterday I was with the Weber family in *Berlin* (2 days), simply to get a little fresh air—since just then there was nothing to do here. There I was also invited to Herr von *Wildenbruch's* (the famous poet).[4] In general, I was received there splendidly.

Best wishes from your
Gustav

Once again, dear mother, Happy Birthday!

Shelfmark: E2-MF-66
Notes

[1] Marie Mahler's birthday was 2 March.

[2] See note to letter 55, below.

[3] Heinrich Braun (1854–1927), Emma Adler's brother, was married to Albert Spiegler's sister Josephine. There is a letter in the Mahler-Rosé Collection written around this time from Marie Mahler to an unknown correspondent ("Herr Doktor"), possibly Heinrich Braun:

> [A]s before, we hear very little from Gustav himself. We don't even know (apart from Dresden) what opera houses have already taken up the opera—and we know even less about its material success, apart from the 10 000 marks that Gustav already has for the piano-vocal score. He has promised to come home at Easter, so we hope to hear all about it in person then.

[4] Ernst von Wildenbruch (1845–1909), German poet and Karl von Weber's brother-in-law.

54 *To Parents*

[Leipzig, 2 March 1888]

Dear Mother and Father,
Just a brief report that the Duke of Coburg-Gotha was tremendously kind to me. He conversed with me for a long time, and after the performance, Staegemann and I accompanied him to the train station and were with him (in the royal salon) for another hour until the train departed.

Apart from that, I am very industrious and am rapidly coming along with my piece. The few people I have played it for were completely taken with it.

So you have received the piano-vocal score and the newspapers all right then? Yes?

Why didn't you let me know?

Next week I am conducting Meistersinger again.[1]

Best wishes from
your
Gustav.

Shelfmark: E2-MF-77
Note

[1] This performance did not take place owing to the closure of the theatres after the kaiser's death on 9 March.

55 *To Parents*

[Leipzig, end March 1888][1]

Dear Mother and Father,
Well! Today my work is finished and I can say—thank God—that it has turned out well. With it, I again hope to take a large step forward. Tomorrow the Staegemann and Weber families are coming for coffee (in fact, I have a wonderful apartment and the Staegemanns and Webers are often over) and I shall then play

the symphony for them a second time. The first time, it virtually caused a sensation amongst them, and they wanted to hear it again immediately.

Naturally, I won't have any difficulty having it performed, since I'm now a "famous" man.

You asked, dear mother, how many there are in the Weber family. It consists of husband, wife, two daughters, and a son. One daughter is 9 and the other is 6; the son is 7. They like me very much, visit me often, and bring me flowers.

Frau Weber keeps me well supplied: poultry, cakes, apples, figs, linen, tea, coffee, etc.—whatever need she happens to gather from my eyes. I often eat there at noon or in the evening too; also at Staegemann's.

Sunday is the first performance of *Pintos* in *Hamburg*; *Wednesday*, the same in *Munich*; and during *May*, the opera is being given in Dresden and Cassel! The other stages, like *Vienna*, will give the opera only next winter.[2]

Of course I'll invite you to *Vienna*; I will certainly go there myself. We will talk about it when I come home next. I certainly hope that this will be sometime next month. I wrote that to Poldi—maybe she can come too.

Best wishes to everybody
from
your Gustav

Write soon.

Shelfmark: E21-MF-675
Notes

[1] HLG I, pp. 271–72, n. 53, mentions an unpublished letter of 28 March from Mahler to Hans von Bülow announcing the completion of his symphony.

[2] In fact, the Hamburg premiere took place on Thursday, 5 April, and the one in Munich on Tuesday, 10 April. *Pintos* was given in Dresden on 10 May, but was not performed in Kassel until the fall. The Vienna premiere was on 18 January 1889. (La Grange is one day off in his date for the Munich performance in the note mentioned above. The situation is exacerbated by what seems to be an erroneous transcription of the letter: Mahler quite clearly writes "Sunday," not "Friday.")

56 *To Parents*

[Leipzig, April 1888]

Dear Mother and Father,
I enclose a programme from the special performance [*Festvorstellung*] of *Pintos*, which was completely sold out and a huge success.[1]

[Also] a new article by Hartmann, about the approaching performance in Dresden, which will take place on 8 May.[2] Maybe I'll go. I have a lot to do right now at the theatre.

I am rehearsing Spontini's "Cortez."

Why do you never write?

Best wishes
from your
Gustav

SHELFMARK: E2-MF-62
NOTES
[1] *Die drei Pintos* was performed on 11, 18, and 30 April. It is unclear which one was the special performance.
[2] Delayed until 10 May. Mahler was unable to attend since the premiere of Spontini's opera also took place that day.

57 *To Parents*

[Leipzig, mid-April 1888]

Dear Mother and Father,
Unfortunately, I still cannot tell you anything definite about my arrival in Iglau—I don't even know whether I can get away from here in the near future, because I have to rehearse Spontini's *Cortez* and Gluck's *Iphigénie*.[1]—As soon as I know anything definite, I will write.

Pintos was just given with great success in Hamburg and Munich.[2] Next time, I'll send you some reviews. Apparently it is being staged this month in Dresden and Cassel. We (Webers, Staegemann and I) will probably all go over to Dresden.[3]

I had a letter from Poldi. I was very happy that she feels so content.

I will bring Emma the potpourri that she wants when I come home.

Why have you not written for so long? I'd like to see something from Justi or Emma anyway—at least a few words.

Best wishes to all
from your
Gustav

How fortunate that Alois is out of the military again.

SHELFMARK: E2-MF-68
NOTES
[1] Gluck's opera was not performed that season, likely owing to Mahler's conflict with the stage director Albert Goldberg and subsequent departure from Leipzig. (The little that we know of this conflict comes from GMB[2]71. There appears to have been some sort of public confrontation between the two men during a rehearsal.)
[2] 5 April and 10 April, respectively.
[3] See note to letter 56.

58 *To Parents*

[Leipzig, 11 May 1888]

Dear Mother and Father,
Yesterday I was at "Pintos" in Dresden.[1] I will come home in a few days, and will spare myself all storytelling until then. I was very busy and have to carry on a terrible amount of correspondence—that's why I haven't written for so long.

The premiere of my symphony in Dresden is 7 December.[2] The premiere of Pintos in Cassel is in the next few months—then comes Braunschweig, Breslau, Bremen, Frankfurt-am-Main, Nürnberg, etc.

I would really like to have a nice, quiet room for two or three weeks, perhaps in Heulos,[3] or wherever. I will have to work a lot. Look around a bit, then!

What is Otto up to?

I believe that I will come at the beginning of next week.

Best wishes
from your
Gustav

SHELFMARK: E2-MF-67

NOTES

[1] 10 May, according to the 16 May issue of the *Neue Zeitschrift für Musik*.

[2] Did not take place.

[3] Near Iglau.

59 *To Parents*

[Leipzig, undated][1]

Dear Mother and Father,

Only briefly, I report that I begin my holiday [*Dienstruhe*] the day after tomorrow and will see you in Iglau in a few days.

Among the many congratulations, I received the enclosed card and letter, which I send for your perusal.

Best wishes
from
your
Gustav

SHELFMARK: E2-MF-78

NOTE

[1]Alfred Rosé wrote "Leipzig" in pencil across the top. It is possible that this letter dates from mid-May 1888 when Mahler left Leipzig.

60 *To Parents*

[Postmark: Munich, 23 May 1888]
[no arrival postmark]

Dear Mother and Father, I am here in Munich for the time being, in order to work towards my purposes. Letters will reach me at this address:

Dr. Heinrich Krzyzanowski
for Mahler in Starnberg, near München

For next year, I have had initial inquiries from *Frankfurt* and *Hannover*

(Court Theatre)—I really don't know yet what I will decide.[1] I hope to be with you soon!

Best wishes from

Gustav
Write soon.

SHELFMARK: E2-MFp-65
NOTE
[1] See letter 52.

61 *To Father*

[Prague, 1 August 1888]

Dear Father,
Warmest congratulations to you on tomorrow's event.[1]

Here the rehearsals are proceeding rapidly.[2]

Sunday I am going to Dresden to play my symphony for Hofrath Schuch—the Dresden performance is as good as certain.

Why does no one ever write me? Is Poldi still in Iglau? What is Otto up to? Is he practising piano diligently? Which of you is coming here on the 18th?

Best wishes to you all

from your
Gustav

SHELFMARK: E2-MF-71
NOTES
[1] Bernhard Mahler's birthday.
[2] Mahler was rehearsing for the Prague premiere of *Die drei Pintos*, which took place on 18 August 1888.

62 *To Justine*

[undated][1]

Dear Justi,
I really should haul you over the coals. Couldn't you have at least written a few lines? Or are you too one of those who always has to have a formal answer first. Do let me know what you are doing and what you are up to from time to time, and if you are unsure of something, ask my advice. Accustom yourself to it—the time will come when it will be of great value to you. By the way, tell me Poldi's address; I have to write her again sometime. Are the boys practising the violin diligently? And the piano? Are you all well? And are things *really peaceful* at home? I want to know everything.

Best wishes to you all
from
Gustav

SHELFMARK: E18-MJ-639
NOTE

[1]The letter probably dates from the Prague or Leipzig period (during Mahler's first year in Budapest, Otto lived in Vienna with Poldi and her family). It is written on paper not found elsewhere in the collection.

BUDAPEST
September 1888–March 1891

Chronology

1888 *September*: Otto Mahler enters the Conservatory of the Gesellschaft der Musikfreunde in Vienna and lives with his sister and brother-in-law Leopoldine and Ludwig Quittner.
1 October: GM named director of the Königlich Ungarischen Oper, Budapest.

1889 *26, 27 January*: Hungarian premieres of *Das Rheingold* and *Die Walküre*, sung in Hungarian and conducted by GM (his first Budapest performances).
18 February: Bernhard Mahler dies in Iglau.
Summer: Vienna, Iglau, Prague, Marienbad, Munich, Salzburg, Bayreuth (*Parsifal, Tristan, Meistersinger*).
September: Otto resumes study at the Conservatory and lives with the Löhr family; Alois begins his military service in a regiment in Brünn.
27 September: death of Leopoldine Mahler.
11 October: Marie Mahler dies in Iglau.
October: Justine joins GM in Budapest; Emma moves in with the Löhrs in Vienna.
20 November: premiere of the First Symphony in Budapest.

1890 *May*: GM and Justine travel to Italy (Trieste, Bologna, Genoa, Milan, Florence, Venice).
Summer: Hinterbrühl with Löhrs; Justine undertakes cure in Franzensbad; GM composes songs from *Des Knaben Wunderhorn*.
Fall: Justine, Emma, and Otto live together in an apartment in Vienna.
October–November: Natalie Bauer-Lechner visits GM in Budapest.

1891 *22 January*: Géza Graf von Zichy becomes *Intendant* of the Opera; conflict with GM begins.
14 March: Zichy and GM agree to the terms of his departure.
22 March: GM leaves Budapest and travels to Vienna.

Letters

63 *To Parents*

[Budapest, end September 1888][1]

Dear Parents,
The position that will be offered me here is an unexpectedly magnificent one—so magnificent that I am afraid to take it, and must consider it seriously.

I would be Director of the Royal Opera, with unlimited authority! Master of as great an institution as the Vienna Court Opera.—1. Kapellmeister at the same time! I report only to the Ministry, and am absolute master.—Fixed annual salary of 10 000 [florins], lots of supplementary income, and *4 months* holiday!—It is really unbelievable!

At the same time, though, the responsibility is terribly great—with a stroke of the pen, I am in charge of a budget of 1 million!—The yearly subvention amounts to 400 000 [florins]!

I have been working with the civil servants and senior officials for two days already, in order to get an idea of the business. I am quite dumbfounded at how much there is to learn!—

More next time! I just received the money order. Write soon! I will write about Otto as soon as I have time. I now must remain free for an indefinite period.

In the greatest haste!

Your Gustav

Shelfmark: E16-MF-614
Note

[1] Mahler arrived in Budapest on 26 September after spending a few days in Vienna consulting with Beniczky (see GMB[2] 74, which undoubtedly dates from this time). See Zoltan Roman, *Gustav Mahler and Hungary* (Budapest: Akadémiai Kiadó, 1991), pp. 25–26, for a discussion of the uncertainties around Mahler's contract.

64 *To Parents*

[Budapest, Autumn 1888]

Dear Parents,
So that you don't worry, I am writing to let you know that I am well and also that my eyes are all right.—I have *never* before had so much to do and to worry about, but it is hard in the beginning because I have found everything in a huge mess. My position is extremely splendid.—I am sending you my contract to look over—send it back to me right away.

Just write often so that I don't worry.—Sometime soon, I have to travel (after New Year's), then I will visit you.

Very best wishes to you all
from your
Gustav

Shelfmark: E17-MF-623

65 *To Parents*

[Budapest, December 1888]

Dear Parents,
Enclosed, a few Hungarian apples and pears for Christmas. Would you like to have some Hungarian salami?

Please get Otto to have a winter coat made in Iglau at my expense.

What is Poldi's address? Please send it to me soon since I can answer neither her nor Otto.

I have an immense [amount] to do. As soon as Walküre is over, I hope to be able to get some rest.[1]

Best wishes
from your
Gustav

SHELFMARK: E8-MF-392
NOTE

[1] In his first interview in Budapest, for the *Budapesti Hírlap,* Mahler announced his plans to stage *Das Rheingold* and *Die Walküre* for his debut. Originally planned for December (but see Roman, p. 198, n. 22), they were eventually given on 26 and 27 January 1889.

66 *To Parents*[1]

[Budapest, fourth week January 1889]

Dear Mother and Father,
Just a few lines—I am right in the middle of the Nibelungen rehearsals. Friday and Saturday is the premiere.[2] The repetition immediately after! If I carry this out, I will achieve a colossal success and strengthen my position. Then, at any rate, I take . . . come . . . [continuation missing]

. . . in the first days of March.—Please do not do anything stupid, and take care of yourselves, above all—don't deny yourselves *anything*.—*Do you need money*? I have now saved another *1000 fl*.—So, don't lack for anything, I . . . [conclusion missing]

SHELFMARK: E8-MF-394
NOTES

[1] The lower half of the card on which this was written is missing.

[2] The premieres were in fact given on Saturday, 26 January, and Sunday, 27 January.

67 *To Parents*

[Budapest, 25 January 1889]

Dear Mother and Father,
Both dress rehearsals were *splendid* successes[1]—all Budapest is stirred up—

Enclosed, a selection of the huge numbers of articles and letters that I have received already.—The Intendant is quite happy.[2]

I will write more soon.

It was another tremendous success!

How are things with you all? Just write more often!

Best wishes from your
Gustav

Shelfmark: E17-MF-628a (typewritten copy)
Notes

This letter was sold by Alfred Rosé and is now in the Pierpont Morgan Library, New York City (MFC M214.M2145). It is published here with permission of the Pierpont Morgan Library.

[1] According to Roman, p. 53, the dress rehearsals were reversed, with *Die Walküre* on 23 January and *Das Rheingold* on 24 January.

[2] Ferenc (Franz) von Beniczky (1833–1905).

68 *To Parents*

[Budapest, 28 or 30 January 1889][1]

Dear Mother and Father,
It was tremendous again yesterday!—All Budapest is treating me royally. The aristocrats, the parliament, etc.—it is a national enthusiasm, as is only possible in Hungary.

Soon, I will tell you about everything myself. I still have to conduct the second performance, and then I am making a little business trip, during which I will come via Iglau and stay with you for 2–3 days.

Write me how you are all feeling!

Best wishes
from your
Gustav

Shelfmark: E17-MF-619
Note

[1] This letter was written either on the 28th, following the premiere of *Die Walküre*, or on the 30th, following the repetition of *Das Rheingold* (but before the news of Archduke Rudolf's death forced the closing of the theatre). The following letter may make the latter more likely.

69 *To Parents*

[Budapest, 29 January 1889]

Dear Mother and Father,
Walküre's success was even greater. Everyone was cheering: *Eljen Mahler*! I got a *huge* wreath with an enormous ribbon.—

Today is the second performance![1]

Following, you will receive two baskets of grapes and a basket of Seville oranges. Let me know if you enjoy them. They are from *Tokaj*.

Best wishes
from your
Gustav

How are you all?

SHELFMARK: E17-MJ-620
NOTE
[1] *Das Rheingold.*

70 *To Justine*

[Budapest, January or early February 1889][1]

Dear Justi,
Write me at once, and be clear about everything since you must now stay in continual contact with me anyhow. At any rate, just don't lose your head; you know, don't you, that one must never lose hope.—Above all, do not let our dear parents notice anything. I am here—you know that—and I would really like to hurry to help you all, but right now I cannot leave. I do not want to do anything now that would be so obvious to our parents. Is *Frau Schiller* with you, at least?[2] And Alois must *certainly* not neglect the business. Tell Schwarz that he should come down more often.[3]

Write me *immediately.*—When the *need is greatest*, I will come to Iglau *immediately*. But not before, because, as you can imagine, it is difficult for me to get away and I must save my holiday for the most important instance.

At any rate, do not lose heart—it has so often improved before, why not this time.

Best wishes, and write *immediately*.

Your
Gustav

Say hello to Frau Schiller and ask her to take care of things.
Do you get any other assistance from people?

SHELFMARK: E6-MJ-284
NOTES
[1] As Mahler's father was still alive, this letter must date from before mid-February (Bernhard Mahler died on 18 February).
[2] Unknown.
[3] Schwarz was Mahler's parents' doctor.

71 *To Mother*

[Budapest, end February–March 1889][1]

Dear Mother,
I am very happy that your recovery proceeds so well. Naturally, I again have a tremendous amount to do.—Have somebody write me exactly which preserves you like. Should I have *graham <u>bread</u>* sent daily now? Asparagus? Salmon? Lobster? etc. How do you like the graham cake? Can you tolerate it?—If only the children would not make too much noise! ~~Still, let the~~ Nevertheless, do not yet speak too much, and do not tire yourself out. What is Justi up too? She ought to take care of herself too. As she likes the preserves, she should help

herself to as much as she likes, and I will send more.—The same holds true for Poldi.

Best wishes to you all
from your
Gustav

Shelfmark: E17-MF-616
Note
[1] Since Mahler addresses the letter to his mother, as opposed to his customary "Dear Parents," it must have been written after his father's death on 18 February. Before this time, only on their birthdays did Mahler write to them individually (accordingly, most of the letters addressed to Marie Mahler have been assigned dates between mid-February and October 1889).

72 *To Justine*

[Budapest, late February–March 1889]

Dear Justi,
I sent the money (250 fl.) to the doctor already yesterday, so you don't need to worry about it anymore.—

In addition, I have arranged that graham bread will be sent twice weekly. Write me whether it *is enough* and arrives still *fresh*. Otherwise, one ought to have it sent from Vienna.—So, I shouldn't send *salmon* and *lobster* anymore, and pineapple?

Just don't deny yourself anything—I do not want that! *Do not go without anything*—it is a pleasure to provide you with luxuries. You should only pay the usual *household expenses* out of the business.—Above all, dear mother ought to have *every wish* fulfilled *immediately*. I am very happy that things are going so well for you all!—Just tell me about it often. Thanks too to dear Poldi for her letters.—My replies are for her as well.

Best wishes to everyone
Gustav

Shelfmark: E18-MJ-630

73 *To Leopoldine*

[Budapest, March 1889]

Dear Poldi!
About three days ago, I wrote you a registered letter in which I told you that I had just sent the 250 fl. fee to the doctor.[1]—So what sort of story is this! Have you now sent the fee *too*?

Write to the doctor at once, then, [and tell him] that a mistake has occurred and that he should return *one fee*!

I don't know when I will go to Iglau; it depends on what Dr. Spitz writes me.[2]—

I got notice from him, by the way, that the *mail will no longer be held back*! What sort of confusion is this then?—

By the way, in such circumstances, always turn to Dr. Spitz as well as to me, because I really cannot do anything else other than to write to him again. Still, it is quite right that you informed me about everything.

—Write to Dr. Pribram now, and wait [to see] whether he will send it—then *send it back to me perhaps* if you are no longer in financial difficulty.

I think that I am able to come at the beginning of April.

Do you have a nice summer place already?—Search diligently, because it is very important for dear mother. Only she should not dream of "*keeping house*" again, as you write. That makes *absolutely no* sense!

Write again soon.

Your
Gustav

SHELFMARK: E8-MF-396

NOTES

[1] Prof. Dr. Pribram, from Prague, is also mentioned in two letters from June 1886.

[2] According to the note to GMB[2] 108, Spitz was probably a lawyer in Iglau.

74 *To Justine*

[Budapest, March 1889]

Dear Justi,

Quite right! Look around a little bit yourself! Sooner or later I will come home and will set everything in order then.

Just see that you all have a nice place for the summer. At my instructions, Dr. Pribram will send the money to you—it is *best* that you send it back to me immediately, for, as things stand, I have absolutely no desire to enrich the "legal estate" (for which, first of all, you all still have no secure claim) with my own hard-earned money. It is certainly better kept here. Also, I have not telegraphed, because from now on I must avoid all unnecessary expenses.

Naturally, in the case of dear mother, *nothing* must be spared, and I will always be *ready*, gladly, if it is about *her* needs or wishes.

I was very happy to see a few lines from you again. I take that as a good sign that you will soon be well again.—

I already have a tremendous amount to do again.—Tell me, what does Otto write?

Write again soon!

Next I will write to dear mother as well.

Best wishes to everybody
from your
Gustav

SHELFMARK: S1-MJ-731

75 *To Justine (and the Other Siblings)*

[Budapest, March 1889]

My dears!

A postal order follows, with the 100 fl. you asked for. At the same time I cannot help but make a serious objection—in your interest, as well as mine! Now, you know that I hold nothing back from you, and happily offer every sacrifice.—However, in order for me to be ready to meet your needs, I simply have to face the duty to *save* and economise. If I spend all my salary now, where am I supposed to get the money that we all might require if the need intensifies over the summer?

And not only that! I must now put aside some extra pennies for all of us anyway.—For two years, I have really tried, but something always gets in the way. I have also taken on Otto's support, which will cost me 80 fl. a month from now on.

So, take note of all this, and do not approach me without pressing needs and demands.

Live now just as before—certainly *Mother* should be wanting nothing; please keep me regularly informed about needs, for which I will naturally provide in abundance.

But be clever, and don't overtax my earning power now. The time will soon come when it will be of use to you if I have *savings* at my disposal. These right now are *absolutely nil.*

I am writing this letter to you, dear Justine, and ask you not to say anything about it to dear mother, so that she is not unnecessarily troubled.—But carefully direct your thoughts to what I have just said.

You certainly understand me.

So, next I am sending more sardines and preserves. Also, beginning tomorrow, graham bread will come daily. Just be sure to get an *attractive*, suitable summer house.

Do write me daily—even if it's just a card.

Since for the moment I myself am in a tight spot, I must remain in debt to the doctor for a while longer.—If, however, you have enough money, send it to him; if not, I will send it to him on 1 April, when I am paid again.

Best wishes to you all,
from your
Gustav

SHELFMARK: E8-MF-393

76 *To Mother*

[Budapest, end March 1889]

Dear Mother,

Otto wrote me that from now on he will regularly send you graham bread and *graham cake*. I too was of the opinion that this matter was taken care of. I immediately ordered a torte from Vienna to be sent to you all by return of post. How are things with the bread? Do you receive it regularly?

Today I am sending sardines and salmon from here; also white melons.

—I am very happy that you all have a nice summer place already. Just be careful that you don't overtire yourself or get a chill in moving.

Of course, I have a lot to do right now. I am rehearsing a new opera.[1] In April, I hope to get away for a few days and put everything in Iglau in order then. Are you happy with Alois now?

Yesterday I was invited to a soiree at the Intendant's.[2]

Now I must go to another rehearsal.

Write again soon!

Best wishes from your
Gustav

SHELFMARK: E17-MF-622
NOTES

[1] *Les Dragons de Villars* (*Das Glöckchen des Eremiten*) by Aimé (Louis) Maillart (1817–1871) was first performed on 31 March.

[2] Beniczky.

77 *To Mother*

[Budapest, 30 March 1889]

Dear Mother,
I am so busy with the preparations for the premiere tomorrow that I can only write a few lines.[1]

I can get away at the beginning of April only with *difficulty. When does Dr. Spitz leave, and when does he come back*? Let me know right away! The address you wanted is as follows:

Frau Hauptmann Marion Freifrau von Weber
Leipzig
Sebastian Bachstrasse 5

But you must send the letter by *registered mail*, since they have already moved from there, and thereby it will be sent on to them at their new address.

Greetings from
Gustav

I will write again tomorrow.

SHELFMARK: E17-MF-621
NOTE

[1] *Les Dragons de Villars.*

78 *To Mother*

[In Hungarian:] THE HUNGARIAN ROYAL OPERA HOUSE
DIRECTORATE
BUDAPEST

Budapest, [April] 18[89]

Dear Mother,
The zwieback is actually for Justi—the cognac is the finest in the world.

Today Otto wrote me; I will send him travel money, and he will come home at Easter.[1]

Naturally, I again have a huge amount to do. Please send me news *daily*, even if it's just a little bit, so that I am reassured.

Tomorrow I will write again—I am in a rush again today.

Is the train seat reserved already?

Best wishes to you all
from your
Gustav

SHELFMARK: E17-MF-617
NOTE
[1] In 1889, Easter Sunday fell on 21 April.

79 *To Justine*

[Budapest, Spring 1889]

Dear Justi,
I am sending dear mother

1 Vienna
1 Berlin
and 1 Dresden newspaper

to be read to her. I am very well. As usual, I have a lot to do. Just keep writing to me often about dear mother's health, and about your own as well.

Best wishes from
your
Gustav

SHELFMARK: E18-MJ-631

80 *To Mother*

[Budapest, end April or May 1889]

Dear Mother,
Here are some reviews of the opera yesterday.[1]—

Now things here are rapidly drawing to a close.—On 18 May, I hope to be in Iglau.

Why have I not got a letter for so long? The weather here is now very nice! Not for you?—When do you move into the new apartment?

Just write again soon!

Has Alois's initial zeal lasted?

Best wishes to you all
from your
Gustav

I also enclose detailed instructions for Justi (for the powder).

SHELFMARK: E17-MF-615

NOTE

[1] According to Roman, p. 137, Mahler conducted *Le nozze di Figaro* on 27 and 29 April; *Die Walküre* on 28 April (probably) and 15 May.

81 *Otto to an Unknown Friend*[1]

[Iglau, August 1889]

Dear friend,

You must not think falsely of me. If I haven't written you, it's because of the very disagreeable and despondent mood that has taken hold of me in view of the very sad events at home. For a while I was really unable to write even a syllable to anybody, let alone a whole letter. Just listen to what is happening at our house. The first thing is that mother finds herself in a condition that gives great cause for concern, almost ruling out the hope of recovery. She really is suffering terrible torments, which occasionally even the doctor calls singular. Justi is half dead from this continual excitement and from staying up at night, and, on top of all that, is suffering from stomach troubles [*Magenkatarrh*]. She certainly is to be pitied. She will hardly be able to stand this much longer. Emma is a completely vulgar, useless creature, whose malicious behaviour is almost impossible to describe. It annoys mother, and is a nuisance for the whole house, etc. Alois is despondently awaiting his imminent draft in 6 weeks. Things are not the best for me either. I will leave my stomach troubles out of it, but to have to watch all of this is enough to drive one to despair. Now you have a rough idea and so will know how I feel and what sort of holidays I am having. So, how are you all? Is your mother in Vienna already? Do you already have an apartment?

At any rate, you will be better off than I am. With friendly greetings, I remain your

Otto

That reminds me. Gustav was here for about 4 days, travelled from here to Prague, and apparently is now in Vienna.[2] If he is not already in Budapest. He seems quite well, by the way.

SHELFMARK: S5-FC-973

NOTES

[1] This letter is the only item of Otto Mahler's in the Gustav Mahler–Alfred Rosé Collection.

[2] Mahler passed through Prague on 17 August en route to Budapest via Vienna. (He was also in Prague on 2 June to hear Ambroise Thomas's *Mignon*, but the content makes an August date more likely.)

82 *To Mother*

[Budapest, 26 August 1889]

Dear Mother,

I have safely arrived back in Budapest.—While the holidays last, I will be living on the *Schwabenberg*, near Budapest, where the air is wonderful.—Mornings, I am always at the opera, and afternoons, outdoors.—

In Vienna, I talked through everything with Poldi; she also immediately went to a good doctor [*Arzt*], who is now treating her.—The trouble is of a *nervous* nature, and completely innocuous.[1]—I am coming to Iglau at the end of September, and on this occasion will see how things are with her in Vienna. If Poldi has not improved by then, then I will go with her to a specialist [*Professor*]. It wasn't possible before, because all of them are not yet in Vienna.—

Everything is arranged for Otto; he will live full-time with the Löwis.[2] He should write at once to Fritz, who will give him more details.

It is quite alright with me that Emma is going to Wlaschim for a while. Hopefully, she'll learn some manners there.

I enclose a clipping from the *Berlin* paper.

I am happy that dear mother is again feeling a bit better. Hopefully, the fall will finally bring a real improvement. For sick people, the fall is the best time of year.

Tomorrow the shah is coming to the opera; we must honour him with a command performance.[3]—The Intendant was here, and accordingly I must do the honours.

Write again soon and in detail.—Otto should head back to Vienna on about 12 September.[4]

Best wishes to everyone
from Gustav

SHELFMARK: E17-MF-618

NOTES

[1] Leopoldine Quittner died on 27 September, probably of a brain tumour (see HLG I, p. 304, n. 18).

[2] During his first year at the Conservatory, Otto had lived with Leopoldine and her family.

[3] The shah of Persia was honoured with an evening of ballet excerpts (see Roman, p. 204, n. 92).

[4] According to the *Bericht über das Conservatorium für Musik und darstellende Kunst . . . für das Schuljahr 1888–1889* (Vienna: Verlag des Conservatoriums der Gesellschaft der Musikfreunde in Wien, 1889), returning students had to register and pay their fees by 15 September.

83 *To Justine*

THE HUNGARIAN ROYAL OPERA HOUSE
DIRECTORATE
BUDAPEST

[Budapest, September 1889][1]

Dearest Justi,
Warmest thanks to Ernestine for her letter.—I very much like having news every day.—*What doctor* do you all have, and what does he say?

I enclose an autograph from *Richard Strauss*, one of the most notable young composers. He probably has a great future ahead of him. Your collection will really grow over time, if it keeps up like this. Write again!

Best wishes from
Gustav

SHELFMARK: E13-MJ-519
NOTE

[1] Date suggested by HLG I, p. 303, n. 10. The mention of several of them needing to see a doctor recalls the situation described by Otto (see letter 81). At any rate, owing to the letterhead, it must date between October 1888 and 1889.

84 *To Justine*

[Budapest, mid-October 1889][1]

Dear Justi,
I didn't in fact know where you are—whether you are still in Iglau, or are already in Vienna. Therefore, I waited to hear from you first, before I wrote you.—

I anticipated the mood that you're in, and it is quite natural that everything has befallen you now that you are alone for the first time in a long time and find yourself in new circumstances.[2] You must not surrender yourself to this mood, because you are young and the sun will shine again for you.

For the time being, I suggest that Friday, the day after tomorrow, you take the express train that leaves Vienna at 9:00 and come and stay with me in Budapest.—Travel *first class*. Someone will take you to the train station and arrange everything.—I will wait for you *here* at the train station—you arrive about 1:30.—

Anyhow, please pick the day I indicated, because I don't have any time to wait for you on Saturday and Sunday.

If this is too sudden for you and you cannot get ready so quickly, then come on *Monday* at the same time.

At any rate, please *telegraph* me right away *when* you want to come.

We can discuss everything here in more detail.

If you'd like, we could look for an apartment together, and have Emma follow later.—And if you don't like it here, then together we will discuss what is better.

Anyhow, for the time being Emma should stay at Löhr's.

So, once again: be reasonable, and don't give yourself over to troubling moods.—Everything will get better for you. Whatever I can do to that end, will be done. Best wishes, and answer *right away*!

your Gustav

Say hello to *everybody*!

Shelfmark: E13-MJ-536

Notes

[1] This letter was probably written between GMB[2] 82 and 83 (postmarked 1 November). Given his mention of Friday being "the day after tomorrow," Mahler must be writing on a Wednesday, thus 16, 23, or 30 October.

[2] Marie Mahler died on 11 October.

85 *To Justine*

[Budapest, end 1889][1]

Dearest Justi,

I enclose some reviews—you receive the Pester Lloyd already anyway. My personal success was very significant.—

Yesterday was a ball at Singers—I danced a lot too. I hope to come to Vienna next week.

Best wishes to everyone
from Gustav

Shelfmark: E13-MJ-518

Note

[1] The dating of this letter is not secure, but it probably dates from 1889 since, as Roman has noted (p. 83), Mahler's popularity in Budapest declined sharply after late 1889. His last significant personal success was the premiere of Nicolai's *Die lustigen Weiber von Windsor* on 24 October 1889.

86 *To Justine*

[Budapest, January 1890]

Dear Justi,

Until today, I've had to deal with a fatal *flu* that hit me all of a sudden.—Morning, in the office and at rehearsal—afternoon and evening, sweating in bed.—[1]

The coffee maker has broken down and won't make any coffee.

I am leaving the matter to be investigated by a commission, and we will see where we are.

I am still not well—the flu is gradually progressing into a case of major runny nose. At any rate, a continual improvement.

Today I had the pleasure of investing 5000 fl. for you at the Commercial bank here. Hopefully, tomorrow the 1000 fl. will arrive for the [illegible] that I had Spitz sell; so, from now on, you really are the well-situated capitalist and Croesus of our family.

Don't forget that *Otto* should look for the forgotten clarinet part from the symphony *right away* and send it.[2] I need it urgently and quickly.

About the rum essence, Spitz wrote me that the agreement was made between Herrmann [*sic*] and Alois, [and] that, as is customary, what is being used will be recorded and an invoice submitted when all is done. You could ask the Herr Corporal sometime how this is with him.—

Enclosed, a postcard that came for you.

I only comment here that I *would like* that you limit your dealings with *Albi*, as well as with other Iglauers, to the bare essentials.—In any case, I absolutely *forbid* Emma to come into the slightest contact with absolutely anyone from there.

In vain, I am expecting the promised letter.

Tomorrow I am sending you the 130 fl., and *100 fl.* to the Löhrs for what I owe Fritz.

Very best wishes to you from
your
Gustav

Up to now, I have seen neither the Singers nor the Felds, but the day before yesterday, Kössler, and yesterday, Mihalowich [*sic*] was with me.[3]

Best wishes to Fritz and Uda, as well as Otto and Emma.

Shelfmark: E16-MJ-604

Notes

[1] According to Roman, p. 88, the flu epidemic was mid-January 1890. (The letter was definitely written after Justine had been in Budapest after their mother's death and before Fritz Löhr embarked on a study trip to Italy with his family in the fall of 1890.)

[2] It is not clear which symphony Mahler means. At this point in his career, Mahler had not conducted many symphonies:

Prague, 21 February 1886: Beethoven, Ninth Symphony
Prague, 18 April 1886: Mozart, Symphony 40
Budapest, 20 November 1889: Mahler, First Symphony
Budapest, 24 February 1890: Beethoven, Fifth Symphony
Budapest, 6 December 1890: Mozart, Symphony No. 40.

[3] See appendix for Singer, Kössler, and Mihalovich. For Feld, see above, letter 10.

87 *To Justine*

[Budapest, January 1890]

Dearest Justi,
Enclosed, 2 letters addressed to you.—I am still not very well. I cannot get rid of this cold.—

I am also worried about how things are shaping up with you all. When will you finally write to me about this in some detail? I would prefer that you address your letters to the Theresienring;[1] telegrams and whatever is urgent, however, to the theatre.

With best wishes
from your
Gustav

SHELFMARK: E6-MJ-606
NOTE
[1] Mahler lived at Theresienring No. 3.

88 *To Justine*[1]

Telegram (handwritten)

Budapest, 8/6 1890 9:40 a.m.
Still here and cannot get down to write more details from Hinterbrühl everything is going splendidly.[2]

Gustav

SHELFMARK: E16-MJt-605
NOTE
[1] Addressed to "Justine Mahler Villa Fellner Franzensbad." Justine had gone to Franzensbad in Bohemia for a month's cure.
[2] Mahler spent most of the summer of 1890 with the Löhr family in Hinterbrühl, near Vienna.

89 *To Justine*

[Hinterbrühl, 10 June 1890]

Dear Justi,
Today, early Tuesday, I have finally arrived and will now tell you how I fared.

Well, if nothing is to be concealed, I upset my stomach in the train compartment and in the dining car on a steak and salad (!) and, upon my arrival, I had to lie down after an extremely severe rash and a terrible headache. I was somewhat better that evening, and I went to [the] Singers. They were in a very gracious mood, and were most delighted by your last letter. Their nieces are still with them. I ate nothing, however, and because of that, we did not once talk about eating, but mostly about my non-eating.

Later the same evening, I met Mihalovich—hoho! hehe!—The next morning, I went to see the Intendant, who was dissolved in anxiety.[1] His pains were so great that, in order to alleviate them, I had to throw in 2 more days.—I was invited to Singers for lunch. I went to Mihalovich's in the afternoon, where Apponyi[2] was already waiting for me. Both asked about you.

Then, with *Mih.* to Margaret Island, where I met the *Felds* (all of them) and exchanged a few words with them. Naturally we talked about you.—That evening I dined with M. at the Hotel Continental, where *Kössler* presented himself. It was very nice. K. was quite sincere when he asked about you, and was quite astonished when I told him that the trip agreed so well with you.—Next was dinner at Singers with me and Mihalovich. After the meal, Kössler (a musician) came, and fetched me for a walk.

We went (in the strongest wind) up the Johannisberg (away from Auwinkel), [and] from there up the Schwabenberg to the Hotel Continental, where *Singer*, the *Deutschs*, and Mihalovich turned up. Everybody asked about you, etc. etc.

Old Herr Deutsch (Singer's father), whom I had seen for a moment at lunch, asked for your address and assured me that he will *certainly* visit you in Franzensbad. Since he already left for Marienbad yesterday, you can count on it that he will descend upon you next week.—If this is disagreeable to you, then be wary, and instruct your chambermaid.

The next day, I had a lunch rendezvous with Kössler at H. Stephan's.—Suddenly, *Herzfeld* arrived.[3] I ate with both of them, then, and took the midday train to Vienna and [proceeded] directly to Hinterbrühl without stopping in Vienna. Without exception, everyone in Budapest sends greetings.

Now, just write about yourself. Tell me what the doctor says about you, how he *finds you*, how long you expect to have to stay there, etc. etc. Many greetings and kisses from your

Gustav

Write whether I should send you money.

Shelfmark: E16-MJ-598

Notes

[1] Beniczky.

[2] See appendix.

[3] Viktor von Herzfeld (1850–1920), critic of *Neues Pester Journal*.

90 *To Justine*

[Hinterbrühl, second week June 1890]

Dearest Justi,

Hopefully you are finally in possession of our letters.—Without a doubt, the postal connection between us must be bad—for example, yesterday I received 2 letters from you at once.—I quite believe you that you are in the depths of despair. I foresaw these feelings. But now, just be nice and reasonable, and consider that all this is inevitable and certainly not so horrible. 4 weeks, even 5, finally come to an end, and if one thereby has become *healthy*, then one can certainly pay for it with a bit of boredom. *So don't be impatient.* Before you know it, you will be with us again.

If you have to stay longer than 4 weeks, and this is just too unbearable for you, then I will just spend the last week with you in Franzensbad. Here it is raining nonstop, and I can assure you that that is not pleasant either. Even here you probably wouldn't be any more entertained.

Hilgermann should be in Fr[anzensbad] by now.[1] The boots, and yesterday, a warm sweater, have gone off to you; ditto, a packet of "Grenzbotens" in a wrapper.[2]

I think that, in order to alleviate your boredom, it would be best if you read French very diligently. What is up with Stifter? Do you not like him anymore? By the way, you will see that you will accustom yourself to life there better than you now think; everyone begins like this. Also, until now, you have not tasted what it would mean to be alone away from home, and that is really necessary for a person.

You can imagine that I am longing to be with you; however, in consideration of what you are gaining by it, I am bearing it with great joy—you must think the same way! Now, be warmly greeted and kissed by your

Gustav

Head high! Grin and bear it!

Shelfmark: S1-MJ-756

Notes

[1] Laura Hilgermann (1867–1937), mezzo-soprano who sang under Mahler in Prague, Budapest, and Vienna. Letters to Mahler from her husband, actor Siegfried Rosenberg, from this time indicate that she was ill; see below, letter 95.

[2] Likely a newspaper.

91 *To Justine*[1]

Postcard

[Postmark: Hinterbrühl, 13.6.90]

[Arrival postmark: Franzensbad, 14.6.90]

D.J.

Today I am going to Kaltenleutgeben again—the rain has now stopped. You've received the boots already. Write me about your health in more detail. H[ilgermann] is hopefully also in F[ranzensbad] now. I wanted to draw your attention to the fact that you really should be diligent about going to the *theatre*. Someone will certainly go with you. Warmly, your

~~M.~~G.

Shelfmark: E6-MJp-303

Note

[1] Addressed to "Fräulein Justine Mahler / Curgast / in Franzensbad / Villa Fellner."

92 *To Justine*[1]

Postcard
[Postmark: Hinterbrühl, 15.6.90]
[Arrival postmark: Franzensbad, 16.6.90]

Dearest Justi,
Today I sent you what you wanted. I am very happy that you are starting to like it better. You should probably ask your doctor whether you ought go to Marienbad.—What effects from the cure do you notice? Write me about it in more detail.

Ever yours, G.

SHELFMARK: E6-MJp-304
NOTE
[1] Addressed to "Fräulein Justine Mahler / Curgast / in Franzensbad / Villa Fellner."

93 *To Justine*

Postcard
[Postmark: Hinterbrühl, 16.6.90]
[Arrival postmark: Franzensbad, 17.6.90]

D.J.
I do very much miss hearing something detailed about you even once, particularly on the following points: I. *Health*. II. What does the doctor say? III. In what circles are you moving, what are you doing? IV. Did you get the money?

I am already taking the cold-water cure.

Here, it's the same old routine!

Ever yours, G.

SHELFMARK: E6-MJp-305
NOTE
[1] Addressed to "Fräulein Justine Mahler / in Franzensbad / Villa Fellner."

94 *To Justine*

[Hinterbrühl, mid-June 1890][1]

My dear Justi, for days I have sat down to write you something substantial, and, with the best of intentions, did not get around to it. Even my supply of stationery failed me, and since the others also ran out, I had to resort to post cards, which I had a supply of.—Of course, on a post card one can only write the most trivial things. But I think that, between us, anything at all suffices.

[line scratched out]

Do I only have to assure you that I so sorely miss you, and that I accompany you in spirit all the time? To the fountain, into the waters, at meals.—But, strangely, such assurances do not want to emerge from my pen. Maybe you can appreciate that—maybe it's the same for you; I can tell this from your letters.—See, you must not be touchy about it, and think of me with *confidence*.—I notice it in you that you feel dissatisfied because of me, and perhaps in dark moods that you doubt whether I really miss you and whether I want you to return to me.

Well, write me honestly about everything, completely without reservation. I really must economize a bit now, otherwise, I would simply visit you in Franzensbad.—Under such circumstances, dear Justi, 4 weeks are a long time, but, look, they will pass by quickly; bear them with serenity. It actually pleases me, and not just because of your health. It satisfies me to know that you have been left to your own devices, because only that steels one for living, and that is especially necessary for you.

You must become strong and independent, and a courageously *steadfast* Justi. Thereby you'll give me strength for all of us.

I am actually living here very distractedly. I cannot concentrate properly because of the frequent disturbances outside. But, still, I have already composed a nice song from "des Knaben Wunderhorn!"[2] That at least makes you happy, doesn't it?

I am walking a lot in the woods and the villages.

Uda is such a splendid being that I really want her to be your friend. Just seek out her company when you arrive. You have the same taste in people as I do, and I know that you will like her very much. She also has an inner tact and sensitivity that, unfortunately, one is very unaccustomed to. Here we are concocting plan after plan—but, of course, everything must remain open for now, until you come.

Your frequent headaches worry me very much. What does the doctor say about it? Is it natural? By the way, do you associate with Brayn?[3]

Once I went to the theatre here with Uda and heard German on stage again for the first time in a long time. It was not pretty! Anyhow, when you come, we'll go together sometime.

Emma is really unassuming, and I can only say that she made a good impression on me. All the same, Uda says that she pulls herself together in front of me. So we'll see.

Freund was out here last Sunday and particularly asked about you.

We have rearranged our mealtimes because of my cure. We have our second breakfast around 11:30. Around 4:00, I have a cold rub-down. Around 5:00 we have lunch, and then, at most, before going to sleep we have a cup of tea or milk.

I am writing this by the lamp—I have to pick this time, because I can't get around to it by day because of the visits I told you about already.

Now, I am going to sleep. Tomorrow morning I have to get up again at 5:30 to have a cold shower and rub-down again.

Good night. Best wishes and kisses.

Your
Gustav

How much should I send to our esteemed "Auntie"?

SHELFMARK: E8-MJ-382

NOTES

1 On 16 June (letter 93), Mahler announced that he had started his cure, and on 21 June (letter 96), Mahler asked Justine if she had received his letter.

[2] Mahler's nine early *Wunderhorn* songs were written between 1887 and 1890. More exact dates of composition cannot be determined.

[3] Unknown.

95 *To Justine*[1]

Postcard
[Postmark: Wieden-in-Wien, 18.6.90]
[Arrival postmark: Franzensbad, 19.6.90]

D.J.
Yesterday I had a visit from Budapest (the stage technician, Christofani,[2] today it's Rosenberg[)].[3] So, I have not been able to write, and you must now be patient until tomorrow. By the way, the cold-water cure is also somewhat straining—so, as you see, you don't have anything on me in that respect.

Best wishes from your
G.

Shelfmark: E6-MJp-306
Notes

[1] Addressed to "Fräulein Justine Mahler / in Franzensbad / Villa Fellner."

[2] Jozsef Christofani, "technical inspector," active between October 1889 and August 1911; see Roman, p. 216, n. 181.

[3] Visiting his wife, Laura Hilgermann.

96 *To Justine*[1]

Postcard
[Postmark: Hinterbrühl, 21.6.90]
[Arrival postmark: Franzensbad, 23.6.90]

D.J.
Received your letters. Hopefully you are now in possession of mine. The photography has its difficulties, though. Because of the [money], which we must take into consideration a bit.—Now there is so much piano playing here that it's unbearable, otherwise it would be very nice. The cure is having a wonderful effect. From Pollini I received a firm offer and have partially taken it up.[2]

Ever your G.

Shelfmark: E6-MJp-307
Notes

[1] Addressed to "Fräulein Justine Mahler / in Franzensbad / Villa Fellner."

[2] See appendix. According to GMB² 58, Mahler had had a firm offer from him as early as December 1886. See below, letters 110 and 112.

97 *To Justine*

Postcard
[Postmark: Vienna, 23.6.90]
[Arrival postmark: Franzensbad, 24.6.90]

D.J.
Yesterday, Sunday, the whole Löwi [Löhr] family was out here with us.—Today, I have to go to Vienna, and am quickly writing just a few lines.—I am very happy that things are going so well for you. Just be really careful *not to overdo it.* Then you can really enjoy Hinterbrühl. Can you not yet find out on what day you will be leaving Franzensbad, so that I can arrange my trip accordingly? Then I will meet you part-way to Prague.

Best wishes from your
G.

Shelfmark: E8-MJp-355
Note
[1] Addressed to "Fräulein Justine Mahler / in Franzensbad / Villa Fellner."

98 *To Justine*

[?Hinterbrühl, 29 June 1890][1]

Dearest Justi,
For 2 days we have had both Kössler Janosch from Budapest and Clementine Spiegler[2] from Kaltenleutgeben visiting.—The former is really sorry to have missed you; nevertheless it is possible that he will visit us again on his return journey.—Tomorrow we are going together to Ebners in the wilds, where I might stay for 2 or 3 days.[3]—Be so kind and send me back the letters that I enclosed last time.—Would it be alright with you if I perhaps met you half way only as far as *Iglau* (because of the cost). Write me about it.

Today I am going to Vienna with Kössler; he sends his best greetings.

Best wishes from your
Gustav

Shelfmark: E13-MJ-521
Notes
[1] Dated on the basis of the following postcard.
[2] See appendix.
[3] Dr. Eduard Ebner and his wife, Ottilie, were part of Mahler's Budapest circle. Their daughter, Ottilie von Balassa, published a memoir of her mother, *Die Brahmsfreundin Ottilie Ebner und ihr Kreis*, which mentions Mahler's visit to her family in the country (cited in Roman, p. 221).

99 *To Justine*[1]

Postcard
[Postmark: Mödling, 30.6.90]
[Arrival postmark: Franzensbad, 1.7.90]

D.J.
Just a quick greeting—I am writing this at the train station. I am travelling into the *wilds* with Koessler—will stay there for perhaps 2–3 days. Koessler asks whom I am writing—he sends his greetings. Otto is *really* coming out on Wednesday all right. I hear that the doctor is keeping you until the 22nd.—*Of course* it *must* be done.—You mustn't lose patience—these 3 weeks will indeed pass too. You must remain very brave.

Ever yours, G.

SHELFMARK: E8-MJp-356
NOTE
[1] Addressed to "Fräulein Justine Mahler / in Franzensbad / Villa Fellner."

100 *To Justine*[1]

Postcard
[Postmark: Hinterbrühl, 3.7.90]
[Arrival postmark: Franzensbad, 4.7.90]

D.J.!
You must still have a bit of patience; yesterday I got back from the wilds, and discovered such a mess of correspondence that I hardly know where to begin.—It was magnificent there. You wrote earlier that it is very difficult for you to get up so early, and now you want to leave at 5:30 in the morning! What am I to make of that? It also worries me that you have so many headaches. If nothing else is possible, better that you stay overnight in Prague before you ruin the day for yourself. We will still make up our minds.

Best wishes from your G.

SHELFMARK: E8-MJp-357
NOTE
[1] Addressed to "Fräulein Justine Mahler / in Franzensbad / Villa Fellner."

101 *To Justine*

[Hinderbrühl, 4 or 5 July 1890][1]

Dearest Justi,
Otto already came to us for good yesterday.—Fritz is coming on the 10th.—So, only you are missing to make the party complete.

—Alois asks when he should come.—I think that I'll invite him for *August.*

—Dear Justi, do you know what would be best? If you came *directly to Vienna* from Franzensbad.—In August I have to go to Prague for sure, and so then I could stop at Iglau much more easily.—In our circumstances, one now must avoid all possible unnecessary expenses, so this would be so much better.

Think about it, and let me know.—I couldn't visit Hilgermann. *What was it* then that you wanted her to tell me?

Here everything is going as usual. To be honest, Uda is a little too hard on Emma. She is being treated as if she were an *au pair.* That doesn't seem right to me by any means. First of all, it is not right for Emma—because of it, she will become completely frightened and intimidated on the one hand, and more hypocritical and false on the other.

—I have a terrible pen.[2]

—It was splendid in the country. Anyhow, the Ebners—who were very kind—want you to come out to [see] them again with me.

In every respect we are all in *splendid* health.—Otto feels very well here too.—

I've had 2 letters from Bianchi[3] here.

Best wishes from
Your
Gustav

Now, just grin and bear it! It's only two weeks!

SHELFMARK: E13-MJ-522

NOTES

[1] Date estimated on the basis of Mahler's return from visiting the Ebners.

[2] The letter has a large number of ink blots, particularly in the two sentences written before this comment.

[3] Bianca Bianchi (1855–1947), coloratura soprano. On 13 November 1889 she sang three of Mahler's songs in concert in Budapest.

102 *To Justine*

[Hinterbrühl, 6 July 1890]

Dear Justi,

Today, Sunday, we are all here together again. Tomorrow I have to go to Vienna on business—so, as you see, I am not celebrating my birthday.

You are still a bit too impatient. You will soon be free of everything, and will be able to enjoy yourself here all the more after such long privations.—Just don't neglect any aspect of your cure, and don't do *anything too quickly*! A couple of days are of no consequence. Let me know how you feel about my idea regarding the *direct* return trip. Perhaps then you can travel to Iglau along with me while I go on to Prague. I also have some other reasons for this, which I will tell you about in person.

With best wishes
from your
Gustav

What did you want H[ilgermann] to tell me? You can just write me, because no one here ever sees my letters.

SHELFMARK: E8-MJ-358

103 *To Justine*

[Hinterbrühl, 8 July 1890]

Dearest Justi,
Yesterday morning, before my departure for Vienna, I received your birthday greeting. With regard to your trip home, in spite of everything, I have decided to ask you to come *directly from Franzensbad to Vienna.*

I have *very important* reasons for this, dear Justi, which I will tell you in person.

Please, do find out how the trains are scheduled, and by all means travel on an *express train.* I will send you the 150 fl. in the next few days.—Just don't worry about the money, we will soon make up for it again. If only *your health* comes back, then I don't regret a single penny.

Also, let me know your exact arrival time in Vienna, and at *which station* you will arrive, since I will then wait for you in *Vienna.*

I can't wait to see you here with us again.—Certainly, this must be a terrible time for you—I know that!

I received both letters from *Bianchi.*

Nina Hof[f]mann[1] is coming out to us for a few days. She is quite ailing, and we want her to profit a bit from the good Hinterbrühl air.—

I have already given up my cure, since on the whole I already feel *better* than I have for years.—Nevertheless, I get up every day at 6:00 a.m. and, rain or shine, go for a swim before breakfast.—Otto accompanies me—he is feeling decisively better too.

Just be nice and sensible for a few more days. Best wishes

from your
Gustav

Shelfmark: E13-MJ-523
Note
[1] See appendix.

104 *To Justine*

[Hinterbrühl, June–July 1890]

Dearest Justi,
I am sending you a letter from Alois, one from Rosenberg, and others, which are from the field marshall and regimental doctor that you know.[1]—They are concerned with the business of Alois's release.—Everything could already have been in order, if Alois had followed our advice at the time.—It's a good thing anyway that one is satisfied with him. Now that it seems that he will not be in Brünn, let's let that go, and have him come to us in August.

Here everything is as usual. I go here and there—mainly to Vienna on business for a day, but I am always back in the evening. For God's sake, don't make a big deal of the fact that you will be a kilo or two heavier; *just don't do anything about it*! It doesn't matter; really, how can one be so vain, when it concerns one's health.

Best wishes
from your
Gustav

SHELFMARK: E16-MJ-612
NOTE
[1] Do not survive. Several of these letters appear to concern Alois's military service.

105 *To Justine*

[Hinterbrühl, mid-July 1890]

Dear Justine,
Please, *in any case* be sure not to travel at night.—It is not necessary to rush, and it would be very bad for you.—Listen to me, and travel during the day! *Don't* trouble yourself about the reduced fare, there would be too many discomforts as a consequence.

—You can imagine that I will be really glad to see you away from this miserable cure [*Bademisere*] and to finally have you with us again—if only it has done you good!—*Just* travel by day, and telegraph or write me *in good time*, the arrival time and the *station* where you arrive.

I will wait for you there; if we miss one another by some misunderstanding, travel on the next train on the southern line to *Mödling*, take a *fiacre* from there to Weissenbacherstraße,[1] where you would *certainly* be expected.

With best wishes
from your
Gustav

SHELFMARK: E13-MJ-524
NOTE
[1] The Mahlers and the Löhrs spent the summer of 1890 at the Villa Lehnhart, Hinterbrühl, Weißenbacherstraße 12. See Löhr's notes 59 and 62 in GMB[2] (pp. 439–40).

106 *To Justine*

[Hinterbrühl, mid-July 1890]

Dearest Justi,
I hear from Otto that you aren't coming until Saturday then. Please let me know the exact hour of your arrival in Vienna, and tell me the train station! I will meet you there. The gloves are nice, but too small. I am sending them back to you; maybe you can exchange them and perhaps buy a few more pairs there.

The money will go off tomorrow too. (150 fl.)—
Fritz has already moved in, but Nina can't come.

We are already anxiously awaiting you—the fatter, the better!
At any rate, write again in some detail.

Best wishes to you all
from your
Gustav

SHELFMARK: E16-MJ-611

107 *To Justine*

[Budapest, end August 1890][1]

Dear Justi,
In the case that I just brought back from Hinterbrühl, there was a little paper packet containing the "Rübezahl"[2] and also 2 letters to me from the Intendant. I left everything, and you took over putting things in order.—Now these things are missing, and I need them very much.

Please, *tell me if you know anything about them* and *perhaps where* they *are to be found.*

I am furious that such things were misplaced. I received your package all right.

My cold is disappearing.

Best wishes to everyone
from Gustav

SHELFMARK: E8-MJ-362
NOTES

[1] Mahler returned to Budapest on 22 or 23 August (see Roman, pp. 97–98 and 216, n. 183).

[2] In the early 1880s, Mahler wrote the libretto for an unrealised opera on the legendary mountain spirit Rübezahl. See Stephen E. Hefling, "The Road Not Taken: Mahler's *Rübezahl*," *Yale University Library Gazette* 57 (1983): 145–70.

108 *To Justine*

[Budapest, September 1890]

Dear Justi,
I must infer from your letter that you are *not well*; I ask you, once and for all, *not* to spare me in the future, but tell me the *unvarnished* truth.—You don't need to be shy with me at all.—I am sending you 11 fl. today for yourself—(I will send [money] for the shoes next time; I don't have any more with me just now).—Mind you, I do not understand the money situation at all—but I am not the least inclined to be disturbed about it at all, as you seem to be. We are finished with U[da] this month—and in the future I will know to protect *ourselves* from her.—

Someday when you are well, explain everything to me calmly.—You write that neither you nor U[da] have any more. So do I still have to send you money before the 1st? If that is the case, let me know by express, and I will send something immediately.

You write: "Write *Freund* that he comes often!" My dear Justi! what you mean *by that*, I don't know. Am I supposed to write him then that *he comes too often* or that he shouldn't come *so often*.—I take it from your letter that U[da] is becoming increasingly amiable once again. Now don't concern yourself with this anymore; the affair is *at an end*—so what of it! I am still balancing accounts all right.

Write me, or have Otto write all the details about you all: how you are getting on; how the girl is; also whether you need more money before the 1st, and how much I should send you for *October*.

On *4 October*, I am probably coming to Vienna for 1 or 2 days. Anyhow, write right away.

Best wishes from
Gustav

At the very least, Otto should write.

SHELFMARK: E8-MJ-372

109 *To Justine*

THE DIRECTORATE
OF THE ROY. HUNG. OPERA
BUDAPEST[1]

[Budapest, 16 September 1890]

Dear Justi,
I just gave your *Vienna address* to your mover and received the following letter, which I send you for your information. Tonight, Don Giovanni[2]—My hands are full.—Best wishes to Fritz—I will write tomorrow. From now on should I always write to Vienna?[3]

Ever your
Gustav

According to the enclosed note, the little purse was sent to Toni.

[written across the top:] Anyway, go or dispatch to this Viennese mover.[4]

SHELFMARK: E8-MJ-359

NOTES

[1] Unlike the Hungarian letterhead used above in letters 78 and 83, this version is in German. Both letterheads are used interchangeably in subsequent letters.

[2] According to Roman, p.138, Mahler conducted *Don Giovanni* on 16 September (and possibly also on 18 September and 3 October).

[3] Justine had remained in Hinterbrühl with Uda Löhr until mid-September.

[4] Since the deaths of Mahler's parents and sister in 1889, Mahler's siblings had been living with the Löhrs in Vienna. In mid-September 1890, Friedrich Löhr and his family left for a year of study in Italy, necessitating the dissolution of the household. Justine, Emma, and Otto moved into nearby Breitegasse 4. See GMB[2] 97 (and Löhr's note 65).

110 *To Justine*

[Budapest, end September 1890]

Dearest Justi,
I don't know now where I should write to you—that is why I don't dare send you the money that you asked for before I have received the correct address from you.—It really is strange that *U[da]* took the money for herself against my wishes. Hopefully, *something will be left over*?! At any rate, don't worry about it; if everything costs us a few gulden more now, that really doesn't matter—

The blame for the business with the mover naturally lies in the unreasonableness of the local tradespeople.—At any rate, the affair is a *lesson* for us that we will remember.

I am letting you know that I am already negotiating with *Pollini*, and if he agrees to my conditions, maybe we will be together all right, in *Hamburg* next September!! But for the time being, still *keep quiet* to everybody![1]

It would really be best if you made me a *short duvet* [*Tuckent*], because it is still a bit too cold.

Why do you *not* write *how you are*? Are you sleeping well? etc.?

Bela[2] was at city hall [*Stadthauptmannschaft*] and he was told that the little book was already *sent* (which the city official told me himself today too)!

Fritz should let the business with Quittmeyer [*sic*] rest for the time being.—I will write him next.[3]

Very best wishes to everyone
from your
Gustav

Should I maybe send 50 fl. school money?
I will send you the 10 fl. when you tell me the address.

Shelfmark: E16-MJ-601
Notes

[1] The Mahler-Rosé Collection contains a draft letter from Mahler to Pollini, dated 26 September 1890, which reads in part:

> In this case, however, you will not hold it against me if I do not want to take the final, decisive step until I have a binding statement from you, since I do not want to fall between two stools.—
>
> Regarding the financial aspect, I regret that I am unable to change my request, since I am not in a position to make a great financial sacrifice in order to achieve my wishes (as I already indicated in my last letter).
>
> Here I receive a yearly salary of *10.000 fl* with a travel allowance [*Reisezulage*] of 800 fl. in addition to an activity bonus [*Funktionszulage*] of 600 fl. (for operatic performances). It is therefore certainly not unreasonable if I ask you for a yearly salary of 14.000 marks. I would like to have the salary divided into 9 installments between September and June, if this would not go against the custom of your box office too much.
>
> Most respectfully yours,
> Gustav Mahler

It is unclear whether or not the letter was sent.

[2] Unknown.

[3] Mahler's former brother-in-law, Leopoldine's widower.

111 *To Justine*

[Budapest, end September 1890][1]

Dearest Justi,

Just as I got back from a walk on the Bastei, I received your letter.—Well, the welcome [news] in it twice outweighs the unwelcome [news].—I'm so pleased that you are doing well! I am especially happy that you go walking with the girl and Emma every day for 2 hours. *I* especially *ask you* to do this daily—even in bad weather.

There is one thing that I don't understand about the bills. Uda sent me a bill for *70 fl.* (including the 15 fl. that she returned to you)—(extra for Emma's expenses), which I *sent* to her in *Venice*. Did she also have extra expenses apart from that? And do you know how they are connected? For the move to Vienna, I sent Fritz 128 fl. as well. That is also not there. Please write me what you know about it. By how much has your blood percentage risen (*Wie viel prozent blut hast du zugenommen*)? I no longer remember exactly how much it was in the summer.—Why wasn't Otto with you at Pfungen's?[2] At any rate, when you go there with Emma, he should come with you *too*. Just build yourselves up well, and *do not give up anything*. Eat just as much meat as you can. I am doing *splendidly*. Write me *when* I should send you the 60 fl. What is that about the accommodation? Did you put aside the 30 fl. for it, or weren't you able to?

Best wishes from Gustav

At any rate, I still hope to come in *October*.

Shelfmark: E8-MJ-370

Notes

[1] The card must have been written after the move and departure of Fritz Löhr and his family (who were in Florence by 3 October, according to the address on a postcard in the Löhr Nachlaß in the Handschriftensammlung of the Österreichische Nationalbibliothek).

[2] Unknown, also mentioned in letter 132.

112 *To Justine*[1]

[Budapest, end September 1890]

Dear Justi,

I have just sent the money to Fritz in Venice—the money that Uda lent you. Hopefully you are already in possession of the *70 fl.* I sent you. Today I am sending you your first stipend (of 250 fl.), as Uda indicated to me.—The 70 fl. I sent you, I subtracted, leaving 180 fl.

In the process, *Otto* has then paid another 2 months tuition [*Schulgeld*] in advance, which we will settle the next time I come to Vienna.

I really would rather send you 250 fl. a month, and from it, always keep 35 fl. for old Löwi so that you have always got your rent together on rent day.

Hopefully these calculations fit with yours; let me know right away so that my mind is settled. *My negotiations with Pollini are nearing an end!* Probably we will be together in Hamburg from next fall on. But don't tell *anybody*.—[2]

I really feel great right now. My old health seems to have returned.

Let me know how you are doing with the housekeeping, and whether you can get by on the planned stipend.

How much does Passy pay for her apartment? If you're a bit too short [of money] at first, just write me without even thinking about it. I will then send you a little bit from time to time!

I send you best wishes, and remain

Your Gustav

Greetings to Otto as well; he ought to write me more often.

SHELFMARK: E16-MJ-602

NOTES

[1] On a blank page of the letter, Justine made notes on their finances ("12 [fl.] Elise / 10 [fl.] Wäsche / 2 [fl.] Emma / 4 [fl.] Otto / 35 [fl.] Passy / 24 [fl.][blank]") and wrote down an address: "Campo Moisè 1464 dalla Signora Rambonsek." This may be one of the Löhrs' addresses in Italy, although it is not amongst the cards in Löhr's Nachlaß.

[2] This is the last mention of Pollini in the family letters until Mahler took up his appointment in Hamburg in late March 1891. The Mahler-Rosé Collection contains two of the three letters to Pollini published in GMB[2] (nos. 99 and 100; the whereabouts of no. 98 is unknown). The last of these, written 7 November 1890, indicates that they had almost reached an agreement.

113 *To Justine*

[Budapest, Autumn 1890][1]

Dearest Justi,

With this, I am sending you the picture proofs. If you want, just keep them for yourselves and let me know which you like best.

Apropos! What is with the rent? Put aside the proper amount each month, dear Justi! This struck me at breakfast today as I was just thinking about the next 1st of the month.

Best wishes from your
Gustav

SHELFMARK: E16-MJ-603

NOTE

[1] Mahler's similar comments about the rent in letter 112 suggests that this letter also dates from the fall of 1890.

114 *To Justine*

THE DIRECTORATE
OF THE ROY. HUNG. OPERA
BUDAPEST

[Budapest, end October 1890][1]

Dearest Justi,

I just had to pay a bill for Otto of 33 fl. 34 to the "*Wetzler*" estate. I would like to ask you to see to it that such amounts do not accumulate any longer; instead, pay *them all right away*.—Money is so tight this month, that this amount causes me real hardship.—In spite of all my economising, I have not yet been able to be debt-free. I recently had to send Fritz *200 fl* and hope that with that I won't have any more claims from there. (These 200 fl. were the last remainder of the money that I borrowed in Hinterbrühl.)—I am now well, but very strained. So don't expect a long letter from me. Best wishes to everybody

from your
Gustav

SHELFMARK: E8-MJ-368
NOTE
[1] Dated on the basis of the next letter (but see the note to it).

115 *To Justine*

[Budapest, 29 October 1890]

Dearest Justi,
I just received your letter. I have *already paid Wetzler* the 33 fl. So don't take any money there, otherwise they will just take it. Emma's report I have not received yet. Tonight is the concert.[1] I'm going to the dress rehearsal [*Generalprobe*] now.—What were you actually missing? You didn't write me anything about it? Why don't I ever find anything out?

Best wishes from
Gustav

SHELFMARK: E8-MJ-369
NOTE
[1] On 29 October 1890 there was a concert at the Opera House to celebrate the hundredth anniversary of Hungarian theatre. The program was shared between Mahler and Sándor Erkel; the former conducted Liszt's *Festklänge*, the prelude to Mihalovich's *Toldis Liebe*, and his *Königshymnus*. (This and the previous letter have been dated on the basis of this concert, although it is possible that the concert to which Mahler refers was the pension-funds benefit concert held on 5 December.)

116 *To Justine*

THE DIRECTORATE
OF THE ROY. HUNG. OPERA
BUDAPEST

[Budapest, Autumn 1890]

Dearest Justi,
Things here have become far too exaggerated. The fellows have disgraced themselves through and through—that is it.

Bauer is on her way again today.[1] She will soon have told you everything. I have my hands full. This time, just best wishes from your

Gustav

Write me in detail about you all.

[across the top of the letter:] At my expense, you can take 2 seats for *every phil. concert* for yourself and one of the *girls*. I will pay for it at *Binder's*.

SHELFMARK: E13-MJ-532
NOTE

[1] Natalie Bauer-Lechner (see appendix) visited Mahler for the first time in late October or November 1890. Mahler's letter of invitation to her (19 October 1890, published in Roman, pp. 107–8) makes it clear that she was already acquainted with Justine.

117 *To Justine*

[Budapest, Autumn 1890]

D.J.
To my surprise, I read in your letter that there is a *day* class in Trier. As early as the summer I asked why he was not signed up for the *day* class and heard that there was only a *night class*; I didn't understand it at all, but I had to be content with the answer. Now I see that there really is a day class.—Well, dammit, why did he sign up for the night class then? Please, clarify this for me.

I only wanted to send Alois 50 fl. at the end of every month; so does he need so much this time at the beginning? I will send the money tomorrow, but hope that from now on he will get by with it.

Best wishes
Gustav

Why did Alois have to borrow from you? With what did you pay for the journey? I await more particular suggestions about Otto.

SHELFMARK: E8-MJ-365

118 *To Justine*

[Budapest, Autumn 1890][1]

Dearest Justi!
Hopefully you are already in possession of the 235 fl. I sent to you, according to your calculation

60 fl. for you
25 fl. for Otto's expenses
150 fl. for clothes and laundry,

so that I have to send you 256 fl. on the 1st.

I am doing just brilliantly well, and am now thinking about visiting you when I can get myself free. I might come completely unexpectedly. At any rate, I will telegraph you from the Budapest train station.

By the way, I am living a terribly philistine life—to bed around 10:30, up around 6:30. I am drinking a lot of milk—it suits me really well.

You write too little detail about your health, and—I almost fear—with too little honesty. How are you all getting on together? Do you feed yourselves properly?

Best wishes from your
Gustav

Say hello to Bertha from me too—I will write soon.

SHELFMARK: E8-MJ-366
NOTE
[1] The dating of this letter is not secure.

119 *To Justine*

[Budapest, Autumn 1890]

Dear Justi,
It is starting to get cold; please send me the quilt right away.—You will receive the money on time by mail, in case I don't come myself.—

I am urging Otto seriously to be diligent and now to make use of his time. Go *walking with the girl* every day! I am splendid, only I have a lot to do.

Best wishes from your
Gustav

SHELFMARK: E8-MJ-367

120 *To Justine*

THE DIRECTORATE
OF THE ROY. HUNG. OPERA
BUDAPEST

[Budapest, second week November 1890][1]

Dearest Justi,
I just sent you *180* fl. by money order; please give 50 fl. of it *immediately* to Nina Hof[f]mann. I don't like it that you owe the tailor, and therefore I would rather send it all.—

From the 1st, you will get 260 fl. every month.—

Today, only best wishes. I have a tremendous amount to do.

Your Gustav

SHELFMARK: E13-MJ-534
NOTE
[1] Dated on the basis of the references to money in the next letter.

121 *To Justine*

[Budapest, c. 17 November 1890]

Dearest Justi,

This time it has been a long time since I have had a letter from you. Are you still unwell? What is wrong with you?

Today is the 1st dress rehearsal of Asraël. The day after tomorrow is the final one, before an invited audience.

It's bad luck that you had to miss the Philharmonic Concert.—Who went in your place? Did you get the 180 fl.? And have you sent Nina the 50 fl. already?

Spitz will send the final bill at the beginning of January, he writes. Things are going excellently for me. All the work is succeeding splendidly this time.

Just write soon!

Very best wishes to everyone
from your
Gustav

Shelfmark: E8-MJ-361

122 *To Justine*

THE HUNGARIAN ROYAL OPERA HOUSE
DIRECTORATE
BUDAPEST

[Budapest, mid-November 1890]

Dearest Justi,

In great haste, I am sending you another newspaper notice. Today I am going to Totis in Esterhazy! Hence the great haste.—Asraël is on next week.[1] A huge amount of work. I am well! Tomorrow I will send money!

Best wishes from your
Gustav

Might it be possible to send you 10 or 20 fl. only at the end of the month? Because of the 50 fl. for Nina, it would be difficult for me now—I'd have to take another advance!

Shelfmark: E8-MJ-360

Note

[1] The premiere of Alberto Franchetti's opera *Asraël* took place on 20 November 1890.

123 *To Justine*

[Budapest, 17 December 1890]

Dearest Justi,

I'm right in the middle of rehearsals for "*Cavalleria Rusticana*." The first performance is set for *Monday* the 22nd.[1] If I manage this, then I will leave here on

Tuesday night, and will be in Vienna Wednesday and Friday.—If not, then I just *must* stay here, and would then see about coming out on New Year's.

Your eye troubles worry me.—What is this about glasses? Do you have to wear them *all the time*? I don't like it at all that you should have to get used to glasses.—

Yesterday was Don Giovanni.[2] Brahms and D'Albert were at the performance. Afterwards, I was together with Brahms, and to my great joy he was *really delighted* with my conducting.—He spoke just like Goldmark did about Lohengrin.[3]—He said that many things had been revealed to him for the first time, and that he had *never* heard Mozart performed so stylishly.—From Brahms, this really means something, because he belongs completely to the old school.

Since you are collecting autographs, I am sending you the enclosed letters, which might have some value for you.

—This month I am as poor as a church mouse and have to avoid all expenses—thus it is not advisable that you come here with me—or so I think.

Write a bit more about how you all are! Are you going to the Philharmonic [Concert] on Sunday?

Best wishes from your
Gustav

Shelfmark: E12-MJ-483

Notes

[1] Postponed to 26 December 1890.

[2] 16 December 1890.

[3] Austrian composer Carl Goldmark (1830–1915).

124 *To Justine*

[Budapest, third week December 1890][1]

Dearest Justi,

Enclosed, a letter from the Generalintendant of the Munich Court Theatre, Freiherr von Perfall, as a contribution for your autograph collection.[2] He wrote it himself, which is an extraordinary honour.—I am still hoping to be finished with the new opera ahead of Monday, and so spend Christmas Eve with you.[3]

If this doesn't happen, however, hopefully you will be reasonable; I hope to come for New Year's at any rate.

Very best wishes
from your
Gustav

Shelfmark: E8-MJ-354

Notes

[1] On the back of the letter, Justine wrote "Lieber Gustav" and a list of names: "[Zsigmond] Singer; Feld; Kopely; [Ede] Pauláy [*sic*]; Benitzky [= Beniczky]." Paulay was the artistic director of the National Theatre.

[2] Not in the Mahler-Rosé Collection. As *Generalintendant*, Karl Freiherr von Perfall (1824–1907) was a strong supporter of Wagner, despite the latter's hostility.

[3] As indicated by the previous letter, the premiere of *Cavalleria rusticana* was originally scheduled for 22 December.

125 *To Justine*

[Budapest, between 18 and 25 December 1890]

Dearest Justi,
I just sent you the money. Right now, I am very stressed and must ask you to content yourself with this sparse news. You know how it goes if I have a lot to do. Furthermore, I have recently been unwell, I had a stomach catarrh or something like that—diarrhoea. Now I am better again, but I must still be very cautious. Someone needs to tell me *Fritz's* address in Rome.

You did entirely right with your visit to Singer—otherwise, in this respect behave entirely according to your feelings.

How *do you like the wine*, and how *long* will *it suffice*? It is from Petanovics, and certainly high quality. *Jahn* is here today;[1] perhaps I might be able to speak with him about the free admission.

Best wishes to everyone from
your
Gustav

Otto should write again sometime. Many greetings to Bertha. I received Hans' symphony just fine.[2]

SHELFMARK: E8-MJ-363
NOTES

[1] See appendix.

[2] Hans Rott (1858–1884). On the basis of this sentence, I have argued that Mahler's real acquaintance with Rott's Symphony in E Major comes from this time, and not from the summer of 1900, as indicated by Natalie Bauer-Lechner. This now provides an explanation for the apparent quotations of Rott's work in Mahler's Second and Third symphonies. See Stephen McClatchie, "Hans Rott, Gustav Mahler, and the 'New Symphony': New Evidence for a Pressing Question," *Music & Letters* 81 (2000): 392–401.

126 *To Justine*

[Budapest, between 18 and 25 December 1890]

Dearest Justi,
Hopefully, you are all better again. You didn't write me at all about you and Otto being unwell.—What is wrong with Otto? Please be more specific.—Also, the "pleasantness" that you have to tell me, don't procrastinate, like Papa Löwi does, tell me right away.—Should I send more wine? How did the Löwis like the wine?

I didn't want to talk to Jahn about it here, but at any rate, I will tell him in Vienna, since I am now on somewhat more friendly footing with him.[1] It would only have been embarrassing for me "to exploit" his visit right away. There shouldn't be any difficulties now in working out your visit to the Opera.

Whether I can come to Vienna for Christmas, I still don't know. Of course I will do it if only it can be done somehow.—But please, just don't make *any expenses*—it is *not easy* for me.

Best wishes from
Gustav

SHELFMARK: E8-MJ-364
NOTE
[1] See letter 134 of January 1891.

127 *To Justine*

[Budapest, between 18 and 25 December 1890]

Dearest Justi,
I decided today not to give the new work until Friday the 26th, and 3 times in a row, so that I plan to leave here at night on Sunday the 28th, and to arrive in Vienna early on Monday the 29th.—I will stay in Vienna Monday, Tuesday, and Wednesday, and will go back again on Thursday. So, we will all begin the New Year together, which is really lovely.

Today I can give you a new autograph and another, better one, from Goldmark.[1]

What is this about your eyes and the glasses? I am very concerned. Perhaps have Otto write me about it immediately. For now, best wishes to everybody

from Gustav

The paper is gold and made of a hair ornament that they wear at concerts here.

She gave me these lines without my asking for them.

Can I stay *with all of you this time*?

SHELFMARK: E16-MJ-600
NOTE
[1] Do not survive.

128 *To Justine*

THE DIRECTORATE
OF THE ROY. HUNG. OPERA
BUDAPEST

[Budapest, c. 25 December 1890]

Dearest Justi,
Merry Christmas! God willing, I will be with you on Monday.—

The dress rehearsal of the new opera went splendidly, and at last I hope for a "decisive success"! Enclosed, a newspaper that should interest you.

Best wishes to everybody from
Gustav

SHELFMARK: E16-MJ-610

129 *To Justine*

[Budapest, November–December 1890]

Dear Justi,
You will gather from the enclosed letter what it is about—only, *I* don't have the skin rash, Frau Lehmann's niece does.[1]—Please, if you can make out from the letter that I sent to Pick, to arrange for everything, [and] perhaps to write yourself—about all of our former household customs, you should describe to me how they were done.—I remember that we ignited a large roll of paper, and that a liquid came out the other end, which was applied to the area, so that within 3 days, everything was back in order. Perhaps send my letter to *Pick* in Iglau, who might remember—or write to *old* Dr. Krauss or Frau Schiller. But *very quickly*—express post!

Best wishes from your
(*hurried*)
Gustav

Shelfmark: E18-MJ-640
Note

[1] Lilli Lehmann spent a month as guest singer in Budapest during November and December 1890. It was the last time that she and Mahler performed together before Mahler went to Vienna in 1897.

130 *To Justine*

THE DIRECTORATE
OF THE ROY. HUNG. OPERA
BUDAPEST

[Budapest, early January 1891]

Dearest Justi,
Do go to any concert that attracts you, but buy *a seat* and not an admission. Enclosed, a letter to me from *Mascagni* (the composer of Cavalleria Rusticana) for your autograph collection.[1] Also, 2 reviews in foreign papers.—The one from the *Dresden Zeitung* is by *Rosenberg*, who has now become a journalist.[2]—The other is from the Berlin Borsencouri[e]r.—A's letter—is again entirely Alois. I'm only curious what sort of plan is rattling around in his head this time.

Write really soon.

Best wishes from your
Gustav

Give Ernestine my best greetings. Nina passed on my request to you, didn't she? Did you have good seats at the Opera?

Shelfmark: E13-MJ-529
Notes

[1] A copy of this letter, dated 31 December 1890, thanking Mahler for the Budapest premiere of *Cavalleria rusticana* survives in the Mahler-Rosé Collection (the whereabouts of the original sold by Alfred Rosé is unknown).

[2] Perhaps Siegfried Rosenberg.

131 *To Justine*

THE DIRECTORATE
OF THE ROY. HUNG. OPERA
BUDAPEST

[Budapest, early January 1891]

Dearest Justi,
I am very concerned to still be without a letter from you all. Enclosed, a letter, the address of which will amuse you. Naturally, I again have a terrible amount to do.—I'm now rehearsing "*Waffenschmied*".[1]—Write soon.

When I left, I had the impression that you were not completely well. Is that so?

Best wishes to everyone from
Gustav

Did you *request seats for Friday*? and receive them?

Give my best wishes to Nina![2] *Now, in this first difficult time*, quite seriously, she should *live and eat* with *you all.* Tell her this from me!

SHELFMARK: E13-MJ-526
NOTES

[1] Albert Lortzing's *Der Waffenschmied* had its premiere on 17 January 1891.

[2] It is unclear if this refers to Nina Hoffmann, mentioned in previous letters, or to the Mahlers' other friend Nina Hoffmann, Siegfried Lipiner's first wife. According to GMB², they divorced in 1890, so it is possible that Mahler is alluding to this event. (In August 1891, Nina subsequently married Mahler's friend Albert Spiegler [and is always referred to as Nina Spiegler in this volume]). Interestingly, in 1889 Mahler wrote to Fritz that "I didn't say a word to Albert about Nina—this was her express wish" [letter of 16 June 1889, published omitting this sentence in GMB², p. 437, n. 48; original in ÖNB-Handschriftensammlung 295/45–7].)

132 *To Justine*

[Budapest, early January 1891]

Dearest Justi,
What doctor is treating you?

Have Dr. Pfungen called immediately,[1] so that he can examine you. Please, have news sent to me every day.—Don't go out as long as the doctor does not permit it.—

Did you receive the wine that I sent you through Petanovics about 3 weeks ago?[2]

Otto, at least, should write a postcard daily with an exact report.

Best wishes to everyone
from
Gustav

SHELFMARK: E3-MJ-145
NOTES

[1] Mentioned above in letter 111.

[2] See letter 125.

133 *To Justine*

THE DIRECTORATE
OF THE ROY. HUNG. OPERA
BUDAPEST

[Budapest, between 11 and 15 January 1891]

Dearest Justi,
Please, at least let me have some news over the course of the day. There are so many of you that, even if there is a lot to do, surely one or the other of you will find the time for a postcard.—I have so many worries that you could at least relieve one of them—with [news of] your well-being.

Today I am sending you an interesting review from Dresden.—Saturday, is the premiere of "*Waffenschmied*".—I have recently caught a cold again—sore throat—yesterday I sweated it out hard, and because of that am again somewhat better.

Best wishes to everyone from
Gustav

SHELFMARK: E13-MJ-527

134 *To Justine*

THE HUNGARIAN ROYAL OPERA HOUSE
DIRECTORATE
BUDAPEST

[Budapest, 18 January 1891]

Dearest Justi,
Enclosed, the German reviews of yesterday's premiere of "Waffenschmied." Tonight *Brahms* will be in my box.

I am completely well again now—anyway, this time it was very slight.—At any rate, it is best that you take in a girl for the afternoon.—Whether you can apply for [tickets] at the Opera a second time is a strange question, since it seems that you didn't even get tickets once.—As I see it, Jahn doesn't exactly hand out the free tickets, but only approves [them].—I will raise this to the manager's office [*Intendanz*] again sometime. Best wishes. Write soon.

Your
Gustav

Say hello to [illegible woman's name], and thank her for the letter.—I am sending the books to Reich[1] right away.

SHELFMARK: E13-MJ-528
NOTE
[1] Unclear.

135 *To Justine*

[Budapest, 20 January 1891]

Dearest Justi,
In the next few days, you will still receive the desired supplement from me. 28 fl. in all, if I have understood you correctly.—The day after tomorrow the new Intendant takes up his duties.—
Then, in just a few days, many things will be determined.—So much is certain: he is taking great care to start off on the right foot with me.

Send me your bankbook next time so that I can have the entry made in it that I told you about already.—As I already told you, from 1 January 91, you will receive 4? % indefinitely. So in a year this comes to *30 fl*, which is not an amount to be squandered.

When will you go out again?

I hope for detailed news soon, and send you all my best wishes

Your
Gustav

SHELFMARK: E13-MJ-525
NOTE

[1] On 22 January 1891, Beniczky was replaced as *Intendant* by Géza, Graf von Zichy (see appendix).

136 *To Justine*

[Budapest, early February 1891]

Dearest Justi,
I am splendid—and have *an awful lot* to do! I *was not* at the ball, so you don't need to envy me.[1]

I did everything possible for Frau Lortzing. Perhaps it succeeded, but I am *not* getting on well with Zychy [*sic*], so I cannot do too much.—Today I am conducting in Ofen.[2]

Best wishes to everyone
from Gustav

SHELFMARK: E13-MJ-530
NOTE

[1] In early February Mahler conducted performances of *Die lustigen Weiber von Windsor* (1 February), *Der Waffenschmied* (7, 12 February), and *Cavalleria rusticana* (8, 14 February).

[2] Ofen is the German name for the portion of Budapest on the right bank of the Danube.

137 *To Justine*

[Budapest, late January or February 1891]

Dearest Justi,
You mustn't make too much of it if I don't write very often just now.—Now is a time when I have to negotiate, and because of that, you already know that I am not in the mood to chat.

So far *everything* is going superbly! I hope that everything will be brought to an end to *my*, and our, content. *You* write me often, so that I can be really *at ease*—I need that now. Bianchi has appeared again.[1]—Singer is saving me again—in fact, everyone is saving me now.

I received the little deposit book. Very best wishes to everyone from

Your Gustav

Perhaps I'll come to Vienna at the beginning of March.

Shelfmark: E5-MJ-246
Note
[1] According to HLG I, p. 331, Bianchi was ill in December 1890 and January 1891.

138 *To Justine*

THE HUNGARIAN ROYAL OPERA HOUSE
DIRECTORATE
BUDAPEST

[Budapest, February 1891]

Dearest Justi,
Enclosed, an article from the Berlin "*Börsencourier*" and [the] *Dresdner Zeitung*.

Here, things are *very* warlike.—As you can well imagine, I am *steadfast*—but *might* goes before right, so I also have to be very *careful*. A soldier and a diplomat at the same time. I hope that everything will be resolved in our best interest.

Best, Your Gustav

[across the top of the letter:] Do write!

Shelfmark: E13-MJ-533

139 *To Justine*

THE HUNGARIAN ROYAL OPERA HOUSE
DIRECTORATE
BUDAPEST

[Budapest, February 1891]

Dearest Justi,
Enclosed, some more reading for you all.—A few more days of patience, and then I am in the *clear* here. For now I must go step by step.—Hope for the *best*. More than that, I can't say now. Prince Hohenlohe and Baron Edelsheim left their cards for me, which is a great honour.[1]

Write right away. Tomorrow I will send you your monthly stipend.—Did you receive the red wine?[2]

Write right away. Very best wishes

from your
Gustav

I hope to come to Vienna in March.

SHELFMARK: E16-MJ-599
NOTES

[1] Konstantin, Fürst zu Hohenlohe-Schillingsfürst (1863–1918), was *Erster Obersthofmeister* to Kaiser Franz-Josef. Leopold Wilhelm, Freiherr von Edelsheim (1826–1893), was an Austrian general.

[2] See the following letter, as well as letter 132, above.

140 *To Justine*

THE DIRECTORATE
OF THE ROY. HUNG. OPERA
BUDAPEST

[Budapest, February 1891]

Dearest Justi,
I am terribly preoccupied right now, so you must content yourself with just a greeting. The packet with the shirts arrived—hopefully you're now in receipt of the *wine*. Write soon.

Ever yours,
Gustav

SHELFMARK: E16-MJ-608

141 *To Justine*

[Budapest, February or March 1891][1]

Dearest Justi,
I have a terrible lot to do. That is why you must be content and not expect any long or frequent letters from me for the next little while. My health is superb. Right now I am in the middle *of battle*, which is being waged very persistently by all sides. That's why it's not desirable that you come and visit me just now. I hope at least to be able to arrange to get away for a day, but it is impossible to predict.—At any rate, I would come on the spur of the moment.

Do you really want to send me another duvet? Didn't you just send me a smaller quilt?

Please, write to Brünn yourself. I have absolutely no time to do so. Incidentally, Monsieur A[lois] will probably turn up on the 1st with his exact address.

Best wishes to everyone from
your
Gustav

Shelfmark: E8-MJ-371
Note
[1] The letter has been dated on the basis of its similarity to surrounding letters and Mahler's comment that he is "in the middle of battle." It is possible, however, that it dates from September or October 1890 during the Újházy affair; see Roman, pp. 100–101.

142 *To Justine*

[Budapest, February or March 1891]

Dearest Justi,
With this, I am sending you another 40 fl. in the hope that the "finances" now can be brought into order.—Here things are now topsy-turvy—open warfare, which is more than a little difficult for me.

I wanted to come to Vienna on Tuesday, but now prefer *to stay here* and keep my eyes open.—

Your continual headache worries me a great deal; *what is with that*? Do write me about it in detail! Has it never lasted so long before?

I recently got a very agitated letter from Alois about the monthly consignments that have been carried out, and other noble behaviour on my part.—

Please write me, or have [somebody] write me, *exactly what* is wrong with you.

Very best wishes
from your
Gustav

Send me the little book, like *Papa Löwi* advised. I myself don't understand it at all.

Shelfmark: E5-MJ-248

143 *To Justine*

[Budapest, 9 March 1891]

Dearest Justi,
My trip to Vienna gets postponed from day to day, and today I don't even know if I will be able to come in the near future.

Tomorrow the Emperor is coming to the theatre—I will do some of the conducting.[1]

Enclosed, some articles. The one from the [*Neues*] *Pester Journal* is by *Doczi*.[2]

Best wishes to you all
from your
Gustav

I am now thinking about the *summer* again. Think up a nice place for a summer vacation.

Shelfmark: E13-MJ-520
Notes

[1] On 10 March 1891, the Opera presented a mixed program in the presence of Emperor Franz-Joseph. Mahler conducted *Cavalleria rusticana*, Mendelssohn's "Hebrides" overture, and an aria from Nicolai's *Die lustigen Weiber von Windsor.*

[2] Hungarian writer Lajos Dóczi (or Dóczy) (1845–1919), best known for his play *A csók* (The Kiss).

144 *To Justine*

[Budapest, 14 March 1891]

Dearest Justi,
Hurrah! I'm free! I was relieved of my duties today under very favourable conditions.[1]

I will stay here a few days more, then I will come to Vienna. Further details in person.—Why didn't you write anything about your visit to Lehmann's?[2]

Anyhow, write in detail!

Best wishes to everybody
from
Gustav

Shelfmark: E8-MJ-374
Notes

[1] According to Roman, p. 129, Zichy and Mahler signed an agreement at 1:30 P.M. on 14 March that provided Mahler with a severance payment of 20,000 florins, an additional 5,000 florins representing his salary until mid-July, and the refund of all of his pension contributions.

[2] Probably soprano Lilli Lehmann (1848–1933).

Undated Letters from Budapest

145 *To Justine*

[Budapest, 1888–1891][1]

Dear Justi,
Enclosed, 260 fl. Sent 25 to Alois. Is everything in order? Or do you need something?

Hurriedly, your
Gustav

SHELFMARK: E5-MJ-250
NOTE

[1] Possibly written between November 1890 and March 1891 (letter 120, of November 1890, indicates that Mahler will send 260 florins per month).

146 *To Justine*

THE HUNGARIAN ROYAL OPERA HOUSE
DIRECTORATE
BUDAPEST

[Budapest, possibly Winter 1891][1]

Dearest Justi,
For your manuscript collection, a letter from *Dóczi*[2]—now one of the most famous poets. How are you?

All the same, I am very worried! Write me in detail *but more often.*

Warmly,
Gustav

SHELFMARK: E13-MJ-531
NOTES
[1] Possibly winter of 1891 on the basis of the surrounding items in envelope 13 as well as the mention of Dóczi.
[2] See above, letter 143.

147 *To Justine*

THE HUNGARIAN ROYAL OPERA HOUSE
DIRECTORATE
BUDAPEST

[Budapest, 1888–1891]

Dearest Justi,
God willing, I am leaving here Sunday at noon, and will be at the Staatsbahnhof

around 7:00. Expect me in the said place, and take care until then.—If something intervenes, I will telegraph.

Ever yours,
Gustav

Shelfmark: E13-MJ-535

148 *To Justine*

THE HUNGARIAN ROYAL OPERA HOUSE
DIRECTORATE
BUDAPEST

[Budapest, 1888–1891]

Dearest Justi,
Enclosed, a letter from Joh. Strauss[1] for your autograph collection, and a review from a Berlin newspaper.

In the next few days I hope to be able to come to Vienna.

Very best wishes from
Gustav

Shelfmark: E16-MJ-609
Note
[1] Does not survive in the Mahler-Rosé Collection.

149 *To Justine*

[Budapest, 1888–1891]

Dearest Justi,
Hopefully you are now somewhat better! Why have I not got any news about it?—Today I am sending you an article from the Dresden Nachrichten. Tomorrow I have an invitation from the Prime Minister, a very high honour for an opera director![1]

I am really completely healthy!

Write soon!

Very best wishes to everyone
from your
Gustav

Shelfmark: E5-MJ-249
Note
[1] As the prime minister is not named, it is difficult to date this letter more precisely. According to Roman, p. 92, Gyula Szapáry was appointed prime minister in March 1890. As Szapáry was more nationalistic and conservative than his predecessor, this may have been an opportune moment for Mahler to pay his respects.

150 *To Justine*

[Budapest, 1888–1891][1]

Dear Justi,
Why don't you write how you are?
For whom do you need the seats?
I chose them in the back rows, since they cost me 20 groschen less there.
I enclose an article that appeared in the Wiener Fremdenblatt yesterday.
Kindest regards. I will come over soon.

Your
Gustav

SHELFMARK: E16-MJ-607
NOTE
[1] Several letters from the Budapest period mention Mahler obtaining tickets for Justine.

Gustav Mahler,
Kassel, 1883–1884

(Gustav Mahler–Alfred Rosé Collection, Music Library, University of Western Ontario. Reproduced with permission.)

Mahler and his sister Justine,
Budapest, 1889–1890

(Gustav Mahler–Alfred Rosé Collection, Music Library, University of Western Ontario. Reproduced with permission.)

Justine Mahler, 1890–1891
(Gustav Mahler–Alfred Rosé Collection, Music Library, University of Western Ontario. Reproduced with permission.)

Emma Mahler, c. 1889
(Gustav Mahler–Alfred Rosé Collection, Music Library, University of Western Ontario. Reproduced with permission.)

Gustav Mahler, 1890s
(© Bibliothèque Musicale Gustav Mahler. Reproduced with permission.)

Gustav Mahler, Hamburg, 1896
(Gustav Mahler–Alfred Rosé Collection, Music Library, University of Western Ontario. Reproduced with permission.)

Gustav Mahler,
Vienna, 1898

(Gustav Mahler–Alfred Rosé Collection, Music Library, University of Western Ontario. Reproduced with permission.)

Gustav Mahler, Vienna, 1898. The photograph is inscribed to his future brother-in-law Arnold Rosé: "To my dear friend and / 'kindred spirit' Arnold Rosé / Vienna, June 98 / Gust. Mahler."

(Gustav Mahler–Alfred Rosé Collection, Music Library, University of Western Ontario. Reproduced with permission.)

Alma Mahler,
Maiernigg, c. 1902
(Gustav Mahler–Alfred Rosé Collection, Music Library, University of Western Ontario. Reproduced with permission.)

Gustav and Alma Mahler, Toblach, 1909
(Gustav Mahler–Alfred Rosé Collection, Music Library, University of Western Ontario. Reproduced with permission.)

Arnold and Alfred Rosé, c. 1904

(Gustav Mahler–Alfred Rosé Collection, Music Library, University of Western Ontario. Reproduced with permission.)

Justine and Arnold Rosé, 1910s

(Gustav Mahler–Alfred Rosé Collection, Music Library, University of Western Ontario. Reproduced with permission.)

Hamburg
March 1891–April 1897

Chronology

1891 *26 March*: GM engaged as conductor at the Stadttheater, Hamburg (debut: *Tannhäuser*, 29 March).
Summer: Munich, Vienna, Perchtoldsdorf (where Justine, Otto, and Emma were residing for the summer), Hofgastein, Marienbad, Eger, Bayreuth (*Tannhäuser* and *Parsifal* [twice]).
August: GM travels to Scandinavia (Denmark, Sweden, Norway).

1892 *January–February*: GM composes 5 *Humoresken* for voice and piano (texts from *Des Knaben Wunderhorn*).
February: Three volumes (fourteen songs) of GM's early songs are published by Schott.
February–26 April: GM orchestrates 5 *Humoresken*.
27 April: Otto leaves the Conservatory without a diploma.
End May–mid-July: GM travels to London with the Hamburg company for a season of German opera. In preparation, Mahler began to study English (*April*).
July–August: GM in Berchtesgaden with Justine and Natalie.
End August: GM's return to Hamburg is delayed until mid-September by a cholera epidemic.
End October: Alois ill with tuberculosis.
12 December: GM conducts subscription concert in place of an ill Hans von Bülow, and on the same evening two of his *Humoresken* songs are first performed at a Philharmonic concert in Berlin.
End December: Justine and Alois travel to Merano for the winter for Alois to recuperate.

1893 *January*: GM revises the First Symphony.
February: GM orchestrates the *Lieder eines fahrenden Gesellen*.
Mid-April: Justine and Alois return from Merano.
End April–end June: Justine with GM in Hamburg; Alois, Otto, and Emma remain in Vienna.
Summer: Steinbach am Attersee; GM composes four *Wunderhorn* songs for piano or orchestra, continues to revise the First Symphony, and begins the Second (Andante and Scherzo).
End August: GM leaves Alois to his own devices.

19 September–mid-November: Justine with GM in Hamburg.
27 October: premiere of First Symphony (as *Titan*), three *Humoresken*, and three *Wunderhorn* songs in Hamburg.
Mid-November–April or early May 1894: Justine travels to Merano and Italy (Florence, Rome, Naples, Palermo, Venice).
December: GM revises *Das klagende Lied*.

1894 *5 February*: GM signs new five-year contract with Pollini.
12 February: death of Hans von Bülow in Alexandria.
29 March: Bülow's funeral and cremation in Hamburg; GM inspired by Klopstock's *Auferstehen* ode.
April: GM revises *Todtenfeier* for the Second Symphony; Otto volunteers at the Leipzig Stadttheater.
3 June: First Symphony performed at the Allgemeine Deutsche Musikverein festival in Weimar.
Summer: Steinbach am Attersee, Bayreuth (*Parsifal*, *Lohengrin*, *Tannhäuser*); GM completes Second Symphony.
1 September: Otto takes a position in Bremen.
September: Justine and Emma move to Hamburg to live with GM.
15 September: arrival of Bruno Schlesinger (later Walter) at the Hamburg Stadttheater.

1895 *6 February*: Otto commits suicide in Vienna.
4 March: premiere of the first three movements of the Second Symphony, Berlin.
Summer: Steinbach am Attersee; GM composes all but the first movement of the Third Symphony.
September: arrival of Anna von Mildenburg at the Hamburg Stadttheater.
13 December: premiere of the complete Second Symphony in Berlin.

1896 *16 March*: first performance of First Symphony without *Blumine* movement in Berlin; concert also included *Todtenfeier* and the *Lieder eines fahrenden Gesellen*.
Summer: Steinbach am Attersee, Bayreuth (*Ring*, with Justine); GM completes Third Symphony and composes "Lob des hohen Verstandes."
9 November: Nikisch conducts the second movement of the Third Symphony in Berlin.
December: GM begins to campaign for a position at the Vienna Hofoper.
14 December: first two movements of Second Symphony performed in Leipzig.

1897 *15 January*: Ernst von Schuch conducts middle movements of Second Symphony in Dresden.
February: publication of Second Symphony.
23 February: GM converts to Catholicism.
9 March: Weingartner conducts the second, third, and sixth movements of the Third Symphony in Berlin.

12–16 March: GM travels to Moscow to conduct.
19–25 March: GM in Munich to conduct the Kaim Orchestra.
28 March–1 April: GM in Budapest to conduct the Philharmonic.
Late March–early April: GM in Vienna several times in the course of his travels.
8 April: announcement of GM's engagement as conductor at the Vienna Hofoper.
24 April: GM's last performance in Hamburg (*Eroica* symphony and *Fidelio*).

Letters

151 *To Justine*

Telegram[1]
Hamburg, 30 March 1891, 9:33 a.m.[2]

yesterday's debut exceptionally brilliant = gustav

SHELFMARK: E13-MJt-544
NOTES
[1] Addressed to "mahler wien breitegasze 4."
[2] Mahler's first appearance in Hamburg was on 29 March 1891 in Wagner's *Tannhäuser*.

152 *To Justine*

STREIT'S HOTEL
HAMBURG

[Hamburg, 30 March 1891]

Dearest Justi,
I hasten to tell you that, after last night's *extraordinarily* brilliant success (about which I already telegraphed you), my contract was finalised yesterday under better terms.[1]

I am engaged as *director* of the opera—and take up the title from next season; until June, I remain "as guest."[2]—Further, every season I have a benefit performance, which under good circumstances corresponds to a taking of 1500–2000 marks.[3] Please, keep *this last fact secret*, and don't tell *anyone* anything of it.

My position is quite *exceptional* at the theatre.—

The weather is dreadful—these conditions in Hamburg are said to be altogether inconvenient.—On the other hand, here one has a wonderful appetite and a splendid stomach.

Society life here charming.

Write soon, and in detail.

Ever your
Gustav

SHELFMARK: E11-MJ-470
NOTES

[1] After Mahler's successful debut his salary was raised from 12,000 to 14,000 Reichsmarks, i.e., to the amount that Mahler had requested in September 1890; see the note to letter 110 and Bernd Schabbing, *Gustav Mahler als Konzert- und Operndirigent in Hamburg* (Berlin: Ernst Kuhn, 2002), p. 165.

[2] According to Schabbing, p. 165, from 1892 on, Mahler was listed in the *Bühnen-Almanach* as "Dir.," which must be understood as *Direktor*, not *Dirigent* (conductor), since the latter was not used at the time (conductors were give the title of *Kapellmeister*). Out of consideration for Pollini, the "director" in the administrative sense, Mahler did not use the title.

[3] In a benefit performance, the proceeds are given in whole or in part to an individual performer, group of performers, or entire company. Generally the beneficiary is entitled to choose the programme.

153 *To Justine*

[Hamburg, 5 April 1891][1]

Dearest Justi,

Owing to your letter of today, I must assume that a long letter of mine (including the *first* Tannhäuser reviews) has been lost.—Above all, I want to reassure you I left you without any second thoughts whatever and in *the most perfect* friendship.—I do know you—and you certainly must know by now that I, once I have spoken my piece, *I* am entirely *finished* with the issue. Not [even] in my sleep *would I have* given another thought to these recent events. Your promise reassured me completely. I only asked you for it out of *concern* for you—*not* because of my own personal sensitivity. At the same time, I do know that I can *depend* on you to *keep* your *word.*

So: everything is back in order.

I have to tell you again and again: above all, *watch out for yourself.* Furthermore, you shouldn't torment yourself with self-reproach. I like it very much that you are a very sensitive human being.—You only must see to it (and I must help you in this) that these feelings are channelled into the *proper* paths.

It is splendid here! The city is really the most marvellous that I know.—

I am already overwhelmed with invitations from the most prominent families.—I have already been to a big dinner.—People here will please you *very much.*—My position at the theatre is undisputed.—I will send you all of the reviews about me. Don't make too much of it if I don't write much. I am really too *busy.*

Today is Meistersinger.

Very best wishes to you all.

Heartfelt greetings to Ernestine. When I can, I will write her and Fritz too. Please send me his address.

Your
Gustav

SHELFMARK: E10-MJ-425
NOTE
[1] Dated on the basis of the *Meistersinger* performance, Mahler's first performance of the work in Hamburg.

154 *To Justine*

[Hamburg, April 1891]

Dearest Justi,
I take it from your last letters that you have not received at least *3 letters*, in which I told you more or less everything in detail.

My contract is firmly concluded for *3 years*; namely, I am engaged as *director* of the opera, and this position will be publicised in the next few months.—Further, apart from my salary, I have a benefit performance every year, which is customary here for the most distinguished members.—People here are extremely sociable and hospitable.—

At the theatre, the attitude towards me is one of great enthusiasm, and in every respect, I can certainly be content with the change.

As soon as next month, I will take an apartment so that we will be all set for the fall.—I still don't know anything about schools for Emma.—As soon as I can catch my breath a little, I will ask about everything.[1]

The city is beautiful—the harbour magnificent—much more impressive than Trieste and Genoa.

I received the enclosed letter from Alois. What do you have to say about it?

Write soon.

Best wishes from
your
Gustav

Greetings to Ernestine.

SHELFMARK: E10-MJ-420
NOTE
[1] Letters from the spring of 1891 make it clear that Mahler intended that Justine and Emma would come to Hamburg in the fall. In the end, however, this did not happen until 1894.

155 *To Justine*

STREIT'S HOTEL
HAMBURG

[Hamburg, April 1891]

Dearest Justi,
Here are some more reviews. Write me how you are in detail sometime.—Apartments here are *very expensive*, but *completely* [. . .][1]

The harbour is wonderful, [and] not to be surpassed [. . .]

Ever your
Gustav

SHELFMARK: E4-MJ-175
NOTE
[1] The letter is torn along the right side, obscuring some words.

156 *To Justine*

STREIT'S HOTEL
HAMBURG

[Hamburg, April 1891]

Dearest Justi,
Enclosed, another 2 newspaper notices that I fished out of the papers here. As you see, I am rising to be a famous star.

Actually, I am a little bit disgusted with the amateurish hustle and bustle at the theatre.—I have already had a rehearsal today.—We will simply see what I will be able to manage. The city is beautiful, and so lively as one can hardly imagine.—But it is *very* expensive here. I could hardly get an apartment for less than *1000 Mk.* Write me right away. By the way, Pollini is still not here, [but] will only arrive in the next few days. Vederemo.

Very best wishes from your
Gustav

SHELFMARK: E4-MJ-176

157 *To Justine*

[Hamburg, April 1891]

Dearest Justi,
Enclosed, more reviews. Clothes and boots are horribly expensive here. You must assemble your winter wardrobe in Vienna. A pair of boots that I had made here cost 20 Mk.—At any rate, wait a bit. Of course, give notice [about your apartment] on 1 May.—Did you already speak with Papa Löwi about Otto?

I sent the 20 Mk. to Alois.

The climate here is extraordinarily healthy. One eats and digests excellently.

I am already constantly invited to dinner here, but for the most part I have to refuse.

Best wishes from
Gustav

SHELFMARK: E10-MJ-452

~ 158 *To Justine*

DIREKTION B. POLLINI
HAMBURG

[Hamburg, April 1891]

Dearest Justi,
I just received your card.—As far as I remember, when we totalled up the numbers *recently*, I paid *everything*, didn't I, so that I wouldn't have to send you anything more on the 1st? So how much do I have to send you altogether now—*net*? If I understand this card, it would actually be *340* fl.!?

Tomorrow I move into Director Pollini's villa. He left today and has placed the entire house at my disposal. From the enclosed personnel list, you can get a sense of what a position I am taking on here.

Dear Justi, you really must help me a little bit—in the next 3 years now I *must earn* my independence in order to be able to finally work on something for myself! We have to *save*, save. I will not make any reproaches—but do take it to heart!

I have a tremendous amount to do!

Also, from now on my address is

Heimhuderstrasse 54

There I am living in a one-storey villa with a beautiful garden—I also eat there! Isn't that really nice of Pollini?

My best wishes to Ernestine and all the Löwis—the same to Uda.

Your Gustav

SHELFMARK: E11-MJ-471

~ 159 *To Justine*

[Hamburg, April 1891]

Dearest Justi,
I have been living in "my villa" already since the day before yesterday. Wonderful accommodations—(I have the whole house—and also eat at home, since Pollini's household staff will carry on.)—I must take care not to get too accustomed to it.

Hopefully you are now in possession of the money I sent you. Enclosed, some more reviews. This very comfortable life that I am leading here, combined with the varied activity at the theatre, is having the best effect on my health, which—touch wood!—improves effortlessly from day to day.

What would you think if we went to the Bavarian Alps in July, then to Hamburg in August in order to set up the apartment (it is wonderful here in the summer), and then for 2 more weeks to the North Sea.—I think that the climate here would soon make you completely healthy, just as I am.

Write again soon. Best wishes to you all from

Your
Gustav

SHELFMARK: E10-MJ-428

160 *To Justine*

[Hamburg, April 1891]

Dearest Justi,
How much should I send this month? I mislaid the notebook where I wrote down the amount.—Let me know what it is right away.—It is very inconvenient, though, if I have to send you the money earlier.—If it must be, I might send it to you on the 1st by *telegraph*.—

The apartments here are *splendid*. I haven't decided yet, though.

Very best wishes to everyone
Gustav

Answer right away!

SHELFMARK: E11-MJ-478

161 *To Justine*

[Hamburg, April 1891]

Dearest Justi,
From *all* sides, I am advised to take *our Elise* to Hamburg—since all of the servants here are said to be very bad. So that's settled; we'll keep it like that, that Elise is with us here in Hamburg from 1 August. I just saw an apartment that I liked a lot, and which also has the requirements that you mentioned in your last letter. It is available 1 August, and so this fits very well with my summer plans. We could have the furniture sent with Elise and then still go from here to the North Sea for 14 days, which should be exceptionally fortifying. So we would all arrive here on 1 August, set up the apartment with Elise's help, and then, while we go to the sea, Elise can set everything up and worry about the prices and places to shop, etc.

In *July* she should go to her parents in the countryside—We will probably be somewhere in the Bavarian Alps.

So, speak with Elise at once, and don't forget to give notice for your apartment in May.

Best wishes to everyone
from Gustav

SHELFMARK: E21-MJ-674

162 *To Justine*

[Hamburg, May 1891]

Dearest Justi,
Enclosed, you have my menu for May—So, you can all imagine my work.—

Now it is starting to be nice here. You will be amazed how glorious Hamburg is.

I probably won't get around to writing anyone.—Send Nina some newspaper clippings about my activity here, and say hello to her for me.

Also, congratulate Lili Heller for me.[1] They're all in such a terrible hurry.—From Prohaska, I had a letter, and clarification, apologies, etc.[2]

Very best wishes to everyone
from
Gustav

Extra greetings to *Ernestine.*

Shelfmark: E10-MJ-451
Notes
[1] Unknown.
[2] Prohaska is mentioned in letters of December 1893 as being from Iglau.

163 *To Justine*

[Hamburg, May 1891]

Dearest Justi,
Hopefully, you are now in possession of the letter in which, among other things, I told you that I found an apartment for us that suffices in every respect.[1]—I also advised you to go to Frau *Pischof's* for a few days at least.[2]—That would do you much good, now that spring is here. I have a lot to do, and because of that, am rarely in the mood to write.—

I hope to be in Vienna around 8 June.—See to it that we can already be in the country by the end of *June.*

Best wishes to *Nina*—she must excuse me that I hardly ever answer, but I really have no time for it.—

Otto is supposed to send me my *songs*—I need them.[3]

Ever your
Gustav

Shelfmark: E10-MJ-459
Notes
[1] No such letter appears to survive, unless Mahler's memory is faulty and he is referring to the following letter.
[2] Apparently a family friend in Vienna, also mentioned in letter 237.
[3] To date, Mahler had written five songs to texts by Leander, Tirso da Molina, and himself; the four *Lieder eines fahrenden Gesellen*; and nine *Wunderhorn* songs.

164 *To Justine*

[Hamburg, May 1891]

Dearest Justi,
Yesterday I rented an apartment in a really beautiful location. *All* the rooms overlook gardens and lawns.—It has everything that you could want.—More details about it in person.—We move in on August 1st.—

I advise you *most strongly* to come to Hamburg for a few days, namely as soon *as possible*, so that you can still enjoy the spring there.

For the summer (actually July and August), I now have my plan; hopefully it pleases you too.—

On 1 June, I leave for your place via Leipzig, Berlin, [and] Munich; I am thinking of stopping everywhere for a few days, so that I hope to be in Vienna around the middle of *June*.

By the way, the apartment is 2 houses away from Pollini's villa, and in the *healthiest* district of Hamburg. A fifteen-minute stroll of gardens and avenues in every direction.

Otto should send my *songs* by registered mail, whether [he is] *finished or not*. I need them.—Best wishes to *Nina*—I have a terrible amount to do and *cannot* write letters.

Best wishes from
Gustav

Shelfmark: E10-MJ-443

165 *To Justine*

[Hamburg, third week May 1891]

Dearest Justi,
In my unsurpassed laziness, just the news that it is almost over now, thank God. The *last* performance is a week Sunday.[1]

After that, it's directly to Vienna, via *Berlin, Leipzig*, Munich.

Please, see to it that we can all be *off* by June 20.

Also that *Emma* receives her leaving certificate.[2]—

Germany's *best* trade school is here—she begins in *September*.

So that is quite satisfactory.

The apartment is on the 3rd floor.

Anyhow, write soon and in detail.

The songs arrived.

Best wishes to everyone from
Gustav

Shelfmark: E10-MJ-445
Notes

[1] Wagner's *Lohengrin*, Sunday, 31 May.

[2] Certificate given to a student who has not yet completed a course.

166 *To Justine*

[Hamburg, 29 May 1891]

Monday, dearest Justi, I am leaving here, first for Leipzig, where my address is the Hotel de Russe. Direct your next letter there.

Tomorrow I will send you the money for *June*—the discussed amount, *210 fl.*

Today I am conducting *Götterdämmerung* again, and Sunday, Lohengrin—then I am *finished*.

Best wishes to you all
from Gustav

SOURCE
Letter sold by Alfred Rosé; present ownership unknown. As there is no photocopy in the Mahler-Rosé Collection, the text of Henry-Louis de La Grange's transcription has not been checked against the original.

167 *To Justine*

[Hamburg, 30 or 31 May 1891] or [Hamburg, 24 May 1892][1]

Dearest Justi,
Enclosed, a priceless essay that Bülow gave to me. I had to laugh heartily over it.

Then, something else for your manuscript collection.

(Petersen is the mayor here.)

Ever yours
Gustav

I leave the day after tomorrow!

The essay must be read out loud!

SHELFMARK: E10-MJ-454
NOTE
[1] Owing to the mention of Mayor Carl Friedrich Petersen (1809–1892), this letter must date from May 1891 or 1892. In 1891, the last performance (*Lohengrin*) was on 31 May, and Mahler left Hamburg on 1 or 2 June. In 1892, Mahler and the Hamburg ensemble left for London on 26 May. Petersen died 14 November 1892. The essay mentioned in the letter does not survive.

168 *To Justine*

Postcard[1]
[Postmark: Hofgastein, 19.7.91]
[Arrival postmark: Perchtoldsdorf, 20.7.91]

D.J.
I just left Gastein. My next address is: *Marienbad general delivery*.[2] Please write right away in detail how everything is going.

—Apropos, eat *no strawberries*! We all got nasty stomach-aches *from them*.

Ever your
Gustav

SHELFMARK: E4-MJp-173
NOTES

[1] Addressed to "Fräulein Justine Mahler / in Perchtoldsdorf bei Wien / Hochstrasse 25."

[2] After paying a diplomatic visit to Pollini, who took his annual summer cure in Bad Gastein, Mahler spent a few days in Marienbad for a cure. While in Gastein, Mahler met his old friend Natalie Bauer-Lechner (HLG I, p. 356).

169 *To Justine*

Postcard[1]
[Postmark: Marienbad, 21 July 1891]
[Arrival postmark: Perchtoldsdorf, 22 July 1891]

Dear Justi,
Arrived here—already received your letters.—It is disastrous that Otto does such stupid things. I *disapprove* of his latest *revelation* in *every* sense.—I would have thought that he might have had enough of his *amusements* for the time being, and think again about the fulfilment of his duties.

Please, let me know right away and in detail about the course of events. I will write again soon. I am very well.

I am living in the "*Königsvilla*," and am staying until 1 August. I met Natalie in Gastein.

Best,
Gustav

SHELFMARK: E12-MJp-484
NOTE

[1] Addressed to "Fräulein Justine Mahler / in Perchtoldsdorf a.d. Südb. / bei Wien / Hochstrasse 25."

170 *To Justine*

KÖNIGS-VILLA
MARIENBAD

[Marienbad, between 21 and 24 July 1891]

Dearest Justi,
Here is an interesting contribution for your autograph collection.—I asked Bülow in a card for a favour, and immediately received this answer. Not many people can boast about receiving a signature from Bülow.[1] What are these remarks that you made to Otto? Please always tell me such things *fully*, don't just allude to them.—You certainly don't need to be afraid that I will misunderstand. It goes *without saying* that you always speak to me as a friend—and you do know that with me, one doesn't easily run into the threat of misunderstanding or hostility.—

I can put myself inside any human heart—and certainly yours I know inside and out.

Much will be unclear to you about Otto, which I can again very well imagine. Just now you are all living together, and get into subjective viewpoints that just rob you of understanding for the point of view of the others.—This is always the case with people, even the *best* and the wisest. Then it is always good to think that a time will come in which all records are closed forever—and there is no more injustice to atone for.

Then one will be more careful of oneself, and more forbearing with others.

Best wishes. Explain your last letter to me frankly!

Your
Gustav

Did Fritz get my letter?

SHELFMARK: E10-MJ-457
NOTE
[1] Does not survive in the Mahler-Rosé Collection.

171 *To Justine*

KÖNIGS-VILLA
MARIENBAD

[Marienbad, between 20 and 24 July 1891]

Dearest Justi,
Please send the newspapers out to me immediately. (—Obviously.)—

Frankly, it is quite astonishing that Emma wanted a doll. In your place, *I* would *not* have bought her such a thing, despite the greatest pressure.—An almost grown-up girl, who is so overripe in one respect, and so childish on the other, remains a riddle to me.

—Otto's trip annoys me.—What kinds of pranks are these? Why so excessive? Even if I took him with me for 14 whole days, he has to go off again?—As long as I have to hand over money for such things, I also wish to be asked *permission*.

Don't retort that you will make up for it somewhere or other.—I *do not* want you to make good for it "*somewhere else*."

Why do I make calculations then, and try hard to deliver you from all life's needs?

Apart from the money, though, there is again such inconsiderateness and egotism in it.—If I had added another 30 fl., he could have gone to Bayreuth with it—furthermore, prepare yourself [for the fact] that you'll have to give him more money.

Will he simply be without pocket money for 3 months?—For what did I intend pocket money for him? I obviously do have my reasons if I refuse him something!? I want the money I send to be used as I *indicate*, and not as the mood strikes somebody or other.—In a word, I hereby express to Otto my *fullest disapproval* of his behaviour. Please keep me informed of the further course of this adventure.—

Regarding Uda's lessons, I really can't say anything definitive about it from afar, and must now leave it to you and Uda.

Mind you, it doesn't seem right that you, and *above all Emma*, give up French before you have reached the desired goal. One should *not* leave things undone.—As I said, I will not decide about it; do what you think.—

That swimming agrees with you so well makes me happy. It is a sign that your health has *decidedly* improved—last year, you couldn't have stood it so well.

The cure doesn't agree with me this time at all, and I am pushing off for Bayreuth the sooner the better.—Many thanks to Ernestine for her letter. Only she should not be put off about writing repeatedly; I will answer sometime when I have better *pens*. There's nothing to be done with this one.

It is really wonderful that Nina is coming over.—Just be sure *you* walk assiduously, even in the rain—it really is the healthiest. Write soon!

Very best wishes to everyone from
your Gustav

SHELFMARK: S1-MJ-760

172 *To Justine*

Postcard[1]
[Postmark: Eger, 25.7.91][2]
[Arrival postmark: Perchtoldsdorf, 26.7.91]

Dear Justi,
I am just on the way to Bayreuth! Please, now send everything there, *general delivery*!

In M[arienbad] it was *too dreadful*.

Warmly,
G.

SHELFMARK: E4-MJp-165
NOTES

[1] Addressed to "Fräulein Justine Mahler / in Perchtoldsdorf a.d. Südb. / bei Wien / Hochstrasse 25."

[2] Now Cheb, in the Czech Republic.

173 *To Justine*

Postcard[1]
[Postmark: Bayreuth, 30.7.91]
[Arrival postmark: Perchtoldsdorf, (31.)7.91]

D.J.
I am just leaving Bayreuth.—

Until further notice, letters to *Eger*, general delivery. I am going on a hiking tour through the Fichtelgebirge. I am doing splendidly.

Ever your
~~Mahler~~ Gustav

SHELFMARK: E4-MJp-166
NOTE

[1] Addressed to "Fräulein Justine Mahler / in Perchtoldsdorf a.d. Südb. / bei Wien / Hochstrasse 25."

174 *To Justine*

Wunsiedel 31/7 91

Dearest Justi,
I have just come from a wonderful hike (6 hours). Louisenburg [Luisenburg], about which I've already told you and which would even awaken Otto's respect, Kösseine, the peak of the Fichtelgebirge (Alexanderbad) and back.—This evening Bertha, along with *Reif[f]*[1] are coming back here from Bayreuth; once here, we plan to go on a longer excursion.—This is as lovely and friendly an area for a longer stay as I could wish.

I really regret it that we have used this summer so impracticably. For next year, I have made up my mind to decide (if we are healthy) to take lodgings for the entire summer somewhere on a restful lake, and calmly spend the time there.—This bicycling aimlessly around the world is not worth anything. I will be really happy to do this, until things start again in Hamburg.—I heard 3 performances in Bayreuth.[2]—Bertha told me about the change in your studies, which meets my full approval.

It's very sensible that Nina is with you now. It will do you good. Just go walking diligently, and use the summer properly.—I'll still be going to Helgoland and Sylt for 3 weeks. On 24 August, I will arrive in Hamburg.—I hope to have a detailed letter from you in Eger, where I am going the day after tomorrow to visit Rudolf Krzyzanowski, who himself is there just now.—Hopefully, there will be detailed news about Otto's trip and adventure.—Now that he has furnished such proof of his valiant independence, he will now hopefully apply himself to his books with great enthusiasm, the required wisdom and discipline for which ought to be provided by [the prospect of] a year of imp. and roy. military service.—What is up with his teacher?

Kindest regards to you all

Your Gustav

You could send me *Alois'* letter for me to look over.

[across the top of the letter:] Say hello to *Freund* from me.

SHELFMARK: E4-MJ-167
NOTES

[1] According to HLG I, p. 356, singer Josef Reiff-Heissinger (see GMB[2], p. 432, n. 3).

[2] *Parsifal* (26 July), *Tannhäuser* (27 July), and *Parsifal* (29 July).

175 *To Justine*

Postcard[1]
[Postmark: Hamburg, 3.8.91]
[Arrival postmark: Perchtoldsdorf, 5.8.91]

Dearest J.
I'm now sitting again here in Hamburg. The day after tomorrow, early, I board ship and depart—for where, I don't even know myself.—This summer I have been loafing around proficiently; even that has its own charm.

I have just taken private lodgings with full board for the winter—very cheap and quite good.[2]

As soon as I have the address, I will give it to you. Hopefully I'll get news from you tomorrow.

Ever your
Gustav

Shelfmark: E4-MJp-168
Notes

[1] Addressed to "Fräulein Justine Mahler / in Perchtoldsdorf a.d. Südb. / bei Wien / Hochstrasse 25."

[2] This is the first reference in the family letters to the fact that Justine and Emma were not moving to Hamburg after all. La Grange speculates that this was because Löhr's decision to prolong his Italian trip meant that he couldn't take in Otto (HLG I, p. 356).

176 *To Justine*

Postcard[1]
[Postmark: Hamburg, 4.8.91]
[Arrival postmark: Perchtoldsdorf, 6.8.91]

D.J.,
I am just about to leave for *Kiel*, and from there, by ship early tomorrow morning for Copenhagen. Unfortunately, I am still without a *letter*, and would ask you for one—since I never know my address beforehand, telegraph me *immediately* at the Hotel Angleterre, Copenhagen, after you receive this, [and let me know] if you are all in good health and if Otto is safely home again.—I am planning to go right up to Norway, and will write you a card from everywhere I will be. Unfortunately I cannot expect any letters from you since I never know in advance where I will stay. I am *in good health* and very much looking forward to my trip.

Warmly, G.

Tentatively, I will arrive back in *Hamb.* on the 25th.

Shelfmark: E4-MJp-169
Note

[1] Addressed to "Fräulein Justine Mahler / in Perchtoldsdorf a.d. Südb. / bei Wien / Hochstrasse 25."

◌ 177 *To Justine*

Deutsche Reichspost Postcard[1]
[Postmark: (illegible), 5.8.91]
[Arrival postmark: Perchtoldsdorf, 7.8.91]
Kiel, 5/8, *on board*, 11 a.m.

D.J.
Just about to leave for Copenhagen.—Spent the night here—then had a marvellous walk.

Took a swim in the sea (13 degrees R[éaumur].)[2]

Splendid weather.

More from Copenhagen.

Hopefully I will find a telegram.

Warmly,
G.

Shelfmark: E12-MJp-485
Notes

[1] Addressed to "Fräulein Justine Mahler / in Perchtoldsdorf bei Wien / Hochstrasse 25."

[2] On the Réaumur scale, water freezes at 0° and boils at 80°.

◌ 178 *To Justine*

Postcard[1]
[Postmark: Korsør, 5 August 1891]
[Arrival postmark: Perchtoldsdorf, 7 August 1891]
Korsör (Zealand) 5/8

Wonderful trip—arrived at 6:00.
Saw the city—sea wonderful—city dismal.—Around 7:30 I travel by rail to Copenhagen.

Best wishes,
G.

Shelfmark: E12-MJp-485a
Note

[1] Addressed to "Fräulein Justine Mahler / in Perchtoldsdorf a.d. Südb. / bei Wien / Hochstrasse 25."

179 *To Justine*

Postcard[1]
[Postmark: Copenhagen, 6.8.91]
[Arrival postmark: Perchtoldsdorf, 8.8.91]
Kopenhagen 6/8 (? I don't know exactly.)

D.J.
—In vain, I have been expecting news and am really rather uneasy. Hopefully nothing has happened, has it?!

Today I wandered everywhere throughout the city and the harbour—only the *Thorwaldsen* museum is worth seeing—and got a rather good overall picture.—The city is really impressive. Tomorrow I am going up the Danish *coast*, partly on foot, and partly by steamboat, and hope to reach Elsinore [Helsingør] (remember, from Hamlet) in 2 days.—My next reachable address is: *Christiania Martins Hotel.*

Write a few lines there *immediately*!

Warmly, G.

[written across the top of the letter:] Is Otto home?

SHELFMARK: E4-MJp-170
NOTE
[1] Addressed to "Fräulein Justine Mahler / in Perchtoldsdorf a.d. Südb. / bei Wien / Hochstrasse 25."

180 *To Justine*

Postcard[1]
[Postmark: Helsingør, 8.8.91]
[Arrival postmark: Perchtoldsdorf, 10.8.91]
Helsingför 7/8

Finally received the telegram. So I am going forward with relief.—Today a wonderful walking tour through the woods and to the sea, during which whole herds of game were to be seen.—Tomorrow, across the Kat[t]egat to Göteborg (Sweden).

This time I'll probably get seasick. Tomorrow morning before the departure of the steamboat, another nice walking tour on the coast for an hour.

Warmly,
G.

SHELFMARK: E12-MJp-486
NOTE
[1] Addressed to "Fräulein Justine Mahler / in Perchtoldsdorf a.d. Südb. / bei Wien / Hochstrasse 25."

181 *To Justine*

Postcard[1]
[Postmark: Göteborg, 9 August 1891]
[Arrival postmark: Perchtoldsdorf, 12 August 1891]
Gothenburg (Swedish coast) Sunday

Spent the night in Helsingör (highest point of Seeland). Morning excursion—to *Kronberg* (Hamlet's terrace), among others.—Noon, across the strait [*Sund*] to Helsingborg (25 minute journey by ship). From there to Halmstadt on a small mailboat.—Rough sea (as usual in the Kat[t]egat)—Was almost seasick.—Walked, and spent the night in Halmstadt. Today, to Gothenburg by train at 6:00 a.m. The journey along the Swedish coast very unusual—nothing but overgrown cliffs and rocks. Life eventful everywhere. People very friendly.

I had almost overslept, since one cannot count on a proper wake-up call in the hotel here. I jumped up at 5:45 and—*believe it or not*, sat in the *train compartment* at 6:00!!! The way of life is *so very different* from ours.—My stomach is not in the best shape.—Today and tomorrow, wandering along the coast on foot and by train.—

Best, Gustav.

SHELFMARK: E4-MJp-171
NOTE
[1] Addressed to "Fräulein Justine Mahler / in Perchtoldsdorf a.d. Südb. / bei Wien / Hochstrasse 25."

182 *To Justine*

Postcard[1]
[Postmark: Göteborg, 10.8.91]
[Arrival postmark: Perchtoldsdorf, 12.8.91]
Gothenburg, Sunday [9 August] 10:00 p.m.—

A wonderful day today. The city is the most unusual one can imagine. In the middle of the ~~houses and~~ streets, suddenly cliffs and rocks—often very spread out. I was on top of the highest—this is something that even the boldest fantasy cannot conceive of. A world in itself. A view roughly like from the Rax. Only more rocky and less hospitable.—From the peak, a broad view of the *bay* right to the broad ocean—Over here, wooded, rocky mountains, moors, [and] valleys, and over there, an imposing city spreading itself out.—A marvellous ramble. Right in the middle, a large, dancing place on a rock spread with planks, where, by chance, I was present at a folk dance. Everywhere full of people.—Tomorrow, by ship through the Schäre to an island "Marstrand" (Sea bath). More than anything I don't want to leave this place. *Indescribable*! Marvellous harbour life!

Best wishes,

G.

SHELFMARK: E12-MJp-487
NOTE
[1] Addressed to "Fräulein Justine Mahler / in Perchtoldsdorf a.d. Südb. / bei Wien / Hochstrasse 25."

183 *To Justine*

GRAND HOTEL, CHRISTIANIA

[Christiania (Oslo), 11. August 1891]
Tuesday

Dearest!
So, yesterday was a day of travel only. Off by train at 8:00 a.m.—around 6:00 I arrived in *Moss*. The journey was very interesting and went by before I knew it.

Always along the coast—a glimpse of a cove here and there, but mostly through country away from the coast.—Nevertheless, a large mighty sea or river every minute—small, rocky, treed hills everywhere.—I wanted to spend the night in Moss, in order to travel by steamer to Christiania in the morning so that I could enjoy the impressive approach, but I was so depressed by the perpetual smell of fish and ships in the little town (similar as in Venice) and by the very primitive accommodations that I decided to leave again by the steamer at 7:00.—Because of the bad weather, it was delayed 1½ hours and only arrived in Moss at 8:30.—I spent the hour and a half at the bay near the ship's dock, and passed the time away in a lively pantomime conversation with the Norwegian sailors working nearby. We had a marvellous conversation; they showed gallantry by speaking English for my benefit, and I spoke Norwegian (with the help of my Baedeker). I was finally sick from the smell of the water, natural for such a narrow bay.—

Finally the ship came—it went off into the darkness; around 12:00 we arrived in Ch[ristiania]—unfortunately, dark night—plus rain and more rain—and it is still raining today, ruining all my beautiful plans. Today I slept in Martins Hotel (still no trace of a letter), but am moving to the Grand Hotel here, because I want comfortable lodgings after so many calamities and with this incessant weather.—What now, I don't know. If it clears up and if my money holds out, then I will go into the country.—If the rain lasts, however, I will take the sea route to Hamburg—unfortunately this goes through the *Skagerrak* and through the whole North Sea! Brrr!

Very best wishes from
Gustav

SHELFMARK: E4-MJ-190

184 *To Justine and Other Siblings*

GRAND HOTEL, CHRISTIANIA

[Christiania (Oslo), 12 August 1891]

My dears,
Yesterday I had hardly sent my letter when yours came.—By way of answer, this above all: *I* am *completely* opposed to you renting a room, for a thousand

reasons.—If there's no other way, just stay in the old apartment and enlist the owner to renovate it, like on the first floor. That will be best of all.

Yesterday, I looked round the city, and made 2 trips to the peaks, from which one has a view of the city and surroundings. A splendid royal castle, "Oscarhall," resembles Miramare extraordinarily. Evenings, when I return to the hotel, I sit in the reading room. When I looked up from my newspaper for a moment, in front of me I saw—*Ibsen*.[1] He is here right now, and is living in the same hotel.—You can well imagine that I was not a little moved by this.—Today I am making an expedition in the vicinity of Christiania.—Unfortunately, my money will not suffice for me to complete my so beautifully planned route through the Norwegian interior.—With *heavy* heart, I must give up my plan, and slowly get ready for my trip home; namely, I will contrive it so that I travel in short stages to the south point of Norway (Christiansund), from whence on *Sunday* a direct ship departs to Hamburg (48 hours).—Perhaps from there I will make another little trip to Helgoland.—But I would *really* borrow from this *Norway*! In splendidness and individuality of nature, as well as of the inhabitants, the Alps cannot compare (for us southerners).

Once one really knows one's way around, life here is extraordinarily cheap and very comfortable. Write now directly to Hamburg (Hotel Streit).

Best wishes from
Gustav

Did you get all my postcards?

SHELFMARK: E4-MJ-188
NOTE
[1] Norwegian dramatist Henrik Ibsen (1828–1906).

185 *To Justine*

GRAND HOTEL, CHRISTIANIA

[Christiania (Oslo), 13 August 1891]

Dearest Justi,
Just about to depart for Drammen (city in the Christiania fjord).

Yesterday was successful—climbed the Frognersaeter–A small mountain near Christiania, about the height of the Anninger, with a splendid view of the whole countryside and the bay. Splendid way up through woods and meadows. People here are all friendly and helpful. On the return trip I made the acquaintance of a university professor from here. I even had to enter his home in order to obtain the directions I wanted.—The trip there and back lasted 8½ hours—with a half-hour rest at the lookout.—

It is extremely gratifying that I am finding own way with the help of my Baedeker, in which I now have considerable practice.

Today I am staying in Drammen, tomorrow by ship to Laurwik (a small sea spa on the Norwegian coast)—tomorrow from there by ship to Christiansund—overnight by ship to Friedrichshafen in Jütland. From there, by train to Tondern, and from there by ship to *Sylt*. I will then stay there 8 days.

I would rather have roamed around Norway for another 8 days, but this time it is too *expensive* for me, since one has to travel by *wagon-lit*, which is very expensive here, because of the terrible distances and lack of any trains.

So I will yet have my sea baths. I will tell you my address in Sylt next time (as long as I don't change my plans).

Best,
Gustav

Shelfmark: E4-MJ-189

186 *To Justine and Other Siblings*

[Fridrichshafen, 15 August 1891]
Friedrichshafen (Jütland) Saturday

My dears,
The last 3 days were the best of the whole trip.—Here are the outward facts.

Left *Christ.* early Thursday by rail to *Drammen*.—Its harbour made a better impression on me than that of *Ch.* itself. The city lies on both sides of a glorious river, the mouth of which is here in the Christiania fjord, and is surrounded on all sides by wooded mountains. I immediately set off up the prettiest of these, and discovered a whole world in itself. A timber forest that almost covers the expanse of the mountain, with odd parts, one moment rocky, the next boggy, that I zigzagged through. Right in the middle, completely hidden, a lake called the Schwarzsee (in German translation)—Again, open places here and there, which on the one side overlooks the whole countryside right down to the ocean, or rather, the bay, and on the other, the various valleys and the river running through them. After about 5 extremely enjoyable hours, I was still on time to board the ~~ship~~ boat to take me to Laurwik.—In spite of the strong wind and rain, I stayed on deck (as through the whole trip in general), and in about 5 hours arrived in Laurwik.—I went to bed immediately since the ship left for Christiansund the next morning at 6:00 a.m.—

This trip through the Norwegian "skerries" was the most enjoyable of my whole tour. On the one side, the most characteristic images of rocks—and cliffs—also islands—one moment barren, the next wooded, the next even covered with houses or lighthouses. On the other, the wonderful, richly articulated Norwegian coast. In between, always little sections of open sea!—The wind blew hard, and when we came out of the skerries into the open sea, it drove along the waves of the Kat[t]egat. At such moments the ship tossed back and forth—fortunately, I was spared from seasickness.—On the ship, it turned out that there was a "Salvation Army" troupe among us—about 8 men and just as many women in very funny uniforms and with just as funny manners. Later on, they took up 3 guitars, a violin, and 1 trumpet and began to tune their instruments.—Because of that, I really became attentive, and saw that they all had large crests (on the men's caps and the women's shoulders) that read: "Frölse's

Army"—I didn't know without asking, although I suspected, that they were the "famous Salvation army," of which you will have just heard as much as I had before now: namely, the name.

So, they tuned for about an hour. All the passengers stood attentively in order to hear them—admittedly, some were puking over the side, as the ship rode up and down over high swells. Finally, they began to sing, the women with squeaky voices, and the men with croaky ones. In fact, it was apparent that they all hardly knew either the words or the music, so that they took the helm alternately, just if they knew how to continue, so that it was mostly a kind of antiphonal singing. 4 women and a man made up the orchestra—the first 3 played guitar and a violin, and the last played trumpet. It immediately stood out that the violin player held the bow right in the middle.—The song was a very funny ballad with a sacred text, of which I understood only the word "Jesus Christ" and Portugal. We arrived in Christiansund at 8:00 p.m.—In the morning the long-hidden sun came out right after our departure.—When we came into the harbour here, we saw the French fleet there.

After a 2 hour stay on land, again aboard ship and through the feared Skagerrack to Friedrichshafen.—I slept remarkably well, in spite of the groaning of the engine, the blowing wind, and the back-and-forth motion, and arrived here today at 10:30 in the best of moods.—Into the city immediately, and then a little walk.—What a contrast—an endless moor—a farmer here and there—a windmill, a house—away over there, the open sea. I walked and walked, and came to a kind of park that attracted me—and arrived—at a cemetery. I wandered around a bit and was inspired and thought of what has passed before me.—Whether the high mountains of Norway—or Jutland moor!—the end is always the same.—About 5:00 I roar off with the train—Now, home through the North sea by way of Sylt and Helgoland.—

Best wishes to all from
Gustav

SHELFMARK: E4-MJ-191

187 *To Justine*

Postcard: Gruss aus Helgoland[1]
[Postmark: Helgoland, 20.[8.]91]
[Arrival postmark: Perchtoldsdorf, 22.8.91]

Arrived in Sylt—soaked to the skin—after a 20-hour journey. Stayed there 2 days.—From here, a splendid journey by sea to Helgoland. Been here 2 days.—Yesterday wonderful weather, today storm and rain—In spite of that, went sailing. Also swam in sea here as well as in Sylt. Stay very extraordinary—Tomorrow, by ship to Hamburg. I hope to find detailed news of you all.—I am very refreshed.—The performances in Hamburg begin Sunday *30* with Fidelio.—Best wishes

from Gustav

[across top of card, above illustration of a ship at sea:] Goodbye sea!!

Shelfmark: E12-MJp-488

Note

[1] Addressed to "Fräulein Justine Mahler / in Perchtoldsdorf a.d. Südb. / bei Wien / Hochstrasse 25," with return address: "Absender-Mahler, Hamburg, Stadttheater."

188 *To Justine*

[Hamburg, end August 1891]

Dearest Justi,

Enclosed, a letter for Jenny that hopefully you will get in enough time to give to her *Sunday before* the wedding.[1] If not, please do send it to her *immediately*, wherever [she is].—I had actually forgotten—not her wedding, but just to write her. I got your and Ernestine's letter yesterday. What kind of *nervous attacks* are these? How do they manifest themselves, and where do they come from? Have you asked the doctor?

I congratulate you on your Jean-Paul reading—it is a hard crust, and happy is he who can digest it.—I am still living here very quietly, and almost contentedly, so long as the performances have not started.—I am reading an awful lot again—you know that does me good when I'm in the mood.—Sooner or later, my interaction with Pollini always seems to become tense. At least there are already all of the indications that this is happening! Well—"as God wills"!—*Continually* beautiful weather here now—the first time since our walk in the Höllenthal.—Isn't that just too bad?—Don't let yourself get grey hair over 6 fl. a month.—

Did you not receive the letter where I advised you to keep the old apartment? Just make use of the glorious September, and stay *out there* as long as possible.[2] For today, just best wishes

from Gustav

Shelfmark: E21-MJ-673

Notes

[1] Mentioned also in letter 189, dated 1 September by Mahler (and verified by his mention of the opening performance of *Fidelio* that day). While it seems that Mahler is referring to Jenny Feld, the letter from her son to Alfred Rosé quoted in the notes to letter 10 says that his parents were married in 1892. As that letter was written in 1968, it is quite possible that his memory was faulty. (There was no performance of *Fidelio* on 1 September 1892.)

[2] Here, and in subsequent letters, Mahler encourages Justine to stay out in Perchtoldsdorf at their summer accommodation as long as possible.

189 *To Justine*

DIRECTOR B. POLLINI
HAMBURG

Hamburg, 1. Sept. *1891*

Dearest Justi,
It is now 6:00—the opening performance of Fidelio begins at 7:30. Therefore I'm "all keyed up."—I received your last letters very quickly one after another.—The first came just after I sent my express letter to Ernestine.—Upon my arrival in Hamburg, of course, I found 2 or 3 letters from you, and *one from Bertha.*—The interval, however, until your first current one amounted to at least 10 days, so I was naturally very worried. And I now see after the fact that my worry was not without foundation, since you yourself tell of a significant indisposition.—Did you get my letter to Jenny in enough time to be able to give it to her?

I really hope so, otherwise there would have been absolutely no sign of life from me at the time of her wedding.

Ernestine's letter pleased me very much. You can also treat yourself to Münchhausen sometime.[1]—Above all, the first books are splendid. Later, especially towards the end, the thing becomes a little bit superficial—these days especially, the "love story" is a bit insipid [*eine Blasse Limonade*].—It is very wise of you all to consult the professor. Otto should just buckle down to work.

I am living very comfortably and eat at home at midday too. I pay 150 *Mk.* monthly for accommodation, breakfast, midday meal, and service.

I am only worried about my apartment in the Heimhuderstr[asse], which is still not rented.—I will still have a hard nut to crack there.

Best wishes to all,
your
Gustav

SHELFMARK: E4-MJ-172
NOTE

[1] Karl Immermann (1796–1840), *Münchhausen: Eine Geschichte in Arabesken* (1839). This work is divided into eight "books." It is possible, however, that Mahler is referring to Gottfried August Bürger (1747–1794), *Wunderbare Reisen zu Wasser und zu Lande Feldzüge und lustige Abenteuer des Freiherrn von Münchhausen, wie er diesselben bei der Flasche im Zirkel seiner Freunde selbst zu erzählen pflegt* (1786).

190 *To Justine*

DIRECTOR B. POLLINI
HAMBURG

[Hamburg, first week September 1891]

Dearest Justi,
I received your letter.—What drove Ary[1] and Jenny's husband apart then?—Regarding the tension between me and Pollini, for the moment it is just a feeling on *my* part that sooner or later it will come about.—Also, Hamburg is not exactly adequate ground for my nature to be able to run free. That is why again I only regard this place as a stopover—certainly I can't deny that I am now tired of this eternal wandering, and long for "a home."—But again there isn't anyone here with whom I have anything more in common than air and light.—By the

way, I enclose a review of Fidelio.[2] The rest are about the same.—It is strange how strong my homesickness for Vienna is this time; I haven't had this feeling for 8 years.

If I only had enough money to permit us to live a modest life from the interest, I would get up from here, walk away, and come to you. Say hello to Ary from me.

For today, I close.

Ever your
Gustav

Shelfmark: E4-MJ-174
Note
[1] Unknown.
[2] According to Schabbing, p. 300, only the 1 September performance of *Fidelio* was reviewed.

191 *To Justine*

[Hamburg, early September 1891]

Dearest Justi,
I received the package from Papa Löwi, but in it I am missing the little package with the papers (from the Hungarian bank—my contract, etc.)—I do remember giving them to him to look after together with the scores! Or did I give it to you? Please clarify this for me.—At any rate, I need them; please forward them to me.—You do have the demission etc. there too, right?—

Also, when you have a chance, please write me how much I have to send you on 1 October.—Nina shouldn't imagine such silly things! Am I easily offended or the like?—Of course I rarely write anything about her, because I always imagine that she is away again when my letter comes. I am very happy that she is with you—and see it, finally, as a good idea on her part.

With my unconquerable laziness about letters, I never manage to write anyone regularly. Anyway, I assume that everyone finds out from you about anything notable that concerns me.

September seems to be starting off wonderfully. Stay out there a good *long* time yet.—I wish that I could be with you for a few days too.

Next summer we must arrange everything more practically from the outset.—

I *only* feel comfortable here in my room.—Otherwise, I feel *completely* alien as never before.—I am very curious how it all will turn out.—I don't have to overexert myself right now—and everything could be very nice—if—if—it just were nicer.—

Hopefully, tomorrow I will rouse myself to write a few lines to Fritz for his arrival.[1]—He will certainly be in a hurry!

Best wishes to everyone.

I am very happy about *your* "progress."

Your
Gustav

SHELFMARK: S1-MJ-744
NOTE
[1] According to GMB[2], p. 440, n. 65, the Löhr family returned from their Italian sojourn in mid-September 1891.

192 *To Justine*

KÖNIGS-VILLA
MARIENBAD[1]

[Hamburg, 12 September 1891]

Dearest Justi,
Enclosed, a review of the last, very beautiful performance of Meistersinger.[2]

Tonight is the new production of *Tannhäuser*.

From your last letter, then, I gather the following calculation: you get on

October: 327 fl = 562 Mk—
1 November 462 " = 742.—

Is this right? Please confirm this again, and I will then send you the requested amount.

Is Fritz now in Vienna? Please let me know about his arrival right away, also how his health is.—What do you think of the fact that now, when I'm mired in work, we have continually had the most beautiful summer weather?

All July and August we had to splash around in rain—that is really bad luck!—

Very best wishes from your
Gustav

Jenny still has my books (among them, keepsakes). Didn't she say anything about them?

SHELFMARK: E11-MJ-475
NOTES
[1] Obviously, paper left over from Mahler's July cure.
[2] 9 September 1891.

193 *To Justine*

[Hamburg, mid-September 1891]

Dearest Justi,
I just received and opened my box from Budapest and, to my greatest dismay, found that many things from my desk (above all the beautiful inkwell etc.) are *not there*! So apparently they must be with the things in Vienna! Please let me know right away if you know anything about this!—

Tannhäuser was also new—enclosed, the reviews.[1]

From the arch-rogue and tramp Taussig,[2] I received the following priceless letter, which I hereby enclose for your edification. Apparently he was in Norway at the same time as I was, so I can count myself lucky that I didn't run into him on a ship somewhere.

It's great that you all are taking such good advantage of the beautiful weather. Do stay out there a long time.

Please send some reviews to the *Singers* sometime.

Best wishes to all of you
from
Gustav

SHELFMARK: E10-MJ-415
NOTES

[1] According to Schabbing, both the first (12 September) and second (14 September) performances of *Tannhäuser* were reviewed.

[2] Possibly, actor and director Emanuel Taussig (1856–1912).

194 *To Justine*

[Hamburg, second half of September 1891]

Dearest Justi,
I am looking for the calculation that you sent me a few weeks ago, and I cannot find it! Please, take a moment sometime and let me know how much I have to send you on 1 October.—This time I am damned short of money, and I cannot get away from money worries.

This time my laundry was badly seen to at home; I had already taken it in shabby condition [*deroutem Zustand*] on my trip, and I can hardly use my clothes any longer since I don't have anyone here to look after them.—I am making you aware of this for the future, so that when I come to visit, you will have to take care that this is seen to and fixed.

I received the batons here (also had to pay 70 marks duty for them)—they are very nice.

Please tell Fritz sometime that you are talking to him alone that I am absolutely not able to pay the 150 fl. in advance because, for the moment, I don't know at all where I am going to find the money that I have to pay on the 1st.—Actually, I can't [even] have the most necessary things that I need made, like *shirts*, handkerchiefs, and new tails, and must go about shabbily.—I will write him again the next time I have a moment.

Is *Otto* learning anything? Tell Fritz too that with the tutoring, I am *only* concerned about the *examination*![1] General education [*Bildung*] and the like is completely secondary to me.—

He must do his examination next fall: I. so that he can finally think of something else; II. so that I am finally free of these troubling money worries.—I would also like to turn my thoughts to other directions.—Papa Löwi can keep the papers, but among them is also a contract with *Pollini*. Send *it* to me, because I might have need of it.

Why did Bauer[-Lechner] appear suddenly, and what is wrong with her?

I have messed myself up terribly with the fatal apartment—I signed a lease for 2 years and, as of today, it is still not rented.

Send me the calculation immediately; if I remember it rightly, I have to send you 350 or 60 fl., right?

It's now very cold here. I have just had to have the heating on, and the stove burns splendidly but—it smokes! Damn it all—it always has to smoke for me!

How are you all feeling?

Best wishes to everyone
from your
Gustav

I received a notice from Iglau that I have to pay a military tax of *120 fl.* for the past 3 years.—

Again no relief! Still more fun!

SHELFMARK: E10-MJ-444
NOTE

[1] This is the first of many references in the letters to the examination that would allow Otto to complete his military service as a "one-year recruit" (*Einjahrig Freiwilliger*). On military service in Österreich-Ungarn, see István Deák, *Beyond Nationalism* (Oxford: Oxford University Press, 1990).

195 *To Justine*

[Hamburg, second half of September 1891]

Dearest Justi,
Your plan about the shirts is quite all right with me.—So, make me 6 *of them*—(neck size no. 40)—and 1 *dozen* handkerchiefs. I have absolutely no *socks*—heaven knows where they have all gone.—So please make me 6 pairs of *good* winter socks too. All this *as quickly as possible*, and send it to me with the things from my desk *and* the little coffee maker, well-packed so that it doesn't break.—

I was pleased about many things in your last letters—I see how rapidly you are developing into a mature human being—but, I also had a less contenting glimpse into your life.—Next time be a little more clear about it, [but] it seems that your relations with one another are very confused. Even if there is something disagreeable to you, confide it to me openly.

One thing that *none* of you should even imagine is that any *one* of you has any insight into human nature!—What it's really about is this: as long as one person believes of another that he is *different*—still, let that pass!—but—despite believing that, one always still makes *demands* of others that are really always only suitable for *oneself.*—*In that* lies the error.—Always remember that every *human being* is a world to himself; one knows a large part of it—namely insofar as it is contained in oneself—but the rest of it remains a life-long secret to someone [else].—If one establishes new rules, they are always suited for the piece of the world that one knows—(namely, because it is one's own)—.—

But this leads too far afield! Just don't fight—don't be *suspicious* of each other—be content with what you have in common, don't criticise what you don't understand, and—*don't make any rules* for "the human race."—To the *Lord*

God you are certainly all the same!—But, seeing with human eyes, everyone is and remains an *unknown* world, yet with some small measure of sameness which makes *understanding* possible.

You are all bound together by this measure of sameness. Do not destroy the *connection* thoughtlessly.

—Unfortunately, since my return—actually since a cold drink in *Marienbad*—I have been suffering from a stomach catarrh, which I am now energetically fighting with a strict diet.

Did you receive the money?

With best wishes to you all,
Gustav

Best wishes to Nina—of course, she, too, is not a good judge of character.

[on a separate scrap of ledger paper:] Right—I forgot the most important thing in my sermon: namely! That which *really particularly* makes someone outraged about someone else, 99 times out of 100, is exactly *that thing* that one is capable of oneself.—It is the same with *mistakes* as with the whole person: namely, that one recognises one's own world in another, and is enraged at one's own image in the mirror—would even like to smash the mirror, if possible.

SHELFMARK: E10-MJ-458

196 *To Justine*

[Hamburg, second half of September 1891]

Dear Justi,
2 days ago I sent a *detailed* letter to you at the old Petersdorf address.—It would be embarrassing if this letter in particular were lost.—Hopefully you can still obtain it, because it contains some questions and clarifications that I really wanted to see brought to your attention.—

Luckily I let my apartment for half a year, so I don't have to worry about it until 1 May 92. Hopefully I'll now be successful in again finding a tenant from that point on.

You can imagine that this was a job that I just didn't need in order to acquire "experience and practice" through this rather out of the way path.

As you asked, the day after tomorrow I will send Papa Löwi 600 Mk.—Since I lost your calculation, please let me know immediately how much is still needed for 1 October.—I will then send the rest immediately.

It annoys me that you cannot obtain the desired renovations to the apartment.

Please send me the things for my desk, as well as the little coffee machine, sometime—*well* packed, though, so that *nothing* will be broken. You know how much many of these things mean to me.

It is really something that I am damned to be alone wherever I am. Nevertheless, I am just as incapable of getting used to it as [getting used to] being hanged.

Alois has announced himself again already with a postcard.—Please, send him his "salary" (as he puts it) immediately. You can make an exception again and send him an extra 5 fl.; add it to what I owe you.

—It is going damned poorly for the lord Intendant in Budapest. I read the papers from there now and then.[1]

I am glad for you and her that Natalie wants to live in Vienna.—You will see that you will get on very well with her.

Write me again in somewhat more detail, and best wishes to you and everyone else

from your
Gustav

SHELFMARK: E10-MJ-424

NOTE

[1] Roman, chapter 4, discusses Zichy's difficulties in Budapest after Mahler's departure. By the fall of 1891, "even the most partisan elements of the press had to admit . . . [that] Zichy's efforts to 'Hungarianize' the Opera and to fill the gap left by the departure of the disliked 'foreign' director and conductor were proving to be conspicuously unsuccessful" (p. 142).

197 *To Justine*

[Hamburg, September 1891]

Dearest Justi

I just received the enclosed court-of-trusteeship [*Vormundschaftgerichtes*] notice, from which you see that something really must be done regarding the estate, since Alois will certainly have received a similar notice.—Please, ask *Freund*'s advice right away, and write Alois that he should put his assets into safekeeping for the time being until he is released from the military!—Then I myself will discuss with him what he should do.—Between us, I am afraid that he will have already contracted debts.—But, my God, we'll just have to see—there is nothing to be done.—I am often very worried about these fellows.—I have a lot on my mind right now, that is why you haven't heard from me. You know that I am always like that, so don't worry about me. I am *healthy*, in fact, more than in a long time. My stomach is treating me splendidly—and I, it.

Write me often, and in detail. I am really happy that, by all signs, you all feel so comfortable, and are so full of vim and vigour.

Best wishes to everyone from
your
Gustav

SHELFMARK: E10-MJ-469

198 *To Justine*

[Hamburg, 14 October 1891]

Dearest Justi,

Yesterday I sent you 55 Mk.—

I am moving from here on 1 November—probably to a little hotel, where at least I hope to be looked after a little more attentively.[1]—

Enclosed, an article from the "*Dresden* Zeitung." (pure *brimstone*—but well meant.)

My stomach is better *daily*. Here's why:—before I ate *much too infrequently* and always *much too much* at a time.—Now I eat a *little* something every 3½ hours and now the improvement is so noticeable that it is absolutely clear that *that* was the reason for it.—

I recommend that you *all* emulate this, especially Fritz.

Better *not* to write to Alois. Anyway, it wouldn't do any good.—Unfortunately, one has to let such people just go as they go! I am pleased that Otto is so diligent. By the way, I think that it would not be too much to ask that once in a while he deigns to report his own news to me himself.

Tristan was performed again yesterday.—This work in particular always stirs me powerfully like no other when I'm conducting.

Thanks to Nina for her letter; I will write again when I am more calm. I received *Fritz's* book and already today I am devoting it to its proper purpose; I will write him soon.—

How good you are to be learning so well! Just carry on, and "chin up!"

Ever your
Gustav

Shelfmark: E10-MJ-460
Notes
[1] Hôtel Royal.
[2] 13 October 1892.

199 *An Justine*

[Hamburg, 15 October 1891][1]

Dearest Justi,
Yesterday I wrote and sent you an article from the Dresden Zeitung. Hopefully you've now received it.—

—Send me the *winter coat*, not the sweater—further, send me my *coffee mill*!—Weren't the manuscript paper and the pencils, etc. with the other things?

You all must have it *very comfortable* there now! How happy I would be for even a few days with you! As a bachelor one is kept very badly here.—

It is splendid that you are enjoying your studies so much. When I come home next summer, possibly you'll already be a total scholar!

My stomach feels really excellent, "knock on wood." The best in 4 years. And *only* because I eat a *little, frequently*. If it keeps on like *this*, I really hope to be *completely healthy* again.

Write again soon!

Say hello to Ernestine from me! How is she?

Ever your
Gustav

Send the enclosed letter to Alois. Once again, I don't know his address.

SHELFMARK: E10-MJ-466
NOTE
[1] Dated on the basis of the previous letter.

200 *To Justine*

[Hamburg, 1 November 1891]

Dearest Justi,
I am horribly busy now.—I received the package.—Up to now I've worn 2 of the shirts. On one, the sleeves were too short and the collar too low.—The other is *perfect*! Vederemo!

My stomach is the best that it's been for years—the only anomaly still is that I absolutely must eat *every three* hours. Since I have been *doing that*, I have been well. Isn't that funny? So *that* was certainly the cause of my trouble, that I *understood* my stomach incorrectly and ate so *infrequently*.—Because of that, I didn't take the medicine, but have it in case something else is wrong with me sometime.

Today I am moving to my new apartment. The address from now on:
Grosse Bleichen
Hotêl [*sic*] Royal

I will write again soon.

Ever yours,
Gustav

SHELFMARK: E11-MJ-477

201 *To Justine*

[Hamburg, early November 1891]

Dearest Justi,

I just got 3 letters from you at once at my new apartment.—

Right now, I am just *not* in the mood to write.—But, things are going well, and I am quite cheerful.—That you ~~are~~ were so worried was of course not necessary—but I do know that once a worry has established itself, it never goes away, but always increases.

I am kept reasonably well in my new home—of course, it's expensive,—but what is one to do? I can no longer turn a blind eye so much to the present—*it* also has to be comfortable, otherwise one trips over one's own feet. I would really like it if I were to get the books from the *Felds*, but I won't *remind* them directly.[1] Maybe you will find a kind way to do so.—Do what you want with *Tieck*. Everyone must behave according to their own sensitivities.—*I* myself would not go there, since for *us*, companionship with these people is not possible.

I *cannot support* it, and that would be, if at all, the only way to be of service.

As you see, I still never have a pen in the house.

Best wishes to everyone.

Why do you not tell me the *amount* that I should send? I always forget it. Tomorrow I will send you 700 Mk, and the rest when I know exactly how much you need.

Best wishes
from
Gustav

SHELFMARK: E10-MJ-467
NOTE
[1] Also mentioned in letter 192.

202 *To Justine*

[Hamburg, early November 1891]

Dearest Justi,
Here I am sending you 700 Mk.—Please let me know right away how much I have to send to you, so that I can forward the possible remainder at once.

My stomach is excellent. Unfortunately I couldn't take out the money any earlier, since I don't like to have clerks do me favours.—Please, wherever it is possible, arrange it so that you always get the money on the 2nd.—Be sure to write me *when* the money arrived.

The socks are probably too thin for the winter; I will buy warmer ones for the cold weather.

I am already using the heat here heartily, since, as you know, I am always freezing in winter.—You must have it really *snug* now. Will the time ever come when I will be free of this helpless *bachelor* existence?

Imagine, I recently received an obituary note from Budapest announcing that the *young man*, whom I pointed out to you that time on the Schabenberg and whom I always liked so much, chorus-director *Salvi*, is dead.

I am pleased that you are all so keen and diligent, and are so cheerful and well because of it.

For this coming summer, I would like a really quiet and comfortable long stay in a pretty and inexpensive place. Think about it a little bit. Maybe you'll even have an idea.

Best wishes
from your
Gustav

SHELFMARK: E10-MJ-465

203 *To Justine*

[Hamburg, 15 November 1891]

Dearest Justi,
Now you've had your first Sunday afternoon gathering.[1] The idea is splendid; I hope that everything has gone well up to now. Really tell me how it was, so that I can at least enjoy with you a little bit from afar.—

Yesterday was the premiere of an opera by Rubinstein, with wonderfully beautiful things in it (it is called Der Dämon). The performance was magnificent and pleased me and everyone else very much.—As soon as the reviews appear, I will send them to you.[2]

The enclosed article came to my attention yesterday, and I am sending it to you for your enjoyment. You will see that it's impossible to escape one's fate.

Write me in good time how much I have to send you this month.

Have you still not heard from Jenny? I *haven't*!

How is Emma behaving? And what about Otto's studies?

With best wishes to you all
from your
Gustav

How is Nina feeling? Fritz?

SHELFMARK: E11-MJ-472

NOTES

[1] In an unpublished passage of her memoirs, Natalie Bauer-Lechner mentions these Sunday gatherings:

> I regularly went over to the [apartment on the] Breitegasse and did and read this and that with Justi. We tried to provide some social entertainment by putting together a "Sunday Tea," with games, music, and dancing—but because it was so far-fetched, and had not arisen in a natural manner, also because the house was lacking an actual head and centre [i.e., Gustav], it did not survive a winter. (Bibliothèque Musicale Gustav Mahler)

[2] Anton Rubinstein's *Der Dämon* was performed only once in Hamburg during Mahler's tenure, on 14 November 1891. Reviews in the *Fremdenblatt* and the *Correspondent* appeared on 16 November.

204 *To Justine*

[Hamburg, 22 November 1891]

Dearest Justi,

Freund tells me that, on Alois' instructions, the *deposit* belonging to him is supposed to have been dispatched to me.—However, since it is still not in my hands, I hasten to report to you that this strikes me as astonishing. Perhaps there is some entirely harmless reason; at any rate, look into the matter.

I still have my lonely, quiet life; I have been rummaging about in my old and oldest papers. How peculiar this made me feel is something with which almost no one can resonate.—Now, however, I'm in "work-mode"—Nina ought not to take it as neglect that I have not yet answered her, but answered Natalie so quickly. This is easily explained by their respective natures. Natalie is such a <u>*simple*</u> human being. Nina is a *twofold* creature; I have already discussed this with her, and she knows it too.—To write her, and really when people haven't actually spoken for *as long* as the two of us (because the last moments in ~~Vienna~~ Perchtoldsdorf showed me at best that <u>*now*</u> she doesn't understand me properly), so to write her, then, is decidedly not inviting, and is simply disturbing for me.—Nevertheless, I think about her often, and in sincere friendship. For

I understand *her* well, and don't make anything of it that she now has so little insight about me.

Nevertheless, greet her *warmly* from me—I don't think that I can snatch the time to write her before the New Year.—

Just think what I have now found out: since my departure from Budapest, it has been circulated there in quite *clear* form that I had asked for *Jenny's hand* and that I had been "refused". Thus, my "melancholy."—This is now being told in Hamburg too!

Isn't that delightful?—Now, it is certainly not unlikely that "Papa Feld" has some suspicious connection to these rumours; he would be capable of such a thing!—

Incidentally, on the *27*. I am conducting a big orchestral concert in Lübeck; since it is "*Day of Repentance*" here, on which operas or concerts absolutely cannot take place, we will all be deposited by Pollini in all possible directions that day. The task of concertising in Lübeck with the whole orchestra has fallen to me, which greatly amuses me.[1]—

By the way, I can report that I am quite *loved* by the *orchestra* here; that has *never* happened to me before. It is thus so much nicer than in Budapest; *ditto* with the *chorus*. The soloists are quite *divided*. The majority *hate* me; the minority—to which, by the way, especially the most talented belong—is on my side.—I no longer *speak* with Pollini—without the slightest thing having happened between us.—It is simply natural for us; and that is not very promising.

Best wishes to you all
Gustav

SHELFMARK: E10-MJ-416
NOTE
[1] The "Bußtags-Konzert des Hamburger Stadttheaters" at the Lübeck Coliseum consisted of Haydn's Symphony No. 101 ("The Clock"), an aria from *Le nozze di Figaro*, Florestan's aria from *Fidelio*, the *Leonore* Overture No. 3, the *Tannhäuser* overture, and excerpts from act I of *Die Walküre* ("Winterstürme" and closing section).

205 *To Justine*

[Hamburg, c. 24 November 1891][1]

Dearest Justi,
Please dispatch the enclosed letter to Alois right away; I have misplaced his address. He wrote me and asked me for advice.

See if it is legible enough; I am in a great hurry!

Your Sunday plans are very good, and please me very much.—Chamber music regularly, that is best for you all.—

How does it stand with Otto's induction [*Assentirung*]? Look after it!—

Apropos—I think that you have now had *enough* of Jean Paul for a while! Remember, there are many other authors in the world.

Occasionally take up something else! Biographical, for example!—If possible, obtain *Lewes* "*Goethe*" or something like it![2]

With best wishes from your
Gustav

Shelfmark: E10-MJ-417
Notes

[1] Dated across the top, in what appears to be Justine's hand, "26/Nov 91." This letter is dated based on the assumptions that this is the date received and that it took an average of two days for a letter from Hamburg to reach Vienna.

[2] George Henry Lewes, *The Life and Works of Goethe: With Sketches of His Age and Contemporaries* (1855), revised as *The Life of Goethe* (1864); German translation by Julius Frese as *Goethe's Leben und Werke*.

206 *To Justine*

[Hamburg, 1 December 1891][1]

Dearest Justi,

Hopefully you've now received the 600 Mk. I sent you! Is it enough?

Yesterday Brahms was at the Bülow Concert,[2] where, to the amusement of the audience, Bülow, who as a treat usually makes all kinds of jokes with me, called down from his first-floor box that I should come up right away: Brahms was demanding to see me.—There both Brahms and Bülow treated me in the most reverential way. Brahms especially had been gushing all day long to all who would listen about my Don Giovanni performance in Budapest.[3] This is now arousing the greatest sensation in local music circles, and I hope soon to earn for myself the title "our" Kapellmeister Mahler etc., in local newspaper reviews, which in a city one usually earns for oneself justly only after 20 to 30 years service, [and] which I, in my accustomed manner, have taken "by storm." —Afterwards, I was together with Brahms at the inn; it is really rare that Brahms, the notorious ironist, takes someone else so seriously and treats him so warmly and sincerely—especially a musician!

So this is something gratifying that I have to tell you.—

Next time I will send the reviews of the Lübeck concert.

In all probability I will conduct some big orchestra concerts in January and February.

How is Emma? What is Otto up to? Couldn't the little lord give me a sign of life sometime?

Did you get my letter for Fritz?—I lost all my addresses!

Best wishes from your
Gustav

Shelfmark: E10-MJ-418
Notes

[1] Dated across top, in what appears to be Justine's hand, "3/12 91."

[2] The fourth subscription concert in the Neue Abonnementskonzert series, conducted by Bülow, took place on 30 November 1891. The programme consisted of Berlioz's *Le Roi Lear* overture, Saint-Saëns' Piano Concerto No.4 (Teresa Carreño), Goldmark's *Sakuntala*

overture, Liszt's *Hungarian Fantasy* for piano and orchestra (Carreño), and Beethoven's Symphony No. 2.

[3] On 16 December 1890; see letter 123.

207 *To Justine*

[Hamburg, c. 4 December 1891][1]

Dearest Justi,
Of course it's all right with me if you look after that particular item [*Bewußtes*] for Fritz.—

Your reports about your jour fixe amuse me greatly.—So, does Otto not play there at all?—By the way, how is the business about his studies arranged? I still have no further news of Alois.—From a distance, I have such a vague feeling that everything is not in order; you know Alois.—Please write to Iglau right away and find out if the money is still there—and in general, *what* Alois actually instigated there! He did write me similarly! Don't forget to let me know about it as soon as possible.

Hopefully Nina is well again, isn't she!?

I still don't know where I will be at Christmas.—Probably my usual way of life will continue throughout, without any interruption at all. By the way, since I'm on the topic, I must give you an account of my meals

8:00 Tea, and a roll with meat on it
11:00 A roll with meat on it
2:00 A glass of very white coffee and a croissant
5:00 A very substantial dinner
9:00 Pilsner Beer and again, cold meat and bread, etc.

If I am conducting, I eat a sandwich during the interval, and have supper after the performance.—Since I have been following this regime, I have been *decisively* better. For a weak stomach, *this* is the *best* cure: to eat *a little bit, frequently*.—Tell Fritz this.—My decisive improvement began from the moment that I adopted this rule at the advice of a doctor.

Best wishes from
Gustav

The enclosed clipping is from the leading Lübeck paper and one frequently read in Germany.

SHELFMARK: S1-MJ-732
NOTE

[1] Dated across top, in what appears to be Justine's hand, "6/12 91."

208 *To Justine*

[Hamburg, c. 4 December 1891][1]

Dearest Justi,
Today only the good news that *about Wednesday* I ~~may~~ will arrive in Vienna to spend a few days with you.[2]—I owe this unforeseen holiday to chance—I am

travelling on a business matter.—See that one evening we can have *all our friends* over together.—Could I stay with you comfortably?—after the new arrangement of your apartment? If not, then take a room for me at *Höllers*.

Notify Alois about it, [and see] whether or not he could come to Vienna for a few hours: I need to talk with him. The business about the money does strike me as rather suspicious.

I will still telegraph my exact arrival.

Best
Gustav

SHELFMARK: E15-MJ-571
NOTES

[1] Dated across top, in what appears to be Justine's hand, "6/12 91."

[2] Wednesday, 9 December. Mahler did not conduct after 5 December (*Don Giovanni*) until 17 December (*Fidelio*).

209 *To Justine*

[Hamburg, 17 December 1891][1]

Dearest Justi,
Just some very brief news of my happy, actually "very unhappy," arrival. It pleases me here less than before. In my room I found a letter from you and Bertha—and one from Nina. Did you all then have a happy evening?—These few days did us all good and helped [me] recover a little bit.—Now diligently back to work again until the summer!

Write again soon!

Best wishes to everyone
from
Gustav

SHELFMARK: E10-MJ-419
NOTE

[1] Dated across the top, in what appears to be Justine's hand, "19. Dezember 91." Again, assuming a two-day delivery time, Mahler must have returned to Hamburg on 17 December in time to conduct *Fidelio* that evening.

210 *To Justine*

[Hamburg, Autumn 1891][1]

Dearest Justi!
In your letter today you [mentioned] again that you hadn't had a letter for a long time.—It seems to me, however, that I wrote you a few days ago.—Right now I don't have too much to do, but in spite of this, I am not in a mood to write letters.—

Please have Papa Löwi look amongst the papers from the Hungarian bank and send me the statement [*Abrechnung*] from 1 July 1891 as soon as possible; I need it urgently!

Otto's letter surprised and pleased me with the clarity and reasonableness of its thought.—

Surely the time has come when official arrangements for the examination should be made? Don't neglect anything!

Enclosed, a card for your collection.

Write soon!

Yours affectionately,
Gustav

Shelfmark: E10-MJ-462

Note

[1] The contents suggest that this was written between September and December 1891. Otto's examination was first mentioned in mid-September (letter 194).

211 *To Justine*

[Hamburg,] 1 January 1892

Dearest Justi!

You're the first person I've written to this new year! The Christmas parcel arrived; the photograph was very welcome, since I don't have one. But there is something *stiff* in your expression which is only intensified by the fact that your current *hair style* is decidedly wrong for you—which I hereby declare again most conclusively!

Your nervous headache worries me very much! What is involved in these conditions that I don't recognise in you? Please tell me, or have someone else tell me, about it in detail. Maybe one of the girls would be so kind as to do this.—Today I am conducting for the first time after the big break (Tannhäuser), and lots is going on again!

Poor Nina worries me as well.

One could really bear everything gladly if one could only see and know his nearest and dearest to be *healthy*. Since you are interested in cards (visiting), I won't withhold the one from the famous man who was here recently without any particular reason.

By the way, at Christmas I received a charming *little silver* match box for little wax matches. Since I already have one for *Swedish* ones, I thought of *you* for this one—would you like to have it? I'll send it to you; only I don't know whether you'd have to pay tax on it.

Enclosed, the register of the bonds purchased with Alois's money, which I again ask Papa Löwi to keep.

My songs will probably appear soon.—

Now the days will start to lengthen again, and we can all look forward again to the summer which will bring us together again, hopefully for a longer time.

My "warmest wishes for the New Year" to *everyone*.

Your
Gustav

Shelfmark: E3-MJ-113

212 *To Justine*

[Hamburg, c. 4 January 1892][1]

Dearest Justi!

Your last letter worried me somewhat—please don't be so laconic in such instances.—First, how does *Nina* feel; what does the doctor say? *2. how do you feel*? Did you maybe have the flu? Then just be careful, and perhaps stay at home! At any rate, pay a little attention to Nina's material needs! Provide her with refreshments and then send me the bill on the first of the month—a good piece of *meat* and *vegetables*—and compote. Maybe also a decent bottle of wine, if the doctor allows it. If she hesitates to take it, just say that it is my wish, and you must do it!

I must admit that a letter from Alois to me has calmed me so far! *If* only what he *says* is *true*; if he's just free from the military, I'll now see what kind of trouble I'll have with him.

Please, dear Justi, tell me in detail, right away, about *yourself* and *Nina*!

Warm wishes
from your
Gustav

SHELFMARK: E3-MJ-114
NOTE

[1] Dated across top, in what appears to be Justine's hand, "6/1 92."

213 *To Justine*

[Hamburg, early 1892]

Dearest Justi!

I have received your letters and have obtained from them a little glimmer of hope, that for a while at least, you will have a period of relative calm.—I may perhaps be allowed to receive Otto's letter sometime this year.—

I am just so overtaxed here and busy with so many different things—I *must* let things go as they are going.—Alois should just *use* his time *well—French and English and Stenography*!

Please let me know right away *how much* I should send you on the *1st*.—

Since I have to pay taxes—and 2 months rent, I am in considerable difficulty this time [about] where I am to get the money from, and would like to send you *whatever can be gotten around*, such as rent, etc., only next month.

Please answer this right away.

—It is very nice that you and Natalie are getting along so well.—

As far as *Faust* is concerned, you *don't* need to hurry *at all*, since I have so much to do in so many different directions that I won't have a chance to read the things for weeks or even months. So no need to hurry.[1]

By the way, keep reporting to me on the general condition of your health.

Best wishes from your
Gustav

Shelfmark: E4-MJ-182
Note
[1] It is possible that Mahler is referring to the line-by-line study of *Faust* in Justine's hand that survives in the Mahler-Rosé Collection (S3-JD-780; 122 pages).

214 *To Justine*

[Hamburg, early 1892]

Dearest Justi!
Alois should just go ahead and get used to the idea that he *won't* be accepting any other position *this year.—On the whole*, this is perhaps the best thing for his future.—Here is what I propose over any other course of action: I. He should *take the business course* that Matscheko[1] pointed out to him (if he hasn't already registered, he should register immediately)—and be *very diligent* at it, II. *French* and *English* are absolute necessities. With all of this, the year is already all taken up!—*If* he can do all of *this*, then I'll find him a good position *here*, that I can *guarantee*—of course, only if I'm still *here* and alive.—

If these qualifications permit him to become employed here or in any other large business centre—(and I will make sure that happens)—this would be 1000 times better for his future than getting however good a clerical job somewhere or other now, where there is *no* chance of a career (à la Hermann in Iglau). He should take comfort and not give himself grey hair—but rather be very *diligent* and *serious* and *truly* use this *gift* of a year to the fullest (the opportunity will *never* come again)! And in short order see to it that he braces himself and makes himself strong for the strain and stress that may be in store.—Incidentally, I expect of him that he will write me *in detail* at least once every 2 weeks about his studies and whatever else he is up to!—I *require* this of him, and hope that at least *he* will acquiesce to my wishes. You all could also bring him along a bit so that he gets the hint.

So: chin up—as far as being without a job: on the contrary, I couldn't wish him anything better, if he follows my advice.

As far as my own health is concerned, you have nothing to be worried about. It couldn't be better.—As for my mood—it has been subject to change since time immemorial! That you certainly know! Also, that I am not the sort who is at the mercy of his moods.

Please do send me this month's calculations.

Yours affectionately,
Gustav

Don't hurry with Faust—I *really* couldn't read it right now. Not until *spring*—please send it to me then.

Shelfmark: E4-MJ-183
Note
[1] Possibly the father or brother of Nina Hoffmann.

215 *To Justine*

[Hamburg, c. 14 January 1892][1]

Dearest Justi!

I was occupied all this time with the rehearsals of a new opera by Tchaikovsky, *Onegin* (a very mediocre effort), the premiere of which apparently will be conducted by the composer himself.[2]

Your last letters—and above all, that from Ernestine, whom I sincerely thank—have calmed me a little bit.—How are you both now?

By the way, last Sunday *Strauss's "Don Juan"* was done in the Philharmonic Concert.[3] It would interest me to hear what was said about it, and what impression it had on Otto.

He should tell me about it himself.

The enclosed clipping is from the *Pester Lloyd*.

Here now we have the most beautiful winter weather.—My condition is excellent.

When will Freund do his examination?

Best wishes from
Gustav

Write soon!

SHELFMARK: E3-MJ-115

NOTES

[1] Dated across the top, in what appears to be Justine's hand, "16/1 92."

[2] In the end, Mahler himself conducted the premiere; see the following letter.

[3] Strauss's *Don Juan* was performed by the Vienna Philharmonic under Hans Richter on 10 January 1892.

216 *To Justine*

[Hamburg, 20 January 1892]

Dearest Justi!

This flu that has claimed so many victims in Vienna now worries me too.—In Hamburg we actually don't hear anything at all about it, so for me the threat is not great.—Just don't economise excessively about the small gathering; a few gulden don't matter, just send me the bill.

Yesterday was *Onegin*—*I* conducted, since the composer asked me to. Result: *succès d'estime*.—Afterwards, a pig-out [*Festfressen*] at Pollini's—one of his specialities.

By the way, Tchaikovsky is a very nice old man, apparently exceedingly prosperous, very elegant manner—reminds me a lot of Mihalovich.

It was good that you all went to *Lumpaci*.[1] It is a splendid comedy, full of wit and splendid fantasy—especially at the beginning.—I regard the first act as the most successful example of what this type of literature has to show.

I read Die [Neue Freie] Presse here all the time. I'm not writing because of that! To judge by "Hanslick," the work ought to have been *ingenious* and *sig-*

nificant! Precisely that is what I call in question! I don't think that he is worthy of such a fiery philippic and raging rejection. Therefore, I am interested in the judgement of a *young* and sensible musician.[2]—January is soon almost over, and June even closer.

Warmest greetings to you all
from your
Gustav

What is *Nina* up to? Say hello to her for me.

SHELFMARK: E3-MJ-116
NOTES

[1] *Der böse Geist des Lumpacivagabundus oder Das liederliche Kleeblatt* (1835), by Johann Nestroy (1801–1862).

[2] It seems that Mahler is referring to the Vienna performance of Strauss's *Don Juan* mentioned in the previous letter. Hanslick's review of *Don Juan* appears in his *Fünf Jahre Musik, 1891–1895. Die moderne Oper*, vol. 7 (Berlin: Allgemeiner Verlag für deutsche Litteratur, 1896), pp. 178–81. Since the review is largely critical of the work, despite praising its orchestration and effect, Mahler's comment must be meant ironically.

217 *To Justine*

[Hamburg, January 1892][1]

Dearest Justi!
I am most pleased about the favourable news. If only it would last.—Incidentally, I have been in a fine state—to wit, all of a sudden *Bülow's* secretary came and asked me to conduct the next concert for him since he is very ill.[2] I, quite happily, devised a wonderful programme right away. Hardly had Bülow read the programme when he announced that he was healthy again, etc., etc.

Of course, I always have to be ready here, nevertheless, because it is possible that sometime or other I will have to stand in for him.

Be good, all of you, and write again soon! Say hello to the Löwi girls for me. It is most good of them to support you so much. What is Fritz up to?

Best wishes from
your
Gustav

SHELFMARK: E4-MJ-184
NOTES

[1] The first section of the letter was published by Alfred Rosé, "Gustav Mahler und Hans von Bülow," *Neues Wiener Journal*, 23 September 1928, where the date was given as 1891. On the letter itself, Rosé wrote 1892 in pencil. The latter appears more likely to La Grange (HLG I, p. 377).

[2] Either the sixth subscription concert (18 January) or the seventh (1 February). In the end, Bülow conducted both.

218 *To Justine*

[Hamburg, January 1892]

Dearest Justi,

Above all, I have to scold you over your letter of today! What kind of foolishness is this! *Why* do you feel "dumb"? Because you can't chatter on in everything, or maybe because you can't understand everything right away?—Why do you feel "superfluous"? For whom are you "superfluous," then?—To the contrary, this time I was very pleased with you and was not disturbed by minor matters.—For a year your judgement has been developing in all respects, and I spent these 8 days in the best mood that I've been in in a long time! So don't think such thoughts! *That* is the only "stupidity" that I discerned in you, and only after the fact!

I have really taken to the "Knaben Wunderhorn," and now have in my [collection] no fewer than 3 copies.—

Apropos! Have you properly kept the *publishing contract* and accompanying letter from the Schott Firm that I gave you in Vienna? It happened so quickly—I think we were interrupted; please take good care of this.[1]

By the way, are you completely sprightly again? It seems to me that you were not quite well?

I can imagine that after such beautiful, carefree, and merry days, the rebound is very difficult for you all. But, however long it is, I will indeed come back, and in the meantime, we will prey upon our companions instead! Work hard so that you'll be able to have it so good again.

Write really soon, and in detail!

Very best wishes from your
Gustav

Don't always have such silly thoughts! One is *often at* one's cleverest when one feels "dumb"! Frl. Seidler[2] certainly *always* feels *very clever.*

Shelfmark: E3-MJ-142

Notes

[1] Mahler's early songs were published by B. Schott's Söhne in February 1892; see Knud Martner and Robert Becqué, "Zwölf Unbekannte Briefe Gustav Mahlers an Ludwig Strecker," *Archiv für Musikwissenschaft* 34 (1977): 287–97.

[2] Unknown.

219 *To Justine*

[Hamburg, end of January 1892]

Dearest!

Please confirm your receipt of the money *right away*, also whether it is enough.

I am now working for myself![1] Thus my lazy correspondence. Naturally I am feeling splendid because of it!

The business with Sax is stupid—act according to your feelings. For me, it is always only a slight pleasure to be on intimate terms with someone I don't know [*mit einem Unbekannten "Du" zu sein*]! Do what you like, as though altogether unintentionally—I am pleased that Nina is better.—I would be very happy to see the question of this summer settled for us in a practical manner. Just take into consideration, above all, that this year we must consider our money *very* carefully.—

I am starting to put something aside for the summer, [but] my local obligations make it sufficiently difficult for me.

I'm already terribly happy about spring—it's already settled in all my limbs.

—I have *Des Knaben Wunderhorn* to hand.—With the self-awareness so typical of authors, I can say, by the way, that it is really having an effect again.[2]

The enclosed letter from Apponyi, whom I telegraphed on election day, is for your autograph album.[3]

I also had a letter from Singer. Further, Professor *Hubay* was with me yesterday—he is performing here.[4]

Best wishes to you all
from
Gustav

SHELFMARK: E3-MJ-141
NOTES

[1] On 28 January, Mahler completed the *Wunderhorn* song "Der Schildwache Nachtlied" for voice and piano.

[2] By 22 February, Mahler had completed five new songs from *Des knaben Wunderhorn*.

[3] General elections to the Hungarian Diet were held on 28 January 1892. According to the London *Times*, 30 January 1892: "One of the most interesting contests was at Pressburg between Count Albert Apponyi and M. Szilagyi, the Minister of Justice. The latter was elected by a majority of 96 votes out of 882. . . . M. Szilagyi, the Minister of Justice, was formerly one of Count Apponyi's staunchest supporters."

[4] Hungarian violinist and composer Jenő Hubay (1858–1937) was the soloist at the seventh subscription concert, 1 February 1892.

220 *To Justine*

[Hamburg, between 7 and 9 February 1892]

Dearest Justi!
I received both your letters, but not yet Natalie's.

What is this about the accommodations?—The question is certainly very complicated this year! I.—When is *Otto's* examination, and where is he supposed to stay in the meantime (this year I absolutely do not have enough money for two households).—Further, aside from us, who of our friends will still be around! To sit ourselves down alone for 3 months makes no sense for us—even less for you.

How many *rooms* does the place have? Can I have one entirely for myself, and is it well separated from the others? Where will Fritz be over the holidays?

This year all of these things need to have been taken into consideration! So remember this and *do what you want to*; I will be content with everything, and would prefer that for once this bother is taken off *my* shoulders.—I too would like to have it comfortable for once! But I am decidedly in need of some *company* and some comfortable accommodations. So, do you understand, Justi? Relieve me of this worry, and deal with it as a housewife.

But, for other reasons, please delay your decision for another half week. I'll tell you why when I have a moment.

I have finished 3 new songs from *Des Knaben Wunderhorn*![1]—

The printed ones will appear before long in all the music stores.

How is everybody's health?

By the way, as soon as I receive detailed news about my question, I will reveal my intention on that point!

Are there no pianos in the surrounding houses? etc.?

Warmest wishes from
your
Gustav

As I see it, all in all you need about another 40 fl. A damned business! I myself am terribly short this month, but will see about sending it to you. Tell me *when* you need it—*right away*, or how long it can wait.

Yesterday I forgot to send this letter.—Today, I received Natalie's letter.—Since the place is so isolated, it is *absolutely* <u>*not*</u> suitable for a stay of *3 months*. I know this from experience! The first month everything is wonderful. The second, one wanders around *lost*, and in the *third* it ripens into desperation, and one would rather bear the thickest city air only to be around people. So: keep going on the *little houses*!

Please greet Natalie warmly for me—maybe I'll get around to writing her sometime.

SHELFMARK: E10-MJ-438
NOTE

[1] "Der Schildwache Nachtlied," 28 January; "Verlor'ne Müh'!" 1 February; and "Wer hat dies Liedlein erdacht?!" 6 February. "Das himmlische Leben" followed on 10 February and "Trost im Unglück" on 22 February.

221 *To Justine*

[Hamburg, mid-February 1892]

Dearest Justi!
Hellfire and damnation!

Why is everything suddenly turned upside down again! Just because I am going to England for a few weeks, does everything have to be changed?[1] After everything, may I not recover from the strain in a *lovely and healthy* region, but have to do with dusty, sunny, piano-y[2] Petersdorf!

And the damned Franzensbad baths! They're not worth a cent. Nina ought to settle down with us on a beautiful and healthy patch of earth.

With my comment several days ago, I merely wanted to say that *now*, since at this point it is for 6 weeks, I also accept a <u>*secluded*</u> region. But *first* and foremost it must be lovely, because I must then recover from the strains of London and muster strength for a new campaign.

For God's sake, go wherever you like with Natalie and look for something really *nice*, so that I can finally just spend a proper summer.

You all just go *ahead* at the beginning of July and make everything nicely comfortable, and I'll get there straight from *London* around the middle of July. At the same time Otto can interrupt his studies for a week (as well as his lessons) and gather his strength with us, and since the area will be on the western line [*Westbahn*], or at least a line within a fare zone [*Zonentarifbahn*], our friends can come one after the other.

And hopefully Nina will come with us too!

I have damned little time to write, because I have to compose. Number *4* is also done, and is quite something![3]—All are in *sketch* form [*Lapidarschrift*]!

By the way, things are not *entirely* settled yet with London, but are now most probable.—I'll leave here then on May 20!

Please make do with the monthly allowance, otherwise, in spite of London [earnings], we'll be hungry this summer. Yesterday I sent the 80 marks. Please let me know if this supplement will suffice. Why do you never state the *sum* that you need; I always have to figure it out!

Best wishes to you all.
Your
Gustav

The songs are for you all! (who naturally have no money to buy them.)[4]

SHELFMARK: E10-MJ-426
NOTES

[1] Mahler and the Hamburg company were in residence at Covent Garden Opera, London, from the end of May through the middle of July 1892.

[2] Mahler's neologism, "clavierige," appears to be making a joke of his abhorrence of all noise while he composes. The word is written in Roman letters, not *Currentschrift*, and is unmistakable.

[3] "Das himmlische Leben," completed on 10 February. (Note, too, that Mahler writes of having to compose, rather than orchestrate, so the letter must date from February.)

[4] Schott had just published Mahler's early songs.

222 *To Justine*

[Hamburg, February 1892][1]

Dearest Justi!
I am moving the day after tomorrow—I cannot stand it here any longer because of the noise, and unfortunately cannot find an apartment, despite searching constantly for weeks.

Thus I am moving back into my first place: *Hotel Streit*.

Of course this is much more expensive again, but what am I do? I cannot sleep here another night, what with the slamming doors, neighbours' boots dropping, the drunks lurching here and there, etc.

So, next letter to the new address.—I am invited to Mayor Petersen's on

Wednesday—a great honour, since he is the *leading* personality here in the Hamburg "republic."

You do seem to be in a crazy [*rappelnden*] mood? I prefer the crazy one, or the restless [*Zappelnde*] one. I am in a restless [one], and my neighbours in a traipsing [one] [*trappelnden*]!

Future generations (not exactly those not born yet, but the squealing, piping, and singing ones on the street right now) do not interest me in the slightest.

—*Packing* tomorrow! Oh! Oh! Oh!

Best wishes from your
Gustav

Who has bought my songs already? Have you already seen people on the street with them?

SHELFMARK: E3-MJ-118
NOTE

[1] Owing to the mention of Mahler's published songs, the letter must date from February 1892 (despite La Grange's suggestion that Mahler moved back to the Hotel Streit earlier in the year; see HLG I, p. 301). Mahler did manage to find an apartment by March: on 16 March, he indicated his return address as "Bundesstrasse 10 III." in an unpublished letter to Antonia "Toni" Petersen (1840–1909), the mayor's daughter.

223 *To Justine*

[Hamburg, end of February 1892]

Dearest Justi!

I am pleased about your enterprise! Just don't let that revolting "Lourié" creature near you.[1] She is unbelievably pushy and is impossible to get away from. I have recently avoided her like the plague. Enclosed, several *reviews* as well as several contributions to your manuscript collection, etc.—No. 5 is finished too.[2] Unfortunately, I have to set it aside again: first of all, a huge amount to do at the theatre, and [second,] there's *no* peace to be found at the Hotel.[3]

By the way, next Sunday I am invited to dine at Bülow's, whom I now frequently see socially.

The entire circle in which I socialise—which, by the way, increases more and more from day to day—is the same as his.—

By the way, among them there are really an awful lot of charming people, and absolutely *not* affected, despite [the fact] that most of them belong to the cream of local society. It was lovely at the mayor's, and I was treated with great warmth. Of course, the more that Hamburg pleases me, the less the theatre does, and I see that I am going to run into a typical conflict there, all right.

By the way, I am really longing to be together with you all for a few weeks of complete peace and comfort, and am annoyed that it is now being postponed for a few weeks.—Please write me right away *how* much money I should send you on the first.

Best wishes to everybody
from
Gustav

SHELFMARK: E10-MJ-423
NOTES
[1] Unknown.
[2] "Trost im Unglück" was completed on 22 February 1892.
[3] It seems that moving back to the Hotel Streit did not solve Mahler's problem with noise.

224 *To Justine*

[Hamburg, March 1892]

Dearest Justi!
In greatest haste! I have a lot to do again right now! You'll get the rest of the *372* fl. before long.—Now please write me in good time how much you need. *One thing* above all! (This is the main reason why I am sending a few lines despite all engagements.)

I *forbid* everyone to associate with Frl. *Lourié* in any way, and ask you to reject her *brusquely*, if there's no other way. *Under no circumstances* visit her, and if she comes, be *cool* and *dismissive* towards her.—Please write me a few lines about this point. She is a quite common Russian Jew, who, by the way, behaved towards me in such a pushy and indecent manner, that I was obliged to snub her directly.

I am in the middle of *orchestrating*! I have probably forgotten to say that they all are *for* orchestra and voice. I call them each "*Humoresken*," the title which the subject matter richly deserves![1]

Best wishes to all
from your
Gustav

London is as good as certain. See to it for me that we spend our 6 weeks in a beautiful *and peaceful* spot, from which hiking is worthwhile.

SHELFMARK: E3-MJ-120
NOTE
[1] The manuscript of the piano version of "Trost im Unglück" is dated 22 February. Between this date and 26 April (orchestration of "Trost im Unglück"), Mahler orchestrated the 5 *Humoresken*. The orchestral manuscript for "Das himmlische Leben" is dated 12 March; the orchestral manuscripts of the other three songs are undated.

225 *To Justine*

[Hamburg, second week March 1892]

Dearest Justi!
Yesterday I received your letter.—Right out from the middle of all sorts of things—*orchestration* of my Humoresken, study of the *Eroica* Symphony, which I conduct in the theatre on Monday,[1] and at the same time, rehearsals of a new

opera[2]—nevertheless, I'm writing a few quick lines because I don't want to leave you completely unanswered.

By the way, it would be good if you could indicate for me a way to send you *such letters* that are for *your* eyes *only*. I'll await this in your next letter, and restrict myself today to just a few remarks.

I daresay I know what is *troubling* you, and in the end it is not a "disaster"! So keep your chin up, it will resolve itself somehow, in one way or another!

Of course, from here, where I don't see anything and don't *hear anything* from you, I can't give you any advice other than "*by all means* do not let yourself get *carried away*;" and remain reasonable! Always remember: however *intense* it gets, nevertheless it's not the end of the world (even of "your" world).

The best thing to do is sit down and simply pour out your heart to me, as to one of your *girlfriends*! That is really the best thing.—So much for the main business! Now, as far as your self-torment that you are this or that is concerned, do console yourself![3] You are as you are—no one can change you! Good or bad *does not exist.*[4] Above all take note: *avoid* every temptation. No human strength is sufficient to resist it; human beings can only get out of danger's *way*! So just keep trying—you are already on the right path, as I have perceived for some time! We stumble all together in every moment, and the best thing that we can do is to always *pick ourselves up again right away*, don't worry about the bumps and bruises for too long, but quickly and merrily carry on once more!

Come now—I haven't departed this life yet—whenever you need a friend, you certainly know where he is.—Moreover, in *16* weeks I will be with you, you know. Until then, *keep your chin up*!

Write me in complete confidence and in detail!

Yours affectionately,
Gustav

SHELFMARK: S1-MJ-734

NOTES

[1] Mahler's annual benefit concert was on Monday, 14 March; see letter 226, below.

[2] *Le rêve* (*Der Traum*) (1891) by Alfred Bruneau (1857–1934).

[3] Mahler had just recently composed the song "Trost im Unglück," which bears the annotation on the title page: *Wir wissen uns zu trösten* ("we know how to console ourselves").

[4] This line surely reflects Mahler's reengagement with the writings of Nietzsche (e.g., *Beyond Good and Evil*) in late 1891; see GMB[2] 108.

226 *To Justine*

[Hamburg, 15 March 1892]

Dearest Justi!

So yesterday was my benefit performance![1] *Sold-out* house and cheering from the public as I have never experienced before.—

At the end I received: *27* laurel wreaths, loads of bouquets, writing cases, embroidery, cigar boxes, books, a piano lamp, a marvellous picture of Beethoven, a Wagner picture (both very large). You can just imagine what a fuss this was—

The *Eroica* succeeded splendidly.—

Unfortunately amongst all of these wonderful things, 2 unpleasant new ones. First, I have a boil on my right thumb, which hurts me something awful.

2.—I am on *quite bad terms* with Pollini. The fellow makes me so angry that I can hardly stand it, and one of these days I'll smash his skull with some nearby wooden or pasteboard object.

Of course this worries me for all sorts of reasons.—There is just never any peace in life!—On the one side a public full of understanding, which really almost spoils me; on the other side a "chief" who is as "reasonable" as an ox.

Write again soon.

Affectionately yours,
Gustav

This *damned* thumb!

SHELFMARK: E3-MJ-140
NOTE

[1] For his benefit, Mahler conducted Beethoven's Third Symphony and *Fidelio* (with the *Leonore* Overture No. 3).

227 *To Justine*

[Hamburg, fourth week March 1892]

Dearest Justi!
Alas, I still never have a chance to write. Monday is another premiere (*Le Rêve*),[1] a new, very difficult, but interesting, work which takes up all of my time.

—I don't get around to working for myself at all.—I didn't keep reviews from my benefit; they all look the same.—I was again very good. We're now past these idiocies, aren't we?

My finger is better again.

Did you receive the 40 marks? Then why did you not acknowledge them?

Write me right away how much I should send on the 1st.

Also, about the "matter in question," I would indeed like to hear something, because I don't know anything about it at all. I am *swamped* with invitations here. I am often received by the mayor's family and treated very well—and by the "best circles," as well.

Also I am often together with Bülow. Well, I'll tell you funny stories about him in the summer.

I long terribly for peace and rest, and for the countryside [*Grünen*]. Please write me *right away* and pull yourself together a little bit.

I received a few friendly lines again from Alois—including the request for money on account of dental fillings and mental anguish. So add in another *10 fl.* for him on the first, and send it to him in my name.

Best wishes to all of you!

How is *Nina*? Fritz?

You are always so brief in your letters—do overcome yourself a little bit, and be communicative.

Affectionately yours,
Gustav

Just keep your head high: the wind *never* blows *one's* head away—*one's hat at most*! Do you understand?

SHELFMARK: E3-MJ-117
NOTE
[1] 28 March.

228 *To Justine*

[Hamburg, end of March 1892]

Dearest Justi!
I am just about to conclude my contract which obliges me to conduct the German season (Nibelungen, Tristan, Fidelio) at the *Royal Opera* in *London* in *June* and *half of July*.[1]—This is one of the most outstanding positions for a conductor, and can possibly bring with it the most pleasant consequences for the future.

So, count on me with the summer place only from the *middle of July*—that is why from now on I am happy with *everything* that you decide on.

This too was why I asked you to wait.—Moreover, for financial reasons this is really extremely welcome, because I was really in a quandary about where I was going to find housekeeping money for the summer.—I get 3000 marks for the few weeks there, I'll still save a couple hundred marks here, and thus I hope that we can face the summer quite confidently.

Unfortunately this means that we'll only get together 6 weeks later—or actually only *4 weeks*, since because of this I won't take any holiday trip to Norway etc. beforehand, as I had originally planned, but will travel directly from London to Vienna!

Naturally I am starting to learn English, because it is quite necessary there.[2] Please send the enclosed review *back* to me *right away*.

I am in the most splendid mood!

Affectionately yours,
Gustav

Is Otto being diligent? And is he progressing?

SHELFMARK: E3-MJ-119
NOTES
[1] According to Andrew Nicholson, Mahler signed his contract on 2 April; see Nicholson, "Mahler in London in 1892," in *The Mahler Companion*, ed. Donald Mitchell and Andrew Nicholson (Oxford: Oxford University Press, 1999), p. 539. Around this time, Mahler wrote to Siegfried Rosenberg: "The engagements in London have all been settled—even before *I* had said anything. Between you and me, Harris would rather have had Hans Richter, who of course would have been a tremendous asset for the London enterprise, in view of his standing there" (Hamburg Staats- und Universitätsbibliothek; trans. Nicholson, p. 539).
[2] Mahler took English lessons with his friend Dr. Arnold Berliner (1862–1942).

229 *To Justine*

[Hamburg, April 1892]

Dearest Justi!

Please do me the *following* favour, which must be done *immediately* and *promptly*! Go to *Nina* and have her [ask] *Hippauf*, whom I engaged that time, whether he would like to come with me to London for *July* [*sic*, June] and *July*.[1] *Either way*, he should write to me immediately. He would receive *300 marks* monthly, and *free passage there and back*.

This London business is giving me a terrible amount of trouble and work since the preparations have mostly been left to me.—

How glad I am about the country—though I still have a huge amount of work before then.

You have not acknowledged either the 40 marks last month, or the 700 this time.—Please do this *right away*, and tell me how much you still need. I am always so broke, to hell with the damned money.

Warmest *congratulations* to Ernestine for her new position; one day we will marvel over it there in person.

At any rate, she must come for a few days in *August*—also Fritz and Uda; Natalie. Or at least alternately, depending on space. I will probably not work those few weeks, but should try to recover properly from the travails of the year.

Hopefully *Otto* will be able to come for a few days, despite his examination—possibly we can use them for a hike with Fritz.

Please just send a budget estimate for *July*, August, and September. We must *really* economise otherwise I *won't* make it, *despite London*.

What is this about the *new teacher? I certainly don't know anything about it?*

When is the *examination* then?

My health is splendid: appetite and digestion excellent, only my nerves are always on edge.—Will I *ever be able* to find an uninterrupted stretch *to work* for myself? Will this damned slavery [*Roboten*] ever have an end?!

I *had* to have a new suit, and overcoat as well, made in the last few days—the old shabby [ones] won't do anymore—*210* marks!! And on it goes indefinitely.

—So why do you never write in detail? Just keep in mind how strained I am here, and that at least from this side I need some order and peace?!

See that you all go to Berchtesgaden in *June* already.[2]—It would be a crying shame indeed if this marvellous opportunity were not used!

How will it be with *Otto* this summer?

Many thanks to Natalie for her favour and letter.

Very best wishes from
Gustav

Shelfmark: E10-MJ-427

Notes

[1] According to Schabbing, p. 353, Hippauf was a violinist engaged in Hamburg for the 1892–1893 and 1893–1894 seasons. From a subsequent letter (letter 267), it seems that he was a contemporary of Otto's, perhaps from the Conservatory.

[2] After the London tour, Mahler joined his siblings in Berchtesgaden for the rest of the summer.

230 *To Justine*

[Hamburg, April 1892]

Dearest Justi!
With regard to Hippauf, please tell him no more than that if *the gentlemen are willing to approve of my proposal as it is*, they are to return the signed contract to me immediately.

I am *not* empowered to alter anything in it.

You have not told me that Papa Löwi is under the weather [*liegen*]. What is wrong with him?

English reading is still very difficult going for me, even though I am attempting a very easy book by *Marryat*.[1]

Very best wishes from your
Gustav

SHELFMARK: E10-MJ-431
NOTE
[1] Frederick Marryat (1792–1848), English author of novels, adventure fiction, historical novels, sea stories, and children's literature.

231 *To Justine*

[Hamburg, April 1892]

Dearest Justi!
About every 6 weeks I receive notice that from now on I should increase your allowance by sum *a* or *b*, which naturally decreases my own.

I never say a word on the assumption that everything has a limit, [but] now the matter is getting a bit too "obvious." Can you all *subtract*?—then kindly take the amount of my monthly income, and subtract what *on average* I have to send you. Don't just content yourselves with noticing the difference in the end, however, but imagine yourselves in my situation for a change: that is, in the situation of a man supposed to spare eating, drinking, clothing himself, and n.b. a *3 month* household for the summer. *Perhaps* you will then find a way to get along with what we agreed upon together—so be it that the *number* of teachers or their fees amounts to less, whichever you wish.

Herewith I have respectfully but altogether decisively taken exception to this.

Verily, apart from my mission of wracking my brains as to how I can earn more money, I have other obligations imposed on me in part by Pollini, in part by God.—

I would be immensely happy about the summer at Berchtesgaden if I weren't overcome from time to time by the dark suspicion that while you all are just gadding about the ideal heights, I'll probably have to linger in the depths with the "monthly bills" and various "budgets."

Listen, dear Justi, don't however sink into inconsolable melancholy because of this, and at any rate don't get it into your head that from now on you'll earn money by mending clothes or by other things that you'll learn as quickly as possible. Just tell yourself cheerfully what's what, and consider how one can *manage* with *what one has*, how to establish a *limit*—or more precisely stay within *the limits* of one's circumstances—*without* gnawing hunger pangs, or becoming mindless for lack of spiritual sustenance, or without declining into the brutal bourgeoisie by oppressing all the serving and working classes.

Let me know the outcome of these considerations as soon as possible, if you please (N.B. establish a limit *here* too) and so *Good bye I muth go englisch spoken—i have 5 hour the third Lesson.*[1] *I am*

your devoted
Mister Gustav Mahler
manager of Royal Opera
*of Conventgarden [*sic*]*
of London[2]

Shelfmark: E10-MJ-429
Notes

[1] A letter to Ernestine Löhr indicates that he took his first lesson on 4 April; see below.

[2] The concluding passage in italics was written in English. Mahler erroneously writes "Convent Garden," the name of a concert hall in Hamburg, instead of "Covent Garden."

232 *Justine to Gustav*[1]

[Vienna, April 1892]

Dearest Gustav! I just this moment received your letter, which actually didn't surprise me very much at all because I completely understand your situation, although no one is helped by understanding alone. There is nothing at all to be done for the moment. Since Otto is in this mess—one absolutely cannot skimp on his education, even though the whole thing is so unpractically arranged <aha!!> that, instead of the course with Fries (for which he would have to pay 20 fl. monthly), he has professors who cost 125 fl. monthly and with whom he isn't even guaranteed to pass the examination!—for the moment, we can't do anything other than to spare no effort to see the thing through as it is now arranged. It will be over at the end of September. <Twice in the margin, Mahler writes, "aha!!">

I didn't want to say anything to you about my *own* affair until it was concluded, *but given your present mood it might perhaps calm* <?> *you a little bit* <?>. The other week I visited the director of the kindergarten class, initiated everything, and *on 11 September will take the special examination* <?>. I will then be finished *in a year* <?>, and *some time later* <?> will take the English-language examination. On the other hand, I already (before this last letter of yours) spoke with Ernestine *who perhaps will look around Merano for a post like hers* for me. I write all this entirely calmly, without any agitation, and not under the influence of a sudden decision. You yourself above all must understand that *I absolutely cannot find my life's work* <!> *anymore in the domestic management of* <!!!> *my brothers and sisters* <!!>. I wanted to keep all this to myself until Berchtesgaden and let you know there, but I felt compelled not to keep it from you any longer after your letter of today. I can tell you one thing: I am absolutely not careless with money. *What I spent this winter on the small gatherings*, I did only with your permission, and since I realised that I couldn't have done without taking part in the festivities.

I must become independent. This thought preoccupies me constantly, never leaves me for a moment. I have the exact same blood in my veins as you do, so you will know how deeply this resolve is rooted in me; I cannot live like this. *I want to be completely independent*. But from you I claim the means to do so, and I also do know well with *whom* [Justine's underlining] I am dealing. *But just look, if this seems like a terrible state of affairs to you as well*, it is also no small matter for me to keep house with *your money*—and with no possibility of doing it any other way. Please *accept a few more months* of everything as it now is; I cannot do anything else. I assure you that *none of us has put on anything unnecessary*, and that I never spend a kreutzer [extra] on food. *We all have huge appetites; I cannot help it* and *am miserable enough about it*. Everything is put towards the teachers. Also, my lessons are arranged so that I have to learn history, geography, and natural history as well once a week with Uda; with that, I have every subject that I need to take the examination. If you were here, you would see everything. *By the way, the time that we are all together will last another year, and then everything breaks up*. Do not think that *your letter has hurt me any more* than *when I receive the money on the first of every month*. I am convinced that no one understands the whole situation as much as I do. However, more soon.

Affectionately yours, Justine

[Mahler's response:]

I. Sensitivity of the *most immature* sort!
II. Complete misunderstanding of my views and intentions! Consequently false interpretation of my words.
III. Too quick to answer off the cuff.—Just read my letter again *properly*, and then answer one more time *reasonably* and *nicely*!!

Don't take "positions" and don't be a little dolt!!

Shelfmark: E7-JM-353
Note

[1] Throughout the letter, Mahler underlines passages and makes marginal notes in blue pencil. All emphases in this letter (underlinings and double underlinings) are Mahler's, not Justine's; his marginal notes are enclosed in < >. Sometime between 9 April and 13 April 1892, Mahler asked Ernestine Löhr to help him explain his position to Justine (S3-MC-776; dated on the basis of the reference to the concert on 15 April):

Dear Ernestine!
You have probably read my last letter to Justi, and of you I can suppose that you have read it correctly. Justi's answer seems to me to have been written in the heat of the moment, and I am less annoyed about its somewhat brusque form (which I naturally attribute only to the momentary mood) than I am about the content, i.e. the fundamental way of thinking (*not* the way of feeling), which I find so *immature*. Furthermore, she knows that nothing irritates me more than this type of childish sensibility—from which I had really hoped *she* had long ago emancipated herself.

Today I sent her letter back to her with my marginal notes, and I beg you to go to her and look at my answer for yourselves, and reprimand her childishness, and read through the letter with her one more time.—Here I am surrounded by work: *Friday* I conduct the *Mozart Requiem* and then the *Bruckner Te Deum*, and I really need to be rested up for it.—n.b. from now I have to use every spare moment to learn English.

I was enormously happy about your job. Please tell me something more about it: *what* you have to do, *what* the position is like, what sort of income you have, etc.

I certainly hope that you'll spend a few days with us in Berchtesgaden, so that we can say goodbye in peace. This year I really earned my summer. I am tremendously happy [about it] all right.

I can never get coherent news from Justi about *everything*—Emma, Otto, Nina, Fritz, etc. Please do sit down and tell me about everything.

My health is again good; and therefore as well my vitality and zest for life.

Best wishes to your papa and the family.

Yours, Gustav Mahler
Bundesstrasse 10 III

A second letter to Ernestine, written entirely in English, again raises the matter (16 April 1892; E2-MC-80):

Dear Mistress Ernestine!

I got your second lettre yesterday and your carte of corr. just now.—I thank you very well for the last *good news as respects our friend Nina.*

I can wery well read and understand your english writing, and you must not be affread that I was angry over your.—I have must laugh at your first lettre, wich could make honour to every "Beschwichtigungshofrath", *although you think not it.—What you have written in this lettre, I self know very well, but you misunderstand my intentions!* Pay attention! *I have nothing to say agains it, if my sister affords ever as much money for to eat or thrink or dresse or learn as for her* pleasure! *I am always pleased, if I hear, that she is* merry *and amuse hereself! She is young and mary and* ought *live in health and gayety! But I become* wery angry, *if I see that you* all *are* unpractical sheeps, *and throw my money out the window. For instance: My brother Otto take teachers like a prince, so many and dear—and this all for a little be examined, wich must undertake thousand and thousand poor fellow; and* add to this, *that I do not even know if he will pass his examination or not!—As for the rest: I know allready, that* now *this all cannot be altered, and we must let all, how it is; but for the future I must beg, to consider about such things, you all with another!*

The last lettre of you was wery agreable for me and I thank you many times for the all news over yourself and the others! Only I am sorry over our friend Nina, that she must suffer again pains and lie in here bett!

I want, *that my sister take care for she, and buys a good win and meat, and which she use, for here recreation. I am werry sorry ower these bad news, and I hop, that she get again soon enteirly well.—*

As respects my english writting,, you can see, i was diligent. I am learning alls in all now not yet 2 weeks (I have begin my lecons Monday 4. April) and I have not even much time to repete my Pensums because I must every day conduct my orchestra in the rehearsels and representations. My teatsher ist wery asthonished over my fast progresses, and I hop, if we shall be together in "Berchtesgaden", we cann speek with another in the beautiful langage.

Last night was the performance of the "Requiem" *and the "Te Deum". I self habe been obliged, to be werry satisfead with the artistes, and the works (both) mad a great impression upon the auditors.*

I have sent already a lettre to Bruckner in which I inform him upon the grand success of his great and beautiful work.

There are certain many mistaken in this lettre, but I hope, you excuse me therefore, und I sent only many greetings for you all!

Gustav

233 *To Justine*

[Hamburg, April 1892]

Dearest Justi!

First off, *how* silly that you didn't go to Semmering *with Natalie*! Two days like that are simply not to be measured in terms of money!

The news about Freund is really welcome; so we are finally in good hands again.—I *really* want him to visit me here in Hamburg; he can *stay* with me *in splendid fashion*.

Your last letters were really funny! I do know all that as well as you all do! I am not annoyed at all that you *spend money*! Money, after all, is only money, and as regards the *future*, I am truly not accustomed to deem the *present* so trifling!

But you all have arranged everything so *stupidly* and *unpractically*. The dozen of you together do not have as much common sense as any old tailor, for example, who has around my income, lives splendidly, has his children educated to the teeth, and yet doesn't have any debts.—You've already said yourself how stupidly the business with Otto is arranged, and I could say a lot more still if I were there!

Note one thing: if you were to write to me today "I have spent such and such for my *pleasure*—I have ordered a pretty dress for myself" and so on, I would only be *pleased* about it. But if now you write: we have nothing to wear—we are stinting on food, you must send us more money again because (for example) the lessons have again become more complicated, then I would simply like to fling it all down out of anger.—Other people have learned things already—must a fortune be spent on it?

Believe me: *students* are the main thing; *teachers* are secondary.

It would be going too far to say anything more on this. Hopefully you understand me!

By the way, I never write you in this manner to reproach you, but *only* to make you aware in the *future*! Moreover, I am not at all *edgy* about it—to the contrary, once I have expressed something like this, I am done with it, and I don't think of it at all!

I think it great fun that you want to take an examination. That is very clever—that is, only if your *health* does not suffer because of it, otherwise it would be very *stupid* again!

Please just don't be a "Miss know-it-all"?! For others always suffer as a result of this. Do write me diligently about Otto and Emma! And above all, *damn it*, don't *spare* me, you dolt, you only *upset* me that way!!

Affectionately yours,
Gustav

SHELFMARK: E10-MJ-422

234 *To Justine*

[Hamburg, end April 1892]

Dearest Justi!
I received the enclosed telegram the night before yesterday. I received it after the financial institutions [*Geldsendungen*] were already closed and so, after I had already lost the evening (during which I wanted to work), had to leave the house the next morning bright and early at 6 a.m., in order to arrange to telegraph the money.

Since then I have been without news, and therefore assume that the young lord is saved from danger for the time being.—Maybe the telegram and its contents were just the necessary aplomb in order to prevail upon me with such an unusual demand.—Please let me know if you know something about it.—Lord knows what else will come of it. This young lord may give me much "amusement" in the course of his eventful career.

—The enclosed letter from Binder is another lovely piece of news too![1]—So Otto is *not* attending his *primary subject*?[2] Why does he even bother going to the Conservatory? Just to drop off his tuition? And why such unforgivable negligence? No time for that because of the military examination, right? Please, some clarification here too.

I am continuously learning English—it is only now starting to get difficult, i.e. I am beginning to not recognise the difficulties.

Since I'm not endowed with the *clumsiness* of the lot of you, I still hope, however, to get over it.

For God['s] sake, just don't take everything so terribly seriously and knock your heads against the wall as if the sky were falling.—If I added together how you all feel and how things are with you all, the resulting sum would almost certainly be -x. Have Freund clarify this.

I hereby offer a prize for him who has a three-day toothache or stomachache without imagining that this is a consequence of unrequited love or the return of world suffering.

When does Freund come back? I am definitely counting on his visiting me here for a few days.—If he came in May, he would just hit the Wagner cycle.[3]—By the way, I have some *splendid* reading for you, but I won't send the books to you until Berchtesgaden where you can enjoy them in more peace, and where you will get more out of them in your initial loneliness. Please send me your total for the *first* soon, and estimate the amount that I have to send you for 1 *June* as soon as possible; since I steam off from here on 27 May, I must know this in plenty of time.

How are you all feeling?

Best wishes to you all
Gustav

Shelfmark: E3-MJ-121
Notes

[1] While a Carl Binder, born in 1875, is listed as a piano student in the Conservatory in the *Jahresbericht über das Conservatorium für Musik und darstellende Kunst* for 1889–1890, 1890–1891, 1891–1892, and 1892–1893, Mahler's later reference to a Herr Binder (letter 237) suggests that Otto's classmate is not meant here.

[2] According to the 1891–1892 *Jahresbericht*, Otto Mahler left the Conservatory on 27 April 1892; see below, letter 238.

[3] Between 15 and 25 May, Mahler conducted the complete *Ring*, *Tristan*, and *Meistersinger*.

235 *To Justine*

[Hamburg, end April 1892][1]

Dearest Justi!

Today you'll get a real load. *First*, the letter from Alois. According to *this* letter, the young man was *not* arrested, and *that* scare was only a later addition. That is the worst of it, that I cannot put any faith in his words.—A frivolous prank I would gladly excuse—but not to be able to *believe* a person, that makes every relationship impossible.—Write him appropriately, and at the same time inform him that I have deducted the *150* fl. out of his *capital* deposited with me.—If he only had some *Mahler*ish blood in his veins, I could do so much for him here in *Hamburg*, where I am on most familiar terms with merchants in the grand manner: firms whose business stretches to all five corners of the earth, whose ships truly sail in all the world's seas. A young man who is *dependable* and energetic can have a great career here—if he has connections.

—2. A letter from Schiller.[2] If you believe it, then send the old fellow some sum that you feel appropriate as a reward for "long life."

I will send you *850 marks* on the first. *38 fl.* of it belong to our brother, for concert tickets. Please see to it that the money is given to him *right away*.

I am still waiting for Otto's letter. He just *shouldn't* be so weighted down. He should just take the matter *more lightly*, without being any *less* diligent. An examination is certainly no "death sentence"! The worst that can happen is—one *fails*! If he had really completely done his duty, and then had that misfortune, I wouldn't bite his head off!—

3.—a moving letter from *Bruckner*, which typifies the complete helplessness of the poor man.[3] It must be hard, mind you, to have to be 70 years old before one is "*played*".—If all the signs are to be believed, *my* lot won't be any different.—

With "*doleful outcry*" I finally lay aside the fair copies of my new scores (5 of them).—Now I will have to peddle them about again to my esteemed colleagues.—Since they are even more idiosyncratic than my earlier ones, utter *humour* in the highest sense of the word (something for which only the exceptional portion of humanity was created), I will probably "have to add them to the others" again!—Truly an edifying prospect, to write a library for one's own drawer.—By the way, I am still in *the best mood* (despite my recent biting invective—maybe they're even a symptom of it), learn English diligently, and wish that I were already back from London and in Berchtesgaden—where the summer is said to be *very hot*!—Hopefully I will not have to suffer again there from *your* damned examinations, which really are *"mine"* too, and that you will have some time left over for *me* too! Eh?!

Heartiest greetings from
Gustav

SHELFMARK: E6-MJ-290
NOTES

[1] Since Mahler mentions completing his *Humoresken*, the letter must have been written after 26 April (the date on the manuscript of the orchestral version of "Trost im Unglück").

[2] Unknown.

[3] The letter, likely written in response to GMB[2] 110, does not survive.

236 *To Justine*

[Hamburg, April or May 1892]

Dearest Justi!
Your letters have gradually all arrived. I hope mine have too—especially my last one, which also includes a page for Otto.—As a consequence of your third letter, I had to think of the matter as *pressing*. All the more surprising, then, that in your last letter you passed right over it to the daily events.—In my view, *this* above all has to be in order now! Please [send me] detailed news about it as soon as possible.—For my part, I received a card from Friesz (almost at the same time as your *former* news), which I enclose here. Should I write Friesz now?[1]

I think that Alois will be there now, so please keep me informed about it from now on. In fact, I insist upon the utmost openness from you—without consideration for me! The matter is *too important*!

The business about Polna has moved me greatly![2] What am I to make of it? Was their relationship so *bad*, then, that she *seeks* refuge in *other people's houses*? If that is the case, then you could have taken her in for a few days at least, until something happened.

At any rate, please look for her right away, and tell her from me that she should go to a *lawyer* immediately and initiate legal proceedings against Pollini! I know from *reliable* sources that she will *win the case*. Since I do not know the details, I cannot advise her any further. She should just go to ~~Pollini~~ a lawyer right away *with her contract*.—

That really is too rough!

Anyway, these were a couple of nice pieces of news!—

I was with Markus's [*sic*] girls[3]—it is *all right*![4]

Since I no longer know where M[arcus] is, and have moreover learned that the girl has already written her, I will let everything else go.

Best wishes to everyone
from your
Gustav

Warmest wishes to Fritz und Uda—now they won't sleep all night again!

SHELFMARK: S1-MJ-741
NOTES

[1] This name, spelled variously "Friess," "Friesz," and "Fries," occurs in numerous letters from this time. The Institut Friesz was a private preparatory course for the military, run by Direktor Friesz, a retired military man (in 1904 it was located on the Schottenbasteigasse in the first district).

[2] Unknown.

[3] Adele Marcus; see appendix.

[4] The two italicised words are in English in the original.

237 *To Justine*

[Hamburg, April or May 1892]

Dearest Justi!

Well, for heaven's sake, give Herr Binder his yearly "discretion"!

I still do not have any *news* from Otto! Damn it, when will somebody tell me what is going on?!

That Frau Pischof's little one was operated on successfully really makes me happy for the dear woman.[1]—It just shows again that doctors have the privilege of understanding *nothing*. Nina should also really pull herself together so that I'll have something from her when I come to Berchtesgaden.

For once I would really like to spend a few careless, beautiful summer days. No one can predict what next winter will bring.

Pollini, who for a long time with *envious* eyes has watched my position with the public grow stronger from day to day, is now starting to *fear* me (it is unbelievable, but *true*)! And will summon up everything possible to *drive me away* from here.

He engaged Muck from Prague for next year;[2] I am really curious how that will turn out.—So *these* in fact are the worries that are being expressed if I sometimes argue about spending too much money.—This year will have to be fine as it is, but next year, *Justi*, we *must* really make savings where possible, and *you* must help me with it. I must be prepared to have to *leave* here without being able to find a suitable position as quickly again. (Of course Ernestine will smile when she reads this sentence, but things don't *always* go as luckily as before; at all events, I do not have any patent from heaven.)—

By the way, send me the exact address that I should use to write you in Berchtesgaden.—In a bookstore, I just bought the book that I already *told* you about, and instructed them to send it to you in Vienna at the beginning of June.[3]—I would prefer that you first read it leisurely in the beautiful natural surroundings of Berchtesgaden.—It will do you a world of good. It is a splendid book—what, I won't say yet.—I am diligently learning English and can be well pleased with my progress.—Everything is *fabulous*: I am getting along really well with reading as well as speaking.—The point of all this is of course London! There I will probably have to start from scratch again.—Do go to *Pischof's* for a few days, it will do you a lot of good.—

Best wishes to all
from your
Gustav

Congratulate Frau Pischof and give her my best wishes.

SHELFMARK: S1-MJ-733

NOTES

[1] Also mentioned in letter 163, May 1891.

[2] Conductor Carl Muck (1859–1940) went to the Königliche Oper in Berlin instead in 1892.

[3] Mahler is referring to letter 234.

238 *To Justine*

[Hamburg, May 1892]

Dearest Justi!
From Natalie I have come to know how things stand with Otto.[1]—It was very wrong to conceal this from me; consequently I was led astray, and was even misled into sending Otto a letter that may lead him down the wrong path. One thing I see now: things must simply run their course. If thereby Otto also gives us lots of trouble and worry, he'll surely inflict the worst on *himself*, and *the day will come* when he will *bitterly* regret it.

Why did he really not want to go to Friesz at all, since it is quite evident that only in this way will he get through the examination?

I won't say another word, however—let him do what he wants. He is old enough, and, in the end, you can lead a horse to water but cannot *make* him drink.

I am only happy that Natalie told me the truth.—But *you*! Consider what mischief you get up to with your *secrecy* and euphemisms. With both of them—*Otto* as well as *Alois*. N.B. that in the end I certainly must learn the result, and some *consideration* for me would be appreciated.

I am very pleased about Emma—just let her continue to be good! It is really refreshing to hear something good sometimes too!—

I was stuck in my room for two days with a cold. Today I am feeling better again.

I've written an answer to Friesz, but haven't sent it yet because I don't know his address.—If you think that I should still send it, then send me the exact address.

Yours,
Gustav

SHELFMARK: E10-MJ-461
NOTE

[1] While Mahler knew in April that Otto was not attending his primary subject at the Conservatory (see above, letter 234), it was some weeks before he learned that Otto had dropped out on 27 April 1892.

239 *To Justine*

[Hamburg, mid-May 1892]

Dearest Justi!
I had a fine shock about the operation! Why didn't you write any more details about it? Was the operation dangerous, and how is Nina feeling? Please send frequent bulletins!

Your letter about Otto's examination created strong doubts in me as well.—*I* certainly *cannot intervene* from here; do what you all think best. I think that, if at all possible, he should take the examination—*nevertheless* he should perhaps enroll with Friesz, so that he could take the course again right away, just in case of a *failure*. How is it with the Conservatory? Has he *lost* the whole year, then, or not? He has not written me, but I would just like to know?!

So, if nothing intervenes, I leave early on 27 May—by ship from Cuxhafen to Southampton.[1] From there it is another 2 hours by rail to London, where I arrive on the afternoon of the 28th. Before then, I have to conduct the [Wagner] cycle here again.[2]

Please give me *Heuberger*'s address right away; he lives on Maria-Theresienstrasse, but I don't know the number.[3]—

The book that I will send you is a *Schiller biography* that just appeared, and is one of the *best* biographies around—truly a rare article.[4]

Enclosed, a newspaper clipping that amused me because I encountered it so suddenly. (I was sitting in the coffee house and by chance happened to read the *Leipziger Zeitung*—I cut the article out right away.)

Best wishes from your
Gustav

SHELFMARK: E14-MJ-546
NOTES

[1] Mahler left Hamburg on the evening of the 26th; see below, letter 241.

[2] *Die Meistersinger von Nürnberg*, 15 May; *Das Rheingold*, 17 May; *Die Walküre*, 19 May; *Siegfried*, 20 May; *Tristan und Isolde*, 22 May (Wagner's birthday); *Götterdämmerung*, 25 May.

[3] Richard Heuberger (1850–1914) was a composer, choral conductor, and music critic at the *Wiener Tagblatt*. In 1896, he moved to the *Neue Freie Presse* as Hanslick's successor, remaining until 1901.

[4] Later letters indicate that it was by Otto Brahm (1856–1912): *Schiller*, 2 vols. (Berlin: W. Hertz, 1888–1892).

240 *To Justine*

[Hamburg, end May 1892]

Dearest Justi!

Hopefully, when I seal the letter today I won't forget the clipping again, which really was very nice. For originality's sake, I enclose another one that appeared *here*.

I leave here on Wednesday or Thursday; please direct your next letter to
(*10 Kr. stamp*) London
De Keyser's Royal Hotel
New Bridge Street

Hopefully I'll find a letter there already when I arrive.—

The business with Otto is too stupid. What do his teachers say, then? Don't they know anything? You've got an ingenious arrangement there with "Prince Tuition"! No one is responsible, and no one worries about it! What does Freund or Fritz say?

I will send you 750 marks for June on the first. At the same time, I ask you to have Freund withdraw the *interest* in Iglau so that you can pay the rent in Berchtesgaden with it.

Hopefully, you'll get by this way, otherwise write me in London immediately. (You first must pay the rent on 1 July, right?)

Let me know exactly what Otto will do.—When are you all going to Berchtesgaden?—What is wrong with Elise?—What kind of illness or thing does Louise have?—

In two letters you write: Louise has [here, Mahler writes an intentional scribble], which I (eventually) roughly deciphered as mums.—Mind you, I don't know what mums is. Maybe you could clarify this for me?

Very best wishes
from
Gustav

I'll probably not write again from here. Next one from London.

SHELFMARK: E3-MJ-123

241 *To Justine*

[Hamburg, 26 May 1892]

Dearest Justi!
The enclosed letter I received back in the winter, and put aside for you all to answer some time—but forgot all about it.

Now I have stumbled upon it.

Write the poor thing a few lines, and say hello to her from me.

I start tonight.

My hands are full.

For the time being my address is
De Keyser's
Royal Hôtel.

[unsigned]

SHELFMARK: E6-MJ-286

242 *To Justine*

DE KEYSER'S ROYAL HOTEL, LONDON, E.C.

London 28. May *1892*[1]

Dearest Justi!
After a 24-hour trip (the sea crossing was magnificent), arrived here, well rested and breakfasted.

Found your letter.

Please absolutely take *Freund's* advice regarding Otto. He *understands* the matter better than *Fritz*, and will look after it *more conscientiously*.

The business with Otto worries me greatly.

—London is no idle illusion; the city is *tremendously* imposing!

Today I am still looking for a private dwelling.

Did you receive the *money*? *Freund* will look after the rent and *Bercht*[esgaden]; I will send you money again on 1 July.

I hope to be with you around the 22nd.

What happened, then, with all the tuition and war loans?[2]

I can just *watch* everything!? Not organise such [things] from far away! And in Vienna I don't have anybody who has both the will and the understanding for it.

I know absolutely nothing about Fritz! He seems not to trouble himself very much about Otto. Perhaps he too is fatalistic about it! That is the viewpoint, you see, of all people who are too lazy to follow a thing through to its proper conclusion. Moreover, this fatalism's characteristic—most commonly—is to exist only at *others'* expense, not at that of those who possess it. If these others are not available, the fatalism disappears too.

I am only fatalistic, then, if something is *over and done with*.—As long as this is not the case, being fatalistic is simply *unmanly* and *unworthy*. Point this out to Otto so that he knows my view about these annoying things.

Best wishes
from
Gustav

Shelfmark: E6-MJ-285

Notes

[1] The italicised words and numbers were printed on the stationery. Mahler wrote the month in English.

[2] The transcription of this word is not completely secure.

243 *To Justine*

Postcard[1]
[Postmark: London, My 30 92]
[Arrival postmark: Vienna, 1.6.92]

Dearest J.
Address for the time being
Coventgarden—Theatre
More details next time!
G.

Shelfmark: E12-MJp-489

Note

[1] Addressed to "Fräulein Justine Mahler / Austria / Wien / VII. Breitegasse 4 II."

244 *To Justine*

Lettercard[1]
[Postmark: London, My 31 92]
[Arrival postmark: Vienna, 2.6.92]

Dearest Justi!
I have now finally arrived in the harbour of a comfortable home—a real English family, who do not speak a word of *German*, and with whom I take all my meals.[2] Very pleasant and helpful people, who, incidentally, permit themselves to be compensated lavishly: 5 pounds (100 marks) per week.

London is indescribably imposing.—Here one gets a glimpse of what "humanity" has become.

I hope to receive detailed news of you all.—I *will tell* you everything in Berchtesgaden.—The first performance is Wednesday, *8 June*.[3]

Yours affectionately,
Gustav

69 Torrington Square

W.C.

Shelfmark: E6-MJ-287
Notes

[1] Addressed to "Miss Justine Mahler / Austria / Vienna / VII. Breitegasse 4 II."

[2] According to Nicholson, "Mahler in London in 1892," Solomon Jacobson and family (see plate 25.1, p. 541). Torrington Square was within the proximity of Covent Garden.

[3] *Siegfried* with Max Alvary.

245 *To Justine*

[Embossed:]

THEATRE ROYAL DRURY LANE / AND / ROYAL ITALIAN
OPERA COVENT GARDEN
LESSEE AND MANAGER
SIR AUGUSTUS HARRIS[1]

[London, first week June 1892]

Dearest Justi!
I am terribly tired from all of the preparations—I think that this is the most difficult thing that I have ever done.—The city is stunningly magnificent—its first impression on me was a bit like when I saw the *sea* for the first time.

I *won't* write again before Wednesday, but I await *detailed* news from you![2] I have *not* yet received Lipiner's letter.

Best,
Gustav

SHELFMARK: E10-MJ-432
NOTES

[1] Sir Augustus Harris (1852–1896) was an actor, dramatist, and impresario. He was the manager of Covent Garden from 1888 and the lessee of Drury Lane from 1879.

[2] The first performance was on Wednesday, 8 June.

246 *To Justine*

Postcard[1]
[Postmark: London, Ju 9 92]
[Arrival postmark: Vienna, 11.6.92]

Yesterday everything *happily* came to its end.—I had to [overcome?] terrible difficulties, more than anyone could imagine. I literally didn't sit down for 5 days.

A sensational success for London.[2]—My lucky star was watching over me.—

I await detailed news. If you read or hear anything about it in Vienna, write me about it!

G.

SHELFMARK: E3-MJp-122
NOTES

[1] Addressed to "Fräulein Justine Mahler / Austria / Wien / VII. Breitegasse 4 II."

[2] The *Times* review described *Siegfried* as a "wonderful success" and noted that "scarcely a single detail, either in the orchestra or on the stage, fell short of perfection" (quoted in Nicholson, "Mahler in London in 1892," p. 544).

247 *To Justine*

[Embossed:]

THEATRE ROYAL DRURY LANE / AND / ROYAL ITALIAN
OPERA COVENT GARDEN
LESSEE AND MANAGER
SIR AUGUSTUS HARRIS

[London, c. 10 June 1892]

Dearest Justi!

Enclosed, reviews of the first performance.

Please send them right away to <u>*Singer*</u> in Budapest after you have looked at them.

<u>*Important*</u>!

Best,
Gustav

SHELFMARK: E18-MJ-644

248 *To Justine*

[Embossed:]

THEATRE ROYAL DRURY LANE / AND / ROYAL ITALIAN
OPERA COVENT GARDEN
LESSEE AND MANAGER
SIR AUGUSTUS HARRIS

[London, June 1892]

Dearest Justi!
I just received Lipiner's letter![1] He complains *bitterly* that you aren't concerning yourself with Clementine *at all* at this difficult time—now, when she is especially *thankful* for a visit!—How on earth can you be so thoughtless!?—I don't understand you! Just go *right away* and *show her* a little care!—I am quite exhausted!

Write soon.

Best,
Gustav

SHELFMARK: E10-MJ-455
NOTE
[1] Siegfried Lipiner; see appendix.

249 *To Justine*

[London, June 1892]

Dearest J.
I am sending you more clippings. It is terribly tiring for me. In Berchtesgaden, you all must make it as calm and comfortable for me as possible, so that I can recover a bit from the strain.

The public is charming toward me, and toward all of us Germans.

If only I were in the country already!

Do write *in more detail*! Confound it, once again!

God-dam.[1]

I don't make the promised progress in engl. language.—I have not time to exercise it, and only very seldom I have opportunity to talk english. Everyday and all day I hold rehearsals with the german compagnie.

I write englich according your notice in your last letter. That you could understand the news-paper I have sent you; I have perceived with pleasure that you are studing this important and not at all difficult language.

Yours
Gustav

SHELFMARK: E10-MJ-430
NOTE
[1] From this point on, Mahler writes in English.

250 *To Justine*

[Embossed:]

THEATRE ROYAL DRURY LANE / AND / ROYAL ITALIAN
OPERA COVENT GARDEN
LESSEE AND MANAGER
SIR AUGUSTUS HARRIS

[London, June 1892]

Dearest Justi!
This very day some money (600 marks) is going off to you. Let me know right away how much I still need to send—I am too tired out to be able to write letters, but I expect detailed news from you.

In the near future a Frau *Marcus* from Hamburg will visit you. This is a family who have shown themselves to be especially friendly toward me, so I would like you to receive the ladies *very well.*

—If only I were already there too!

Yours affectionately,
Gustav

SHELFMARK: E3-MJ-124

251 *To Justine*

[Embossed:]

THEATRE ROYAL DRURY LANE / AND / ROYAL ITALIAN
OPERA COVENT GARDEN
LESSEE AND MANAGER
SIR AUGUSTUS HARRIS

[London, June 1892]

Dearest Justi!
From day to day I wait for a letter from all of you—but in vain!

In addition to all the current excitement, these worries to boot! Did you receive the 600 marks? Where is Otto? Why don't you write? Today 20 £ (over 200 marks) are going off to you, just in case. Please confirm receipt right away.—

Here work and difficulty all over the place.

Please address all letters to the following address:

London, W.C.
Alfred-place 22.[1]

It seems to me that a letter from you was lost.—I have been at my new address for 3 weeks, [and] wrote you at that time (still in Vienna) to address my letters to Covent Garden—[This] seems also to have been lost.[2]

All arrangements here are very complicated for a foreigner—most especially sending money. I find myself almost depressed because of the terrible efforts—but nevertheless am quite healthy!

Dammit, don't leave me awaiting news.

Best,
Gustav

SHELFMARK: E14-MJ-547

NOTES

[1] According to Nicholson, "Mahler in London in 1892," 22 Alfred Place was a lodging house near Covent Garden run by Mrs. Mary A. Gusterson (see plate 25.2, p. 541).

[2] Mahler's comment is difficult to decipher since when he first arrived in London, he stayed at De Keyser's Royal Hotel and then at 69 Torrington Square, unless perhaps by new "address" he simply means London. GMB[2] 111, postmarked 9 June, was written from Torrington Square (although from the contents, it appears that it was written the week before), and in GMB[2] 114 (14 July) Mahler gives Alfred Place as his address. On 30 May, Mahler sent a postcard to Justine asking her to address letters to Covent Garden; see above, letter 243.

252 *To Justine*

[Embossed:]

THEATRE ROYAL DRURY LANE / AND / ROYAL ITALIAN
OPERA COVENT GARDEN
LESSEE AND MANAGER
SIR AUGUSTUS HARRIS

[London, June or July 1892]

Dearest Justi!

Your last letter—about Nina and Ernest[ine]—just arrived.

I didn't send anything to Otto—however, 200 marks to you. Please settle what is to be settled, and let me know how much I still have to send you.—

I am glad that you all are so content.—I certainly can't join you before the end of July.

At any rate, let's arrange it so that you all meet me in *Salzburg*!

Best wishes to you all
from
Gustav

SHELFMARK: E10-MJ-456

253 *To Justine*

[Embossed:]

THEATRE ROYAL DRURY LANE / AND / ROYAL ITALIAN
OPERA COVENT GARDEN
LESSEE AND MANAGER
SIR AUGUSTUS HARRIS

[London, beginning of July 1892]

Dear Justi!

All your letters have arrived!

I sent you around 120 marks again—I don't quite know! You wrote in your letter before last that I should send Otto 30 fl.—then all is in order! The next day I got a letter from Ernestine—I should immediately send Otto 165 fl. right away, etc.

Just in case, I have just sent you 6 £ (120 marks)—and hope that that takes care of you all until my arrival.—Unfortunately I am only bringing a small number of these beloved notes with me—with which, willy-nilly, we must make do until the end of September. Apparently we are finishing here on the 22nd,[1] whereupon I will make my way to Berchtesgaden on the first and fastest train. A journey, at any rate, of at least 36 hours.

Hasn't Frau Markus [*sic*] from Hamburg been there yet!

When is Otto actually coming to Berchtesg[aden]? And what sort of new arrangement is this, that he already started Friesz's course in June? The story is confused of course—you all seem to have cooked and salted the soup (and *I*, it seems, have to spoon it out).

I am hugely busy here, but I take every opportunity to come out into the fresh air.

Write soon.

Best
Gustav

If you still find yourself in need despite this, telegraph me.—I hope to be with you on the *25th*.

SHELFMARK: S1-MJ-735

NOTE

[1] With a performance of *Tannhäuser* at Covent Garden.

254 *To Justine*

[Embossed:]

THEATRE ROYAL DRURY LANE / AND / ROYAL ITALIAN
OPERA COVENT GARDEN
LESSEE AND MANAGER
SIR AUGUSTUS HARRIS

[London, third week July 1892]

Dearest!

So, early *Saturday* I leave here.[1] Spend the night in Cologne.

Off Sunday early.—In Munich the next morning—off again right away, and after that I hope to arrive in *Salzburg* on Monday around midday (c. 1:00), where hopefully one of you will be waiting for me.—I suspect that the mail no longer goes to Berchtesgaden in the *afternoons*.

If *this* is the case absolutely only *one of you* should wait; *otherwise* all of you could make the journey to Salzburg together.

Ask about the trains again. I am coming on the *first* express train [*Courirzug*], which departs Munich for Salzburg early Monday (around *9:00*). If I don't come *on it*, then await me on the next one.

Received Otto's letter!

Best wishes
from Gustav

SHELFMARK: E14-MJ-548
NOTE

[1] 23 July.

255 *To Justine*

Postcard[1]

[Postmark: Munich, 25. Aug. 92]
[Arrival postmark: Berchtesgaden, 26. Aug. 92]

M[y] D[ears]
Since the news that's arrived doesn't sound very inviting, I will stay here for the time being and await the development of the matter![2] My address for the time being: c/o Krzyzanowski, Schnorrstrasse 9.

Please, *on your part* the greatest *precautions* from now on!—No milk—no fruit—no wine!—You all could drink *beer*—all very moderately! At any rate, send me news right away!

Ever yours
Gustav

SHELFMARK: E4-MJp-177
NOTES

[1] Addressed to "Fräulein Justine Mahler / Berchtesgaden / Villa Hechler am Salzburg [*sic*]."

[2] Contrary to Natalie's account, it is clear that Mahler learned of the cholera outbreak in Hamburg in Munich, and not in Berlin (NBL, p. 23). The outbreak began on 16 August and was not completely eradicated until October. More than 8,000 died.

256 *To Justine*

[Berlin, 27 August 1892]

Dearest Justi!
Yesterday I did not travel on right away, as I intended, but stayed here.—

Since I suspect that you might be worried because of the news from Hamburg, I wanted to tell you that I telegraphed my friend Berliner in Hamburg and asked him for detailed news of the cholera that broke out there; whether I stay here or travel on to Hamburg will depend on his answer.[1]

At any rate, don't forget that the epidemic strikes mainly that portion of the populace that does not have the intelligence and the means to protect themselves from it.—Whoever lives healthily and openly, keeps on a strict diet, and has enough money to enjoy only the best and the purest has nothing to fear.

The inhabitants of the stinking "old city," [which is] *full of narrow streets* and *bad* sewers, near the harbour are affected by the cholera—thus, about a half an hour away from my house, which lies in the healthiest part of town.—So *don't worry*; you all know how careful I am. By the way, you'll get daily bulletins!

If Berliner's telegram—upon which I can depend completely—is *reassuring*, I will depart tonight.—If not, I will stay *here*.[2]

Further details tomorrow.

Yours ever
Gustav

SHELFMARK: E3-MJ-125
NOTES

[1] See Mahler's letter of 27 August to Berliner, GMB[2] 116.

[2] Mahler stayed in Berlin until 29 August. That night he set off again for Berchtesgaden, where he remained until mid-September. According to NBL, p. 24, after Mahler learned that Pollini was going to reopen the theatre on 15 September, Justine and Natalie went along with him to Munich. There they learned that the epidemic was still raging, and Mahler decided to delay his return despite Pollini's threats.

257 *To Justine*

[Berlin, 20 September 1892]

Dearest Justi!
The journey ended happily. Feld[1] met me at the train station and everywhere I met people from Hamburg who were just about to go back there. Feld is travelling with me tomorrow too.—The epidemic has now lost its virulent character, and with a little bit of care one can go there *without any* danger.

Hopefully you have already had correspondingly reassuring news from the newspaper and, like me, are no longer worried.

I am very curious about your news regarding *Waging*.[2] You all must have had a wonderful day. It is too bad that all the beauty of the last few days was spoiled for me by the perpetual uncertainty.

Nevertheless, however, the time in Berchtesgaden was splendid, and the whole world maintains that I have put on weight over the last weeks. How is Natalie's esteemed [*P.T.*] stomach?[3]

Please, for God's sake, send your next letters to Hamburg, where I plan to go tomorrow as long as I get favourable news again today.

Best wishes to you both
from your
Gustav

SHELFMARK: E10-MJ-433
NOTES
[1] Leo Feld (1858–1896) was second *Kapellmeister* at the Stadttheater from 1886 to 1892.
[2] Waging am See is near Berchtesgaden.
[3] *Pleno Titulo,* "with all due titles," was a courtly form of address in the Austro-Hungarian empire.

258 *To Justine*

Hamburg, Thursday [22 September 1892]

So, dear children, arrived happily [*glücklich*] in Hamburg, happily disinfected, very happily [*überglücklich*] dined, and am just sitting and deliriously happily [*sauglücklich*] smoking a cigar in my beautiful 3 rooms—i.e. of course only in one at a time.—

Anyway, if somebody had been afraid, the fear would have disappeared at the moment he entered Hamburg's precincts.—It's already as if nothing had happened—everything goes on as usual, and one is *downright* ashamed of oneself to have hesitated so long. The *pestilence* appears to have come to an end, which naturally won't prevent me by any means from continuing to live with pedantic caution.

For tomorrow a whole bunch of rehearsals are already announced for me.—I have not yet met Pollini face to face, but will call on him later (5:00). Feld met me at the train station. He will come tomorrow.

At any rate, I will write you a card daily and more often—but I assure you that it is quite unnecessary to have the least concern.

In Berlin I called on Frau Marcus's family—found them all very well and spent a pleasant evening with them.—Is Frau Marcus still with you?

I am quite happy to be back to routine.—My quarters have become something beautiful, [and] cosier than I've ever had.

As soon as you get to Vienna, dear Justi, send me my writing desk and book armoire right away.

Frau *Schack* has been here for a week, together with the whole family.[1] I'll write more soon.

Your letter did reach me in Berlin and it was friendly sustenance [*Wegzehrung*] for me on the journey.

Best wishes to you all from
your
Gustav

Say hello to Frau Marcus and Toni from me.

I am wallowing in contentment!

[written across the top of the letter:] I eat at *home*!

SHELFMARK: E5-MJ-233
NOTE
[1] From later letters, it appears that Frau Schack was Mahler's landlady.

259 *To the Siblings*

[Hamburg, 23 September 1892]

Dear Children!

So, day two also reaches its happy end.—The epidemic seems to have come to an end from the day I returned here! I have such power to disinfect!

Joking aside, I am splendid; I eat marvellously at my landlady's—a splendid *Bechstein* piano is in my room.

On Wednesday I conduct for the first time—*Meistersinger*, in fact.[1]

Imagine, *Feld* was *dismissed* by the strict Pollini because he didn't return punctually. With me he was very merciful right from the start! You all can gather from this just how unevenly things are judged here. Feld will try to appeal.

—Admittedly, it feels a little bit lonely here—well, I must get used to it.

I present you all with the card that Nina forwarded to me already after my first departure for Hamburg. So even then her sensible nature was already knocked out of harmony by me. What do you all say *to that*!? Shouldn't this sensible nature have been helped previously by a senseless thrashing? I am beginning to consider corporal punishment an absolutely necessary means of human education. The card was posted in Berchtesgaden on *25 Aug.*—thus, one day after my first departure!—

Please just give the silly goose a little piece of *my* mind when you pass through on the way to Vienna.

Everyone here marvels at my good appearance and plumpness!

Of course, never before have I remained so well.—

Did you all receive all my letters?

Best wishes from your
Gustav

Say hello to Frau Marcus and Toni.

SHELFMARK: S1-MJ-736

NOTE

[1] Mahler conducted for the first time on Wednesday, 5 October (*Meistersinger*).

260 *To Justine*

[Hamburg, Autumn 1892][1]

Dearest Justi!

Of course a doctor should be consulted about Otto *right away*. Moreover, Otto shouldn't tire himself under any circumstances; in this state, no one can accomplish anything.—

Could he perhaps postpone the examination until he has a good rest?

In any case, the doctor must be obeyed. If he indicates that the examination must not happen, then for God's sake, Otto should give it up and recover his health above all, and at most occupy himself with music.—In this case, one will just have to hope that he will *not be taken* when he is called up for military service.

Ultimately, health is surely the main thing; *without that*, no one can do anything. The whole business was again treated badly.—After the never-ending, futile grind Otto ought simply to have had a *proper* holiday, and rested, and not put his wholly frayed nerves back in the yoke right away.

Please just see to it that this is arranged reasonably. *Under no circumstances* should he over*tire* himself; if he fails the examination, well, he can just do it again. If the doctor orders complete *relaxation* and rest for him, then he should simply let the thing run its course, and rest and renew himself spiritually. Go walking with him daily for *2 hours* in good air.

At any rate, let me know about it *right away*. He should just be reasonable. One cannot do the impossible, and under the prevailing circumstances I completely understand that the brain cannot do anything if for years it has been continually maltreated in the stupidest manner.

So he should make music and go walking to his heart's content!

The rest will turn out all right, you'll see. The others, Hippauf—etc. etc. got away *free*!

Best wishes from your
Gustav

Shelfmark: S1-MJ-757
Note

[1] The date of this letter is not certain, although it must date from the fall of 1892. I have placed it here in light of the postscript in the next letter (261).

261 *To Justine*

[Hamburg, September 1892]

Dearest Justi!
I just got Nina's letter, which worries me quite a bit about your situation. It is really quite terrible that you returned home from the summer in need of relaxation.

For that, for the most part we indeed also have Nina—tender, sensitive, always living completely for the well-being of others—to thank. (By the way, I have received 2 letters from her—the second concerning the Alois affair, in which she asks me what I think about the matter.)—Naturally I don't have anything at all against your plan to go away again, wherever and with whomsoever you want, as long as it is good for your health. Think about the latter carefully—I doubt that you will feel well in Albi's company, especially in *Iglau* or anywhere else.[1]

~~In this case~~ Incidentally *Iglau* is no place at all for you now—it is *much too harsh*. Look for a *milder* climate instead—Merano would surely be the best.—How would it be if sooner or later you were to get things started in Vienna and then simply let them run their course—you wouldn't be able to change [them] anyway—and make your way as soon as possible to Ernestine in Merano. At any rate, just ask the doctor, and, not least, *yourself* too, and do what seems best to you.

—Does Emma continue to prove trustworthy? Alois will certainly soon have a post—only Otto is left; I still leave to his discretion, as long as there is time, to shift over *completely* to Friesz's.—Then you would indeed be completely free.—Emma will just be able to dwell for [a] few weeks with Elise and the girls, and you can do something about your health.

I will send Alois 50 fl. in the next few days.—If only he would just spare me his damned windbagging [*Windbeuteleien*]; even from the short account I see his truly deplorable, childish, and immature manner "between the lines."—He should consider that just now he has gone through 1/8 of his wealth—just 7/8 remains! This way, soon everything would be "remaindered."

—So, now just let things run their course and don't worry yourself about anything other than your *health*—have *rest* and *comfort*.—Let me know soon how you are!

Yours affectionately
Gustav

It is very impractical to consult a doctor about *3* patients in one sitting—thereby he can't even examine *one* properly!!

I wrote a few lines to Friesz.

SHELFMARK: E4-MJ-179
NOTE
[1] Albine Adler, a family friend.

262 *To Justine*

[Hamburg, end September 1892]

Dearest Justi!
I. *Where* do you all want to go next summer? II. What did Elise do?—Please, for God's sake, *no* hints! Instead, either *clear and comprehensible* or *not at all* (quite in the Podmanicky [*sic*] style).[1]—From Alois, I again received the enclosed small token of attention! Please, tell him *one thing* above all: from now on *telegrams* from him will be *completely* ignored by me.—If he wants something from me, he is to *write*—namely, in *detail* and exhaustively. *Lies* will be avenged bitterly! Just what has he done with all the money? (Bear in mind: at the time he transferred only 4000 fl. to me, so already then he kept about 350 fl. for himself.) How unfortunate that one can never demand an explanation from this *false* man, because one knows that he will only tell one what suits him! But really—I am quite serious—my *patience* will soon be at an *end*! Impress this on him powerfully! By God! I will have *nothing* more to do with him, if he carries on like this! Above all, I hereby demand of him that he give me an *account* of all the money that I sent him recently. *450* fl. all together! Whatever it may *be*, I will forgive him—but *not* of a *lie*. If he *still* has debts, he should own up to them, but I will *only* respond to a detailed explanation.—I won't give him a *single* kreuzer of his money without knowing why! Of course, he is of legal age and has the right to it.—If he *demands it*, I will send him the entire amount *by return of post*—but then *I* am *finished* with him.—You would hardly believe how many midday meals this *rogue* has spoiled for me.—

Just do impress on him that he *should no longer presume* to send me a telegram—it would be *completely* ignored, *no matter what* it says.

Hippauf and all the others have all reported here already. The poor fellows were quite unhappy—they were only sent all over the place by their colleagues! Well, the sun is shining on them again now.—

It is reliably reported that *Mirsch* (the critic who died of cholera), already suffering from diarrhoea for a week, nevertheless was not deterred from eating an *entire melon*![2]

Imagine: an educated man!

I sent the 300 fl.—hopefully you're already in possession of them! How much do I still have to send you, when is the latest that you must have the rest?

What is *Freund*'s address!

Best wishes to all.—Otto should let himself be heard from once in a while—[and] certainly *not* be *insulted*.—I detest touchiness!

Best,
Gustav

SHELFMARK: E18-MJ-643

NOTES

[1] Baron Frigyes Podmaniczky (1824–1907) was the first *Intendant* of the Opera in Budapest. He resigned in 1886. Zoltan Roman speculates that Mahler may have been referring to Podmaniczky's "well-known qualities as a hard-working, no-nonsense 'straight shooter'" (personal communication, 28 January 2002).

[2] Paul Mirsch (1857–1892) was the critic at the *Hamburger Nachrichten*.

263 *To Justine*

Always date letters! [Hamburg,] 1/X 92

It is often important indeed!

My dears!

Today I got your 2nd and 3rd letter, which were forwarded to me here.—Naturally, I was very happy about the contents—(please always address them from now on to Bundesstrasse *10* III). Hopefully, Josephine is now with you and is enjoying herself a bit.[1]—

I don't have *too much* to do, and always have afternoons and evenings for myself—the latter I spend in the most stimulating manner with Dr. Berliner.

I tell you frankly, I am ashamed to have had such fear, and also, so to speak, to have run from it! Just in case, I set it down here once again: whoever is meticulously *careful* and *clean* is absolutely *not threatened* by cholera! For heaven's sake, if it should ever show itself in Vienna, don't lose your head—as I did!

Well, after all it really was beautiful in Berchtesgaden! Along with this letter, another is going to the bank in Budapest; in the next few days 300 fl. will be sent to *your* address, dear Justi. Please send me your calculation right away if you can't manage with 300 fl.—Even in this case, please send me the items that inevitably and necessarily must be paid *right away*. Everything else please leave, if possible, until 1 November (—so then, certainly, a charming menu will have come together!)

Further, please send *Dr. Freund's address* as soon as possible.

Your habit of writing on sealed letters, dear Natalie, is beginning to please me very much.—From now on, if possible, please develop this bad habit almost into a vice! *What do you think of Nina's postcard*?

Hr. Pollini is very *polite* towards me—accordingly, please send me my bookcase!!

The meals at my landlady's are quite good! I feel like always continuing this!

For now, best wishes from
your Gustav

SHELFMARK: S1-MJ-737
NOTE
[1] Possibly Albert Spiegler's sister Josephine.

264 *To Justine*

[Hamburg,] 2 Oct. [1892]

Dearest Justi,
Your letter of today (the 2nd that I received) is incomprehensible to me.
Up to now, I have sent *daily letters* to you—you write that you are still *without* a letter! How can this be?

Further: what is this about Elise? Please, dear Justi, *at last* stop—at least in *letters* to me—dropping hints about which one can break one's head before an explanation arrives. Either *immediately* let me know everything necessary for an explanation, or *don't* hint *at all* whatsoever!—So, what has gone wrong with Elise?

Here everything is already going its old merry way again.

The newspapers have exaggerated and sensationally played everything up in an *irresponsible* way. This will be a lesson for me for my whole future.

I assume that you are now in Vienna, and so I am addressing [this] there.

What was the matter with *Josephine*?

If you need to, then go away with Alois for 14 days too—at the worst, the other two could eat upstairs with Bertha!

Did you receive the money (300 fl.) yet?—

Best wishes to Natalie from me, and to you all as well.

from your
Gustav

SHELFMARK: E4-MJ-186

265 *To Justine*

[Hamburg, 6 or 7 October 1892]

Dearest Justi!
~~To~~ Yesterday a 2nd telegram (answer prepaid) came from Mr. Alois.[1]—Naturally I sent him the money by mail right after the *first* telegram.—I am curious what you will tell me.—

I know that you would like the Brahm so much.[2]—Of course, as you may recall, I had intended it for you while you were alone at first at Berchtesgaden, and not for you to read it in the company of a confused and screwed-up Charlotte Kalb.[3]—Now you see how differently one sees and enjoys such a thing *alone*. This should be a warning to you about reading a book for the first time *in company*—even if the companion isn't such a wound-up, foolish girl [*Urschel*] as N[ina].

Feld is initiating proceedings against Pollini, which in all probability he should *win*.

Enclosed, a review of my first performance—but hopefully after that you will do without being sent these gentlemen's reviews.[4]—They are all alike, and are really not worth reading.

Still only a few of the wealthy families have yet returned. More and more I continue to see how cowardly and dumb is this particular fear of *cholera*.

Hopefully, I'll soon get more detailed news; very best wishes from

Gustav

SHELFMARK: E4-MJ-178

NOTES

[1] "Mr." in English in the original.

[2] Otto Brahm's biography of Schiller, mentioned earlier.

[3] Unknown.

[4] A review of the 5 October performance of *Die Meistersinger* appeared in the *Fremdenblatt* the next day.

266 *To Justine*

[Hamburg, c. 25 October 1892]

Dearest Justi!

Today 50 fl. are going off for you, so that you'll have some money already on the 1st; on the 1st, I'll send the other fifty.

You first wanted *150* fl.

And *290* fl. more

Is the amount for the rent also included in the 290 fl.? And in this case, couldn't I at least send you this 50 fl. next month. This time I really am more broke than ever before!—Please let me know as soon as possible.

So, today I am sending 50 fl.

On the 1st, another 340.—If you notify me that you really do need the other 50 fl. now, I'll send it to you too in the next few days.

The Marcuses still don't seem to be here—I at least have heard nothing from them yet.—Are you perhaps corresponding with them?

So Joachim really announced herself for the 2nd Bülow concert, and put *my* Humoresken on the program.[1] Herr Hansel [*Hannsch*] von Bülow was again so kind as to not accept them because of "their special [*eigenthümlich*] [read: odd] style."—

I'm sending you Bülow's letter; please let Natalie read it and then send it back to me.[2]

Isn't this yet another instance of friendly encouragement [in the face] of questionable talent?

Best wishes from your
Gustav

SHELFMARK: E8-MJ-373
NOTES

[1] In the end, mezzo-soprano Amalie Joachim (1839–1898) performed *Lieder* by Schubert (one) and Brahms (two) and one of the Countess's arias from *Le nozze di Figaro* instead of Mahler's songs at the concert on 7 November.

[2] Bülow's letter, dated 25 October 1892, survives in the Mahler-Rosé Collection (E5-MC-258):

> Hbg. 25 Oct. 92
>
> Esteemed Herr Kapellmeister!
> My numerous attempts (*not* superficial) to comprehend, and to feel, the special [*eigenthümlich*] style of the songs that you so kindly sent me have turned out to be so futile that, with regard to the composer as well as the performer, I feel unable to accept the responsibility of their performance at the 7 November concert.
>
> As a result of this conviction, I have requested that Herr Wolff, the concert manager, turn to you personally to rehearse and conduct the piece.
>
> Yours faithfully
>
> H. v. Bülow

Bülow wrote to Hermann Wolff on the same day; see letter 426 in Hans von Bülow, *Briefe*, ed. Marie von Bülow, vol. 8: *Höhepunkt und Ende, 1886–1894* (Leipzig: Breitkopf und Härtel, 1908).

267 *To Justine*

[Hamburg, October 1892][1]

Dearest Justi!
I just got your letter; it reached me alone at home (in the evening), just like you wrote it.—My reply to Otto's letter will be in his hands already.—I would *never* have thought that it would be he who would give us the most worry.

I was recently at Marcus's for dinner.—I became so nervous and fidgety from the awful boredom that right in the middle of it (i.e., *after* eating) I had to get up and run around the city for an hour and then return. If they knew the real reason for my being fidgety, they wouldn't be surprised at it any more. I am glad that Alois is being so reasonable—if only it would last!—Health-wise, I am quite splendid.—If only you would just pull yourself together for once.—

I had a letter from Singer, the contents of which should interest you. I'll enclose it for you.

Also, I got a few lines from Nina regarding Hippauf. Please say hello to her for me, and tell her that I'll look around for him a little bit, but I can't do much for him because circumstances are too tight here. Maybe later.

If I'm conducting an orchestra and my glance happens on young Hippauf, I always think of Otto: how in Hippauf's presence he always put on an air of one who is superior and how *far away* he still is from being able to do anything properly.

By the way, I can imagine what sort of face he'll walk around with after my letter.

The enclosed review is of a performance of Tristan that Harris has now mounted in London[2]—Incidentally, I have another chance to *go* there this year! That would of course be a means to recover a bit from this financial disaster that I've now cleverly fallen into.

What are Fritz and Uda up to? The Löwis? What do you hear of Ernestine?

With very best wishes,
your
Gustav

Please let me know if everything is now in order with the money, whether you have enough, etc.

Shelfmark: E4-MJ-185
Notes

[1] The date of this letter is not clear, particularly given Mahler's comments about Hippauf. By the end of October, a return visit to London was doubtful; see below.

[2] Augustus Harris mounted four performances of *Tristan und Isolde* at Covent Garden between 10 October and 9 December 1892.

268 *To Justine*

[Hamburg, c. 28 October 1892][1]

Dearest Justi!
Under *no* circumstances will I allow you to become the overnight caregiver.[2]—*By all means*, bring in a *good*, reliable nurse into the house.—Please write daily, at least a postcard.

Best, in haste
Gustav

Shelfmark: E6-MJ-298
Notes

[1] Mahler's letter to Emil Freund of 28 October is very similar in content, making it likely that they were written on the same day; see GMB[2] 119.

[2] Alois had been spitting blood and was soon diagnosed with tuberculosis.

269 *To Justine*

[Hamburg, end October or early November 1892]

Dearest Justi!
I am already in possession of your comforting news, and wish from the bottom of my heart that it lasts.—Special "care" is being taken that there is a limit to everything.—

Once *again* I ask you to take on a *nurse* for the worst time, and under no circumstances will I permit you all to watch overnight.

I hope that you will follow my wishes.—In addition, go walking (at least an hour) with Emma everyday around the same time.—

Observe all of this meticulously!

Which photograph did you like best? Which one did Fritz pick? I'll also send one to the Löwi girls, who are supporting you so admirably. Just send me news everyday!

Yesterday I was invited to the *Hertz-Marcus*'s—this tells you everything.—Dinner was around 6:00.—By 8:00 I was already so wild with boredom that I ran away around 8:30.—

England is very doubtful. Nevertheless, if I have to go there, then perhaps you should come here during the spring (when it is *glorious* here—perhaps with Alois)! Of course we must wait to see what course Alois's condition takes!—If it should become necessary for him to go to the *south*, you can go with him then.

Who knows if *Merano* might not be in order.

Best wishes from your
Gustav

Otto shouldn't interrupt his studies! Emma either!

SHELFMARK: E10-MJ-442

270 *To Justine*

Postcard[1]
[Postmark: Hamburg, 3.11.92]
[Arrival postmark: Vienna, 5.11.92]

D.J.

Hopefully you have received the money; I sent you the entire amount you wanted (440 fl. in total), right? Unfortunately I had to withdraw from the bank again. Please confirm receipt of the money.

I wrote Otto. From now on, I insist that he attend school until the examination, and that he take it. Whether he succeeds or fails is all the same (or, rather is unfortunately not all the same). Write again soon.

Yours affectionately
G.

SHELFMARK: E12-MJp-490

NOTE

[1] Addressed to "Fräulein Justine Mahler / Wien / VII. Breitegasse 4 II."

271 *To Justine*

Postcard[1]
[Postmark: Hamburg, 15.11.92]
[Arrival postmark: Vienna, 17.11.92]

D.J. Just today I got Freund's letter. Now then, one must sit back and watch how Otto behaves there. I still can't quite predict whether I can come to Vienna in the course of the winter. It is scarcely probable for December, since, as you know already, my relationship with Pollini is one of loveliest discord. My health is on the best footing. I still always dine at home at noon. Let me hear something again soon. (Also, answer the question about the "day" course.)

Yours affectionately,
Gustav

Your letter just came—write tomorrow then. Today I am sending you the money that you spent for the trip (70 marks). Let me know if it is *enough*!

SHELFMARK: E4-MJp-180
NOTE
[1] Addressed to "Fräulein Justine Mahler / Wien / VII. Breitegasse 4 II."

272 *To Justine*

[Hamburg, c. 23 November 1892][1]

Dearest Justi!

Your last letter deserves special marks for diligence because of its detail, and above all because of the high spirits (or more precisely, the good health) that is reflected in it. Here it is then: mark: excellent.

I also got Alois's letter, and see from it that you all are busily pursuing French-English.

I am surprised not to hear anything from Otto about how he is getting on now.

I think that he will get through the examination after all if he pulls himself together now.—To choose the evening course was an utter *blunder*, one that absolutely cannot be excused or comprehended.—He should have gone into the day course *right away*, after all.—

Your letter of the 21st just arrived. Again pure Justi! Who is the singer, then, who has rented above you—or more precisely, what is her name?

Please just see that Otto doesn't miss a lesson, and that he does his homework.—

My stomach is performing splendidly, and *you* would be astonished at what good colour I have.—

On Thursday I conduct a new production of Joseph and his Brothers here.[2] (A splendid work, a real *chef d'oeuvre* of French art.)

Please say hello to Natalie for me. I will write her next.—Also, the photos will now finally arrive. Please let me know some time how much I have to send you on the 1st.

I am still continuing my little ablutions every morning; the effect remains excellent, and is not wearing out at all.

Best wishes to everyone
from your
Gustav

It is again *uncertain* and doubtful if I'll go to London.

SHELFMARK: S1-MJ-738
NOTES

[1] Dated on the basis of Justine's letter of 21 November. Generally it took two days for letters from Vienna to reach Hamburg.

[2] *Joseph in Ägypten* (1807, as *Joseph*) by Etienne-Nicolas Méhul (1763–1817) was first given on Thursday, 24 November.

273 *To Justine*

Postcard[1]
[Postmark: Hamburg, 24.11.92]
[Arrival postmark: Vienna, 26.11.92]

D.J.
Tomorrow you will receive a selection of my newest photos. A very large one, which the photographer made especially for me, you'll get next week; I'm dedicating it to you very specially.—Please get Fritz and have him choose one of the photos for himself, the one he likes best.—Give it to him, and if you want, I'll send you another of the same. The news about Feld pleases me greatly. I am really very devoted to her, and it troubled me not to know anything about how she was doing.—Write again soon.

Best wishes, Gustav

SHELFMARK: E4-MJp-181
NOTE

[1] Addressed to "Fräulein Justine Mahler / Wien / VII. Breitegasse 4 II."

274 *To Justine*

[Hamburg, Autumn 1892][1]

Dearest Justi!
I just received Otto's report card.—As much as it distresses me, it is not unexpected after the recent revelations.

At this point, as far as I'm concerned, in order to arrive at a decision, I must first wait for a precise and detailed explanation from you, in which I'd like to hear how *Otto himself* feels now about the matter. As far as I can see now, on the surface of it, we must completely forget about leading Otto to a one-year voluntary recruit examination [*Einjährig-freiwilligen Prüfung*].—We must let the matter go as it may.—It is certainly not out of the question that Otto might escape from a future induction into military service [*Assentirung*].[2]—If he is "*taken*", I do have a definite plan all right; I'll let you know about it sometime.

Henceforth it seems to be a question *of which* direction Otto should now *pursue*; *what should* he study! According to the law, *when* does his induction *take place*? And thus, how long does he have until then to improve in his métier, music? Would it not be advisable that he now re-enter the Conservatory! Maybe if he went back to Fuchs,[3] he would be allowed back into the class that he left the year before.—In addition, since it seems that, relatively, he shows the most talent for languages, he could learn French and English, and thus at least pick up a foundation of general education. This of course must go hand-in-hand with *reading* and familiarity with literature, etc.—Maybe Fritz could take up his private study with him again, and, pursuing just the general goals of education [*Bildung*] and intellectual stimulation, this time achieve better results.—But in any case, something must happen.[4]—

Please let me know everything that *he* thinks, what *you all* think. *Then* I will make my decision.—It is really very worrying—just be sure that you remain healthy. ~~The Michel's plan Mr. Alois~~

Best wishes,
Gustav

(Please don't let Otto get *wind* of this letter—for the time being, don't say anything to Fritz either.)

Shelfmark: E4-MJ-187
Notes

[1] The date of this letter is not clear, although it seems that Otto had failed his examination by this point.

[2] In fact, Otto was rejected for service; see below, letter 369, as well as Löhr's note 69, GMB[2], p. 441.

[3] Robert Fuchs (1847–1927), Austrian composer, organist, and conductor, taught composition at the Conservatory of the Gesellschaft der Musikfreunde. In addition to Mahler and his brother, Fuchs also numbered Wolf, Zemlinsky, Sibelius, Schreker, and Franz Schmidt amongst his students.

[4] In an unpublished portion of her memoirs, Natalie Bauer-Lechner wrote:

> [Otto] couldn't manage the preparation for the one-year voluntary recruit examination (which any idiot can do) [even] with the most expensive teachers, which G[ustav] engaged for him. . . . Later I taught Otto violin for a while—as a favour to him and G—so that at least he could serve his three years as a musician, since nothing at all came of the voluntary examination. But here too he was so unspeakably lazy and would not practice, although he knew how much for him depended on it, that I have never had to put up with worse torment in lessons. (Bibliothèque Musicale Gustav Mahler)

275 *To Justine*

Postcard[1]
[Postmark: Hamburg, 3.12.92]
[Arrival postmark: Vienna, 4.12.92]

D.J!
The message just came again—Bülow can *not* conduct, and I must be prepared! Tomorrow he might be healthy again! It doesn't matter.—I have to sit myself down again and work! The devil with it! I am glad about the good news! If only

I could also send you some too—(that is, that I am conducting the concert!). Tomorrow, of course, it has got to be decided.

Best, G.

SHELFMARK: E11-MJp-473
NOTE
[1] Addressed to "Fräulein Justine Mahler / Wien / VII. Breitegasse 4 II."

276 *To Justine*

[Hamburg, 4 December 1892]

Dearest Justi!
I just got the letters from you all. I think I read from yours that you still have a lot on your mind.—What sort of continual fears are these "that I don't like to talk things out like that"—or that "that might appear too sentimental" to me—etc.! *You* really *are an ass*![1] I simply don't like it if someone is *untruthful*; secondly, admittedly I think it best to work against *weak* feelings as quickly as possible, and above all not to fall into them.—However, if they are there at some point, why shouldn't one speak about them to a good friend (as indeed I am)? That really would be the opposite extreme! Do always say exactly what's on your mind! You need never fear that I would misunderstand something, or even make fun of it. Even if it only comes out of the *moment*, and in the next instant is already no longer true, I'll already know how to interpret it!—

Hopefully the business with Alois is happily coming to an end indeed—and it is maybe a good thing that the illness broke out *now*, while he isn't yet involved in the "world" and in "business"! The germ of illness that was just in him, *had* to come out, and it is therefore for the best that the crisis happened now, when such careful attention is paid to him in such loving surroundings.

So we will just have to hope that it will work out for the best.—He himself shouldn't be impatient! Such a disaster, which breaks over one like destiny, and for which one bears *absolutely no* blame, he will surely be able to bear *like a man*! Especially since nothing at all is lost, other than a bit of time and money.—He will make up for everything when he is healthy again. He can always be assured of *my help*, so far as I am able.—

Regarding Otto, I will sleep on the matter a few days before I make a decision. Monday or Tuesday I will then let him know my decision myself.

—Just be sure that you stay healthy.—You know that this is the most important thing of all!—And finally, don't lose heart! *Better* and *peaceful* times will come again!

Best wishes to you from your
Gustav

Say hello to the Löwis and to Fritz and Uda!

I also sent photos to *Singer* and *Deutsch* in Budapest! Out of pure interest: that is, I remember that formerly *both* offered to find a proper job for *Alois* when the time came!—Yesterday Herr *Hellmann* from Prague visited me; he's here on business.[2]—He also promised me that he could find a job for Alois at any time.

[across the top of the letter:] Hansel [*Hannsch*] von Bülow is healthy again, for a change, and is conducting the concert Monday![3]

SHELFMARK: E11-MJ-480
NOTES

[1] Mahler writes partly in English: "You are eben auch eine Ass!"

[2] Unknown.

[3] The fourth subscription concert took place under Bülow's direction on Monday, 5 December.

277 *To Justine*

[Hamburg, 6 or 7 December 1892]

D.J!
Bülow's firm cancellation for the next concert (Monday 12th) just came. It seems then, that for *certain* I'll conduct on Monday.

Therefore I am extremely busy (have to learn the program from memory).[1]—You must be patient for letters until then.—Also, I won't have a chance to write Otto before next week, and ask him, in the meantime, to do everything that Freund says.

Best wishes to all
from
Gustav

Very hurriedly!

SHELFMARK: E6-MJ-289
NOTE

[1] The program for the fifth subscription concert consisted of the Overture to *A Midsummer Night's Dream* (Mendelssohn); Lalo's *Symphonie Espagnole* and the first movement of Paganini's D Major violin concerto, played by Carl Halir (Karel Halíř, 1859–1909); Wagner's *Siegfried Idyll*; and Beethoven's Fifth Symphony.

278 *To Justine*

[Hamburg, 8 December 1892]

Dearest Justi!
The desk and bookcase just arrived (the veneer quite dull).—The *keys* to the desk *are missing*! Where are they?—Please send them right away!

—Alas! Too many gifts! The news just came that *Joachim* is singing 2 of my Humoresken at the Philharmonic Concert in Berlin on Monday the 12th (the same day that I am conducting the Bülow Concert here)![1] And I cannot be there! And neither the conductor, nor Frau Joachim knows my intentions. At the same time, my colleague *Henschel* [*sic*] has become ill, and *tonight* I have to conduct an opera that I don't know in his place—and apparently everyday, too, until he is better![2]

You all can just imagine *how* horribly worked up I am now. Before *Monday*, I won't be a human being—don't expect a letter!

Best,
Gustav

Send the keys right away!

SHELFMARK: E6-MJ-288
NOTES
[1] Amalie Joachim sang "Der Schildwache Nachtlied" and "Verlor'ne Müh'" at the fifth Philharmonic concert in Berlin, conducted by Raphael Maszkowski.
[2] Theodore Hentschel (1830–1892) died on 19 December. The unknown opera to which Mahler refers was probably Puccini's *Le villi*, which had been first performed on 2 December (not listed in Schabbing's appendix 1).

279 *To Justine*

[Hamburg, c. 10 December 1892]

Dearest Justi!
I am sending you the photo that you wanted, and one that you haven't seen yet.—Henschel [*sic*] is so ill that the outcome is doubtful! I must now continually take over his operas *without* rehearsal. Accordingly I am not "eager to write [*schreiblustig*]"!

But you write diligently!

Best wishes to everybody
from your
Gustav

SHELFMARK: E6-MJ-301

280 *To the Siblings*

[Hamburg, c. 13 or 14 December 1892]

So, dear children, for your amusement I am sending you: I. the 4 reviews by Hamburg's "Radameythes" of the local concert!—and then two little sets of words of wisdom from the Berlin "Minose," which I just got hold of now![1] You'll see—I have already found my "Herzfeld" again.[2]—The other admits at least that he perhaps must have another look at the business.—Well—Let's forget it!

About the concert here, I can also report that the public behaved marvellously, and certainly was *very* enthralled by all my artistry.—I am just happy that all the excitement is finally over.—

What sort of *English note*[3] is this from Natalie that Justi and Alois want to travel only *after* Christmas! Tell me, why not *right away*? It really makes no sense at all to put it off?!—*Don't* hesitate—go *right away* and spend Christmas in beautiful Merano![4]

Please tell Natalie about the reviews. Tomorrow I'll send Freund my photograph.

Yours affectionately
Gustav

SHELFMARK: E6-MJ-302
NOTES

[1] Schabbing, p. 292, lists three reviews from the Hamburg papers on 13 December: Krause (*Fremdenblatt*), Sittard (*Correspondent*), and Pfohl (*Hamburger Nachrichten*). Rhadamanthys and Minos were rulers of Crete and sons of Zeus and Europa, although Rhadamanthys had to flee. Owing to his honesty and fairness, he became one of the judges of the underworld; here Mahler is obviously being ironic.

[2] Mahler is alluding to his Budapest friend and supporter Viktor von Herzfeld, music critic of the *Neues Pester Journal*.

[3] Mahler's meaning is unclear.

[4] Justine and Alois were in Merano from late December until mid-April 1893 while Alois recuperated from tuberculosis.

281 *To Justine*

[Hamburg, c. 15 December 1892]

Dearest Justi!
The telegram of a good gnome [*Heinzelmännchen*], who, like all such house- or kitchen-spirits, anonymously prowl around the world for important events, told me that it's your birthday (or rather that by this time it is more or less over).[1]

Now, you will certainly know, dear Justi, that everyday I grant and wish for you all the best that the world has to offer—and how much more on your birthday, when you are really one of the most important beings, and hopefully have even received chocolate.—But I certainly won't neglect to expressly assure you of all this after the fact, otherwise you might not have known.

By the way—the keys arrived yesterday by post from Vienna. Where are the *duplicates*, in case they are lost here?—

In Merano just be sure that you do stay on the *south* side!

And in all circumstances, travel 1st or 2nd class so that you all can sleep properly.—In these situations, one just should not economise on the trip so that the stay in the new place is not spoiled right at the beginning.

Write again soon.

Yours affectionately
Gustav

What did you all say about the reviews!?

SHELFMARK: E10-MJ-439
NOTE

[1] Justine's birthday was on 15 December.

282 *To Justine*

[Hamburg, mid-December 1892]

Dearest Justi!
Yesterday I sent the money to Alois.—Please borrow what you need from him in the meantime! I'll send 500 marks to you in Merano on the 1st!—In Merano, you don't need to think about money; allow yourselves to be happy there and to become well. If the money runs out, then write me and I'll send more.

So I will send *200 fl.* to Vienna, then? Is that quite enough?

Both the photographs that I sent you've hopefully now received too!—

It just occurs to me: did you tell the doctor that as a child Alois coughed terribly and had swollen and blue fingertips, etc.? It seems to me that this is not unimportant for a possible diagnosis.—

Hopefully I really don't have to tell you about precautionary measures (especially for *the journey*). *Do not* stint *whatsoever* on *the journey*. I even think that you should travel *1st class*.—In particular, the 2nd class cars are poorly heated and ventilated.—The arrangements in 1st class are far better, and this seems to me to be very *important* for *Alois*!

You'll have good times in Merano. I *am* curious what you all will have to report *from* there.

I got Emma's report card. I am very pleased about it. I'll send it to her with the requested photograph.

Who will report to me about Vienna? I expect this, and really desire it from Emma! She should briefly report to me about *everything* that happens on a daily basis.

For today, very best wishes
from your
Gustav

What day *do you all leave*?

I take it that I should sign the *report card*.

SHELFMARK: S1-MJ-739

283 *To Justine*

[Hamburg, after 20 December 1892]

Dearest Justi!
Unfortunately I lost your address, and so do not know if you will get my letter.—At least I am happy to know that the two of you are at last situated.—Of course I am extremely curious to learn how things have turned out now.—Please tell me about Sax and Ernestine too. What sort of letters could these be that he showed you?

I am really extremely well! Just think: for about 2 months I have completely renounced all sweets (with the exception of fruit), and, at least judging from its success, this seems to me to be the most important thing for stomach problems. In addition—*moderate quantities*! Otherwise I don't deny myself anything at all—how "*difficult*"[1] that would be—enjoying everything *in moderation*!

As a consequence of a "discussion," I am on human terms with Pollini. Hopefully it will now last for a while.—

This does seem to be a good sign for Alois that so far on the first night he didn't spit up any blood. He really shouldn't grieve over the lost posts.—I guarantee it: when he is back to normal again, he'll get 10 others in its place. I will send along a few hundred marks on the 1st; if you need money again, write me in good time and another packet of money will arrive.

Be sure not to economise excessively, and *only* think of getting healthy and bright.

You may have already learned that Hentschel is dead. At my recommendation, a young Viennese Herr Erben (also a student of Epstein) was engaged in his place.[2]

Best wishes to *Sax* and Ernestine.

Yours,
Gustav

SHELFMARK: E9-MJ-413
NOTES

[1] Mahler plays on the ambiguity of *schwer*, which can also mean "heavy" or "severe."

[2] Hentschel died on 19 December and was replaced by Robert (not Franz, as given in HLG I, p. 403) Erben (1862–1925).

284 *To Justine*

[Hamburg, 25 December 1892]

Dearest Justi!

As you will see from the enclosed (which I ask you carefully to return to Papa Löwi for safekeeping), Alois sent *4000* fl. to my bank.—Since his inheritance amounted to *4300* fl., he has thus kept *300* fl. of it.—It is now *your* task to figure out what *Alois* did with *this 300 fl.* (above all, Freund should intercede).—The lad really is and remains a cross to bear; I never escape from anger and worry! Such a thoughtless fellow! Write him right away on my behalf that he should instantly make a complete and *truthful* accounting of the whereabouts of the rest, and ask him *why* he didn't tell me anything about it at our last meeting.[1]—

On Christmas Eve last night I sat around at the inn all by myself: or rather, as usual had 2 glasses of pilsner and a steak at the Vienna Café, and went to bed around 10:30 and finally had a proper sleep. Hopefully yours was more fun.

I am really looking forward to the summer. From Near Year's on, I will be terribly busy again.

Today I am invited to a very fine dinner.[2]

I am enclosing a clipping from a Berlin paper about Tolstoy's life!

Best wishes to everybody
from your
Gustav

SHELFMARK: S1-MJ-758
NOTE

[1] Since Justine and Alois were together in Merano at the time, Mahler likely made an error here.

[2] At Henriette Lazarus's home; see below, letter 285.

285 *To Justine*

[Hamburg, early January 1893]

Dearest Justi!
Today just a few lines. I am very busy. I spent Christmas Eve at [the house of] the widow of a Dr. Lazarus, an elderly woman with two equally elderly and unmarried sisters—their brother is *Dr. Schiff* from Vienna (probably in fact known by Sax).[1] It was very quiet and so I fared very well.—On New Year's Eve I was invited to a large party, also on the spur of the moment.—

Hopefully you have now received the money and my letter.—I think that you will manage with the money for the time being.—As soon as you again need more, write me 8 days beforehand. Alois should just be sensible and remember that his most important job right now is just to get well! Everything else will certainly manage by itself.—Unfortunately, I have heard nothing more about Otto! Can you not tell me anything about him?

It is too bad that you can get together so infrequently with Ernestine.—Have I already told you that I am getting along reasonably well with Pollini? This only as a consequence of a "spirited discussion," mind you, in which I risked being "vacationed."—Accordingly, I was at the point of preparing to appear suddenly at your place in *Merano*.—

Anyhow, have a look around where Alois needs to make his summer residence! (Maybe we could all be there, then!) By the way, some time soon I will also send such a picture to Ernestine, seeing that you are such a mean and resentful colleague!—

Tell me about everything diligently. Is there not dancing in Merano? (naturally only by various "accompaniments")

I greet you all warmly
Your
Gustav

The enclosed was in an English newspaper.[2]

SHELFMARK: E5-MJ-252
NOTES

[1] According to HLG I, pp. 403–4, this was Mahler's first visit at the home of Henriette Lazarus, a widow of Austrian origin with whom Mahler was to become close friends. Her unmarried sisters, Virginie and (first name unknown) Schiff, lived with her.

[2] Not found. The clipping may relate to the possibility that Mahler and the Hamburg troupe would again be engaged by Sir Augustus Harris to offer a summer season of German opera at Covent Garden, as had been the case in 1892; see letters 288 and 292, below.

286 *To Emma*

[Hamburg, c. 6 January 1893]

Dear Emma!
I received all your letters. Since, as you might imagine, I am very busy and now must write Justi all the more often since she is away, you need not make too much of it if you do not often receive an answer. Don't let this stop you from writing

me diligently and in detail, however. And above all, accustom yourself to being *completely honest* and so telling me everything *unpleasant* as well, just as Justi does.

That you are going to dance school, I approve of completely. On the other hand, I think that it is unsuitable that you go to a ball with a stranger. *First*, you have no business whatsoever going to a ball yet—you must still be patient; all that can come later.

2. If your sister, or a woman *I* know cannot go with you, then I already reject this from the outset as improper. Be so kind and focus yourself for a while longer on the academic studies that you have begun with such success.

When the proper time comes, I myself will take you to balls and go into society with you. Hopefully you'll also behave, so that our friendship will by no means be brought to an end but will instead be strengthened and made steadfast through *openness* and *truthfulness* on your part.

I wanted to know somewhat *more* about Otto's lessons and the progress of his studies. What is Freund doing?

Be warmly greeted by your brother
Gustav

SOURCE: Typewritten transcription in the Bibliothèque Musicale Gustav Mahler

287 *To Justine*

[Hamburg, 6 January 1893]

Dearest Justi!

I just received a letter from Emma in which, among other things, she writes about attending a ball "with the mother of a friend"! I answered her immediately and refused her request. I hasten to inform you as well, just in case you might have written her otherwise out of thoughtlessness.

Under no circumstances will I yet permit *Emma* to attend balls. I can hardly comprehend how such a thought could have been entertained in Vienna. A *school girl* at a ball! And in the *present* circumstances!

By the way, I'd be glad if on the days that you are unable to write in detail you would now send a postcard (quite laconically) with a brief health *bulletin* about all of you.

Today I am invited to the Marcus's.

Healthwise, I am splendid.

No more sweets!

Warmly, your
Gustav

Friday 6/I 93.

Has care really been taken to arrange *decent supervision* for Emma?

For heaven's sake, don't *muck that* up.

Such ideas clearly indicate that these Viennese dolts calmly let themselves stand around with mouths agape like the imbeciles that they are.

SHELFMARK: S1-MJ-740

288 *To Justine*

[Hamburg, 9 or 10 January 1893][1]

Dearest Justi!
The lost letter still has not reached me and seems therefore to have been read and destroyed by whoever found it. Emma seems to be indebted to you for a few things (what, I do not know), or so I conclude from many remarks in your letters.—What do you say to the new Otto affair? I am giving my assent, and only want to wish that this story just finally reaches its end in one way or another. In any case, it's the best thing for Otto, who this way will at least learn violin and clarinet, and moreover will not get entirely out of touch with his craft.

The holidays are now approaching again with huge strides. By all indications, I am *not going to London* and will therefore steam off to you on 1 June.[2]

If Alois would only be so sensible as to enjoy beautiful Merano in calmness—and you should conclusively lead the way as a good example for him!

Please write daily—at least a correspondence card!

I greet everyone warmly,
your
Gustav

SHELFMARK: E5-MJ-244
NOTES

[1] The date of this letter is not certain. I have suggested 9 or 10 January on the basis of the contents of the next letter, although the discussion of the approaching holidays could mean that it was written later in the spring.

[2] After his successful visit to London with the Hamburg troupe in May, June, and July 1892, Mahler was frequently invited to return but never did so.

289 *To Justine*

[Hamburg,] 13.I.93

Dearest Justi!
Your letter of 11.I just arrived, and with it, the one of 8/I from you that appears to have been lost. I received Jenny's letter and was really most pleased.

Hopefully you have also told her how much we have missed hearing from her, and how warmly we have always remembered her.

The business with Otto is perhaps the best that one could have done. Honestly speaking, *I* always regarded this as a solution to the problem, only *I* didn't wish to say so because, *in the first place*, I didn't want to confront our lord brother with the obvious (perhaps only to be reproached for it later) and secondly, because I was convinced that before he was completely *worn down*, he would have been too presumptuous and, in any case, would have curtly rejected everything.

I am always quite happy when I sense a little improvement in you (in Merano)—one can always clearly tell in your letters, dear Justi, how things are going.

Even if it is still difficult, please, at least [send] a postcard with brief news. Write daily.

Monday is *L'amico Fritz*.[1]

Frau Marcus always asks after you with true sympathy—she really is a friend such as one rarely encounters.

Natalie writes often; from Emma I have received about 3 letters—really the most childish content! And *that* comes from "the circle of acquaintances." No thank you! I don't want him [Otto] wasting time doing nothing.

Be greeted warmly by
your
Gustav

SHELFMARK: E5-MJ-234
NOTE

[1] Pietro Mascagni's *L'amico Fritz* (1891) received its Hamburg premiere under Mahler's direction on Monday, 16 January 1893.

290 *To Justine*

[Hamburg, 16 January 1893]

Dearest Justi!
I received the letter from you and Alois! Alois should certainly not get grey hair [over it]! All will be well again! Simply tell him that he can *always* depend on me, and if he is uneasy for his future, he should rely on me in that respect! I certainly will not leave him in the lurch!

Tonight is *L'amico Fritz* under my direction (for the first time).

I wonder, dear Justi, if you oughtn't to come to Hamburg for a few weeks when you leave Merano?—Frau Marcus always insists that you stay with her, and this would greatly simplify everything.—And for you, it might be a "recovery," and—who knows—the climate here might suit you as well as it does me. Naturally, I would not advise this before *March* or *April*!

Be warmly embraced
by your
Gustav

Enclosed, Otto's letter—it is not without comic flavour for me! So solemn and proud (for a future member of the "band")

[across the top of p. 1:] Please send Otto's letter back to me because of the account.

SHELFMARK: E5-MJ-235

291 *To Justine*

[Hamburg, c. 17 or 18 January 1893]

D.J.
Enclosed merely a "good review" of *L'amico Fritz*.—This *critic* (Pfohl) (the successor of Mirsch, who died of cholera) seems to have turned out to be a cou-

rageous "Mahlerian" after all.[1] *How long* it will last only the gods know. I am already much too accustomed to unexpected changes on the part of favourable critics to put too much stock in it. I congratulate you very much on the little gathering! I am happy how much you enjoyed yourself.—

The snag in the *Otto* affair seems gradually to have come to light again after all. I must be kept well informed about this.

More in detail soon, my dear.

Warmly,
Gustav

Hello to everyone!

Shelfmark: E5-MJ-236
Note

[1] Ferdinand Pfohl (1862–1949) was music critic of the *Hamburger Nachrichten* and a friend while Mahler was in Hamburg; he subsequently became highly critical of Mahler's compositions. See Ferdinand Pfohl, *Gustav Mahler: Eindrücke und Erinnerungen aus den Hamburger Jahren*, ed. Knud Martner (Hamburg: Verlag der Musikalienhandlung Karl Dieter Wagner, 1973). His review is not listed in Schabbing.

292 *To Justine*

[Hamburg, end January 1893]

Dearest Justi!

You still have not indicated how much I have to send *to you* in Merano on the first.—In any case, you ought not to wonder if you do not then receive the money on time. For after all I can not simply send some sum at random, but must first await [to hear] how much you require.—

In a letter that I received yesterday, Natalie gave me a hint that it might be arranged that you could finish your stay in Merano rather more cheaply. Provided that Merano is really *good* for you both, and therefore that you should stay, for many reasons I agree that you ought to look around there—Ernestine and Sax will certainly lend a helping hand—and leave the expensive pension in the foreseeable future and look for a cheaper private situation.

I just wrote to Natalie that she should suggest this to all of you, and at the same time lend you a helping hand as one who is practised in such matters.

Please write me what you think and what you intend to do about these matters.

What does the doctor say about Alois's summer residence this year?

In choosing, take care at least that it is *cheap* and restful.

So there seems to be really *nothing* with England. It is therefore to be assumed that I am with you for three months.

The more isolated and restful the place, the better it is to me. This year, I will do without society as in Berchtesgaden. However, take care that a good *friend* can be with us now and then.

This year really ought to go a little better! My relationship with Pollini is still good!

I give you all my kindest regards. The enclosed photographs are for *Ernestine* and *Sachs*.[1]

Warmly,
your
Gustav

Shelfmark: E5-MJ-245
Note
[1] Presumably, Sax.

293 *To Justine*

[Hamburg, 27 January 1893]

Dearest Justi!
Your news is now rather more comforting, and in particular, things seem to be going not too badly now. If it would do you good, stay quietly with Alois in Merano. Perhaps it would suffice to find accommodations for yourselves near Warmegg,[1] so that expenses might be cheaper. In any case, the main thing is to become completely well again.

The story of Otto's harmonisation of Sax's artistic products has amused me greatly.[2]—This professor seems to have quite the nose; Herr Schutt almost has a Russian potato on his face.[3]

By the way, is Prof. Curtius a son of the famous philologist *Curtius*?[4]

I had already heard about the novellas that you mention; they should be enchanting.

I regard *L'amico Fritz* as a decisive step forward after *Cavalleria* [*rusticana*] and am now convinced that the so-called *conductors* have again conducted the work to ruin; owing to its great subtleties, [it] is very difficult to perform. With a sympathy (which you will readily understand) for this now "failed" and ill-treated composer, I have mustered my entire personality to be successful "in the face of the rabble."—So far, this seems to have succeeded, for the work is repeated again and again owing to the growing interest of the public. By the way, *Jauner* from Vienna was at the last performance; he heard the work first under the thick-skinned Richter and then under Mascagni in the Prater.[5]—Charmingly, he repeatedly reassured me that at every moment he had believed that *Mascagni* was at the podium, so closely had I reproduced *his style* down to the tiniest detail. It is quite clear to me, too, that a *lot* of points of contact exist between Mascagni and myself.

At any rate, *here* for the first time the work had a *success*—actually, for the second time, for the performance in the Prater under Mascagni surely was also very gripping. Only in that instance it was not so easy to distinguish what is to be attributed to the personality of Mascagni, which so fascinated the Viennese.—

Incidentally, it is very nice that you all have now settled into society there a little bit, or so it seems to me.—Has Alois made some acquaintances?—By the way, you have not yet told me anything of the test results. Apparently then *no tubercles* were found? Please, write me about it.

Warmest greetings to you all
27/I 93. from your
Gustav

From Emma I received the following letter today, which I send because of its "cuteness" about you! Is it not comical? Here one is truly at a loss!

Of course I am serious about your coming here! It is merely a question of choosing a convenient time.

SOURCE: Photocopy of autograph letter sold by Alfred Rosé; now owned by Henry-Louis de La Grange. Text previously published in *Gustav Mahler Unbekannte Briefe*, ed. Herta Blaukopf (Vienna: Paul Zsolnay, 1983), pp. 112–13.

NOTES

[1] A pension in Merano.

[2] Apparently Otto had set several of Sax's poems to music. Mahler's intention to do likewise for his friend seems never to have come to pass; see GMB[2] 88.

[3] Unidentified. A Russian potato, or fingerling, is pointy, narrow, and crooked.

[4] Ernst Curtius (1814–1896) was an archaeologist—not a philologist; see letter 306 below—and professor at Berlin University; from 1844 he was tutor to the future emperor. His brother Georg (1820–1885) was a philologist and linguist. It may be Ernst Curtius's son, Theodore (1857–1928), with whom Justine was acquainted in Merano. See *Neue Deutsche Biographie*, s.v. Curtius (Berlin: Denker & Humblot, 1953–).

[5] Franz von Jauner (1831–1900) had been director of the Vienna Hofoper from 1877 to 1881, then the Ringtheater and the Karltheater. He seems to have attended the *L'amico Fritz* performance of 26 January 1893. The opera was first performed in German (under Richter) at the Vienna Opera on 30 March 1892; Mascagni conducted it (in Italian) on 15 September 1892 in the Ausstellungstheater in the Prater.

294 *To Justine*

[Hamburg, 30 January 1893]

Dearest Justi!

I just received your letter.—You seem to have misunderstood my suggestion.—It referred only to the case of a *continuing* stay in Merano—above all, *for Alois*!—It must at least be taken into account that he may have to spend a *long* time there, and in that case, he'll have to accustom himself to simpler circumstances. I really don't need to explain to you why.—Of course I naturally did not think that you ought to abandon the establishment at once.—Most probably Natalie, in her somewhat fumbling way, caused this misunderstanding.—

Now, as for yourself: as long as you really feel well there, and it is beneficial to your health, I am fully in favour of you staying there for another 7–8 weeks (until around the middle of April) and arranging for the summer house directly from there and then settling into it.

My suggestion to come to Hamburg merely arose because I thought that I discerned that you did *not* feel quite well in *Merano*. In any case, constant change is disadvantageous (and *now* especially that things seem to be going so well for all of you), so *stay*, and enjoy Merano's lovely spring.

A single obligation I put on you! Do everything for your *health* and do *not* let yourself be tyrannised by Alois, as in fact seems to me to be the case.

So—now you know what I think. Write me regularly and not always euphemistically holding back, since in the end I always guess the truth anyway, and you might have caused me unnecessary worry.

Warmly, your
Gustav

30/I 93.

SHELFMARK: S1-MJ-742

295 *To Justine*

[Hamburg, 30 January 1893]

Dearest Justi!

Ernestine's letter just *came* too! God, what eloquence!

Note
Thinking: poor
Logic: 4
Character: 1
Moral Behaviour: exceedingly worthy!

If I would only no longer be bothered by moral-methodical arguments!—Ernestine seems to have become quite an exceptional member of the "Society for the Improvement of the Morals of Dung-Beetles" and the "Establishment of Rose-Eating Amongst Bluebottle Flies."[1]

—If I say: could you not do such and such?—this is simply a question for which I await *your* answer (without some sort of sympathy) with complete confidence.—If you say to me: *no*, for *this* and *that* reason, you are reacting loyally and understandably—as, till now, you have hardly been seen to do. So: say to me, it is *one* way or the other! And that's that in the future.—If I see (or think I see) something better, then, again, I'm the sort to assert *my* view, but without wishing to *persuade* you in the least to my opinion. On the other hand, etc. etc.,—it is too boring to thresh through the same business for ever and ever.—So: in this specific instance: it is clear to me that it is better that you *stay* in the pension! So, for God's sake, stay—*without feeling guilty*. I am perfectly content to spend money if you thereby really gain health and happiness. It is silly to break off right in the *middle* of it.

Now stay there until you see a *lasting* and decisive effect—don't be stupid.

Alois should be reasonable and not indulge himself in "interesting" moods, but instead try to get well and leave *others* to get well too.—

From Budapest, he will receive 200 fl. in the next few days. I will send you 340 marks on the first, and 450 to Vienna.

So this will suffice for February. Write me, then, how much I have to send to you on 1 March (or if it doesn't suffice—*when*!)

Warmest greetings from
Gustav

30/I—At night.

SHELFMARK: E5-MJ-237
NOTE
[1] Mahler's precise meaning is not clear, although he is certainly mocking Ernestine Löhr for some perceived moral squeamishness.

296 *To Justine*

[Hamburg, early February 1893]

Dearest Justi!
I received the enclosed letter from Otto (as a response to my last one). I have just written him again and urged many things on him.—The fellow gives me such worries!

So, I sent *265 fl.* to Vienna, and 340 Mk. to you (I think that you'll get 200 fl. for it). Please let me know if this suffices for February.

Later I had to laugh again at Ernestine's emotionalism.

By the way, what kind of theatre do you have? I see from the almanac that the director is a certain *Hertzka* who was in Iglau at the time when I conducted *Boccaccio* there.[1] If you would enjoy it, go there regularly!

The enclosed letter from Mihalovich ought to interest you too.[2]

The "identity card" was supposed to serve as protection for the photographs instead of a cardboard envelope.

How is your reading going? Should I send you something or are you fairly well provided for there?

By the way, do you not think that Otto should learn some more French from Uda? About two weeks ago I got a letter from Nina concerning "arguments"—I answered her in a somewhat humorous but conciliatory manner, so that the lid is back on the pot. I just received her response as well: rather turgid and in any case without understanding the basis of our conflict. But where does one start with these people! It is almost like *Mephisto* in the second part of *Faust* who in the end, in order to save himself from the other cast members, escapes into the *proscenium* towards the public. All just to live in peace.[3] (Probably he will soon feel uneasy about it there.)

Your Gustav greets you warmly

(I learned this way of writing from Natalie!)[4]

SHELFMARK: E6-MJ-296
NOTES
[1] Mahler conducted Franz von Suppé's *Boccaccio* in Iglau on 19 September 1882. Hertzka is unidentified.

[2] This letter appears not to have survived but may be a response to Mahler's of 17 January 1893; see Roman, *Gustav Mahler and Hungary*, pp. 156–58.

[3] Mahler is alluding to the episode after Faust's death when Mephistopheles is forced into the proscenium by the angels strewing roses petals, which burn as they touch him. While he is so distracted, the angels bear away the immortal part of Faust (Goethe, *Faust* II, *ll.* 11676–844).

[4] The last lines are written upside-down across the top of the second page of the letter, and the last few words are written right-side up across the top of the first page.

297 *To Justine*

[Hamburg, early February 1893]

Dearest Justi!

My last letter is still unanswered.—Nevertheless, your last letter in which you wrote of your intentions regarding your return to Vienna provided a combination of prospects.—

It is not so unreasonable, what you suggest there.—You could really see after all that Emma has *proper* accommodation, and since Otto will have reported for military service, you could join me in Hamburg, where we could then both establish ourselves *bachelor-style* in a good pension and await the further development of things.—You would certainly find stimulation and society here, and it would simplify everything greatly.—*Strictly between ourselves*, I have already had the feeling that the circle of friends in Vienna has become rather "heated" for you just now. There are certainly some "diverse cloths" together there.

And to even let yourself be enslaved by the silly household is really not necessary. You could simply send the furniture to the *custom's office* where, like me, it can likewise happily await the development of my affairs. And if I ever am *stable* again, then we can have the furniture calmly join us.—It only remains to worry about Alois! And in fact, I will now look around to see if I might not find a position for him in the south.—Please *ask the doctor* immediately what *Buenos-Aires* in *South America* is like, and whether he recommends residence there for him for the next few years.—Coincidentally, I have some contacts there now, and might be able to arrange a position for him.

What's up with *Cairo*?

However long you want to remain in Merano, please make sure that it depends only on whether the stay is pleasant or not! If it is doing you good, then don't worry about staying as long as you like: and *get well* again at last! Nursing duties must now have their end! I will no longer tolerate it.

Write me about it.

If you have found a summer residence, then you could come here for a few weeks in April or May if need be, and we'll *leave* together for the holidays.

Your Gustav greets you warmly

Write to Frau Marcus sometime, she really deserves it!

[across top of p.1:] Is Frau *Ellmenreich* not there now?[1] If this is the case, please give her my kindest regards.

Shelfmark: E5-MJ-239

Note

[1] Franziska Ellmenreich (1847–1913) was a well-known German actress particularly famous for the pathos of her acting style. She enjoyed great success in the roles of Joan of Arc, Maria Stuart, Sappho, and Iphigenie, and was based in Hamburg from 1887 to 1892, again in 1894, and from 1901 to 1912 (*Neue Deutsche Biographie*, ed. Historische Kommission bei der Bayerischen Akademie der Wissenschaften, s.v. "Ellmenrich, Franziska").

298 *To Justine*

[Hamburg, between 6 and 12 February 1893]

Dearest Justi!
Please go to the theatre as often as you like.—I regard Ellmenreich extremely highly as well, and can imagine that you would enjoy seeing her. Have you already met her somewhere? Would you have an opportunity to do so? If not, seek her out—she is a marvellous woman—and also give her my kindest regards. We have often encountered each other here in society.—Brahms has been here for a few days (he visited me as well) and is again enormously friendly with me.[1]—Tomorrow I am invited to an *intimate* dinner with him at Petersen's.

Hopefully Bertha has given notice for the apartment—in any case I have just written her about doing so.[2]

I constantly hear the most infuriating things about Otto.—Even the other day I received a letter from him which goes well beyond the youthful insolence he has managed up to now!—Well—you all brought him up beautifully together! He will experience a *bitter school* of life! I am quite worried that the fellow will *spoil* my holidays this year, [and] I am looking forward to them tremendously.—I'm still thinking that you should come visit me here in May, if the situation is favourable, and then we'll leave together.

Please, *write daily*!

Warmly,
Gustav

SHELFMARK: E6-MJ-295
NOTES

[1] According to Renate Hofmann and Kurt Hofmann, *Johannes Brahms Zeittafel zu Leben und Werk* (Tutzing: H. Schneider, 1983), p. 220, Brahms was in Hamburg between 6 and 12 February 1893.

[2] Mahler's letter survives in the Mahler-Rosé Collection (E12-MC-509):

> Dear Bertha,
> I just received a letter from Justi in which I was asked to give my assent that we give notice for our apartment for the February deadline (which goes until the 12th).
> Here it is (the assent!)
> Give the notice! For the rest, everything is still hanging very much in the balance.—Justi seems to have her old condition again. I despair to think that even *this* sort of nonsense is not at an end. Thank you very much for "mothering" the two savages [*Wildlinge*]. I have enough to annoy me here, far away.
> Write me sometime, and chat a bit.—Give my best wishes to *Papa, Fritz, Louise, and Uda.*
>
> Ever yours,
> Mahler

299 *To Justine*

[Hamburg, February 1893]

Dearest Justi!
So I just wrote Bertha that she should give notice for the apartment (in case she has not done so), and so the die is now cast!

You must insure that we choose a spot for the summer with a decent but not too expensive inn nearby, so that you don't have to worry about the *midday meal*. Remember how much you had to rush about last year.

—What's this again about your condition? Is Merano not helping you *at all*?—I still don't know whether Hamburg wouldn't be as healthy for you as it is for me. At least my stomach gets better all the time. I eat with great appetite.

As far as Budapest is concerned, you can well imagine that I would not think of going back there [even] in my sleep![1] However, I shall carefully guard against pronouncing that just now. No! I want them to come to me first and make me an offer. Only *then* will my *triumph* be complete! *What sort of answer* they will get, you can just imagine.—

Of course, just as nothing can be determined in advance, so too it is as regards whether I will be in a position to behave in reaction to an offer as I currently plan to.—It might happen sometime that I would be without a post again, and then I might be forced, just as in '88, to say *Yes*.—

I still do not know *Rantzau*, and so can say nothing about it.[2] Do not tell anyone anything of my views about Budapest.

Please always write truthfully about your condition, and without concealing anything from me.

Emma's letter is enclosed!

She's always the same.

I greet you warmly, as well as Alois and Ernestine and the Sachses too.[3]

Gustav

SHELFMARK: S1-MJ-759

NOTES

[1] Given Zichy's difficulties at the Opera in January and February 1893 (after the government changed in November 1892), it may be that a faction from Budapest had approached Mahler about returning there. If so, this letter is the sole surviving piece of documentary evidence. See Roman, *Gustav Mahler in Hungary*, pp. 141–49, 155.

[2] *I Rantzau* is a one-act opera by Pietro Mascagni, first performed in Florence in 1892. It would receive its Hamburg première under Mahler on 19 April 1893.

[3] Mahler probably means the Saxes.

300 *To Justine*

[Hamburg, 11 February 1893]

Dearest Justi!

Today for your entertainment I am sending you the letters from the two Viennese "frogs."[1]—To Alois, I'm also sending 100 fl., just as you indicated. He asked for *300*. Please explain this to him, and tell him that I must urge *the greatest* economy. On all possible grounds.

Have you already written Frau Marcus? The tidying up of the house business and Emma's board I forthwith leave *to you*! Natalie is much too *irregular* for such things, and you are entirely right not to listen too much to her "advice."—In the end, what sort of blessing has she gained by her "freedom"? These really are very risky articles of faith on which she has based her existence! It seems to me that they are shaky everywhere, and will only get worse.—

About Otto, I am now absolutely at my wit's end! It's an awful shame about the boor! Incompetent, ignorant, and respectful of no one![2] What is there to do? The "lash" in the military might perhaps do it! *I* give up! From afar, where I can't supervise and restrain, these women have only made him completely crazy: Nina, with her "understanding," and Natalie with her unbelievable "firmness." I think that you should *not* send him my *letters*, and make it quite clear to him that I know *everything about him*. And that I know about his wanton thoughtlessness as well, and also that he strikes such a presumptuous tone in his letters to me, and—*despite* the fact that he denies it—is so insincere towards me, that I am very angry about it all.

——How extraordinary: the postman just arrived and gave me Emma's last letter (of 9 February).[3] I am furious at Otto! Please, write Emma immediately that from now on nothing happens without *me* or you consenting *beforehand*.—

Natalie seems not much concerned about our house—How about the Löwi girls? Do they not care either? Please, if at all possible, arrange something about these matters.

Warmly, your
Gustav

Your most recent letters sounded like you are cheerful once again. I am enormously pleased! It is really high time that you just come out of this "frog" state once and for all.—

For a while I was *hoarse* and made a humorous comment about it, thus Emma's concern. Of course, I got better ages ago.

SHELFMARK: E5-MJ-251

NOTES

[1] Otto and Emma. In an unpublished section of her memoirs, Natalie Bauer-Lechner records that "with good-natured, brotherly humour, he used to call [his siblings] 'riffraff' or 'frogs'."

[2] Mahler uses almost the identical phrase in a letter to Bertha Löhr from around this time; see notes to letter 301.

[3] See below, letter 301. (It took two days for letters from Vienna to reach Hamburg.)

301 *To Emma*

[Hamburg, 12 or 13 February 1893]

Dear Emma!

I was very angry as well that Otto highhandedly took a stranger into the apartment without asking me, and it was very right of you that you went to sleep at Nina's. As Bertha has since told me, Letitzky was there only one night.[1] I hope that your studies were not disturbed by it. By the way, why didn't you tell me anything about it? This is just the thing that I am interested in.—How long does your school year last? I would like to know this because I have to make my arrangements for the summer accordingly.—

I was displeased to discover that you are not on the best footing with the Löwis. The reason for this must be the same one that is to blame for the fact that you always wait for an answer from Justi before you write back: in other words, you often completely misunderstand your own standpoint.

You are still not completely "grown up"—and even if you were, this would not stop you from behaving modestly and considerately towards your older sister and girl friends.—You would then see that this would have pleasant consequences for you too.—This is an old fault of yours, and I will not deny that it has already become better; however, if you would take my advice to heart, then learn over time to be *modest* and *considerate* towards others. I *do not know* what would become a girl or a woman more.—That your studies are taking such a good course pleases me greatly, and gives me hope that, in the end, a "solid human being" will yet emerge from you.—

With warmest greetings (also to Papa Löwi, as well as to *Bertha* and *Luise* [*sic*]), I am

your brother
Gustav

SOURCE: Typewritten transcription in the Bibliothèque Musicale Gustav Mahler
NOTE

[1] Unidentified. A letter to Bertha Löhr, written around this time, survives in the Mahler-Rosé Collection (E12-MC-510):

Dear Bertha!

I just learned from Emma that she had to move to Nina's because Otto took Letitzky into the apartment! Please telegraph me briefly *immediately* if this is true. In order to take steps, I would like to find out at once whether this is the case. My God, how could you agree to such a thing!?

I had never imagined that I would be given such a cross to bear with the boy! *Incompetent, ignorant, and respectful of no human being*! No consideration towards any one! I am beside myself!

Warmly,
Gustav

Please, telegraph immediately, *only not* so that the telegram arrives in the middle of the night.

302 *To Justine*

[Hamburg, mid-February 1893]

Dearest Justi!
That Merano has such a good effect on you pleases me greatly! *It really does not trouble me* about the money, so, now that you are there, do not be prevented from staying into April as long as you wish.

The whole Mascagni fuss is getting to be too much. To him himself, the thing seems *not* to be so loathsome. Can you believe it, that this is what someone who doesn't like such situations does? At any rate, this shines a questionable spotlight on the young man.[1] Well, we will soon see!—We have time!—

For three weeks Natalie has taken the greatest pains to prove the "immortality of the soul" to me! Power to her! Otto, on the other hand, in his last letter, disclosed to me that there is *no God*, certainly not a righteous one! And I, the heretic, stand between the two (both naturally are convinced that they have made a great impression on me) and say: you're both right; that is, I have tried to show Natalie my way of thinking, of course without success. I am curious what you all will think of my summer plans.—From Bertha I still have no acknowledgement of *receiving the money*—and *neither from you*! God damn it!—As well, I do not know whether Bertha has enough (200 fl.). Did *Alois* receive *100* [florins] on 15 February?[2] Answer my questions, otherwise I'll stop writing at all. By all means buy Ernestine an *attractive* umbrella. I am certainly very curious for once to get to know you as a *healthy* human being.—I hope that I will seem "very together"!

Warmly, your
Gustav

Shelfmark: E5-MJ-242
Notes

[1] The details of the "Mascagni affair" are not clear at present. The last performances of *L'amico Fritz* took place on 12 February in Hamburg and 3 March in Altona.

[2] See above, letter 300.

303 *To Justine*

[Hamburg, mid-February 1893]

Dearest Justi!

Unfortunately, you seem to be right about Natalie: that after so many of the most serious tests she has not yet become "reasonable" is connected with the wholly *one-sided* development of her being; in every one of her actions, one can discern an unfortunate predominance of her desire over her reason.—Already during the summer I made it perfectly *clear* to her solely in what sense a friendly and comradely relationship between us could be imagined. Unfortunately, she did not take the right lesson from it. She lacks the sensitivity, and just as this has always severely tripped her up, it seems once again to have led to a "catastrophe," because a week ago she stopped writing me. I would have thought a woman capable of more tenderness of feeling. Maybe I've offended her with my indifferent reception of her philosophical musings about the "immortality of the soul" (which she insists on proving to me). Since I have already passed the stage during which one always tries to force agreement with others on such subtle things, and for my part would rather leave every man to his own God if only he leaves me to mine, so naturally I was unable to reply to her exposition in the histrionic tone in which it was delivered, and finally brought about the end of the debate with a rather charitable metaphor. This may have been too much—Since before she was always very demanding of an immediate response to her philosophical musings, in this respect it can only be agreeable to me to be relieved of such a grandiloquent exchange of letters. It is now once again up to you to give recompense to the one hurt, and in the end build a bridge once more over which the hostile parties may wander back and forth over the dangerous abyss. Naturally, *I* am not "*angry*"!

As far as your coming here next year is concerned, again I propose that you visit me here for a few days just before the holidays and have a look around.

I even consider this *necessary*, so that you see things with your own eyes and so that at our leisure we can take the right measures for a companionable residence—it's necessary to look for a comfortable *Pension*, to initiate ties to society, etc.—

Please write me what you think about it. Or *have you given it up*? Your vigour pleases me greatly. If it only would be firmly established!—Well, at least we now know where and how you will regain your health, if ever you should be "brought low" again.—

Many greetings to you all!

Was the *200* fl. enough for Bertha? This time, please send a precise estimate in *time* before the next *first of the month*.

Warmly, your
Gustav

Shelfmark: E11-MJ-479

304 *To Justine*

[Hamburg, mid-February 1893]

Dearest Justi!

I am *very against* your leaving Merano as long as the weather in Vienna has not become *really warm*. You would see that you would quickly lose all of the improvements to your health again as soon as you caught a chill.—Just ask the doctor there; he will probably confirm that. So don't be careless. Natalie (who, moreover, only [now] is writing again) will recognise that too. I *do not* think that you should *depart* before the middle of April. This year I have to stay here until the *middle of June*, so there is still enough time for you to possibly come here. So think about it. You can stay with the *Marcuses*, although I will still think that over.—Please, drop them a few lines again; these people are so unbelievably nice to me, and deserve it.

Your Gustav warmly greets you

I am also writing my opinion today to Natalie.

Shelfmark: E6-MJ-297

305 *To Justine*

[Hamburg,] 23./II 93

Dearest Justi!

So, Alois will be sent 350 fl. from the bank in Budapest, and I'll send you *200 fl.* on 1 March. Now, please *indicate* to me *immediately* how much I ought to send *to Vienna*! Why must I always ask you this every month? It really is extremely annoying. You could simply indicate on a card *how much* I have to send, and *to where*.—

Furthermore, I sent Alois 170 Mk = 100 fl. on 15 February; did this package arrive? Please confirm!—

I am afraid from your terse way of expressing yourself in your last cards that you are again *unwell*? Is that so?

For such a "dreaded" author like me, it is always very flattering to hear that my songs are received so well. I always want to express my admiration to those whom my compositions please! Recently they even pleased a musician here. I was quite touched![1]—

Enclosed, another letter which is the answer to my answer.—It will amuse you, to a certain extent. I wrote him [Otto] again about it (where should one begin?)—once again seriously and lovingly, if also very decisively—told the truth and "made my position clear." If this letter is fruitless, then enough with him! The military will clear up his wildness.—

Anyhow, however, my letter seems at least to have had the effect (according to Natalie) that the fellow now practices diligently and no longer spends his nights out of the house. You will be interested in the passage in the letter where he says that *now* he would have taken the examination if someone had allowed him to repeat the course, as he wanted to. What do you say to that?

Just think! Natalie has the awkward plan to come here at Easter.[2] Now, as you know, nothing is more abhorrent to me than the *talk* that is created on such grounds—especially now that you might spend next winter here with me, I'd like such gossip out of the way. It is embarrassing for me to have to ask her not to visit here.

It is really gratifying that you have found such an agreeable companion in Prof. C[urtius]. You seem to get on very well with him.

Many comments in Otto's letters (like the distinction between "fatherly and brotherly" love or the "contempt of art and science") will be incomprehensible to you and are in fact proof of how poorly Otto can read.—

Please write regularly, i.e. daily! Kind regards to Ernestine and the others.

Warmly, your
Gustav

As well, you'll receive another letter from Deutsch in Budapest.[3]

SHELFMARK: E10-MJ-436

NOTES

[1] Mahler is quite likely referring to his early songs, published the year before by Schott. It is possible that the musician he mentioned was J. B. Foerster.

[2] Easter Sunday fell on 2 April in 1893.
[3] According to letter 89, Singer's father.

306 *To Justine*

[Hamburg, end February 1893]

Dearest Justi!

I wrote Otto a serious letter today as well; naturally, I expect my *words* to have no effect. He might be melancholy, misunderstood, and restless for a few days, but then will be his old self again.—

One can't deny that his education in Vienna was ruined right from the beginning. Fritz, on the one hand, the girls on the other (Nina especially) have completely twisted him. One must just hope that his good predisposition and the bit of "Mahler-ness" that lies hidden in him will yet turn everything around for the best.

Tell me sometime whether one might honour Ernestine with a small gift? Perhaps something from me might please her.

How very lucky that you have found Prof. Curtius such an *agreeable* companion, since you seem to me to have been anxious and fidgety in Merano at the beginning.—By the way, if he is Professor in Kiel, he must then be a son of the famous *archaeologist* Curtius, who was Professor at the Berlin University and the teacher of Kaiser Friedrich.[1]

I enclose some letters from King Ludwig to Wagner, which provide a moving and at the same time shocking contribution not only to Wagner's biography but also to the natural history of humanity.[2] So writes a man, who twenty years later could no longer see himself among human beings.—What all must have happened in these twenty years that such a warm heart shut itself off and in the end had to sink into madness.—Just note—it must be much more difficult for a king to be a *human being* these days than for the others.

So, I send Alois 340 fl. on 1 March, and how much to you? Please let me know in time!

At any rate, you seem to be quite cheerful now! Hopefully it will continue!

How much then does Alois still owe?

Warm greetings to you, as well as to Ernestine, the *Saxes* and Alois

Your

Gustav

Shelfmark: E10-MJ-414

Notes

[1] See above, notes to letter 293.

[2] I have been unable to trace these letters. According to the catalogue of Wagner's letters, which includes a detailed listing of where letters were first published (including newspapers), nothing appeared in 1893; see the *Chronologisches Verzeichnis der Briefe von Richard Wagner. Wagner-Brief-Verzeichnis* (*WBV*), ed. Werner Breig, Martin Dürrer, and Andreas Mielke (Wiesbaden: Breitkopf and Härtel, 1998).

307 *To Justine*

[Hamburg, 2 March 1893]

Dearest Justi!

So, you really are well!? Then how very fortunate that you went to Merano.—

Only, now that you're just there, do not impose any constraints on the possible extension of your stay.—This Frl. Fritze, the painter, has already written that she met you.[1]

The house of which she spoke—that of Dr. Lazarus's widow, Frau Lazarus and her unmarried sisters, all three between 40 and 50 years old—is the one here that I visit most often (especially recently). They are very cultured and kind ladies, who lead a kind of bachelor's life and have become very good friends of mine.—If you visit, I would introduce you there above all.—I wrote to Singer in Budapest ages ago about Alois, but have not received an answer yet.—He'll have to look around himself too.—Perhaps one might be able to get something right away through Matscheko?

Otto should really be more manageable now. I still have no answer to my last letter, but I hear from the perceptive Nina that my speech has made an *impression* on him.—If only the poor fellow did not have the military in front of him, I would have no doubt that the must would yet yield a wine.

—So, Prof. Curtius must be a son of the *historian*, archaeologist, now living in Berlin? I am astonished that you are now dining with him! From your comments, I had concluded that you associated with each other in a friendly fashion at other times. His visit, if he passes through Hamburg, will be very agreeable to me.

—As of today, I have still not received a bill from Vienna, so I sent 200 fl. just in case. Can it *not be arranged* that every month, at the *right time*, I receive the details about how much I have to send? Also, you have acknowledged neither the packet from *15 February* nor the two from 1 March.

The day before yesterday I was at a party with *Rubinstein*.[2] It was very interesting—he played whist and every now and then the whole party looked through a peephole (through a crack in the door that leads into the gaming room) with admiration at his large hands, which can play the piano so exceptionally.—

In her last letter Natalie declared herself very hurt that I continue to ignore her plans to visit at Easter. Today I have finally told her the truth! It is strange that she, who otherwise possesses such healthy common sense, has almost no *delicacy of feeling* and cannot negotiate the *risky obstacles* in society, which is quite dangerous for women.—You still have not told me what I could send to Ernestine. I would like very much to render her a small gift and I would best like to chose something that she really needs.

I greet you all warmly
Your Gustav

2/II 93 [*sic*]

SHELFMARK: E5-MJ-238

NOTES

[1] Unidentified.

[2] Anton Rubinstein (1829–1894), the Russian composer, pianist, and conductor, was in Hamburg to conduct the eighth subscription concert (an all-Rubinstein program) on Wednesday, 1 March 1893. On the party, which took place at Henriette Lazarus's, and Mahler's supposed antipathy to Rubinstein, see Ferdinand Pfohl, *Gustav Mahler: Eindrücke und Erinnerungen aus den Hamburger Jahren*, ed. Knud Martner (Hamburg: Karl Dieter Wagner, 1973), p. 53.

308 *To Justine*

Postcard[1]
[Postmark: Hamburg 13.3.93]
[Arrival postmark: Meran 15.[3].93]

D.J!
Here some *spring* has finally arrived—in consequence, I am lazy about writing. Things are splendid. I am happy that you are well. Stay as long as you like!

Best greetings
from your
G.

SHELFMARK: E11-MJp-474
NOTE
[1] Addressed to "Fräulein Justine Mahler / Meran (Tyrol) / Obermais, Pension Warmegg."

309 *To Justine*

[Hamburg, 23 March 1893]

Dearest! I just received your letter in which you announce your departure on *Thursday* (thus, today)—and one from Natalie in which she indicates your rendezvous for *Good Friday*![1] Whatever will happen in the end? Please, be reasonable and *don't* try to do *too much*! In particular, undertake nothing in *cold* weather! And don't *over-exert* yourself in *Vienna*! Let *nothing* lead you astray in that regard.—

Since it is difficult for me to obtain money in the middle of the month, I ask you then to do what you indicated in your letter. I will then send Alois 400 fl. and as much as you have already indicated to all of you in Vienna.

If you have not yet said anything to Natalie, absolutely do not do so (about your trip to Hamburg in May)—It would of course not suit me if she came with you. For various reasons: above all, though, because I cannot burden the Marcuses with you both and you would have to stay with Natalie in an expensive hotel, whereas you will be so splendidly looked after by very kind people in the Marcuses' imposing home.—I am curious how long your improvement will last. So, Alois is staying in Merano until the middle of June, when he can join us in the country?—How will you then arrange things for Otto and Emma?

So finally Natalie actually won't be coming with us for the entire holiday?

I am still hoping to obtain a decent space of time from you in Merano.
Special greetings to Ernestine and the Saxes.

Warmly, your
Gustav

23/III 93.

Ellmenreich is appearing here throughout May, so you can see her a few times and perhaps also get to know her in person.—I was recently together with her at a party and passed along to her how much you would have liked to introduce yourself to her.

I received the following letter from Frau Bülow in thanks for a wreath (with a splendid inscription) that I sent Bülow at his first public appearance.[2]

SHELFMARK: E3-MJ-126
NOTES

[1] 31 March. Given the following letter (310), it is quite possible that this rendezvous was set to search for a summer vacation spot.

[2] The subscription concert of 20 March 1893 (all-Beethoven program) was Bülow's first appearance in public following the illness that forced him to turn several concerts over to other conductors (including Mahler). This was his last subscription concert before his death the following February.

310 *To Justine*

[Hamburg, early April 1893]

Dearest!
I've just come from Frau Dr. Lazarus and her sisters.—We are all agreed to spend the *summer* in the *same* place, if it's possible.—So please look around where you are renting for *me* to see if there isn't also a nice four-room (or so) apartment to be had for the 3 ladies—and tell me about it in detail. Arrange the business so that possibly everything for Frau *Lazarus* can be arranged by writing.—To me it would seem very agreeable: the 3 would be *very* well suited to us, and it also would be of the highest importance for you as a *starting point* for Hamburg. Please, all of you make an effort towards this end!

See to it that the *location* is absolutely *beautiful* and *mountainous*—and above all that there's *water*! (for swimming!)

Best
Gustav

SHELFMARK: E10-MJ-434

311 *To Justine*

[Hamburg, early April 1893]

Dearest Justi!
First, the latest: the *Singers* from Budapest visited me for *one* day.—Naturally I "fêted" them.—They really seem to have made such a long trip in order to visit me.

Alois already told me about his summer plans.—So, do you think that this is reasonable for him too?—Just write him that I am quite in agreement.—The place on the Attersee seems to be a marvellous choice. If the gods don't make short work of it, it will be a pleasant summer for us. I am already looking forward to bathing and rowing.—The steamer connection is also marvellous, particularly for *bad* weather; I have a number of acquaintances in Unterach with whom we might do things.—

It would be *very* good and I would be glad if we could find an apartment near *us* for the *Lazarus* women I wrote you about.—You will certainly get to know them here; they are the ones with whom I associate the most, and who would be a great resource for *you*, if you were here next year.

Just don't dally in Vienna! When must all of you move out? And how will you arrange the whole apartment question? About when are you planning to come here?

So, you are opposed to Emma's living with Nina? Probably because of N's poor health? Please say hello to her for me. I am *far too* tied down to be able to write.—Please let me have news about *Freund*; I haven't heard anything of him for a long time, just that he was in *Meran* a few days ago. *What was he doing there*? Please be sure to answer this question!

As of now, I owe Natalie *122* fl.! Ask her if this is right. I hope to be able to give it back to her before the holidays.

Enclosed, a letter from Mihalovich.

Best wishes to you from
your
Gustav

How is Emma doing now with her studies?

Today I received a telegram from Natalie that again leads me to fear "intermezzi." I am curious what will become of it.

I too have heard here about this *job*-placement *society*. Shall *I* do something in that regard?

SHELFMARK: S1-MJ-743

312 *To Justine*

[Hamburg, early April 1893]

Dearest Justi!

I just received a second letter from Natalie regarding the apartment on the Attersee!—According to it, you did receive a rather detailed letter from me in which I communicated my views about it.—Anyhow—do what you both think best—I will be content with everything.—Hopefully you have already received the printed material I sent.

Say hello to Natalie; and give her my warmest thanks for her kindness.—I have so much to do these days, especially with these matters. I have now done everything about it that was in my power.

Best wishes from
Gustav

[across top of letter:] How is it then with *Otto* this summer? Can he come—or what do you all think about it? Please let me know about it in detail.

What is Freund up to?

SHELFMARK: E3-MJ-143

313 *To Justine*

[Hamburg, 12 April 1893]

Dearest Justi!
I am quite astonished that I am without any news of you all.—Hopefully Otto received my letter.

It is a trial that the boy has lived all along without any *external* firmness and restraint.—At any rate, he has not become acquainted with the "force of external circumstances" and will *bitterly* repent this.—His plan is such a silly [and] immature piece of work that one really must be familiar with this *impudence* in order to believe such a thing. So he, who so far to me has *very* little *ability* and even less *wisdom*, and absolutely no experience in practical matters, and who moreover is supposed to be *inducted into the military* in the fall, "is founding" a society with grandiose, crazy plans.—And for that *I* am supposed to hand over 200 fl. at once (200 fl. *of all things*?). I would like to meet these people who have rediscovered themselves as an "established assembly"—In exchange for it, piano and violin practising would be abandoned.—They are out of the question in view of such weighty events. He still has no *respect* for others. He never asks anybody. Whatever he does not like, he "misunderstands."—However, *my* tolerance is at an *end*—or actually it will now begin. *I am saying nothing* more! I am abandoning him to his colossal flight for the time being.

I am certainly not handing out any *money*! And if he imagines for instance that I would spread roses over his military path, he is gravely mistaken! He will serve on *at the expense of the military* (apart from the fact that I doubt anyway that one *not* serving for a single year can serve at his own expense), in addition to which I would give him a little subsidy, as I did for Alois. He should *not count* on more!

Tell him that!

Please, just don't *overexert* yourself now (since I am convinced that you have immediately plunged in over your head and shoulders, and already look like a frog again); *take care* of your health.

Enclosed, a letter from Bruckner about the performance of his mass.[1] Also one from Alois; I am in complete agreement with him. What is this about *93* fl.?

Is this not another swindle? I thought that I paid the doctor's fee already?

Write soon! Say hello to the Löwis.

Warmly, your
Gustav

12/IV 93.

SHELFMARK: S1-MJ-745
NOTE
[1] Bruckner's letter of 7 April survives in the Mahler-Rosé Collection (E5-CM-261). It was published in facsimile and discussed in Andrea Harrandt, "'Gustav Mahler. O! mögen Sie nur der Meinige bleiben . . . ': Unbekannte Briefe zu zwei Aufführungen von Bruckners Te Deum in Hamburg," in *Gustav Mahler: Werk und Wirken. Neue Mahler-Forschung aus Anlaß der Internationalen Gustav Mahler Gesellschaft*, ed. Erich Wolfgang Partsch (Vienna: Vom Pasqualatihaus, 1996), pp. 50–63.

314 *To Justine*

[Hamburg, 15 April 1893]

Dearest Justi!
First: Regarding packing, arranging the furniture, souvenirs etc., I leave it all to you.—Do as you will.—I would only like to give you particular advice to take *absolutely* nothing if at all possible—not even the desk. At the most, a picture or a similar treasured keepsake that one can easily transport *to* and *fro*, since for the time being we must be prepared for an unsettled life and such baggage is very arduous. It is much better if one keeps oneself entirely free of such inconveniences.—

Sooner or later something really must be determined about my future residence. Either I stay in Hamburg (which would *not* be very agreeable to me because of the circumstances in the theatre) and then we must set ourselves up here and have everything sent once and for all, or I leave here and in that case one cannot yet know under what circumstances.[1] It is also possible that you might not feel comfortable here and want to go to Merano again, or Vienna, for a while. So it is quite good *not* to carry baggage with you!

2. As for Emma, I also leave everything to you. Only, after what you told me about Nina, I am *decisively* against you sending her to her. Another solution absolutely *must* be found. If that is out of the question, if worse comes to worse, send her to the Löwis again for a year.

Naturally I would *pay* them and *not* perchance ask for a *reduction* of my *debt*. You should reassure her about it in conversation, since she possibly might be somewhat worried and emotional about it.

3. About Otto: I also leave everything to you. Offer him a monthly allowance, but above all arrange the entire *business of being declared fit for military service* before you leave Vienna—also that he enters at *state expense*, otherwise he'll trick us again. It is absolutely *out* of the question that I take him on my back *for three years* now under such expensive conditions, since one just *cannot know anything* of the shape that my possible *departure* from Hamburg in a year might take, and in no circumstances do I want to feel obligated *again thereby* to pitch my tent again only because of how much money I'd earn—apart from the fact that this doesn't always *succeed*! So I ask you to make *this clear* to him. Hopefully he himself will understand and govern himself accordingly.

4. About the trip: it's very nice that you are going to Iglau with Natalie first. But since to catch the direct train to Berlin and Hamburg you would have to board in the *middle* of the night, I suggest that first of all you go from *Iglau* to *Prague*, *stay over night* there, and from there take the direct train to *Berlin*, where *I* myself might be able to meet you.

However, I *do not* accept your refusal [to send] regular news, but insist on §11 "one will go on drinking"—or rather, will go on writing.[2]

Warmest greetings from your
Gustav

15/IV 93 Tomorrow is the malefactor's benefit performance![3]

SHELFMARK: S1-MJ-746

NOTES

[1] Mahler's contract in Hamburg was due to expire in 1894.

[2] Mahler's meaning is unclear.

[3] See below, letter 315.

315 *To Justine*

[Hamburg, 18 April 1893]

Dearest Justi!

Thank God, the benefit performance is over.[1]—*Sold-out house* (which finally allows me to pay the *1000* mk. debt that has accumulated in recent months). Massive applause. Reviews are enclosed. Sittard, my infernal judge, was not there out of *cowardice*.[2] 27 wreaths, including a superb one from Bülow with the inscription:

to the Pygmalion of the Hamburg Opera,
in sincere admiration, Hans von Bülow.

Terrible hangover—three whole days chucking out flowers and wreaths. Nausea faded at last. Room again without droppings, desk in order—me too. Today the *Rantzau* dress rehearsal;[3] treadmill in full operation.

—From Alois the following letter: what do you say to the "*450 gulden*" he asks for? If you also think that it is too much too, then please write him about it in my name! Still always the thoughtless rogue!—

I am pleased about your continual good health! Just keep it up, and do not work yourself to death.

Your Gustav greets you warmly

Say hello to Natalie! When the confusion is past, I will write more!

Did you get Tilda's *wedding announcement* from Wlaschim?[4] Should we not send a wedding gift! I would have done so already, if I knew what to send and were not so *broke* as well!

SHELFMARK: E3-MJ-127

NOTES

[1] At his benefit performance on 15 April, Mahler conducted Beethoven's Symphony No. 5 and *Fidelio*.

[2] Joseph Sittard (1846–1903) was the critic for the *Hamburger Correspondent*. His initial support for Mahler soon turned to enmity. (See the first note to letter 280 for an additional perspective on the "infernal judge" comment.)

[3] The premiere was the next day, 19 April.
[4] Unidentified. Wlaschim is in Bohemia.

316 *To Justine*

[Hamburg, April 1893]

Please, dearest, just send me the list of what I have to send to you all for the first.—Alois writes that I should send him 500 fl. of his money. Now please, write me how much of this *is for you* and how much Alois needs. As well, [tell me] whether 500 fl. is what it should be, or *more*, or perhaps even somewhat less! In other words: an accounting—so that every time one knows where one is at.

From Vienna I hope to learn from somebody in good time *how much*! In any case, insist on it.

I am pleased that things are going so well for you all. What is this about a walking tour to Italy that Alois wants to undertake? Where does the doctor recommend that Alois stay in the summer?

Warmly, your
Gustav

In haste!

Shelfmark: E5-MJ-247

317 *To Justine*

[Hamburg, c. 21 or 22 April 1893]

Dearest Justi!

I am completely beside myself about Alois! I wrote the rascal *very sharply*. Leniency would be very much uncalled for in the face of such embarrassment and thoughtlessness. *Where* will these two fellows yet bring me to? The enclosed letter from Alois I send to you for your opinion of *what* is to be done, and ask that you return it to me immediately. I know too little of the circumstances, and *must* leave it to you! Please proceed firmly and *ruthlessly*! At any rate, I am against giving Alois the money directly; instead I will send it directly to Merano.—In fact, I believe that I have had the amount that you indicate sent to you. You arrange the rest yourself!

Since Alois shall actually arrive in Lucern on 1 July, I wonder whether it is a completely needless bother of a journey and waste of money that he still comes to us beforehand. I leave this to you as well to arrange as you will. Do you think that one really should send him the entire *400 fl*? It might well be necessary—judging from Ernestine's letter—in case he did not pay the bill there on the first.

—In my last letter I forbade him to go on the *walking tour* and directly ordered that he should go with Sax to the appointed place. I am now curious whether he will obey the order. *If not*, I am withdrawing my support from him! I am beginning to get absolutely fed up with being dragged behind, continually, through thick and thin, tied to the stirrup of my lord brothers' winged horse.—I have no desire to follow this bold flight any farther. *I, too, am still young*, and not in the mood to be a grumpy moralist. I, too, would enjoy my life, and am not ready to wheeze around with the cares of a nearly dead old man.—I still have *my flight*, damn it all.

I now believe that it was a *big* mistake that I was so forbearing and trusting with those two fellows.—With Otto the fruits are already to be seen.—*Five years* ago I urged him to enter the Military Examination *Preparation Course*. Otto, who with his bad memory will no longer recall this (*Fritz*, who took Otto's side at the time perhaps might), struggled against this, tooth and nail. *I* should have *commanded*. Well, that is past now. He is supposed to blow the trumpet for three years, then. Well, he ought not to imagine that I will continue to maintain him on *these* terms throughout these three years. I have done everything in my power to let this cup pass from him and from me. *He* didn't want it! Fine—*he*'ll have to bear the consequences! It might be his only salvation if he now gets a taste of *what life* is, and what it means to have to *slave away* and *fight* on his own.

The Richter affair appears to be approaching a peaceful end.[1] "Indispensable" Hans will be aided in bearing his heavy cares and family burdens (my God, with an income of around 30 000 fl. can such an ingenious strongman [*Recke*] really not manage—"at least he may console himself that he has remained an *artist* and has not stooped to *hackwork*." Ha, ha, ha!) with a few *thousands* more, and the noble man will be preserved for the noble Viennese.

Tilda's wedding already took place—last *Monday*!

As far as a suitcase is concerned, I would like to suggest that you buy a *splendid* one *here*, where one can have a good selection, otherwise one merely throws money out the window.

Natalie is an exceptionally dear and good creature!

When you travel, I would firmly advise you to make two *stops*: one to stay overnight with Natalie in Prague, and from there to travel to Berlin, where you would be met either by *me*, or by Frau Marcus's sister, where you could spend the night *splendidly*.—From there to here it is only 3½ hours.

Write soon and in detail about everything!

Warmly, your
Gustav

Say hello to Löwi girls and Papa!

Pictures for them and *Nina* will follow soon!

Today I sent Alois a *brochure* and regulations for this "tradesmen's registry office," as well as a *form* to fill out! Please insist that he takes prompt notice of it.

SHELFMARK: E3-MJ-144

NOTE

[1] Hans Richter was almost lured by the Boston Symphony to leave Vienna. The Viennese press reported on 14 April that he had resigned and accepted Boston's offer. In fact, Richter had signed a contract with Boston on 13 April 1893 and wrote a resignation letter the next day. The Opera administration refused his resignation on 20 April; Richter accepted the

decision the next day and cancelled the American contract the day after. The incident is discussed in Christopher Fifield, *True Artist and True Friend: A Biography of Hans Richter* (Oxford: Clarendon, 1993), pp. 256–59. Mahler seems to be quoting from a newspaper report. Correspondence around Richter's attempt to resign is found in the Hofopernarchiv, Z. 242/1893 (Haus-, Hof-, und Staatsarchiv, Wien).

318 *To Justine*

[Hamburg, April 1893]

Dearest Justi!

In haste, I am only sending you the letter from our lord brother, Alois—this seems to have been written *before* he received my very severe one (which *at any rate* now must be in his possession).

As I see things, one now must just let the fellow run, and wait until he gets stuck. I don't think that he is to be helped.

At any rate, tomorrow I will send you the first instalment of the amount for 1 May. Do with it what you think best. *To you on the first* (is this enough time?), I will also then send *400 fl.* Hopefully this will get you to Hamburg.—If not, write me well in advance. I will no longer lift a finger for Alois. That he is not coming to Steinberg [*sic*] is fine with me.[1] He would only disturb my summer—and this year I want to enjoy it properly and without care for once. This will now still depend on how much the other young Titan [*Himmelstürmer*] allows it to be. But at any rate, I can bear everything, just so long as I am dealing with an *honest* man, but Alois's falseness is simply malt plus hops down the drain.—See *how right* Father was in his judgement about him.

At any rate, I am quite happy that Otto is being more reasonable again. What is up with his induction?

Warmest greetings from your
Gustav

Shelfmark: E10-MJ-468
Note

[1] The summer of 1893 was Mahler's first at Steinbach am Attersee.

319 *Alois to Gustav, then Gustav to Justine*

[Hamburg, April 1893]

Dear Gustav!

Whatever caused you to write to me in this fashion, I have no idea; a lightning strike could not have been more unexpected.

First of all, I have paid *all* my bills and do not owe a kreuzer.[1]

Secondly, for teachers I bill you for *less* than I really pay, because I feared that it would be too much for you.

Thirdly, I have not done any thoughtless, deceitful things at all, only unwise ones. I had already given up my walking tour before you wrote me about it, as you saw from my last letter.—

Still, I cannot make accusations, since you probably received the most distorted reports.

I received the package and thank you warmly. I will establish contact with this society, but not put my name down for any position.[2]

I *insist* on the claims in my last letter, and can only tell you that I am absolutely calm and rational.—

I am not staying here in Warmegg, but am going to much higher and cooler Atzwang from whence, as I already wrote, I will go directly to Lucern on 10 June.[3]

I would say further that, if you send the money to Ernestine, I take it that you want to reprimand me like a little kid; I will prove to you that I am no such thing. Do not fear that I will ever be a burden to you. I've already had enough to swallow and for the most part, undeservedly.

If it is too much trouble to administer my few gulden, you can just send them to me and I will deposit them elsewhere.—

I have a heart so full of bitterness that I would have to write you twenty more pages, but I shall prefer to remain silent.

Your brother
Alois

[on reverse:]
Dearest Justi!
I am forwarding to you as quickly as possible the two letters I just received.—Hopefully you have not yet sent the money and are still able to address it to *Alois*. As you see, we are thus all agreed to let Alois go his own way now. It should have happened ages ago—it would have been better for *everyone*.[4]
By the way, I agree that you should *not* stop in Prague (since Natalie will not accompany you), for nothing would be gained by it. Prague is much too far from here too, and the journey would still last too *long*. Maybe you should instead travel here in a sleeping car in a single, direct train.

Your Gustav greets you warmly

[across top of page:] See that you can be here by Sunday *14* May. That is *Die Meistersinger* and following that a complete *Wagner cycle* winds up.[5]

SHELFMARK: E10-FMJ-437
NOTES

[1] Alois writes "kr," which could mean either "kreuzer" (the old currency) or "kronen" (the new one, adopted in August 1892). Since all of the amounts in the letters are given in old currency (florins), the former is more likely.

[2] The "tradesmen's registry office" mentioned above in letter 317.

[3] Unidentified. It may be that the cooler and drier place mentioned by Alois (which appears to read "Atzwang"), like Warmegg, is a pension.

[4] On 26 April, Mahler wrote similarly to Ernestine Löhr (unpublished letter in the Mahler-Rosé Collection, with envelope addressed to "Frl. Ernestine Löhr / in Meran / Pension Warmegg" [E8-MC-397]):

> Dear Ernestine!
> Thank you very much for your friendly efforts.

My lord brothers give me continual worry and trouble. I am letting Alois go his own way. One cannot help him. Where he got his ways, I cannot understand—never in my whole life, was I so thoughtless or inconsiderate, and even less so, deceitful! This last was just too much for me. If I cannot *believe* a man, then I am absolutely finished with him.—That Otto also is beginning to float through the world in bold flight will already be known to you. For him too there is no other means except to learn from life itself. My only comfort is that Justi is now finally really beginning to get well! At least everyone says so. In the end, this will turn out to be the only comfort of the year, which otherwise really has not strewn roses in my path. Fight after fight. What do you think of the idea that Justi give up the Vienna household and for the time being begin a *bachelor life* with me here? Honestly speaking, I have many concerns about it. What should she do? What will she live for? The concerns of the household will be taken from her, since we will live in a pension here. *With what* should she fill her time now? Do you have any idea?

I am very sorry not to see you this year. Or might you still be able to come to us on the Attersee for a few days? Would you want to? I assume that you have a few weeks of holidays and want to visit your family in Vienna—a detour our way would not be too much out of the way!?

I hear with regret that poor Sax is unwell again. Please greet him warmly from me; his wife as well, although I don't know her.

Warmly, your
Gustav Mahler

Hamburg 26/IV 93

[5] *Die Meistersinger* was followed by *Tristan* (16 May) and *Der Ring des Nibelungen* (17, 18, 20, 24 May).

320 *To Justine*

[Hamburg, April 1893][1]

Dearest Justi!

Yesterday I sent *600* marks, out of which I ask you to send *150 fl.* to Sax yourself.—It is marvellous that you took the place on the Attersee; describe it to me in your next letter! Is the location called <u>*Parschall*</u>?

It's too bad that apparently you didn't get the letter I addressed to Hotel Pitter in Salzburg, nor did Natalie get the express letter I sent to Vienna. Please take note of it now, and let me know *what now is to be done*. It is *very important* to me!

I've just come back from an excursion (to the Ostsee) and am quite content.

Yours affectionately,
Gustav

Shelfmark: E10-MJ-421
Note

[1] Justine's whereabouts in April are not exactly clear. She seems to have left Merano towards the middle of the month, travelling with Natalie. She was in Vienna on the 25th (see letter 321) and was in Hamburg no later than the 29th, as she wrote to Ernestine Löhr from

there on that date. It is possible that she made a brief visit to Iglau en route to Hamburg; see below.

321 *To Justine*

Postcard[1]
[Postmark: Hamburg, 23.4.93]
[Arrival postmark: Vienna, 25.4.94]

D.J. I do not know if it is practical just now to buy another *suit* for Otto, because in the *fall* he will no longer *wear* it! In this respect, I think it would be better *not* to get new things any more—he should instead do his best with what he has. In any case, do not neglect to keep after him as regards *punctual* induction.

Warmly, your G.

Also, about the *underclothes*, tell me whether or not he can use these in the military.

Your bill: in fact the *total* is *wrong*: I have to send *397* fl., not *375*! Figure it out again! [2 lines obliterated by ink] . . . and I would buy the suitcase *here* first!

SHELFMARK: E6-MJp-308
NOTE
[1] Addressed to "Fräulein Justine Mahler / Wien / VII. Breitegasse 4 II."

322 *To Justine*

[Hamburg, April 1893]

Dearest Justi!
As well as the *11th*, I am also free in the evening on the *12th* and *13th*. *14th* (Sunday) is Die Meistersinger. This then would be the first opera that you would hear here.—So I advise you to leave on the *10th* or *11th*.—For instance, if you were to take the direct *Vienna-Hamburg* train, which leaves Vienna at night and arrives here the next afternoon around *4:00*, then by all means travel *in the sleeping car*. But it is to be considered whether you wouldn't be better to spend the night in Berlin so that you would arrive here fresh.—I don't know how you are now after travelling all night.—If there is a train (which you can easily find out in Vienna) that departs from *there* in the *morning* and arrives in Berlin in the evening (which is possible), then I advise you to take *it*. In this case, you would be met by Frau Marcus's sister and presumably sleep there. The next morning you would then steam off by express [*Courirzug*].[1]

Please don't forget to bring the manuscripts of my *songs*. I have to have the "fahrenden Gesellen" cycle copied again, since I *don't* have it any more. (I gave it to Joachim that time.)[2]

That you will stay here *with me*, I've already told you.

Supply yourself with woollen *underclothes*—one really needs them here, and it will also be good for the trip.

Hopefully you have already received the 400 fl.[3] If you should still need money (I think that you will need more for the trip by sleeper), then Natalie could lend you some, which I will then send her from here.

Best wishes to you all from
your
Gustav

Don't forget to arrange everything about the induction.—Otto should arrange things so that he can be at the Attersee at the end of May or the beginning of June. Emma probably has to stay in Vienna until the middle of *July*?

How will you look after her living arrangements? Couldn't she stay at Löwis? Would that be best then?

Shelfmark: E21-MJ-672

Notes

[1] Justine obviously decided to go earlier to Hamburg, as she wrote Ernestine from there on 29 April.

[2] In August 1892, Mahler and Amalie Joachim had a meeting in Salzburg, arranged by Max Steinitzer, where she rehearsed the *Lieder eines fahrenden Gesellen*; see HLG I, pp. 393–94.

[3] Mentioned in letter 318.

323 *To Justine*

[Hamburg, April 1893]

Dearest Justi!

I just received your letter.

I agree with you more or less about Immermann's Münchhausen, although you do throw out the baby with the bathwater. In Oberhof everything is not *merely* sentimental—and he is especially not to be overlooked as an agreeable contrast to the Münchhausen part. The figure of Lisbeth is also very nicely drawn as a living tie between the two, almost completely independent, parts.[1]

I am glad that you are slowly finding pleasure in (more deeply lying) humour. With time, Don Quixote should finally also be accessible for you, shouldn't it.—

I forgot to tell you earlier that by this time I have arranged everything here so that you will stay here *with me*. You will have a small, pretty room, and, moreover, can spend the days in *mine*. This will do for the few weeks.—It just doesn't seem right to me that you should live with strangers.

Please, properly check the trains to see if you can arrange it to come from *Vienna* to *Berlin* without having to do without a night's sleep; that would be best! In Berlin, you would then be met by Marcus's sister, a very charming young woman, and then sent onwards the next day.

Yours affectionately,
Gustav

Shelfmark: E21-MJ-671

NOTE

[1] Immermann's novel is also mentioned in letter 189 of 1 September 1891.

324 *To Justine*

[Hamburg, April 1893]

Dearest Justi!

The business about the gap between letters is not clear to you; it took place as follows: I wrote that letter to Otto, whereupon I immediately received that reply from you—hereupon, you went to Iglau—*Otto did not write*—Natalie did not write—and you did not write either.—This gap in letters lasted about a week (without my being able to count it out to the day)! You can just imagine how I worried throughout *these* days, all the more so because of your *curious hints*.

—I can hardly comprehend, either, that you did not at least write a *postcard* to me from Iglau, or at least directly after your arrival! This is not just any small matter these days! *No* letters were lost, only your *memory* left you in the lurch.—By the way, had you given me the report about your stay, which I only received in your 2nd letter after my inquiries, right away, I would have spared you this.

I was surprised that you had nothing *at all* to tell me about your stay there.—Your fear of *appearing* too *sentimental* to me about such things really is completely superfluous.—I really do not require that people shouldn't *feel anything*! I just hate it when they are *self-serving* and *self-indulgent* in their feelings.

[unsigned]

SHELFMARK: E19-MJ-660

325 *To Emma*

[Postmark: Vienna, 15.6.(1893)][1]

Dear Emma!

As Justi already told you, it is my wish that you should stay with our friends in Vienna; at present, I consider that this is the best for you in every respect. Fritz tells me that they are all pleased with you, and this gives me great happiness.

I ask nothing more of you now than that you should preserve this contentment in the future.

Naturally we will spend [our] vacation together. And if from time to time it can be arranged, you can also come and stay with us here for a few days in the interim.—

So, again, behave yourself so that Fritz and Uda will be pleased with you!

Best wishes to you and Otto

from your brother

Gustav

SOURCE: Typewritten transcription in the Bibliothèque Musicale Gustav Mahler

NOTE

[1] Information about the envelope comes from the Sotheby's catalogue entry. It is unclear whether this is the first or the second (arrival) postmark. Since Mahler arrived in Vienna on 17 June (according to GMB[2] 123), the latter is more likely.

Assuming that the Sotheby's catalogue information is correct, the letter could only have been written in 1893, as Justine and Emma were already in Steinbach on this date in 1894 (and in 1895, Otto was dead).

326 *To Alois*

[Steinbach, 23 August 1893]

Dear Alois!

Before my departure for Hamburg, I feel compelled to tell you the following, so as to prevent any misunderstanding or disappointment on your part in the future:

I. When your savings are exhausted, do not, under any circumstances, count on getting even a kreuzer more from me. I assure you categorically that I am neither in a position to support you financially, nor have I the slightest intention of doing so, and you would make a severe—and for you, disastrous—error if you secretly held to that idea.

That is why I advise you to look around for a post, or another source of income, in time, so that you won't find yourself in an embarrassing situation on the day that you spend the last penny of your means.—

II. Dr. Freund asked me most urgently to transfer to him the 80 fl. that you borrowed from him in Budapest. Since I am legally obliged to do so, I did, and you have to subtract this amount from your credit with me. At the same time, I instructed him to send you on 1 Sept. the 250 fl. that you wanted. You would therefore claim another 320 fl. from me, if your calculation is correct, which I will have a look at and check only in Hamburg, where I have the relevant notes.—

Possible exhortations or advice, or explanations of my point of view, I will save myself, since, first of all, they won't do any good, and you would probably even dismiss them according to your own perception of your "dignity."—It only remains for me to express to you my best wishes for your well-being, and my hope above all to see you yet as a useful member of human society.[1]

Your brother
Gustav

Steinbach 23 Aug. 93.

SHELFMARK: E15-MF-597

NOTE

[1] This letter appears to be the culmination of Mahler's decision to let Alois go his own way (see above, letters 317 and 319). On 22 September, Justine wrote to Ernestine Löhr:

> Alois had the last of his money sent to him today. I am afraid for his future—it is appalling how foolishly the fellow acts. He is already reproaching us now that we ordered him to go to Merano and spend such a pile of money there; to date,

he has spent 4000 fl. in a year. Naturally, neither I nor anyone else can take these reproaches to heart. Gustav is firmly resolved not to give him a kreuzer more, whatever happens.

After this point, Alois is mentioned only infrequently in the letters (see introduction).

327 *To Justine*

Postcard[1]
[Postmark: Munich 25. Aug. 93]
[Arrival postmark: Steinbach am Attersee, 26.8.93]

D.J!
Trip was very pleasant.—Baumgarten arrived punctually. He is a lieutenant with *Jelacic* in *Vienna*! Is that not Otto's future regiment?—I am leaving *early* for Berlin, since there is nothing of interest to me here, and will be there already this evening.—There I do hope to find news from you.—Tomorrow evening I then travel onwards.

Best wishes to all from Gustav

[added in pencil across top:] In Salzburg I met Heuberger.[2]

Because of the shoddy circumstances in Salzburg, I could only check in my suitcase from *here*!

SHELFMARK: E3-MJp-130
NOTES
[1] Addressed to "Fräulein Justine Mahler / Steinbach am Attersee."
[2] Richard Heuberger (1850–1914), composer, critic, and conductor.

328 *To Justine*

Postcard[1]
[Postmark: Berlin, 26 August 1893]
[Arrival postmark: Steinbach am Attersee, 28.8.93]

D.J.—Arrived here yesterday after a very pleasant trip (without heat)—Met by Feld at the station.—Travel onwards midday today. Found your card early this morning. Am very curious how your visit in *See* turned out.

Best wishes to all from
your
G.

SHELFMARK: E15-MJp-573
NOTE
[1] Addressed to "Fräulein Justine Mahler / Steinbach am Attersee / Salzkammergut."

329 *To Justine*

Postcard[1]
[Postmark: Hamburg, 26.8.93]
[Arrival postmark: Steinbach am Attersee, 28.8.93]

D.J!
So! Now happily (or actually quite unhappily) arrived in Hamburg.—My room again in a most beautiful state.—*Schacks* are *moving* themselves then at the beginning of November, and assure me that the new apartment should be *very quiet*.[2]—That is splendid, and we will see then. Now I am sitting in the Alster pavilion, where I have a rendezvous with Berliner.—Opening on 1 September with *"Meistersinger"*.

Write soon.

Best
Gustav

SHELFMARK: E12-MJp-491
NOTES
[1] Addressed to "Fräulein Justine Mahler / Steinbach am Attersee / Salzkammergut."
[2] Mahler's landlady.

330 *To Justine*

[Hamburg,] Monday [28 August 1893]

Dearest Justi!
Today I received your 2 letters (the pince-nez was also enclosed).—I am quite unhappy that nothing became of the dwelling in See! I have the greatest fear of taking the place in Steinbach again, and again I categorically advise you against doing so. It would be *terrible* to have *no* quiet, for I see that it is certainly not to be thought that I'll get any here in Hamburg.—Just as I am sitting here at the place that you well know at the writing desk, a military band is playing in the zoological garden, in the same place lions and exotic oxen are roaring (too bad that there aren't any rattlesnakes—they surely would rattle)—a throng of about 10 boys and 15 girls shout in front of the window all day as loud as they can; in the house, a woman on the 2nd floor is singing, and a gentleman is playing the piano—this last a quite new achievement.—

My ability to work seems hopelessly at an end, and now I see that I was resigned to the noise during the two years I spent in the apartment, otherwise I couldn't have stood it so readily.—

I was already twice together with Berliner—he is even more unpleasant and sullenly pedantic than before! Next time I would sooner do without his company and stay all by myself.—I have just been digging around a little bit in my old papers, sketches, works etc. and therefore have become quite sentimental-melancholy.

For you, dear Natalie (to whom this letter also belongs), I enclose a ribbon for your pince-nez.—Better not bring tobacco with you, dear Justi! One has no taste for it here. But don't forget my cigars! Tell me all about your lives in Steinbach! You all don't realise how nice you still have it there.

I met Wagner at the theatre already today.[1]

What do you hear of Frau Markus [*sic*]?

Friday, then, I start with *Meistersinger*, and on Sunday the "newly rehearsed" *Freischütz* follows![2]

I already had a business dispute with Frau Dr. Schack! Namely, she wanted nothing less than that I pay her for the holidays, which, however, I am not of a mind to do.—So: the gentlest little lamb shows some cat's claws—(she claims she is passing on her husband's instructions, which is indeed possible).—So because of this I don't know yet whether I am moving too, and may be in the situation of looking for an apartment.—So!!! Just now a locomotive is whistling on the connecting line! That's it!!!!!

Your Gustav

Shelfmark: E15-MJ-574

Notes

[1] Viennese actor Carl Wagner (1865–1928) joined the Hamburg troupe in 1892 and was a close friend of Mahler's.

[2] 1 and 3 September, respectively.

331 *To Justine*

[Hamburg,] Thursday[,] 31 Aug. 93

Dearest Justi!

I just received the letter in which you indicated to me that the apartment in Steinbach was taken. So: alea jacta est [the die is cast] and you all will have to arrange everything properly, and already begin to manoeuvre [things] a little.—I am already all set up. It is cold here too, and I have stopped bathing (more out of comfort than out of fear of the cold water).—

The suitcase still hasn't arrived—unfortunately I had to have it checked in by a railway attendant in Munich (remember number *36*) and just couldn't have the delivery period assured; but, as everyone there assured me, this wouldn't be necessary, the suitcase would be received in 8 days.—Vederemo!

Enclosed you'll receive Otto's letter from Vienna, for which I ask you for additional clarification.—Whatever will come out of it!

The posting in Cairo would be very nice, but Alois should *only* take it up if he has prospects for the future there. Also only if he receives a *salary*; for I calculate that he no longer has the financial means to start somewhere on a volunteer basis.

As I gather from your letters, you *don't* appear to be *very* well.—I advise you in all seriousness to give up these goddamned *pills*. They have completely ruined me and again I have my old haemorrhoids.

I heard at Oppenheimer's that Frau Marcus isn't thinking of coming back for the moment, since she is doing so remarkably well there.—But the season certainly won't last much longer there either.—And I think that in the meantime you could go *to her*, or if you prefer, we would have to find something here for the short term.

I already bought and read Brahm's *Kleist*: a splendid book, like his Schiller![1]—I was at the watch-maker who makes charming little watches for 25–30 marks; you can look for something there when you come.

Tell me, what is Otto living on in Vienna? Hopefully Ernestine just won't let herself be misled by him to some stupidity or other.—I now see that, for this rascal, contact with me in this regard was *poison*!—Boys who still require the rod just don't have any business being in the company of adults.—Just don't be lured into giving him money. From me, he'll get his allowance and not a penny more! Write again soon, and in somewhat more detail!

Affectionately yours
Gustav

Where is Natalie? And what is her address?

SHELFMARK: E15-MJ-575
NOTE
[1] Otto Brahm, *Heinrich von Kleist* (Berlin: Allgemeine Verein für deutsche Literatur, 1884).

332 *To Justine*

[Hamburg, 3 September 1893]
Write the *date*!

Dearest Justi!
I like your plan very much! Only don't be rash *about the furniture*! As long as we don't know what is happening next year, we can't do anything about it.—*If* he is having something built anyway, Danbauer shouldn't shy away from a few more gulden and lay out the *whole* as a *cottage* [*Häuschen*] and not as a *guest house*; in fact: first, lay out the room as a *mezzanine*, and 2nd, pay for a small *anteroom*, as small as it may be.—Since we will pay him 50 fl. rent a year for what constitutes an investment of 1000 fl., he can certainly spend more on it.[1]

Frau Schack has now given *me* notice, and so I have to move out on *1 Oct.*—so don't do anything with the *furniture*.—In everything else, you all have my agreement.—

I cannot get rid of the thought that at the *summer peak* we will again have to suffer with the noise from the inn.—Take precautions again along these lines!—Don't put the cottage right at the water—the *waves would disturb me terribly*.—

I am right back at work.—

Imagine, my brush must have been left in Steinbach for washing, and now I have to buy a new one! Costs *6 marks*, unfortunately.

What is with Otto!

Why have I not had any news for so long?

Best wishes to you all from
your
Gustav

Sunday, 3 Sept. 93

SHELFMARK: E3-MJ-128
NOTE

[1] This is the first mention of the *Häuschen* that Mahler had built at Steinbach am Attersee. The property belonged to a minor, Anna Scheiche; Danbauer acted as her trustee. On 21 September 1893, architect Josef Lösch sent Danbauer a detailed estimate of the cost for the *Musikpavilion*: 395 fl., 94 kr. See *Gustav Mahler in Steinbach am Attersee: Dokumente, Berichte, Photographien* (Vienna: Internationale Gustav Mahler Gesellschaft, 1985).

333 *To Justine*

Hamburg, 7/IX 93

Dearest Justi!

The mail from Steinbach is unbelievably unreliable.—Usually 2 or 3 letters come at the same time—and then 2 or 3 days without anything at all! Do find out about this!—Right now I am curious how, and whether, the cottage [*Häuschen*] will be! Natalie has made me aware (and is quite right) that it is necessary to establish *contractually* that the cottage will be *finished on time* (I don't know when you have to ask the doctor) in order still *to dry out*; otherwise, it could happen that I might have to move out after a few days because of rheumatism.—What do you mean that *you* ought to furnish the apartment?—Would we then have to buy some furniture?—That would be a costly joke!

2. The security deposit must already be set down now *in writing*; then, just in case we move out, there would be no concern about a settlement with Thanbauer [*sic*, Danbauer].—It also must *be said* that, just in case we didn't take the apartment again, naturally we would not pay *anything* for the cottage.—

I do have some good news to tell: imagine, in the last few days I received a statement from *Schott* for my songs. Around 300 copies were purchased recently, and I got a royalty of 120 marks.—And just a day later, 130 marks royalty for 2 performances of "Pintos" in Dresden!

What elation! But this was also the *answer* to my prayers, since I didn't have a penny more, and had to pay the bill *here* for August, and still live all September.—

It is terribly noisy here now! You can imagine how I am suffering. I have already advertised. About 14 offers have come in now. Perhaps I will still find something.

I have heard from various sides that Frau Marcus is now here. It surprises me that she still has not shown me any sign of life.—At any rate, I will wait for one before I go to her.

I am glad that Otto is back again. I understood his letter to say that he now wanted to stay in Vienna after all.

What luck that Ernestine behaved so sensibly and bravely. The fellow [Otto] would have been capable of doing the stupidest things.—Is he playing *violin* and piano diligently then?—Berliner is now quite cheerful again. Nevertheless, I only see him rarely, since we both have too much to do.—I have still not been to the Elbe.—I *dine* at home at *midday* because it is just so comfortable there.—Do *not* tire yourself out *in Vienna*! Don't forget to bring me the boots.

Best wishes to you all
Your
Gustav

SHELFMARK: E15-MJ-572

334 *To Justine*

[Hamburg, 8 September 1893]

Dearest Justi!
I have just come back, quite tired out, from 20 visits to the available apartments that came in—all in vain—without finding a single suitable one!

The only one that is partially suitable (if still not quite satisfactory) is actually the apartment over Bülow's, which is terribly expensive: *150 marks* a month for 2 rooms.—I am now wondering what I will do, that is, where I will be sitting 4 weeks from today.—

I am still without notice of Frau Marcus, although I know that she is already here.—I cannot understand this, and am now almost inclined to attribute her consequent recent silence towards you to the same reason.—Or might there be a misunderstanding?

What has happened to the architect's plans? Certainly do not leave Steinbach without the matter being set down in writing!—In the case that I am unable to find a room here, I wonder if it wouldn't be most practical to take a small one-year-lease apartment [*Jahreswohnung*] in a quiet place, and furnish it, even if it were only for 9 months. Moving some necessary furniture, that is to say, beds, wash-stand, *etc.*, would be worth the expense if it were effective in obtaining *QUIET*. Right now I am just about like a hounded deer.

What is Otto doing? That is, what is he really *doing*?

Hopefully, I will hear soon.

Warmly, your
8/IX 93. Gustav

Is it true that Professor Virchow from Berlin stayed on the Attersee?[1]—By the way, yesterday I was invited to Pollini's with *Tchaikovsky*.[2] For the moment, I am in excellent graces!

SHELFMARK: E15-MJ- 576
NOTES

[1] Rudolf Ludwig Karl Virchow (1821–1902), famous Berlin doctor and scientist, often termed the "pope of Berlin medicine."

[2] Mahler conducted Tchaikovsky's *Iolanthe* at the Stadttheater on 7 September.

335 *To Justine*

[Hamburg, 15 September 1893]

Dearest Justi!

I was together with Frau Marcus by chance for the first time only on the occasion of a visit with *Her*[t]*z* at the *Park*hotel on the Elbe.[1]—

Since she made absolutely no reference to your staying with her, I could not raise it.—Since then, I have not been with her, and have heard nothing.—

If she hasn't written anything to you about it by now either, I take it that perhaps circumstances have arisen in which it is perhaps not convenient for her to have you there as a guest for so long, and so I have now arranged things so that you will stay with *me* again.

How is too complicated to explain now.—Anyhow, rest assured that it will work *quite well*, without disturbing me.—Also it is only for a few days.—We will discuss everything only upon your arrival in Hamburg. At any rate, let me know the *precise location* and *time* of your arrival. I will be waiting for you.—

I will *probably* reach an agreement with Frau Schack after all, and we will move together into the new apartment, which is so *quiet* and beautiful that I will gladly compromise and be able to say "pater peccavi" [Father, I have sinned]. What is more, I have been looking for apartments for weeks and haven't found *one* that would have been even *halfway* quiet.[2]—

Why don't I ever hear anything at all about *Otto*?

For now, just farewell.

Best wishes to *everyone* in Vienna, and promise to telegraph.

Yours,

15/IX 93 Gustav

SHELFMARK: E5-MJ-240

NOTES

[1] Adele Marcus's father, Daniel Hertz.

[2] On 10 October 1893, Justine wrote to Ernestine: "by the way, Gustav reached an agreement with his landlady and is moving along with her into her new place."

336 *To Emma*

[Hamburg, 19 September 1893][1]

Dear Emma!

We just received your telegram. Your worry is naturally quite unnecessary. We are both excellent and just dined excellently at Frau Marcus's.—Tell me, who on earth in Vienna is making such a fuss about the local "cholera"? It is now found worldwide, isn't it, and whoever lives sensibly and in moderation certainly has nothing to fear! So don't worry any more. Warmest greetings to *Frau Hof*[f]*mann* from me—to the Löwis too.

With best wishes,
your brother
Gustav

Tell me, haven't you had daily news from me? Tomorrow perhaps I will write more. You know, when I have a headache it lasts a while. I am just about to go out with G.

Y[our] J[usti]

SOURCE: Typewritten transcription in the Bibliothèque Musicale Gustav Mahler
NOTE

[1] As Justine was with Mahler in Hamburg, this letter can only be from 1893. She arrived on 19 September. According to an unpublished portion of Natalie's memoirs, Gustav fell ill with cholera that September (see HLG I, p. 426). An excerpt from Justine's letter to Ernestine of 22 September indicates that he started to feel unwell the day after she arrived, which means that letter 336 must have been written on the 19th:

> On the first day of my stay here I had a nice fright. The first news that met me here was that cholera had broken out again, although not as severely as last year. The next day Gustav complained of stomach pains and diarrhoea. . . . After two days the situation heightened: he had a fever too; now you can imagine my fright. . . . I am just glad that everything came to a clean end. The whole thing seems to have been a cold.

On 11 October, she mentioned to Ernestine that Gustav had spent five days in the hospital. This is curious, as there does not appear to be a five-day gap in his schedule during this period: according to Schabbing, he conducted *Der Freischütz* on 22 and 25 September.

337 *To Emma*

[Hamburg, mid-November 1893][1]
Fröbelstrasse 14 III

Dear Emma!
Please dispatch the enclosed letter, which I just received, right away to Alois, whose address you of course will know. Justi left yesterday, and so from now on, please write me weekly, just like before. Naturally you cannot count on regular replies since I am far too busy, as you can well imagine.

Warm greetings to Nina from me—and best wishes to you too from

Your brother
Gustav

What is Otto up to? And why did he not answer my letter?

SOURCE: Typewritten transcription in the Bibliothèque Musicale Gustav Mahler
NOTE

[1] This letter was written after 10 November (as Justine wrote to Ernestine on the 7th that she was attending the gala performance of *Fidelio* that night) but before 18 November (as Gustav wrote to Justine in Merano that day).

338 *To Emma*

[Hamburg, November 1893]

Dear Emma!
You gave me great pleasure with your splendid report.—As you requested, I am enclosing a photograph of myself. Buy yourself a nice frame for it, and send me the bill.

As I just wrote Justi, from now I will expect that you will send me a detailed letter, at least twice a week, about *everything* that is going on. In this way, you will virtually stand in for Justi.—

I remain, with best wishes,

your brother
Gustav

SOURCE: Transcribed from a facsimile of the original letter (Jerry Bruck, New York)

339 *To Justine*

Postcard: Hôtel du Parc / Wiesbaden[1]
[Postmark: Wiesbaden, 18.11.93][2]
[Arrival postmark: Meran, 19.11.93]

Dear J.
Before the concert[3]—after which I must head to the train compartment right away—just the news that I arrived here safely, walked hard in the *beautiful* (famous) air, and had a tremendous appetite all day.—

The public here is supposed to be very cool. (They don't exactly have to be!) The orchestra plays the things quite well.—Pollini called me back because of a *cancellation*. So you all waited anxiously in vain. Yesterday I was with Schott in *Mainz*, to where I walked directly across the Rhine from here (15 minutes by train, and then 30 minutes on foot). Beautiful city! *It appears to me* that he does *not* want to publish the things! Well, vederemo. Tomorrow I will write again about the trip.

Best, G.

[written across the top:] Best wishes to Ernestine.

SHELFMARK: E14-MJp-549
NOTES

[1] Addressed to Fräulein Ernestine Löhr / für Justine Mahler / Tyrol / Meran / Obermais / Pension Warmegg."

[2] From the contents, the card was written on 17 November (the day of the concert).

[3] Mahler was in Wiesbaden to conduct Paul Bulss in three of his *Humoresken*—"Der Schildwache Nachtlied," "Trost im Unglück," and "Rheinlegendchen"—at the third *Curhaus* concert; Franz Nowak conducted the rest of the program.

340 *To Justine*

[Hamburg, c. 18 November 1893][1]

Dearest Justi!
So, nothing in Wiesbaden. It appears that the Humoresken alienated the public.—It's true I was "called" back once—but you know such *succès d'éstime*.—

Strecker will not publish the things,[2] according to a letter that I will send you next time.—

Enclosed, the program and the review from the "Musikzeitung" that Pfohl mentioned.—Finally, a letter from Otto, which I am also sending you as an authentic expression of Ottoness.—

According to Natalie's reports, he is supposedly doing *nothing at all.*

Soon I will tell him that, from 1 February, he will receive *50 fl.* a month from me until he obtains a position. No more under any circumstances—let him manage with it as he can.—

Now I am already anxiously awaiting news from you!

Affectionately,
Gustav

Best wishes to Ernestine!

On no account should you leave Merano until you are *entirely* recovered and back to normal.

SHELFMARK: E15-MJ-577
NOTES

[1] Mahler was back in Hamburg the day after the Wiesbaden concert, as he conducted *Eugene Onegin, Iolanthe,* and *Romeo and Juliet* in memoriam of Tchaikovsky, who had died on 6 November.

[2] Ludwig Strecker (1853–1943) was director of the music publisher Schott.

341 *To Justine*

[Hamburg, 23 November 1893]

Dearest Justi!

Hopefully you received my letter to Merano; I am sending this one to Florence. I am quite furious that you have already hurried away from Merano. Don't *cycle* on in such an expensive manner.—*Health* is the main thing, not *education*![1]

Up to now, I haven't been out at all. Yesterday I did conduct *Die Schöpfung*—in *Altona* in fact, where they allowed it after the Hamburg Senate forbade it.[2]—It sounded wonderfully there and the performance was splendid.—I am also sending you Otto's 2nd letter! What do you think of this shameless fellow[?]—I just wrote him and *refused* his request (for money)![3]

Do you know already that *he* and *Alois* have *moved in together*? Now together they will grumble about us something awful.—

I also turned Nina down (in more detail)—she asked me for 50 fl. for Alois.

I didn't find your *pince-nez.* Is it the one that you had made on *Dr. Sänger's* orders? If this is the case, then send me the *prescription right away*, so that I can have *another* made for you. (Perhaps it does not need to be made of gold.) You've really got to have it for Italy.—Perhaps *nothing* will come of Russia after all.[4] The subscription seems to have gone badly.—

At night I was often with Berliner, usually without anyone else. My rooms have been *very quiet* for a few days, about which I am very happy.—My health and digestion are excellent. Greet Frau Marcus and Toni warmly from me.

Your
Gustav

[across top of first page:] Be sensible and treat your *health* as the most important thing!!! (The same for Frau *Marcus*!)

SHELFMARK: E3-MJ-129
NOTES

[1] During her Hamburg stay, Justine wrote several times to Ernestine indicating that she was unwell. In Mahler's mind at least, the principal reason for her Italian sojourn (which lasted until well into May 1894) was for her to regain her health. Justine was in Florence by early December (her second letter from there to Ernestine is dated 5 December).

[2] The annual *Buß- und Bettags-Konzert* in Altona was on 22 November. In addition to *Die Schöpfung*, the program included two oratorio arias by Mendelssohn.

[3] On 5 December, Justine wrote to Ernestine that "[Gustav] is in despair about Otto."

[4] Justine's letters to Ernestine indicate that, since September, Pollini had been considering taking the Stadttheater company to St. Petersburg during Lent.

342 *To Justine*

Hamburg 5/XII 93.

Dearest Justi!
Hopefully you have now received my last letter.—Who put it to you that I was not well? If it was Natalie, that is because I wrote her that my haemorrhoids are bleeding again, which was already the case at the end of your visit.—However, since I have started to exercise again (everyday before breakfast for the last 14 days), the bleeding went away at once. It seems, then, that *exercise* (Swedish gymnastics in particular) is the best medicine for this illness; you should take note of this too.[1]

—At any rate, health-wise I am very well, eat at Streit's, and take iron, which seems to do me good. Writing letters always takes too much of my time—not only that which I spend, but also that which I need in order to get into a working mood again. So please don't over do it, and enjoy your life and beautiful Italy without looking back or looking forward, etc.—

You can easily imagine that I am not in the rosiest mood because of the Vienna business.—In order to bring you directly up to date on the situation in Vienna, I am sending you the letter that I recently received from Nina.—From this you will see how things stand in Vienna better than from 10 descriptions.[2]

I am now preparing "Das *klagende* Lied," as previously the *Titan*, in order to have it ready for a possible performance.[3] You can imagine how many afternoons and evenings it takes.—At the same time, I am now rehearsing two new works[4]—so think about how much time I have to write letters.—

I have really not yet had time to visit the *Her*[t]*zes* in the Victoria Hotel and to answer Frau Marcus.—I will do the former soon; as for the latter, she will not take it amiss. Mind you, *you* have time to write, and it is also more necessary to have frequent news of you, a *traveller*, and much more exposed to the vagaries of life, than for you [to have news] of me, who continue to journey forward in the way of life and pedantic regularity that you now know so well.

I was at Lazarus's once, and once at *Behns*. There I met Herr *Sahla* again, the one who conducted the last concert so really miserably.[5]—Pollini recently spoke directly to me about "re-engagement," but for the moment I answered only evasively.—I can decide only with *great difficulty*.—

Did you receive a registered letter from *Prohazka* from Iglau, which I *forwarded* to you?[6]—Herewith I am sending you a letter from *Emma*, in which you will immediately detect the "projectile" [*Tells Geschoss*] right away. I am sending both in 2 envelopes. Hopefully my letter wasn't lost by the sloppy Italian conditions. *Write about the day!*

Best wishes to you, and Frau Marcus and Toni.

Your Gustav

SHELFMARK: E5-MJ-241

NOTES

[1] In an unpublished letter to Natalie Bauer-Lechner, 9 December 1893, Mahler indicated that the exercise worked: "As a result of the exercise, the haemorrhoids are completely gone."

[2] Two letters from Justine to Ernestine shed some light on the Vienna situation:

> In a sentimental letter, Nina wrote Gustav that he should bring Otto to Hamburg. I cannot get used to such ideas at all. Will there ever be light in this chaos? There is a funny story about Emma too: she let me know that she is attending *the ball* without even mentioning that it is fine with G.—I hope—or asking me. She told me "I couldn't answer you sooner since I didn't have 10 kreuzer for a stamp, I bought material for a dress for the ball with my pocket money," etc. I am thinking less than ever about spending next winter with her. Nina fulfils her every wish and just simply writes to G. how much he should send! (5 December 1893)
>
> I find it only right and meet that Otto is now seriously beginning to grasp life from the right side—no thanks at all to him. Of course the only salvation was that Gustav finally put a knife to his throat (namely by saying to him that he would receive 70 fl. and not a kr. more on the 1st of each month). (8 December 1893)

[3] On Mahler's revisions to *Das klagende Lied*, see Edward R. Reilly, "*Das klagende Lied* Reconsidered," in *Mahler Studies*, ed. Stephen E. Hefling (Cambridge: Cambridge University Press, 1996), pp. 25–52. Mahler had extensively revised his First Symphony (*Titan*) throughout 1893 (primarily January and August) in preparation for its performance in Hamburg on 27 October; for a discussion of this revision, see Stephen McClatchie, "The 1889 Version of Mahler's First Symphony: A New Manuscript Source," *19th-Century Music* 20 (1996): 99–124.

[4] Verdi's *Falstaff* (first performance in Hamburg, 2 January 1894) and Smetana's *Die verkaufte Braut* (first performance in Hamburg, 17 January 1894).

[5] *Hofkapellmeister* Richard Sahla (1855–1931) conducted the fourth subscription concert on 4 December 1893.

[6] Prohaska is also mentioned in letter 162.

343 *To Justine*

[Hamburg, between 6 and 8 December 1893]

Here is the repertory, dear Justi. I am very eager for your first letter from Rome.[1]—You really should write Prohaska and tell him that the letter that I forwarded to you right away (to Florence) has not arrived.—Perhaps it contains important information regarding Otto! What do you have to say about his last letter? What do *you* think about it? *I* am worrying about whether he might not indeed be capable of something stupid.[2]—At any rate, I will wait for your opinion before I do anything about it.

I sent you the photographs. I received the "singing angel" and am very pleased with it. Should I have it framed?

Write soon. Best wishes to Frau Marcus and Toni from me.

Your
Gustav

SHELFMARK: E3-MJ-138
NOTES

[1] A letter to Ernestine, dated 6–8 December, ends with the comment that she should send her next letter to Rome; see below, letter 344.

[2] See below, letter 348.

344 *To Justine*

[Hamburg, 9 December 1893]

Dearest Justi!
Finally in Rome! So now you are also "one up" on me! Do really enjoy your good fortune—since not everyone is given the opportunity to see Rome. *Bieber* already sent me three large photographs for you—3 smaller ones that I ordered are not here yet; I will ask right away when they will be ready, and send them then—The three large photos will go off to you today.

I am still taking iron.

Just make sure not to neglect Italian.

I still feel excellently and for the present have not noticed anything of the influenza that is supposed to be rampant here—up to now the theatre has been completely spared of it. Pollini is leaving for Petersburg again today, where the matter ought to be decided once and for all.

Bülow is now in Hamburg again. It is going very badly for the poor fellow—now he has a kidney disease!

I recently met Herr Her[t]z in the street, as merry and cheerful as ever.—I still have not gotten around to going to the hotel.—Also, apart from Berliner, I don't see anybody; and him only rarely.—I am working diligently just now on "Klagende Lied"—and such things always consume all of my time and strength, as you know.

I am getting along *excellently* with Pollini—he has never been *so thick* with me. It seems obvious that he wants to *keep* me *here* at any price. If I conclude a further contract with him (which I dread), I'll see to it that I have the right to conduct some concerts every year.

I received a *registered* letter from Otto today, which I enclose for you. Please return it to me, by the way. From it, you will see that the business has recently reached another "stage."—It is unclear to me, mind you, what he will live from, but—until he asks for it *himself* again, he will not get *a kreuzer* from me.[1]—It would be good if you looked after him a bit, and perhaps supported him, in order to prevent stupidity.

Perhaps this is best for him—but I have only a little confidence in his consistency. Please, write me about it.

Best wishes to you all from
your
Gustav

Saturday 9/XII 93

I am curious about *how long* a letter takes to reach the other.

Shelfmark: E15-MJ-578
Note

[1] In an unpublished letter to Natalie written the same day, Mahler lamented, "God, if I only had *some* peace in my family!"

345 *To Emma*

[Hamburg, 15 December 1893]

Dear Emma!
You assume that the reason why I have not answered you yet is probably that I am ill.—This is not the reason at all; quite the opposite: I feel quite cheerful right now. But I am working now, and *then*, as you know, I am not available for anything or anybody.

In this respect, I have to ask of those with whom I associate that they completely accept my desires and habits in these things.—

Accordingly, please do write me as regularly, as before, [but] don't wait first for an answer from me.

It is quite valiant of you that you have resolved to always be truthful and open toward me from now on. Certainly do carry out this intention—and not only toward me, but also toward everyone with whom you want to live.—This is the first requirement in order to make a relationship between 2 people possible.

Of course, I hope that you were not *untruthful* toward me before now; that you were not *more open* is just because it is difficult to be open toward someone whom one does not know well enough yet. Whether this is your "guardian" or your brother is quite immaterial.—It also lies in the nature of things that you would rather put your trust in a girlfriend or sister of your own age, instead of in a brother who is so far beyond you in age and in so many other things.—

Since we are already speaking of it, I must honestly confess to you that your relationship with Justi does not please me very much.—I am afraid that if you continue this way, you both will get farther and farther from one another in life—meanwhile, because of the circumstances, you both actually have to live *with each other.*

Why aren't you more communicative, more open, but also more considerate and more unassuming toward her? She is and remains, after all, your older sister, who is far superior to you not only in years, but also in experience and understanding.—It seems to me that you forget this too often!

As far as your wish to eventually live together with us is concerned, I am afraid that its fulfilment is still far off.—Above all, I still do not know where *I* will be *next year.*—My situation is still too uncertain for me to be able to think about setting up my hearth anywhere; under these circumstances I do not intend to bring you here with me.—

To be sure, you are much more conveniently held responsible than Justi, since you can take a position in Vienna that will provide you with support, internally and externally. *Be sure not to delay* in turning your attention to it!

Unfortunately, Justi doesn't have such a possibility as you—on the other hand, this traipsing around the world will also not be possible in the long term.—Now something else important.—In your letters I miss, above all, *detailed news* about *Otto and Alois.* You know that the two of them don't write me. But I would like to know, and must know, what is happening. So *don't forget this*!

By the way, take care to inquire whether both of them perhaps need something *in the way of underwear, clothes*, or anything else essential, [and] let me know as soon as possible.

Incidentally, in what way has Alois's health worsened, as you write?—

Warm greetings to Nina from me—and best wishes to you too from

Your brother
Gustav

15.XII.93.

SOURCE: Typewritten transcription in the Bibliothèque Musicale Gustav Mahler

346 *To Justine*

[Hamburg, 17 December 1893]

Dearest Justi!

Hopefully you have also received the little photographs!

I am now resolved about *Das klagende Lied*! That is, actually all my work consists of intelligent copying and the finishing of the whole with the help of my experiences as a conductor.—For (on the whole) I can *alter* nothing at all in the work.

I can tell you that I am *absolutely astounded* by this work, ever since I have had it in front of me again. When I consider that it was written by a 20/21-year-old man, I cannot understand it; it is so *idiosyncratic* and *powerful*! The nuts which I have given to crack here are perhaps the toughest that my soil has yet brought forth.—God knows whether I can ever bring *it* to performance.

In the next few days Pollini will be back again from his 2nd trip to St. Petersburg.—Then at any rate the business will finally be decided.—

With regard to the extension of my contract, I have finally decided to make it a condition sine qua non that if my compositions are being performed somewhere I must be allowed, under any circumstances, to travel there and conduct them.—If he does *not* allow me that (which very easily may be the case, given his principles), I will not *sign* a new contract!—Well, we will see indeed. I imagine that you are inspecting the Italian conditions—it seems to me that one could really live there on a really modest income.—Perhaps I should spend time there someday too—That would be wonderful!

Berliner went to Breslau for the holidays, so I am spending them in complete, and contented, solitude.—

My health is *excellent*! The iron does seem to be very effective.

Write again soon.

Let me know whether you've heard anything from Otto. I told Emma off for not writing you.[1]

Best wishes to you and Frau Marcus and Toni.—

I have to go out a little bit before tonight (Sunday 17th).

Your
Gustav

SHELFMARK: E15-MJ-579
NOTE
[1] See the previous letter.

347 *To Justine*

24/XII 93.

Dearest Justi!

Well, this time I have been without news of you for quite a long time.—I am afraid that the reason for it may be that you are "unwell."—

I am writing these lines to you on Christmas Eve. Later I am going to Lazarus's, where I was invited with Wagner.—

Imagine—the photographer sent me a few more of the little photographs (the same shot) that you have already.—If you need them, let me know. Otherwise they can stay here. It seems that nothing will become of *Petersburg this year*!

From the repertory list that I am sending you, you will see that the first two weeks of January really put my shoulder to the wheel. I have underlined in blue what I am conducting.

What do you have to say about Gottl. Adler![1] The business has upset me greatly. At the same time I received a wedding notice for Malesa from *Wlaschim*. The wedding is in Prague, Hotel Stein, on 1 January 1894.—The groom is named Josef Hoffman. So perhaps send congratulations!

Berliner has gone home for Christmas. Most kindly, he gave me a charming book, "Auch Einer!" by Vischer.[2] I didn't give anything to anyone! Natalie gave me a couple of books too—I already told her off for it. Emma, whom this time I wrote rather at length, answered me again. I suspect that, at my reminder, she will now be more forthcoming with you.

The work on "kl. Lied" is progressing *very slowly*, but steadily. I still hope to be finished with it before the beginning of the new year.—Then [have it] copied quickly and parts made.—I hope that this elegant enrichment of my library won't cost me too much (200 or 300 marks at the most).

There will be some really fine instances of artistry [*Kunablen*] among them. (In order to understand this joke, one has to look up what "incunabula" are in the encyclopaedia.)[3] Incidentally, bad enough!—so don't look it up at all!

Hopefully Frau Marcus is not "angry" that I don't write.—Since I am now very engaged with posterity, the here-and-now must have a little patience.

Natalie is complaining too, but she won't for long—why? She'll get used to it in the end.

Best wishes to you from
your
Gustav

Also to Frau Marcus and Tönchen!
(Tönnchen??)

SHELFMARK: E3-MJ-131
NOTES

[1] Physicist Gottlieb Adler (1860–1893) died in Vienna on 14 December. He had just been named professor at the Universität Wien (which he had attended at the same time as Mahler).

[2] Friedrich Theodor Vischer (1807–1887), *Auch Einer! Eine Reisebekanntschaft*, 2 vols. (Stuttgart & Leipzig: Hallberger, 1879).

[3] Something in its early stages; undeveloped.

348 *To Justine*

[Hamburg, end December 1893]

Dearest Justi!
I just got your letter from Rome.—I sent another *letter* and also *7* small photographs of you to Pensione *Michel*. In addition, a little while ago Dr. Schack sent you your forgotten bodice [*Taille*]. Please let me know if you have received all this—or rather, what steps you have taken to do so.—

By the way, how did it happen that your last letter had a *Milan postmark*. Please clarify this for me—this is most curious![1]—

The business with Otto irritates me, the more news I get (and demands on my part for enlistment) the more exasperated I get about the fellow.—I will send him *70 fl.* on the *1st* as usual. But there is *no* way that I am going to write him even a single word. On the contrary, I am so *furious* anyway that he better not show his face to me for a long time. Instead of stopping, these difficulties become more and more complicated, and in the end I won't be able to think about anything other than how I could help him regain his footing.—

By the way, if you are writing him, then elucidate for him how impudent and illogical his behaviour is.

Reproaches from me, even the strongest, have not even *wounded* him.—2. his recent, repeated method to always arrange his life and pursuits over my head without obtaining my permission or my consent in anything whatsoever.—e.g. I hear he is living with Alois; he neither asked my opinion nor communicated with me at all about it.—He goes to Munich without asking me, etc. etc. Set this all out for him.—If you all want to start anything at all with him, do what you want. *I am at the end*! *Neither me* nor a *line* from me should he look to get until he becomes otherwise.—

I don't really understand what you all mean by the "stupid things" that he could undertake.—Do you perhaps mean suicide? That I do not believe—but *even if—how* am I supposed to prevent such a thing from happening in the future to an undisciplined person?[2] I shall certainly not be prepared always to tremble and quake about whether or not Herr Otto is satisfied with me.—My *righteous indignation* towards him (you know how patient I was) has reached its climax! Bad enough that he occupies my thoughts so much and really and truly takes away every moment of peace I have in which to work!

It is quite telling that when it is a matter of angering me, he remains *persistent* and *single-minded*, but when it comes to *accomplishing something*, this he cannot achieve.—You can get this across to him too.

Under no circumstances will I write him any more. All of you, take note of this.

I have already taken steps about his engagement; it has definitely been promised to me for next winter. I don't know what to do with him for the summer, however.—He ought *not* [to come] to Steinbach. Mind you, it will be difficult to find some way out for him.

The Behns and Lazarus send their greetings. Write us soon.

Warmly, your
Gustav

SHELFMARK: E5-MJ-243
NOTES
[1] Justine's letters to Ernestine do not clarify this question, as they were all sent from Rome until the end of March 1894.
[2] Justine's fears were prescient, as Otto did commit suicide on 6 February 1895. See introduction.

349 *To Justine*

[Hamburg, early January 1894]

Dearest Justi!
Enclosed, a letter from Nina that will elucidate the situation for you.

Along with the money, I sent Otto an 8-page letter (admonishing him very seriously, mind you)—to which no reply has come.—

From the New Year's card enclosed as well (I take it that Otto was with the group as well) I see that his Grace [*Gnaden*] has still not admitted me to favour [*Gnaden*] since only his name was missing on it.—Please investigate this!

Falstaff was really a personal triumph here for me.[1]—[Eleanora] Duse appeared 3 times here in the Thaliastrasse. I was at *each* performance. *I wished that you* could have been there, you Italian.—*I* was simply enraptured by her. None of the reports of her is exaggerated.[2]—

Did I write you already that *nothing* is happening with Petersburg? *Put off* until next year.

The cold here is almost unbearable. *Do you all have a stove in your room? What is that about your finger?* I am afraid that you all now will *freeze* horribly.

It seems that I have somewhat offended Natalie again because of a too insensitive correspondence.

Best wishes to you and the two ladies.

Yours
Gustav

SHELFMARK: E3-MJ-133
NOTES

[1] The premiere of *Falstaff* was on 2 January.

[2] Italian actress (1858–1924), particularly known for her leading roles in plays by Ibsen and D'Annunzio.

350 *To Justine*

Postcard[1]
[Postmark: Hamburg, 4.1.94]
[Arrival postmark: Rome, 6.1.94]

D.J!—A few quick lines only so you won't worry.—Falstaff went over *splendidly*. I am very well.

Beginning today it is *10 degrees cold* here! I am chattering! Have you received the money already? And is it enough? Tonight I am at the Lazarus's.

Warmest wishes from
your
G.

Klagende Lied entirely finished and already at the copyist's!

SHELFMARK: E15-MJp-580
NOTE

[1] Addressed to "Fräulein Justine Mahler / Rom / Pensione Unione / Piazza Montecitorio."

351 *To Justine*

[Hamburg,] 14/I 94

Dearest Justi!
Here [is] the new repertory list.—The Bartered Bride is on 2 days later, then.[1]—Did I write you already that [Eleanora] *Duse* appeared here 3 times? I was there each time, and have never had such an impression from an actress.—It really would have been something for you as a connoisseur of the Italian language.—

The performances now are quite good. The personnel take the greatest possible pains (the fruit of the fuss that they have had with me!).—

I just got your letter with the enclosure.—Otto is displaying all the stubbornness and narrow-mindedness of his youth (i.e., at his age, I was farther along!). Regarding Alois, I will send you *40 fl.* more on the 1st; please send it to him as payment for his debt in Lucern—but *from <u>you</u>*, as [your] savings (don't let him know that I gave it to you). Nina writes me that *new debts*, which he professes *not* to have known about, are turning up constantly now. A fine gentleman! Our Viennese friends [*Die Wiener*] really appear not to have known of the depths of common stupidity he demonstrates—for years he has thrown away money, apparently with both hands. What could he have done with it? Nina wrote me that the 20 fl. are already taken up by repairs for sewing machines etc.

Somewhat depressed and sentimental news has arrived again from Natalie. She really is a poor creature. Moreover, I am really afraid of this summer, because I cannot bear to be in *contact with her*.

Strauss conducts here next and has announced himself to me in a friendly manner: "my only friend among all the gods."[2]

Now, off to rehearsal!

Write again soon, and say hello to Frau Markus [*sic*] and Tönchen!

Yours affectionately,
Gustav

SHELFMARK: E3-MJ-132
NOTES

[1] The premiere of *Die verkaufte Braut* took place on 17 January.

[2] Richard Strauss conducted the seventh subscription concert on 22 January 1894. The program included his own tone poem *Aus Italien*. Mahler's quotation alludes to Wotan's lines addressed to Loge at the beginning of the second scene of *Das Rheingold*: "Von allen Göttern / dein einz'ger Freund."

352 *To Justine*

[Hamburg, mid-January 1894]

Dearest Justi!
To crown it all, Lohse has become sick again, and now I have to conduct every day.[1] Despite this, I am quite bright and lively.

Strauss is here now; yesterday I played my Humoresken for him. He was very delighted, and, hopefully, will do something for them.

From Nina's letter, which I will enclose, the situation in Vienna will become clearer to you.—

Let me know right away how much I should *send* to you.—

Did you give *the book to Frau de Boor already*?[2] Also, a few weeks ago I sent you the *tea* you wanted! Did you not receive it?—

Naturally, now I have even less time to write.

Best wishes from
your
Gustav

Say hello to Frau Marcus and Toni from me. How are they?

SHELFMARK: E3-MJ-134
NOTES

[1] *Kapellmeister* Otto Lohse (1859–1925), married to soprano Katarina Klafsky (1855–1896).

[2] Unknown, but also mentioned in letter 379.

353 *To Justine*

[Hamburg, end January 1894]

Dearest Justi!

For almost 8 days a cyclone raged through our city—yesterday it reached its peak, and today the most wonderful weather has arrived. Have you felt nothing of it down there?—

It is not right that now you are only thinking of next year; you should enjoy the present to its utmost. Berliner told me about your letter today. So you are returning as a real Italian? I think that this winter has given you something for your entire life.

I am now in the process of securing my concerts for next year. For the time being, either I will take over the Wolff concerts, or Pollini will arrange 4.[1] Even that would ultimately be enough. I still always eat at the Streit [Hotel]. Shouldn't you come here in May in order to arrange everything for the fall? Or do you think that I can do everything on my own?

For my benefit performance, I am performing the *7th Symphony*.[2]—I was often together with Strauss. I would be lying, however, if I were to say that many points of contact arose between us.—More and more I see that I stand entirely alone amongst present-day musicians. Our goals diverge. From my point of view, I can only see everywhere either old-classical or New-German pedantry. Hardly has Wagner been recognised and understood when yet again the priests of the only accepted true faith come forth and surround the whole terrain with fortresses against real life, which thus always consists of the fact that one always reshapes the Old (even if it is greater and more significant than the New) and creates it anew out of the necessity of the moment.[3] Strauss in particular is just such a Pope! But, at any rate, a likeable chap, insofar as I could discern. Whether it's all genuine remains to be seen. All this is said strictly *between us*, because he is "my only friend among all the gods"—and I do not want to ruin everything with him. By the way, he speculated a little bit about my succession here—and I—for my life would gladly have stepped down for him, if only I had found a little spot to accommodate me.[4]—In this regard, I have tried *everything* so that my conscience may be clear. But it does seem that all doors are closed to me for the moment because of my Jewishness.—

From Munich—Possart, for example[5]—where I had an agent make some direct inquiries came the answer: "*although I am taken with Mahler's outstanding importance*, I am not in a position *to be interested in* him!" A similarly evasive answer from Berlin! So—since the world rejects me, I will return to the Venusberg![6] There I am certainly still in luck, since after all, as you see from Strauss, the position here is not too bad.

[unsigned]

SHELFMARK: S1-MJ-748

NOTES

[1] In early 1894, Mahler was negotiating a renewal of his contract and one of his conditions was that he be allowed to conduct several concerts; see below, letters 355 and 357. In the end Mahler did take over Wolff's subscription concert series for the 1894–1895 season.

[2] Mahler's annual benefit took place on 3 March 1894.

[3] When this letter was published in Herta Blaukopf, "Rivalität und Freundschaft: Die persönlichen Beziehungen zwischen Gustav Mahler und Richard Strauss," in *Gustav Mahler–Richard Strauss. Briefwechsel 1888–1911*, ed. Herta Blaukopf (Munich: Piper, 1980), the phrase "allein seligmachenden Pfaffen [priests of the only accepted true faith]" appeared in parentheses. These parentheses were added in pencil, apparently by Alfred Rosé, and are not Mahler's.

[4] Unbeknownst to Mahler, Strauss was negotiating with Pollini about coming to Hamburg (it is unclear who approached whom); see Mahler's letters to Strauss of 3 February (two) and 6 February in *Gustav Mahler–Richard Strauss. Briefwechsel 1888–1911*. See also Herta Blaukopf's discussion in the same volume, pp. 148–50. In the end, Strauss obtained the position he had been hoping for in Munich.

[5] Ernst von Possart (1841–1921), *Intendant* of Munich Opera.

[6] An allusion to Wagner's *Tannhäuser*: carnal satisfaction, but no spiritual salvation.

354 *To Justine*

[Hamburg, end January 1894]

Dearest Justi!
In haste, I am sending you the new repertory list, in which there is finally some breathing room for me.—I was with Strauss quite a lot.

The enclosed photograph is the one, then, that you mean. Should I have some more made for you?

I have still not received a bill from Sänger[1]—but a heap of others. *Bülow* is going to Cairo—he has *kidney disease*![2] The poor fellow! The *Lazaruses* are going with him (they always have to be at the centre of things).—It is very sad that he will have such an end: to die in the melodramatic company of these old women—considering that he lived with Liszt and Wagner. More soon.

Affectionately,
Gustav

(I have to head to the theatre to conduct!)

Shelfmark: E3-MJ-136
Notes

[1] A Hamburg doctor who also treated Hans von Bülow.

[2] Bülow left Hamburg toward the end of January, en route to Alexandria via Berlin, Vienna, and Trieste. He died in Alexandria on 12 February, only several days after his arrival. See Marie von Bülow's diary entries from this period in Hans von Bülow, *Briefe*, ed. Marie von Bülow, vol. 8: *Höhepunkt und Ende, 1886–1894* (Leipzig: Breitkopf and Härtel, 1908), pp. 455–59.

355 *To Justine*

[Hamburg, 6 February 1894]

Dearest Justi!
First of all, the news that yesterday I concluded another new 5-year contract with Pollini in which I am assured of 4–6 concerts yearly, whether here or somewhere else.—The negotiations were stressful! He wanted nothing of it, but I was *tougher* than he was and pushed it through so decisively that I almost

expected an utter crash.[1] Sometime you will learn the details.—By the way, Pollini is charming towards me.—I am persona gratissima and *just as hated* (as never before) by the *singers*! Well! Forget about it.—

Something else important! *Write nothing* to Vienna about the contract! Otherwise, as you well know, I will pay for it again. Even Emma would then completely neglect her studies and prepare herself *to come here with me*—which I *would no longer even consider.* For the time being, she should calmly take up a position in Vienna, continue living with Nina, and I will simply send her what is necessary.[2]—

Later we will say that I signed for a *further* year and consequently am not able to make any changes to the status quo.—

Now, if it is at all possible, I *must save* as much as *possible* during these *5 years* in order some day finally to become independent. It may be the last opportunity! This will now be *your mission*, to be *concerned* for this and, possibly, to take the finances into your hands! *Can you do this*? This would take the greatest burden from me! I already have a plan!—The Sans woman is already looking for apartments and houses, and already has all kinds of things up her sleeves.[3]—I have decided to set myself up *on modest footing* right away.—To buy nothing new and above all keep my sights on a *quiet apartment* and focus on thoroughgoing *savings* in everything else.

A sad bit of news is that as of the fall Berliner is moving to *Berlin.*—By the way, I have passed your request on to him, and so you will receive detailed news of me and everything else.

I received, and paid, a bill for *90* marks from Dr. Sänger.—

Now the question is what to do about next year; whether *a flat* or a cottage etc. etc. Discuss this sometime with Frau *Marcus*, and write me about it in detail.—That would also be a load off my mind to have everything arranged for next year at this point.—

At any rate, next season I am conducting *4* concerts in *Convent Garden* arranged for here by Pollini.[4] Every now and then I've been at Her[t]zes and also met Frau Michls there.[5] Everyone is very well and merry. Warmest wishes to all of you. I hope that Carnival continues to be merry.

Your

6/II 94 Gustav

Shelfmark: E10-MJ-440

Notes

[1] According to Mahler's letter to Strauss of 6 February, on the 5th he was presented with a signed contract in which Pollini accepted all of his conditions; Mahler indicated to Strauss that he was about to countersign the contract that day (6 February).

[2] A letter from Justine to Ernestine of 22 February 1894 reveals something of the situation:

> I am still terribly uncertain what will happen with Emma next year. I do not know what I ought to do. On the one hand, I would not for anything force G. into living with a person to whom he is not at all close and whose presence would certainly cause agitation? On the other hand, it hurts me terribly that the girl always has to struggle amongst strangers.

An earlier letter suggests that Justine had already decided to join Gustav in Hamburg that fall:

> Gustav cannot make up his mind to sign the contract with Pollini. I am already very eager how it will all end. Afterwards, I will fix my plans for next winter. At any rate, if G. has to stay in Hamburg, I am thinking of setting down [there] for the season—but without a household. It really would not be smart to set oneself up so expensively if one knows in advance that it cannot possibly last for long. Gustav will not stay there for long under any circumstances. (4 February 1894)

In the end, both Justine and Emma moved to Hamburg in early September.

[3] Unknown Hamburg acquaintance of Mahler's. She is mentioned in several letters from this time, as well as in GMB[2] 248. In the note to this letter (letter 234) in *Selected Letters of Gustav Mahler*, Knud Martner identifies her as Elizabeth Sans, a Hamburg pianist and composer.

[4] A concert hall in Hamburg, not to be confused with the London opera house.

[5] Unknown, but also mentioned in letter 367 and in GMB[2] 136 (as Michaels).

356 *To Justine*

[Hamburg, 7 February 1894]

Dearest Justi!
Here [is] the latest repertory list and Mihalovich's letter.[1]—

Hopefully you already have my letter of yesterday.

I am now very frequently at Behns and feel very much at home there. Recently we even "played chamber music."

Right now a Berlin sculptor is living with them, who, moreover, wants to sculpt me too! All in all, I have to sit for at least *12 hours*. I don't think that I would be able to bear it.—The Sans woman is still pestering me about lessons and apartments.

I do not understand that you are now so frequently unwell again! Perhaps the Roman climate is not good for you?

With best wishes,
Your
7/II 94.Gustav

Shelfmark: E3-MJ-135
Note

[1] Does not survive. Mahler answered Mihalovich on the same day as this letter; see Roman, pp. 161–63.

357 *To Justine*

[Hamburg, early February 1894]

Dearest Justi!
I just received your letter in pencil.—I am very concerned. Shouldn't the Roman climate be good for you?[1]

Just think: hardly had I signed the contract with Pollini when Böhme came and asked me, on behalf of *Wolff*, to take over the Bülow Concerts permanently. There was great consternation when I showed him Pollini's signature, *still wet*, on the contract.—Yesterday he was here again and declared that Wolff is prepared to make any concessions to Pollini. I left it to his discretion to look into it here and now tomorrow Wolff is coming to Hamburg to persuade Pollini, but I am afraid that it will all be in vain, since the two of them do not get along with each other.[2]

At any rate, I am conducting concerts next year—perhaps *Pollini* will *have* to arrange them himself.

I received Alois's enclosure. *Do you have enough* money? Why don't you write me *anything* about it? Always indicate to me the sum that you want anyway.

Write me *right away*.

Yours affectionately,
Gustav

Now, hopefully a *calmer* time really will come, since the immediate future is decided.

Congratulations on the marriage proposal! From whom? I image that for a woman this is something like a successful *performance* for me?[3]

SHELFMARK: E3-MJ-137
NOTES

[1] According to her letter to Ernestine of 10 February, Justine had been ill with bronchitis and fever.

[2] Berlin impresario Hermann Wolff (1845–1902). As we have seen, a condition of Mahler's contract was that he be allowed to conduct concerts next year. When he signed his contract on 6 February, Mahler assumed that nothing from Wolff would be forthcoming. While Mahler ultimately did take over the Bülow concerts, it took a number of weeks before the situation was resolved; see letter 364.

[3] In fact, Justine received two proposals, as she wrote to Ernestine on 4 February:

> Now, something new that will amuse you greatly. Since I have been in Rome, I have had two marriage proposals from Italians. . . . I will now describe both of them to you; they are still nearby laying siege to me. The first, Prof. Zucarelli, is 35 years old, the director of a girl's seminary, an author, and an idealist. He told me that he fell in love with me when we walked into the room for the first time. . . . The second—whose photograph I enclose for you to look at—is a young painter, 25 years old (by the way, he is now painting my portrait). . . . I am often afraid, [and] in the course of this I *never* gave him a spark of hope, since I am entirely indifferent towards him. At the masked ball, I went to dance with another man and he followed and said to me that he would kill himself if I touched anyone else; I was not to provoke him, or there would be an accident. . . . The painter told me that I was the realisation of his ideal, that he would love me madly my whole life, and when I told him that I was completely indifferent to him, that I couldn't feel anything for him, he said to me that I should just allow him to love me, that would be enough for him.

358 *To Justine*

[Hamburg, 13 February 1894][1]

Once again I can't work. The negotiations and the continual unrest have definitely driven me out of the mood—it always takes a long time before it settles upon me again.

I am terribly happy about Steinbach—*only I am afraid of Natalie*!—Next year here you will diligently pursue Italian and English, and maybe I will too. You have quite the lead in Italian, mind you.—Here I will have to cede the hegemony to you.

What do you have to say about the letters that I sent you?

Yesterday I read in the Pester Lloyd about the *first* premiere presented by Nikisch: an old Lortzing opera that flopped *completely*. Now Nikisch too will get to know the backside of existence in Budapest. Until now he hasn't done anything other than attend banquets and play the director.—I don't envy that!

A new constellation has set in for Berliner—he may be staying here after all!

Next year I intend to have *chamber music* every week at home—naturally only with the *smallest circle*! Is that all right with you, then?

Sans's address is Bundesstrasse No. 18

Best wishes to you and to the two ladies.

Your
Gustav

Hamburg, 13/II 93 [*sic*] (Wagner's death day)
Tonight Siegfried.

SHELFMARK: E10-MJ-435
NOTE

[1] Although Mahler clearly writes "[18]93" at the end of the letter, from the contents it must have been written in 1894. (For example, *Siegfried* was not performed on this day in 1893.)

359 *To Justine*

[Hamburg, c. 16 February 1894][1]

Dearest Justi!

I just received your letter with the enclosure, which I return to you right away.—The letter is priceless, though.—One certainly cannot take the fellow seriously. And it is very convenient that you stand with him such that one can yet keep a bit of an eye on him.—According to our method, you can also support him with money every now and then when he's headed for disaster—so that one can just keep his head above water without giving him an opportunity for wastefulness.—

It must always appear that you are sacrificing yourself and that *I will not find out about it*!

Yesterday I went for a walk through the parks in Flottbeck with Berliner, and afterwards we ate together in the Park Hotel. There I thought of the time you were with me, and looked forward to when we will be able to walk there together again.

We will have to take advantage of every free afternoon for such an excursion.

The oxygen that I took into my blood manifested itself this morning as a superb mood, and will crystallise itself, I imagine, into a healthy appetite at midday.

I already wrote you that I still eat at Streit's [Hotel] and am well looked after there.—Today I am invited to *Wagner's*; Toni will be very envious.

A few days ago my intrusive guests, the haemorrhoids, presented themselves again. I am banishing them straight away by *gymnastics* and am very pleased to have found such a tried and effective means against them. I am also very happy about Steinbach—only I am very worried about Natalie.—By the way, what are we doing about *Otto* then? That will be a difficult matter!

Your chill seems to have been a bad one, and I have the impression that you still are not *back to normal*! Please be candid about it!

Best wishes to you from
Your
Gustav

How is Frau Markus [*sic*]? I hear about Toni now and then from her grandfather, who naturally talks about her letters once in a while.

[written in pencil:] Did you get my last long letter (about Strauss)?[2]

SHELFMARK: E6-MJ-291
NOTES

[1] The date "18.2.1894" was written across the top of the letter in Justine's hand; this is likely the date it was received.

[2] It is possible that Mahler is referring to letter 353.

360 *To Justine*

[Hamburg, c. third week February 1894]

Dearest Justi!
Bülow Funeral concert next Monday. Strauss has cancelled. *I am conducting the Eroica and Leonore Overture 3.*[1]

Until then, I have a lot to do and to worry about again.

It is curious that someone always has to become ill or die before I can conduct a symphony.—

Why do you write so little? Your plans really are magnificent! One could really envy you!

So, at any rate, you are not coming before *fall* and so I will take an apartment myself. Did you already write Sans. She will take care of everything that you need.

Best wishes to you from
Your
Gustav

SHELFMARK: E15-MJ-581
NOTE

[1] The concert (the ninth subscription concert of the season) took place on Monday, 26 February. In addition to the *Eroica*, the program consisted of a Bach organ prelude and the first two choruses of Brahms's *Ein deutsches Requiem* (the *Leonore* Overture was not performed). According to Blaukopf, "Rivalität und Freundschaft," p. 153, Strauss cancelled to avoid having to conduct a work by Brahms and possibly trouble his relationship with Cosima Wagner.

361 *To Justine*

[Hamburg, 23 or 24 February 1894][1]

Dearest Justi!
Here, quickly, is the repertory list.

Today was the 1st *rehearsal of the Eroica*. Everything is going splendidly, and I am quite content.—

I will have Berliner send you all the reviews of the concert, since I don't read them, as you know. What will the gentlemen bring up this time?

A gala performance of "Fledermaus," with the first cast, for the benefit of the "Presse."[2] *I am conducting*—so that will be quite jolly.

Best wishes to everybody
Gustav

If you can, please send me a photograph or *engraving* (on card), as large as possible, of the beautiful painting (of *Music*—for the moment, I don't know what it is called)—the same one that Lipiner gave me (small) and that you wrote me that you saw in Rome or Florence.[3]

Shelfmark: E15-MJ-582
Notes

[1] The date is speculative and assumes that Mahler began rehearsals for the Bülow memorial concert (Monday, 26 February) at the end of the week before.

[2] The benefit performance of *Die Fledermaus* ("Zum Besten des Unterstützungsfonds des Journalisten- und Schriftsteller-Vereins von Hamburg-Theater in Altona") was on 13 March.

[3] There is no mention of this in Justine's letters to Ernestine. There are two artworks with musical subjects connected with Mahler: the first, a large representation of St. Cecilia, hung in his study (see photographs 92 and 93 in *The Mahler Album*, ed. Gilbert Kaplan [New York: Kaplan Foundation, 1995]); the second, a monk playing a keyboard, apparently by Giorgione, is mentioned by Bruno Walter in his book on Mahler.

362 *To Justine*

[Hamburg, 26 February 1894]

Dearest Justi!
The enclosed will clarify everything!

Tonight is the concert.[1]

You *don't* need *to come here*. I will look for the apartment all by myself.

Still nothing is decided with *Wolff*. The critics will probably "shred" me again, and Wolff will lose his confidence.

But that is immaterial, since Pollini has assured me of *4* concerts for next year.

Best wishes to you from your
Gustav

Shelfmark: E15-MJ-595
Note

[1] The Bülow memorial concert.

363 *To Justine*

[Hamburg, 27 February 1894]

Dearest Justi!

Yesterday "victory on all fronts"!

The Eroica was truly an Eroica!

The evening proceeded most curiously. I myself, as the conductor, was behind a wall of plants that surrounded Bülow's bust and hid me, and the public, with appropriate sensibility, abstained from any sign of applause. But the quiet stillness and the sighs of relief *after* each movement testified clearly how powerful the impression was.

Wolff from Berlin was there too, and now kicks himself terribly that he didn't engage me long ago.—

Now he will summon up everything in order to obtain me from Pollini.—

The local wailing women [*Klageweiber*], Fräulein Petersen and the Schiff ladies, are already extremely embarrassing to me! It was a question of climbing the walls or laughing oneself sick: I've done both.

I am curious how Sittard will shift himself around this time, since because of the mood of the public yesterday he does have to be somewhat prudent.

Things with Berliner are going as usual. I have more annoyance than enjoyment in his company. Just as soon as I go out in a nice, lively mood, I get his cold shower of logic and righteousness such that I almost cannot bring myself to regret his departure—which, as of now, is definitely approaching in the summer. His marked intimacy in other's company also bothers me.

But still, I will *miss* him—the others understand me even less.[1]—I am now at Behns a lot and am beginning to get used to it. I like them more and more and I think that I am preparing a little place in their house for our joint residence in the future—one that will warm us in the winter, and shade us in the summer. They are really sweet towards me.

Apropos, I am now being "*sculpted*." The visual arts seem to like my contours more than the musical ones do. *Allers* wants to paint me too (but I'm not interested).[2]

Your letter yesterday (about the beautiful sculptures) shows great cheer. This winter ought hardly to be given up as lost for you.—

Saturday is my benefit, after which I *will* again breathe some fresh air.—

Best wishes from your
Gustav

Hamburg 27/II 94

SHELFMARK: S1-MJ-747

NOTE

[1] Two excerpts from Justine's letters to Ernestine illuminate Berliner's personality and relationship with the Mahlers:

> Did you find Dr. Berliner's letter nice too? Too bad that one couldn't marry him, but I never could bring myself to do so, despite his sensibleness: his looks are too disagreeable to me. That he is very good natured must certainly be granted. He likes G. a lot more than G. likes him. (8 December 1893)

Dr. Berliner also came over from Berlin and asked me to marry him (I was going in to dinner with him). I asked him not to say anything to G. and made it clear to him that I could never be his wife. (21 March 1895)

[2] Unknown.

364 *To Justine*

[Hamburg, 3 March 1894]

Dear Justi!

Today, on the day of the benefit performance, just a few lines.[1] Afterwards, there is a banquet at Behns' for my friends only. For entry, one will be asked if one is an admirer of my tempos; if not, one won't be admitted.—I think that this is very nice, and next year intend to break off all contact with people who do not regard my tempos as the one true church.

Today Böhme was here in order to ask me on behalf of Wolff to direct the next subscription concert.[2]—After a long fight with me, Pollini deigned to hand me over to Herr Wolff for *500* marks—so the "better principle" triumphed in him. I find this terrific fun that Herr Wolff now has to pay an extra 500 marks to P[ollini] for every concert—and if he had thought about the matter earlier (*before I concluded my contract*), he could have had me *for nothing*.

Today he sent me *300* marks for the last concert. However, they, as well as the money from today's benefit, are for *debts* (which are naturally not lacking—or, unfortunately I am not without them!)

Enclosed, another article from the "Pester Lloyd."

The good Nikisch has only been there for *a few months* and he's already on his last legs! Ugh! I don't envy him!

It is not at all all right with me that Otto and Alois are moving in together again. Otto hardly writes me at all anymore. I don't even know if he receives the money that I regularly send him on the 1st.

I have a charming apartment here up my sleeve (near the Alster *alte Rabenstrasse*) which would suit us wonderfully.—The only unfortunate thing is that your room would face *north*; although with a beautiful view of the countryside. The apartment has extraordinary merit in every respect. You will have 2 rooms in the front, and then next to them is the *dining* and *sitting room* (so 3 rooms altogether). *I would have* 2 spacious rooms in the back by the garden. Your room adjoins a large, beautiful balcony.—The apartment is in a one-storey house. An older, childless couple live on the parterre. We would have the *first* floor, and a few steps higher lies the *kitchen* and maid's room, completely *separate*, and beside it there is another room (possibly for Emma or a guest).

The house belongs to Consul Elkann,[3] whom Frau Marcus may know. Up to now his daughter (or daughter-in-law) has lived there.

Let me know right away if I should take the apartment.

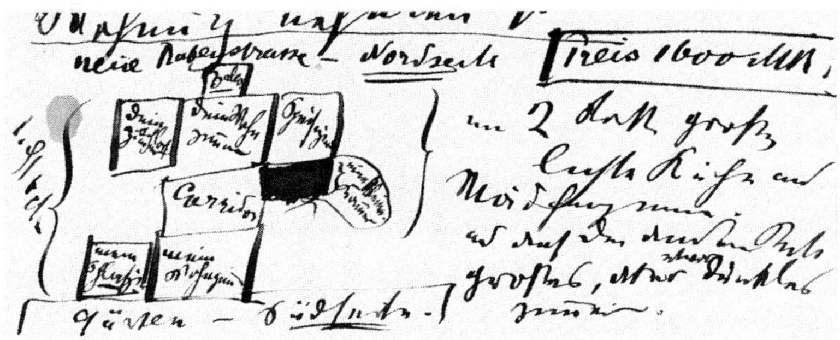

_____________ Price 1600 marks.

Neue Rabenstrasse—<u>North side</u>
[draws plan; see figure 1]
Garden—<u>Southside</u>.

on the 2nd floor, a large, bright, kitchen
and maid's room. and on the other side
a large, but somewhat dark room.

Figure 1. Detail of Mahler's letter to Justine, 3 March 1894 (E15-MJ-583; Gustav Mahler–Alfred Rosé Collection, Music Library, University of Western Ontario. Reproduced with permission.)

Frau Sans doesn't think that we could ever find an apartment that would suit us so well.—One wonders whether you could live in a north room. (I don't know if it is completely <u>due</u> north).—Or *is* this not so important in the winter?

Write right away.

It is very wrong of Frau Marcus to allow herself to go and spoil [everything]. I don't understand how you and Toni could have let it happen so calmly. <u>If I</u> had been there, I would have spoken sharply right away.

Affectionately, your
Gustav

Hamburg 3 March 1894

Shelfmark: E15-MJ-583
Notes

[1] In addition to *Fidelio*, Mahler conducted Beethoven's Seventh Symphony. (Martner, *Gustav Mahler im Konzertsaal*, erroneously gives the date of the benefit performance as 1 March.)

[2] In the end, the tenth subscription concert on 12 March was conducted by Anton Rubinstein.

[3] Unknown.

365 *To Justine*

[Hamburg,] 4/III 94.

Dearest Justi!
The painting came yesterday.—You are depicted quite superbly. Mind you, the painter didn't exactly find the most flattering moment. At any rate, you seem to have had an awful cold at the time. I am very happy about the painting, by the way, and for the time being it is on the piano.[1]

Saturday is Otto's *call-up* [*Stellung*]! as he just informed me. Did I write you already that I got him set up at *Staegemann's* in the summer?[2]—We would be best rid of him that way.—

The enclosed letter from Frau Cosima Wagner, which I received yesterday and which is couched in a particularly friendly tone, I place for your disposal for your natural-history cabinet. Now, slowly, you have gotten the entire family together, except for *him*, who, fortunately, also belongs a little bit to *my* family. (Do you understand this?)[3]

Above all, I see from the letter that, for the time being, Bayreuth is prepared to restore me to grace. What will become of it later cannot be assessed yet. Unfortunately, however, as a consequence I absolutely must appear in *Bayreuth* this *summer*, which will determine and modify my sojourn on the beautiful Attersee a little bit, at any rate.

The painter must be very *talented* indeed! Tell me something about him! If you see him again, convey him my thanks and appreciation, even though we do not know each other.—Hopefully he has enough good taste and manners to court you properly.

—By the way—I just looked at the painting again—I do find it really *splendid.*—

If one knows a person inside and out, in all situations, *the way I know you*, the first glimpse of a painting of him is always disconcerting, since it is only the expression of a single mood and view.

But one thing is certain: there has never been a photograph of you that is as faithful as the painting. It also appears to be made quite splendidly (although I cannot really judge).—

Best wishes to you from
Your
Gustav

Special greetings to Tönchen, and thanks for the friendly hello. I am registering the letter because of the enclosure! *Did you get my previous letter?*

[upside-down, across top of last page:]

I am already terribly happy *about* summer! London is definitely given up![4]

SHELFMARK: E15-MJ-584

NOTES

[1] The portrait of Justine, painted by the young painter who had asked Justine to marry him (see above, notes to letter 357, was a frequent topic of conversation in her letters to Ernestine from this time. Justine had it done in order to be able to send it to Mahler for his March benefit concert (letter to Ernestine of early February).

[2] See below, letter 370.

[3] The letter does not survive in the Mahler-Rosé Collection. Mahler seems to imply that Justine now has letters from Cosima and Siegfried Wagner (although one does not survive), at least, but not one from Richard Wagner.

[4] Mahler had received another offer from Sir Augustus Harris to return to London with the Hamburg company. An unpublished draft of a letter (in English) to Harris, written on the same date as this letter, indicates Mahler's demands: "I am with pleasure to your disposition. . . . My terms are: 50 £ for week and voyage and other expenses free." Mahler's postscript to Justine indicates that he knew that Harris would not accept his price (which was the equivalent of about 1,000 marks a week; see letter 371).

366 *To Emma*

[Hamburg,] 4.III.94

Dear Emma!

Find *Otto* right away and tell him that I am in negotiations on his behalf with the Stadttheater in *Bremen*, where I would like to obtain for him the position of chorus director and 2nd conductor. Since I haven't had any more news from him for weeks, I would like to know right away when his "*call up*" [*Stellung*] in Vienna takes place, and also whether he is in agreement with my steps.—Bremen would be very sensible for him, also because it is very near Hamburg, which may be reached in 1½ hours.

I have concluded my contract again for next year.—Everything is so uncertain for me here, however, that now I have definitely decided *not* to settle down here. I still don't know where Justi will be next year.—At any rate, you will stay in Vienna—just see to it that you do achieve a respectable result in the examination in order to obtain a respectable position.[1] We will certainly talk through all this in the summer properly. I am now up to my ears in so much work that I can again only write you these few lines.—The benefit turned out very well. Everything went splendidly, with wreaths and applause in abundance.

Write me about Otto right away, and order him to communicate with me right away. Have you all received *my money* all right? And how is Nina? Best wishes to all of you

Your brother,
Gustav

Source: Transcribed from a facsimile of the original letter (Jerry Bruck, New York)

Note

[1] Mahler was clearly being disingenuous; see above, letter 355.

367 *To Justine*

[Hamburg, early March 1894]

Dearest Justi!

This time I was really worried that no letter arrived for so long. You all will certainly know that old Hertz is ill. For a while it appeared very alarming—unfortunately, I couldn't talk to anyone in the family and only heard everything from the waiter.—Yesterday, however, I spoke to young Hertz and learned that, luckily, the danger is now passed.—Frau Marcus will have been quite upset by the news. Naturally, Frau Michls is here.—We have the most beautiful spring weather here, which I am enjoying heartily. I will be all alone again during the Easter holidays since Berliner is at his parents' and the Behns have something else on.[1] The weeping willows [*Trauerweiden*] Lazarus and Schiff have become too tiresome for me.

Emma is a terrible problem; I do not know what to do. From afar, it might just be best to let things go, otherwise one would only do the wrong thing.—For the time being, there is nothing to be done about school—she must just repeat it! Moreover, for us to take her in seems very questionable to me, since a lasting status quo would possibly be created under these circumstances; and so we should consider such a thing carefully.[2]

By the way, I have a very pretty apartment up my sleeve (Sans!).

Definite decisions about Otto will have to wait until he survives the trenches [*Stellung*].

As far as your travel plan is concerned, consider really carefully if it is not dangerous now to go to Sicily. At any rate, you all will be careful and sensible.

What is Frau Marcus actually thinking of doing with Toni next year, then? Probably they will settle in here as well?

Should I still send the money to *Rome*?[3] You didn't write me anything about it! From your last letter, you don't seem to be quite "well" now!?

Enclosed, a new photograph that was made for the sculptor who is doing me. It is the only copy and is *not touched up*! How do you like it—should I have more like it made?

Warmest wishes to all of you. Frau Marcus doesn't need to worry! Of course, I go there twice a day in order to inquire.

Affectionately, your
Gustav

SHELFMARK: E15-MJ-589
NOTES

[1] Easter Sunday was 25 March 1894.

[2] On 10 February, Justine had written to Ernestine: "I am beside myself: the girl is anaemic and because of that is neglecting her school. It will be another bitter disappointment for G. that she too won't pass her examination."

[3] On Tuesday, 21 March, Justine wrote to Ernestine that they were leaving on "Tuesday or Wednesday" (28 or 29 March) for Naples. Her next letter was sent from Naples on the 30th. These letters make no mention of a trip to Sicily.

368 *To Justine*

[Hamburg, 10 March 1894]

Dearest Justi!
Enclosed, another new repertory list.—Yesterday I had a nice shock when I read the news of your bomb![1] I cannot believe that you did not telegraph me <u>*right away*</u>.—That was really thoughtless of you. You must have thought that I would read the news right away in all the papers?!

I received your photographs. Thank Frau Markus [*sic*] very much. I'm not attending *any social gatherings at all*. Am also not invited!

The tent of flowers was from an anonymous female donor [*Spenderin*], and in fact obviously from the one who often sends me "poems" and by whom I have been quite showered with "verse" in the last little while.—Otherwise there were also lots of anonymous things there.—From Hertz I received a splendid box with excellent cigars.—From *Berkan* [*sic*] a priceless, golden laurel wreath (he is that admirer of mine who pays respect to me all the time; perhaps you remember the bouquet that time on the day of the concert[)].[2]—

Frau Dr. Lazarus is already back from Rome. I immediately got a card from her that she must see me as soon as possible.—I went to her this very afternoon, where she appeared before me with this certain little face, fixedly distorted with grief—looking at me with agitated understanding. I gave her a bit of a cold shower when I made it clear to her that I am not interested in corpses and do not want to know all the details of the funeral procession, etc. She said right away that this was also her view, and that all sentimentality was like a thorn in her eye.—Whereupon we were both very content.—The old dolt! Let the wailing women leave me in peace!

I am now in the middle of Fledermaus.

Right, I got an offer from *Harris* to conduct there again during the *season*.

I asked for a high fee (6000 marks and all expenses paid).[3] If I let the holiday be ruined than it should also yield a decent amount of money too—which I could well use this year.

But I don't think that he will agree to this; and that is good too!

Affectionately, your
Gustav

Also, I am *not* taking the apartment in the Neue Rabenstrasse. We still have time, to be sure.

Hamburg 10/III 94.

Shelfmark: S1-MJ-749
Notes

[1] On 8 March, a bomb exploded at the Italian parliament on the Piazza Montecitorio (also the location of Justine's pension). In a letter of 12 March, Justine described to Ernestine what happened:

> Five minutes beforehand we went home through the square. I was standing in my room undressed to my undershirt in order to dress for dinner, Toni was next door to me. Suddenly, the window rattled, flew, and shattered into the room—a terrible noise, then screams in the street. In the darkness, I grabbed a skirt and a jacket, threw it on top of my undershirt, and rushed out. Panic! We had to spend the night without any glass in the windows.

[2] Wilhelm Berkhan was a Hamburg merchant and friend of Mahler's. Berkhan and Hermann Behn paid the costs of the Berlin premiere of the Second Symphony on 13 December 1895. (Both Mahler and Justine consistently spelled his name "Berkan," although it always appears as "Berkhan" in the Mahler literature.)

[3] As Mahler had requested 50 pounds (1,000 marks) per week, a six-week visit (as in 1892) must have been planned.

369 *To Justine*

[Hamburg, 10 March 1894]

Dearest Justi!

Just the good *news* that *Otto was released* and starts already in the next few days at the Stadttheater in *Leipzig* as a volunteer.—His contract in *Bremen* is *perfect*[1] too.

So, for the time being everything is in order. Enclosed, a 2nd letter from Cosima (an answer to my answer)—and another one from Frau v[on] Bülow; both may interest you.[2]

Apropos! You haven't *written* me yet if the *tea* that I sent you at your request a few weeks ago arrived safely?

I also see from your last letter that you apparently are *not* going to Sicily? Why?

What would you think if I don't take *any apartment* now and you look for one *yourself only* in the fall when they are always in abundance here? Don't you think that this would be more practical?

Your painting will be disparaged universally.—I really like it!

Affectionately, your
Gustav

10/III 94. London is definitely *off*!

SHELFMARK: E15-MJ-585
NOTES
[1] English in original.
[2] Neither letter survives.

370 *To Justine*

[Hamburg, 14 March 1894]

Dearest Justi!
So, for the moment we have Otto underway, as you will see from the enclosed letter.—In the next few days he will indeed arrive at Staegemann's in Leipzig, and, as of 1 September, is engaged for 3 years as chorus director and 2nd Kapellmeister.[1]—

Well—he has it easier than I [did] at his age.—In the 1st year he will have a monthly wage of *80* marks, *120* in the 2nd, and in the 3rd, *200*!

I also must write something about the "other one."[2] Apparently just now he is busy lining up engagements in Vienna. I am curious how long his sails will stay *full*. Now *nothing* will be of any *use* if *he himself* isn't competent.

Did you get the tea?

Here we have continually beautiful weather.

I would also like to know how things are going with your health? Mine is continually splendid—all winter without a *speck* of *medicine*.

Affectionately yours,
14/III 94 Gustav

SHELFMARK: E15-MJ-586
NOTES
[1] Otto was engaged in Bremen as of 1 September; until then, Mahler obtained a temporary position in Leipzig for him with his old director Max Staegemann (not the other way around, as indicated by HLG I, pp. 446–47).
[2] Alois.

371 *To Justine*

[Hamburg, 15 March 1894]

Dearest Justi!

Judging from your postcard today, *2* of the letters that I wrote you after the bomb attack were lost.—

The *first* was rather long (in which I also reproached you for not *telegraphing* me at once, since you must have known that the newspapers would publish wire reports of it right away)—in the *2nd* I included the *repertory list*; or has this one arrived in the meantime?[1]

Please let me know.

You would not believe *how* exhausted I am now. The day before yesterday was "Fledermaus," with great acclamation!

I did *not* take the *apartment*—Frau Marcus was quite right. Please thank her very much for the "Concerto" that I received. Also, both of your photographs arrived safely.

I just read that Director *Paulay* from Budapest died.[2]

I don't go into society, and am only *rarely* invited. People seem to have gradually realised that the pleasure of my company is only a very moderate one. Frau *Haller* doesn't slacken off at all, also not the famous *Behrendt*.[3]—To the former, I am going tonight; to the latter, naturally never again, obviously, without indicating the true reason. She'll have to figure it out.

I also wrote you that I received a proposal from London for the season there and asked for *1000* marks a week and completely *free room and board*.—As I expected and hoped, Harris's refusal arrived, so now hopefully the whole matter is finished.—Pollini placed too *high* a demand on Wolff—namely, an extra 500 marks *per concert*, apart from my fee.—That was too expensive for Wolff! At any rate, however, I am conducting 4 concerts next year that Pollini himself will arrange at the Convent Garden, so in the end that's good enough.

The enclosed letter from Nina arrived today.

The latest is that I have obtained a position for Otto as 2nd. Kapellmeister in *Bremen* just in case he is free.[4]—He would have to commit himself for *three years* and would *immediately* get a small wage. By any measure, this is advantageous for him, and he has already approved with the words "alea jacta est," like *Caesar*. I am curious whether he will be as cocky there.

For today, best wishes and thanks to Frau Marcus.

Yours,
Gustav

15/III 94.

SHELFMARK: E15-MJ-587

NOTES

[1] Both things described by Mahler are in his letter of 10 March, letter 368.

[2] Ede Paulay (1836–1894), actor, director, and dramaturg, died on 12 March in Budapest. He had been director of the Hungarian National Theatre since 1875.

[3] Both unknown.

[4] Mahler appears to have forgotten that he told Justine this the day before. (His comment about Otto being free is not completely comprehensible, since he knew on 10 March that he had been rejected for military service.)

372 *To Justine*

[Hamburg, 19 March 1894]

Dearest Justi!
From the enclosed you will discover another new mess. I just wrote Nina and forbade her to consult Tedern again, and recommended that Pfungen be consulted.[1] Maybe you know another doctor.—

I am quite furious with the lot of them.—I do not understand the whole business at all. By the way, why have I been 3 days without a letter from you? Did you get my last letters?

So, London is off!

At present we have wonderful weather, and I diligently binge on the air.

By the way, yesterday I was at Schmidt-Parks again! Even today I remain altogether awkward in social gatherings.

Write soon!

Affectionately, your
Gustav

19/III 94.

SHELFMARK: E15-MJ-588
NOTE
[1] Dr. Pfungen is mentioned in earlier letters.

373 *To Justine*

Picture postcard: Gruss vom Süllberg[1]
[Postmark: Blankenese, 21.3.94]
[Arrival postmark: Rome, 23.3.94]
21 March

D.J.
Beautiful spring weather on the Elbe with welcome company! 1 o'clock (now), breakfast *outside*!—Afterwards, through the parks on foot as far as Altona. (Departed from there around 11 o'clock.)

Affectionately, your
G.

Best wishes from the Elbe to the Tiber! Dr. Herm. Behn
and more for Sicily!
Luise Behn

SHELFMARK: E12-MJp-492
NOTE
[1] Addressed to "Fräulein Justine Mahler / Rom / Piazza Montecitorio / Pensione Unione."

374 *To Justine*

[Hamburg, 28 and 29 March 1894]
28/III

Dearest Justi!
Greetings to you in *Naples*, which herewith you "are seeing," but hopefully are not instantly "dying"!

I have more than enough to do for Bülow's funeral and cremation.[1] The dress rehearsal just took place![2] The weeping willows [*Trauerweiden*] (alias old dolts) are already fully inflated. They will shrivel up again dreadfully when he is buried. Right now they are offended by the weather—that it isn't raining. Hopefully I will hear more about you soon.

29/III

Finally the great day has arrived. We shall celebrate the obsequies from 9 o'clock in the morning until about 5 o'clock (at which time there will be a funeral banquet at Behns).

Now all my hopes are that the weeping women don't perhaps establish a Bülow museum (and exhibit his chamber pot and laundry lists, perhaps). What won't people do with the likes of a sick or dead Bülow.—People leave the young and living to pull through on their own.

Strauss is engaged in Munich and is taking over the *Berlin* concerts![3] No one knows yet what will happen with the ones here! At any rate, it is all the same to me! If only spring is always as radiant as this year's!—

Budget jottings have just come again from Harris—I enclose the last note. The business now looks a little bit better. I would possibly go only for *June*—I would just arrive on the Attersee 14 days later—and last year I had to stay here even until 15 June. But I will *not* change my conditions.

I also enclose the last letter from Strauss. *Kretzschmar,* to whom he alludes, is an excellent conductor and currently Germany's leading writer on music.[4]

Surely I've already written you that the "Titan" might be performed at this year's *Tonkünstlerfest* in Nuremberg (end of May).[5]—

Old Her[t]z is almost recovered already. I am there often. He is in a good mood. Frau Michels never leaves his bedside, and this seems to do him a lot of good.—

Best wishes to you and to the two ladies.
Your
Gustav

Shelfmark: E15-MJ-590
Notes

[1] It was at Bülow's funeral and cremation on 29 March that Mahler was inspired by Klopstock's *Auferstehen;* see Josef Bohuslav Foerster's record of the event (republished in Norman Lebrecht, *Gustav Mahler: Erinnerungen seiner Zeitgenossen* [Munich: Piper, 1993], p. 90) and Mahler's letter to Anton Seidl, GMB[2] 216.

[2] Mahler conducted Siegfried's funeral march from *Götterdämmerung.*

[3] Strauss had signed a contract on 20 March to become *Hofkapellmeister* in Munich.

[4] Musicologist and conductor Hermann Kretzschmar (1848–1924).

[5] Strauss, at the time still in Weimar, had persuaded Hans Bronsart von Schellendorf (1830–1913), the Weimar *Intendant,* to perform the First Symphony at the annual festival of the Allgemeine Deutsche Musikverein, held that year in Weimar. The performance took place on 3 June 1894. Mahler had submitted his score to Bronsart in February; see his letter to Bronsart of 2 February in Irina Kaminiarz, *Richard Strauss Briefe aus dem Archiv des allegemeinen deutschen Musikverein (1888–1889)* (Weimar: Böhlau, 1995), p. 92.

375 *To Justine*

Postcard[1]
[Postmark: Hamburg, 30.3.94]
[Arrival postmark: Naples, 1.4.94]

D.J.
Hurrah! *Wolff* was just with Pollini and arranged with him that I will definitely take over the "Bülow Concerts" from now on! *So* I had my way about it after all! More details when I myself know something.—The funeral ceremony was very effective. Lots of applause. At the end I was called (by Böhme, who told me that Wolff had to speak to me). Hopefully the reviews will be good too.—It was Bülow's 4th burial.—There is still only one more (the interment of the ashes in the aristocratic "corner" in Ohlsdorf!). Things have to be taken even to that extent!

Affectionately yours
G.

[across top:] Wolff has to give Pollini a quarter of the takings.

Shelfmark: E12-MJp-493
Note
[1] Addressed to "Fräulein Justine Mahler / Neapel / via Caracciolo 9 / Proprietà Tiberina."

376 *To Justine*

Postcard[1]
[Postmark: Hamburg, 2.4.94]
[Delivery postmark: Naples, 4.4.94]

Dearest Justi!
Hopefully you've now received *my letter* with the enclosure and the postcard that I sent to the address you gave me in Naples.—If *not*, obtain them from the post office—there is interesting news in them.—Meanwhile, I am still struggling with Pollini about the concerts—not everything is in order yet. Today I met old Her[t]z looking exceedingly cheerful and outwardly, I think, quite back to his old self.—Everything has gone for the best unbelievably quickly. Let beautiful Naples do you all well! You are all really to be envied there!

Affectionately, your G.

Shelfmark: E15-MJp-591
Note
[1] Addressed to "Fräulein Justine Mahler / Napoli / via Caraccioli [*sic*] 9 / Proprietà Tiberina."

377 *To Justine*

[Hamburg, c. 19 April 1894][1]

Dearest Justi!
I am sending the repertory list to you in Palermo just in case. I am curious whether you will receive this letter. Write me about it right away!

Otto left today for Leipzig. I am now anxious for his first reports.—

This may now be the most beautiful part of your trip! In Vienna, you will be marvelled at as a monstrosity.

The little May repertory is quite demanding [*anmuthend*] for me—

The Attersee should please me twice as much then.—

You!—I tell you again, this time I am really uneasy about Natalie. All of her friendly browbeating is abhorrent to me. See to it that she doesn't come *before July*! Where are the Marcuses staying this summer? Old Her[t]z is again quite bright and lively.

—I'd like to see anyone else do that!

Best wishes to you all
Your Gustav

Did you all "pay tribute" again?

Shelfmark: E15-MJ-593
Note
[1] In the next letter, dated 23 April, Mahler notes that Otto has been in Leipzig for four days.

378 *To Justine*

[Hamburg, 23 April 1894]

Dearest Justi!
I sent a letter with *some enclosures* to you in *Palermo*. Have it forwarded to you right away.—

Meanwhile I received a form from the post to tell me that the package with the tea is stored in Rome, and they're asking where it is to be sent.—So, should I have it sent on to you? For your own good, I very much regret that you all did *not* go to Palermo. Well, I will wait for you about the apartment! Right now I am again much in favour of a cottage [*Häuschen*]!

Otto has been in Leipzig for 4 days without writing me even *the slightest word*! What do you have to say about that.—He has simply had 100 fl. sent from Vienna and sent me his *address* without the slightest addition on a postcard.—

Yesterday I wrote him what I thought about it; most likely this won't have any further effect upon him.—But I am really happy that we are rid of him for the summer.—The chap has really no inkling of *what* troubles and sorrows I have taken out of his way.

Best wishes from
Your
Gustav

23/IV 94

You write me that I should send 300 marks to you in *Venice*? When? Right away? Also, don't forget that with *general delivery* a registered consignment will *only* be handed over upon the presentation of a *passport*.

SHELFMARK: E15-MJ-592

379 *To Justine*

[Hamburg, between January and April 1894]

Dear Justi!
I just received this card and photograph from [Frau] de Boor! What's with these 2 *offprints*?

Please let me know about it right away, or if you have these two copies *with you*, please send them back to me, *otherwise* I will be *most* embarrassed!

Dear Justi, I do not understand such carelessness at all![1]

I really cannot always clean up after you. I do have enough to do just on my own, don't I!

Hopefully I will also hear how you all are.

I received Frau Marcus's letter and send her my warmest greetings; I will write her next.

Affectionately yours
Gustav

SHELFMARK: E15-MJ-596
NOTE
[1] This sentence is bracketed and marked *auslassen!* (leave out) by Justine.

380 *To Justine*

[Hamburg, 6 May 1894]

Dearest Justi!
Today you'll get a whole pile of interesting news. The content will be explained by the letters and you can get an idea of it from everything.

At the same time I am sending you 400 marks by money order. Don't make anything of the fact that you requested a bit more.—We will surely make it up next year and anyway there is no comparison to the benefit for your life that you have gained from this.

By the way, Staegemann was here recently for a directors' meeting and told me that Otto is much liked in Leipzig because of his sensible, calm and unassuming being.—

Moreover, I was at Schümann's for an evening with Staegemann, Count Hochberg,[1] and 2 other intendants.

About Natalie, I don't know what you intend to tell her.—Don't forget that certain things must only be broached *gently*, even amongst the best of friends who, in the positive sense of the word, can be brutally honest with each other, and I would rather that you did not *expose* yourself in this delicate matter. You will see that this is best.—But I certainly confess to you that Natalie's coming is absolutely abhorrent to me. Apart from the matter in question, (or perhaps precisely because of it), I detest the constant mothering, browbeating, inspecting, and spying. I wouldn't take it this year.

Put off her arrival as long as possible—don't discuss anything about her relations with me, but impress upon her not to *grumble* about what I do or don't do. I'd really prefer it if she just didn't come.[2]

I am sending you the letter from [Frau] *Luksch* at Natalie's instruction.—I have seen charming little houses here, but really would rather wait until you come.—Frau Marcus should make sure that she comes to live near us. Perhaps you could look together in the fall. I would go as high as 18 000 marks rent, for apartments such as I need are rare—and it really is too important for me.—Best wishes to everybody!

Your
6/V 94. Gustav

[at the top of the letter:] Just enjoy the last, beautiful days with *contentment*, and don't worry about a few pennies.

Shelfmark: E10-MJ-441
Notes

[1] Bolko, Graf von Hochberg (1843–1926), *Intendant* of the Berlin Opera.

[2] Since there is nothing on this subject in the published or unpublished portions of Natalie's memoirs, Mahler biographers have assumed that she was not invited to the Attersee in 1894. Justine's letters to Ernestine, however, make it clear that Natalie was there for at least part of the summer. For example, on 11 June, Justine wrote: "G. asked me why I allowed N. to practice in his *Häuschen*—she told him herself." It is not clear whether Mahler was there at the same time, although a letter written the following summer suggests that he was: "everything is almost like last year, only Gustav is very nice to Natalie and they both spend a lot of time together" (8 July 1895).

381 *To Justine*

[Hamburg, May 1894]

Dear Justi!
Quickly, before it's too late, I'd like to ask you not to tell *Natalie* what I said in my last letter. First of all, I would really hurt the poor creature, and 2nd, it would not do any good (just between us).—Therefore, be as considerate as possible. Under no circumstances should she come *right away*—at first I would like to be alone with you and Emma for a few days, and then she should come, for God's sake.—But instruct her, at any rate, that I will not be *mothered*. Only with respect to *meals* do I welcome *control*. In that respect, I'm doing splendidly and if I have a good summer and you are prudent next year, I will become completely healthy again.

On the *28th* I indeed leave for Weimar and stay there a week.—The whole Musikfest lasts *5 days* (1–5 June inclusive). The main pieces are *Guntram* by *Strauss* and my symphony. At any rate, it will be very refreshing for me, even if the consequences probably will not be very significant. But *by and by* I shall perhaps yet prevail. I am taking Otto to Weimar with me. I will stop in Leipzig for a day. On the evening of the 7th I go to Munich and continue on from there right away to Salzburg early on the 8th (not via Innsbruck, which would be a very roundabout way).

So if you believe that I should come via Vöklabruck, perhaps you can wait for me there. In the meantime, please put everything in order, procure a *piano*, and if possible set up my pavilion so that I can *sleep* in it; then you could use my former room as a *bedroom* and would not be disturbed so much by the inn guests.—Bring me the following with you: 1) bathing suit (full) 2) *manilla* [*sic*] *hat* 3) tobacco and paper for cigarettes 4) *antiphon*[1] 5) felt slippers 6) tooth powder and brush. *Natalie* knows what an *antiphon* is; she should see to everything with you.—I'll let you know anything else I remember.—

Greet *Ernestine* warmly for me, and tell her that she ought at least to haunt us for a few days in Steinbach.

Affectionately yours
Gustav

Say hello to Emma and Nina for me. Still *nothing* definite about next year!

[upside-down above salutation on p. 1:] Natalie should bring Fritz's *Hölderlin* with her for me—then everything that she can find by Brentano and Arnim. Maybe Lipiner could lend me some interesting things—his choice!

SHELFMARK: S1-MJ-750
NOTE
[1] Ear plugs.

382 *To Justine*

[Hamburg,] 26/V 94

Dearest Justi!
I just had the bank send you *500 fl.* They should arrive at the same time as you. I am leaving as well *Tuesday* around 9 o'clock in the morning.

The enclosed clipping from the Pester Lloyd should amuse you. The first summary of my initial season there sounded a bit different!—

I will probably take the Berlin-Vienna line after all. I will send my Weimar address—where I will stay about a *week*—to you in Steinbach. At any rate, write me in detail again from there.

What Nina has to receive, you can send out to her from Steinbach.

I am letting Otto come to Weimar although he seems to be sulking again, since I still have no answer to my last letter, which rebuked him for his foolishness (regarding the piano affair).—He has no holidays, but goes from Leipzig directly to Bremen.

Of course, I will certainly see in Weimar.

Best wishes to you from
Your Gustav

Please ask Freund if he got my package (the receipts).

Why don't you write anything about Alois?—What kind of nonsense is this about the new "entries into the estate"?

SHELFMARK: E15-MJ-594

383 *To Justine*

Postcard[1]
[Postmark: Berlin, 29.5.94]
[Arrival postmark: Steinbach am Attersee, 31.5.94]

D.J. From the train compartment en route Berlin-Weimar, where I arrive this evening. I am staying at the "Sächsischer Hof," where I am lodged as a guest of honour.

Early tomorrow morning I already have the first rehearsal.

I am definitely waiting for news of you all there. I am staying through Monday, *4 June*.

Affectionately,
G.

SHELFMARK: E6-MJp-309
NOTE
[1] Addressed to "Fräulein Justine Mahler / Steinbach am Attersee / Oberösterreich."

384 *To Otto*

Postcard[1]
[Postmark: Unterach am Attersee, 30.6.94]
[Arrival postmark: (Leipzig,) 1.7.(94)]

D.O! I hereby announce the safe delivery of a healthy, strong last movement.—Father and child both doing as well as can be expected—the last still not out of danger. At the baptism, it was given the name: Lux lucet in tenebris.[2]—Silent sympathy is requested. Floral offerings gratefully declined.

Other gifts will be accepted, however.

Affectionately,
G.

Steinbach 30. June 1894[3]

SOURCE: ÖNB-Handschriftensammlung, Autog. 486/16
NOTES
[1] Addressed to "Herrn Otto Mahler / Leipzig / Poststrasse 12."
[2] The day before, Mahler wrote almost identically to Friedrich Löhr; see GMB[2] 129.
[3] "Light shines in the darkness" (see John 1:5).

385 *To Justine*

Postcard[1]
[Postmark: Bayreuth, 29 Jul. 94]
[Arrival postmark: Steinbach, 30.7.94]

D.J.—Obtained your letter and preceding postcard in Bayreuth.—I received *nothing* in *Munich*, although in the postcard you seem to refer to a preceding one.—I am letting Otto come—I do feel sorry for the poor fellow. It must be horrible in Leipzig.—I got the 60 marks back already. Here the weather is wonderful again, but hot.—Right now I am going to Parsifal.[2]—It is terribly expensive here, just like at the most fashionable spa! Money just disappears left, right, and centre!

Affectionately, Gustav

Keep on writing to general delivery.

SHELFMARK: E18-MJp-632
NOTES
[1] Addressed to "Fräulein Justine Mahler / Steinbach am Attersee / Oberösterreich."
[2] Mahler had rehearsed tenor Willi Birrenkoven (1865–1955) in the role of Parsifal as a favour to Strauss, who was an assistant at the 1894 festival; see Eduard Reeser, "Gustav Mahler und Cosima Wagner," in *Gustav Mahler Unbekannte Briefe*, ed. Herta Blaukopf (Vienna: Zsolnay, 1983), p. 214. In addition to *Parsifal*, Mahler saw *Tannhäuser* (30 July) and *Lohengrin* (3 August).

386 *To Justine*

Postcard[1]
[Postmark: Bayreuth, 31. Jul. 94]
[Arrival postmark: Steinbach am Attersee, 1.8.94]

D.J.—I am just about to go to Marienbad to visit Nina.—I have been received with great distinction here, especially in Wahnfried.—I attended both performances in the Wagner box. After Parsifal I was at the restaurant with the family, yesterday I was invited there for lunch. It was very interesting.—

I am meeting Otto on Saturday in *Munich*, according to his postcard that just arrived. Sunday at the latest we will *both* be in Steinbach.

Let me know if it would suit you to meet me in *Ischl* and then go by *foot* to Steinbach.—If so, that would be best; if not, we will come directly to Steinbach.

Best wishes,
Gustav

(Sure enough, I forgot my nightshirt.)[2]

SHELFMARK: E6-MJp-310
NOTES
[1] Addressed to "Fräulein Justine Mahler / Steinbach am Attersee / Oberösterreich."
[2] Mahler had a bad habit of leaving his linen in hotel rooms.

387 *To Justine*

Postcard[1]
[Postmark: Marienbad, 1.8.94]
[Arrival postmark: Steinbach am Attersee, 2.8.94]

D.J! Right now we are in the Café Waldmühle and are breakfasting together. On Sunday I am travelling from Munich to Salzburg.—Here I have spoken with 100 people from Budapest—and at midday I am eating with—Singer and Deutsch—Feld and Kalmann are here! Everyone sends greetings!

Affectionately, Gustav

[from Nina:] *So dear Justi, it is* very *nice here with Gustav; thinking of you often. The smallest presents are always the nicest. Addio N.*

Shelfmark: E6-MJp-314
Note
[1] Addressed to "Fräulein Justine Mahler / Steinbach am Attersee / Oberösterr."

388 *To Justine*

Postcard[1]
[Postmark: Bayreuth, 3. Aug. 94]
[Arrival postmark: Steinbach am Attersee, 4.8.94]

D.J. My stay in Bayreuth is successful in all respects. I am invited to Wahnfried almost daily, and my digestion is excellent.—Today is Lohengrin, and the day after tomorrow I leave.

Think over the business with Otto carefully, then you will understand why I let him come. I was with Nina for a day. Hopefully I will still see the Behns. *Freund* ambled in yesterday too. Reiff and his wife and sister-in-law are here too. I travelled together with them from Marienbad.—Frau Wagner accommodates me really warmly, and these moments are very interesting.

Best wishes to everybody
Gustav

Shelfmark: E6-MJp-311
Note
[1] Addressed to "Fräulein Justine Mahler / Steinbach am Attersee / Oberösterreich."

389 *Otto to Justine*

Postcard[1]
[Postmark: Bremen, 25.8.94]
[Arrival postmark: Vienna, 27.8.94]

D.J!
My address is: Grünenweg 5.

For the time being, greetings.
Otto

The trip was rather terrible for me; I almost became mad! At any rate, I am awaiting news from you about the course of events.

SOURCE: Bibliothèque Musicale Gustav Mahler
NOTE
[1] Addressed to "Fräulein Justine Mahler / Wien / IV.Theresianumgasse 6 III." At the time, Justine and Emma were staying with Nina Hoffmann and preparing to move to Hamburg.

390 *To Justine*

Postcard[1]
[Postmark: Hamburg, 28.8.94]
[Arrival postmark:Vienna, 29.8.94]

D.J. Arrived in Berlin with a "flu" and was invited to Wolff's for lunch—ate nothing. I found everything very obliging on this front. The flu intensified into a migraine.—Last night I paced my room in my accustomed manner until 4 o'clock in the morning.—Quite well again now! Everything very friendly in the theatre, from which I see that I am still in grace at court. I hope to have news from you soon!

Yours affectionately, G.

SHELFMARK: E6-MJp-312
NOTE
[1] Addressed to "Fräulein Justine Mahler / Wien / IV.Theresianumstr. 6 / 3. Stock."

391 *To Justine*

Postcard[1]
[Postmark: Hamburg, 30.8.94]
[Arrival postmark:Vienna, 31.8.94]

D.J.! Just see that you are here soon—because, as Frau Sans told me yesterday, it takes at least 8–14 days *after* renting the apartment before we can move into it. Since *each one* has to have *new wallpaper* and *flooring*, and the landlords always wait for their tenant's wishes in this regard. I have some really nice ones up my sleeve.—If possible, please bring me 50 light, dry *Regalitas* (cigars) with you. Here, as well as in Berlin, it has been *cold* since my departure that I am going around in an overcoat.—So the weather conditions are entirely different.—

Best wishes from
G.

I got your 2 letters. Did the mail from *Marienbad* arrive?

SHELFMARK: E6-MJp-313
NOTE
[1] Addressed to "Fräulein Justine Mahler / bei Frau Hofman [*sic*] / Wien / IV.Theresianumgasse 6/3. Stock."

392 *To Justine*

[Hamburg, 1 September 1894]

Dearest Justi!
Here is the first repertory list. The next one you can buy yourself.—It seems to look rotten about apartments.—At any rate, I will wait for you.[1]—They are all beautiful—but quiet?—today is the opening performance—Tannhäuser! Everything is going excellently: the *orchestra* and *singers* are better than last year.

Yesterday I played my *2nd* for *Förster* (whom I told you about—an excellent musician and man).[2] It made a *significant* impression on him.—He compared it with the 9th!

At any rate a work of mine will be performed in Berlin, as *Wolff* told me.

The eating arrangements here are horrible again! I see *how* good your cooking is for me.—If only we *were settled in* already!

Come as soon as possible.

Don't forget to give Fritz *a gulden*.

Write soon.

Yours affectionately,
1. Sept. 94. Gustav

Pollini is exceedingly *gracious*. We have a new conductor (Pohlig) from Bayreuth—a splendid musician and human being, who is very nice to me.[3]

SHELFMARK: S1-MJ-751
NOTES

[1] Justine and Emma arrived in Hamburg at the beginning of September. According to Justine's letters to Ernestine, they found an apartment on 12 September: Parkallee 12/III.. They remained at this address until the end of August 1895, when they moved to Bismarckstrasse 86 (Hohe Luft).

[2] Josef Bohuslav Foerster (1859–1951), Czech composer, writer, and teacher. He moved to Hamburg in 1893 and was active there as a critic until 1903.

[3] Carl Pohlig (1864–1928) was engaged as *Kapellmeister* in Hamburg as of September 1894.

393 *To Otto from Justine and Gustav*[1]

Hamburg, 1 Oct. 94

Dear Otto, *I* myself will acknowledge your last letter to G. You certainly cannot expect an answer from *him* to this last letter; he is simply furious about your boundless ~~insolence~~ and ~~also~~ has complied with your "request" to leave you alone. **<He was [incomplete]>** ~~In addition, he asks me to tell you not to send any more telegrams, but to say everything in letters~~. **<At his orders>** ~~At his request~~, **<for the time being>** I am sending you 30 marks, since G. suspects that you don't have any money. **<He is also prepared to send you more if you need it, and ask for it.>** ~~If you still need something, he will gladly set you a small monthly allowance until you earn something yourself~~. You must *write* me in good time, then, *not tele*graph. What *I myself* would have had to say about your behaviour would not have been so gentle. There is only one excuse for it: *your youth*! How can you still behave this way, after having lived here and seen Gustav's terrific worries and struggles! You whom he always trusts, in whom he has always believed as in himself. Upon getting your letter that time, he telegraphed everyone possible, but couldn't get anything else for you. It is inexcusable that you dared not go to Director Löwe <**despite Gustav's orders**>.[2] By the way, the director wrote Gustav that you are also unbelievably ungrateful. You can't do anything about it, it lies in your nature. I advise you to sit yourself down and write Gustav a reasonable letter, *without* empty phrases, about yourself and what you are thinking of doing—and not about the meaning of the century. He probably deserved something different from you, that is clear. There is lots to be said about it. That you would cause him such hurt and worry, and painful hours, naturally we did not expect. I can tell you that it hurts one to look at him, and he really needs to be spared agitation. I do not think that you are at all aware of what you are doing. Confirm <**the receipt of**> this letter and the money <**that I am sending as a money order**>, more precisely, ~~to G. without causing him distress.~~

Best wishes
J.

<From your last letter it is not at all clear what you are thinking of doing, and how you will earn your living: [illegible word(s)]. If you need money, then write Justine and you will get a monthly allowance like before as long as you don't have a position that will feed you. After your behaviour you can no longer expect that G. will obtain a position for you. See to it yourself as you wish. He asks me to tell you all this.>

SHELFMARK: E8-JMF-395
NOTES

[1] Justine's letter is written in purple ink; Mahler's emendations are in black ink. In the transcription, Justine's underlining has been rendered in italics and Mahler's corrections in boldface. All cancelled text was deleted by Mahler. The placement of Mahler's paragraph at the end is unclear.

This is the last mention of Otto in these letters. From this letter, and a September letter from Justine to Ernestine, it seems that Otto was considering leaving Bremen for a post in Breslau. Justine comments several times in letters to Ernestine from that fall that they had not heard from him. Otto shot himself in Nina Hoffmann's apartment on 6 February 1895. For further discussion of Otto's suicide and Mahler's reaction, see the introduction.

[2] Theodor Löwe (1855–1936), director of the Breslau Stadttheater.

394 *To Justine*

Postcard[1]
[Postmark: Ischl, 3.7.95]
[Arrival postmark: Steinbach am Attersee, 4.7.95]

2nd postcard![2]
It is so pretty here that I have a suggestion for you all: come here *for a few* days in order to get a little change from monotonous Steinbach. I have taken 2 cheap rooms for *both of you* and *Natalie* in the inn where I stayed last year; I will stay with Kössler. So I will wait for you all on Friday (the day after tomorrow) around *1 o'clock* on the *parterre* of the Hotel "*Post*". It would be best, especially if the weather is bad, to come by *postal* [train]—or however you want. Albi can finish her visit there. However, in case you don't want to—if perhaps it would suit you better later, telegraph me right away at the *Hotel Stern.*—Kössler sends greetings. Brahms is immensely kind. I feel splendid. I was already at the doctor.

Affectionately, Gustav

[written in pencil:] Please, bring me some more underwear, a sponge, and toothpaste.

SHELFMARK: E6-MJp-315
NOTES
[1] Addressed to "Fräulein Justine Mahler / Steinbach am Attersee."
[2] The first postcard does not survive.

395 *To Justine*

WATER CURE INSTITUTE OF ISCHL (COLD STREAM)
Proprietor and Medical Director:
DR. HEINRICH HERTZKA & DR. ALFRED WINTERNITZ

[Ischl,] Tuesday night [9 July 1895][1]

Dear Justi!
I just received the *delivery notification.*—Since I will only get the package *tomorrow* morning, I will probably send it *return* again.—

So far, things are going excellently. I have already given notice for Friday and early Friday will leave here and go to *Gosau* by foot.—On Saturday I will climb the Zwieselalm. Sunday from Aussee to Grundelsee and back by various ways to Ischl. From here I will then come back to *Steinbach* via the Langbathsee on *Monday.* All this provided that the weather stays bearable.—I would suggest that you all come here on Sunday and wait for me, and then together we will head home on foot.

If you would like that, then write me right away—addressed to *Hotel Stern,* in fact, where I will stay on Sunday too.—

If the weather should be really beautiful, and if I still feel like going on [*Gehlustig*], mind you, on *Monday* I would go on foot through the Fludergraben from Aussee to Ischl and back to Steinbach only on Tuesday. In this case, we could make our way *towards* each other in the Fludergraben, which would be very merry and then [go] together to *St.*, or you could arrive in Ischl only on Monday and wait for me there.

At any rate, however, in this case I would still telegraph or write you all again.—

So, if you don't hear anything else from me, I will be at the Hotel *Stern* on Sunday night and will ask for you.

According to the telegram I just received from Natalie, it appears that Freund *is coming on Saturday*; please advise him right away that I will not be in Steinbach until Wednesday, and that he should arrange his trip accordingly.—

I am very surprised that I still don't have news of you all, please write a *card* (in fact) right away, addressed to the *cold water sanatorium* so that I can march forward calmly! *My portfolio*?

I feel splendid!

Affectionately,
Gustav

SHELFMARK: S1-MJ-755
NOTE

[1] On 8 July, Justine told Ernestine that Gustav had been in Ischl for ten days.

396 *To Emma*

[Hamburg, Autumn 1895]
Hamburg, den . . . 1895
Welckerstrasse 6B[1]

Dear Emma!
Mildenburg is *not* coming to dinner *today*. *I am coming alone*. If possible, Justi should make herself free tonight to be with her, since she is not well.

Best,
Gustav

SOURCE: Typewritten transcription in the Bibliothèque Musicale Gustav Mahler
NOTE

[1] Anna von Mildenburg's address; the letter was likely written on her stationery. As I have not seen the original letter, it is impossible to know whether the date is correct. Justine's letters to Ernestine indicate that Mildenburg was often there for dinner. (Mildenburg had joined the Hamburg Stadttheater in September 1895; see the introduction for Mahler's relationship with her.)

397 *To Justine*

Postmark[1]
[Postmark: Berlin, 7.12.95][2]
[Arrival postmark: Hamburg, 8.12.95]

D.J!
All was going splendidly up to now until my migraine. I do not crave this weary hotel life! You forgot to send along the *vest* that goes with the new jacket.

The *mutes* have to be transported *carefully* so that they won't be *bent*. You all are coming on Monday, then?

Affectionately, your
G.

Shelfmark: E14-MJp-550
Notes
[1] Addressed to "Fräulein Justine Mahler / Hamburg / Bismarkstr. 86."
[2] Mahler was in Berlin, preparing for the premiere of the Second Symphony on Friday, 13 December.

398 *To Justine*

[Hamburg, Autumn 1895][1]

Dearest Justi!
I arrive tomorrow afternoon around *3 o'clock*.

Behn is coming with me—he had a big surprise for me; but I am not yet supposed to say anything about it.

Anyhow, I was received splendidly.

Affectionately,
Gustav

Shelfmark: E10-MJ-453
Note
[1] From the contents, the note seems to date from the fall of 1895. That fall, Hermann Behn (with the help of Wilhelm Berkhan) paid for the publication of his two-piano reduction of Mahler's Second Symphony, as well as the full score. They also covered the costs of the December premiere of the work in Berlin.

399 *To Justine*

[Berlin, second week March 1896][1]

Dearest Justi!
So everything has gone well! (Only the tickets are not going well—but rather as in former times). I was at Pierson's—everything permitted.[2] Weingartner and Lessmann not at home.[3]—My stomach is again not in order. I wrecked myself at the *Pallas Hotel breakfast*!

In the hotel it is *very* quiet and comfortable after all. Natalie seems to be coming only on Thursday.

Still no trace of Behn!

I am really surprised to be without news of you all.

You could still *inform* me of your arrival.

Affectionately,
Gustav

SHELFMARK: E14-MJ-551
NOTES

[1] The letter was written after 9 March, but probably before 12 March. Mahler was in Berlin preparing for the performance of the First Symphony (without *Blumine* for the first time), *Todtenfeier*, and the *Lieder eines fahrenden Gesellen* on 16 March.

[2] Henry Pierson (1851–1902), director of the Königliche Schauspiele, Berlin.

[3] Felix Weingartner (1863–1942), conductor and composer; Otto Lessmann (1844–1918), critic, composer, teacher, and editor of the *Allgemeine Musikalische Zeitung*.

400 *To Justine*

Postcard[1]
[Postmark: Berlin, 12.3.96]
[Arrival postmark: Hamburg, 13.3.96]

Dear Justi!
Bring 2 copies of my published *Lieder* with you. You will find them in a package in the chest in the piano room.—Don't misplace the *tax notice*, and remind me of it when I come back.

Affectionately,
your
Gustav

[pencilled at top, and crossed out in ink by Mahler:]
8 places on the E[illegible]
4 places, middle parquet Marschalk
Saturday *8 o'clock* Gernsheim

SHELFMARK: E12-MJp-494
NOTE

[1] Addressed to "Fräulein Justine Mahler / Hamburg / Hoheluft, Bismarkstrasse 86."

401 *To Justine*

Postcard[1]
[Postmark: Berlin, 1/6 96]
[Arrival postmark: Hamburg, 2.6.96]

Dearest Justi!
As you know already, I am leaving here already early tomorrow morning! I can't stand this prowling around! I was at Frau S[chlesinger?]'s; I *liked* her *very much*. She improves decidedly on closer acquaintance.[2] O. Bie too.[3]—This evening, together with Marschalk, and then steam off to Leipzig. I am *certainly not* staying there *long*! Off to *Munich* right away! I am thinking of arriving in Steinbach around *Monday* the 8th. Before then, write me sometime (to *Vienna*).

Tomorrow I am in Dresden, and Wednesday in Prague. I will arrive in Vienna on Thursday night.

Best wishes, also to Frau *Marcus* and Toni.

Write me!

Your
Gustav

SHELFMARK: E12-MJp-495
NOTES

[1] Addressed to "Fräulein Justine Mahler / *P.A. 13.* [?] / Hamburg / Bismarkstrasse 86." Mahler's circuitous route to Steinbach was chosen to allow him to meet colleagues and supporters. At the time, he was actively trying to leave Hamburg—ideally for Vienna—as well as to arrange performances of his works.

[2] Frau Schlesinger is mentioned in several of the letters. It is not clear whether this is Bruno (Schlesinger) Walter's mother.

[3] Oskar Bie (1864–1938), professor of art history in Berlin; also wrote on music.

402 *To Justine*

Postcard: Gruß aus Dresden[1]
[Postmark: Dresden, 3.6.96]
[Arrival postmark: Munich, 4. Jun. 96]

Everything went well. Nikisch will perform Nos. 1 and 2 in the Gewandhaus—from the II., and 4 and 5 from the III. in Berlin.[2]—Schuch is performing the *whole II*![3] The local intendant listened too.[4] It even pleased him personally. Scheidemantel will sing the *fahr*[enden] *Gesellen*![5] I am travelling overnight to *Vienna*!

Affectionately, G.

SHELFMARK: S2-MJp-766
NOTES

[1] Addressed to "Fräulein Justine Mahler / München / Schellingstr. 70 / bei Krzyzanowski." Justine was en route to Steinbach.

[2] The Berlin performance took place on 9 November 1896; the Leipzig one on 14 December 1896.

[3] In the end, Schuch performed only the second, third, and fourth movements on 15 January 1897.

[4] Nikolas, Graf von Seebach (1854–1930).

[5] Baritone Karl Scheidemantel (1859–1923).

403 *To Justine*

Postcard[1]
[Postmark: Weissenbach am Attersee, 12.7.96]
[no delivery postmark]

To my great concern, I have just realised that I did not solemnly hand over my *portfolio* to you. Please take it *into your room right away* and always take it with you when you go away.[2]

Please send a card to Ischl ([Hotel] Stern) *every day* with how he *is feeling*.[3] Best wishes to the whole crew.

Your,
G.

Shelfmark: E12-MJp-497
Notes
[1] Addressed to "Fräulein Justine Mahler / Steinbach am Attersee."
[2] Likely containing Mahler's manuscripts; also mentioned above in letter 395.
[3] It is unclear to whom Mahler is referring.

404 *To Justine*

Postcard[1]
[Postmark: Hallstatt, 12.7.96]
[no delivery postmark]

I am sitting at the beautiful lake in Hallstatt, have an excellent coffee and roll [*Milchbrod*] inside me, and am in marvellous spirits.—Journey to Ischl awful, but beautiful. Arrived around 10:45. Then, to Brahms, received in a *very* friendly fashion, and was asked for a symphony. Slept a little bit in the afternoon, then by bicycle to Hallstadt. [*sic*]—Tomorrow by bicycle to St. Gilgen and then by train to Singer's.—You all absolutely must come here again. It is really divine.

Met Frl. Eisler and Seiffert on the esplanade.[2] Was very charming (namely, I was)—naturally, they were too.

Affectionately, G.

What is the noble [*P.T.*] case doing?[3]

Shelfmark: E12-MJp-496
Notes
[1] Addressed to "Fräulein Justine Mahler / Steinbach am Attersee."
[2] Unknown.
[3] See the note to letter 257.

405 *To Justine*

Postcard[1]
[Postmark: 14/7 96, handwritten, and stamp:
"Postconductor im Zuge / Salzburg-Ischl No. 6"]
[no arrival postmark]

My dears—Back from Hallstadt [*sic*] (also by bicycle) and dined at [Hotel] Stern—director Löwe from Breslau was sitting there! Well I heated him up not inconsiderably about Schlesinger! He *is secure*. Löwe firmly promised me everything.[2] Monday, to Salzburg *by train*, very expensive! Spoke to Singer and was saved. Terrible migraine at night, with pacing back and forth! Today, quite well again, by train to St. Gilgen and from there to Ischl by bicycle.—Tomorrow to Mihalovich on the Aussee. Thursday I will probably come to *Steinbach*. More details by letter!

Affectionately, G.

Shelfmark: E12-MJp-498
Notes
[1] Addressed to "Fräulein Justine Mahler / Steinbach am Attersee."
[2] Mahler had arranged for Bruno Walter to be engaged in Breslau for the 1896–1897 season as first *Kapellmeister*.

406 *To Justine*

Postcard[1]
[Postmark: Ischl, 2.8.96]
[Arrival postmark: Steinbach am Attersee, 3.8.96]

Dearest Justi!
Arrived in Ischl tonight; tomorrow I will probably wend my way to Aussee by separate train. Back the same day. Early the day after (Tuesday), at the summer residence [*Hoflager*] in Steinbach again. I hope that Stapel's celebratory dinner will finally go ahead; but *punctually*, at the time that is proper to it.[x]

Affectionately, Gustav

[Natalie:] [x] *(that is proper* to him, *the petty tyrant—that's what it's supposed to mean!) He gets the chance to haggle and rejoices in it. Well.*

Shelfmark: E12-MJp-499
Note
[1] Addressed to "Fräulein Justine Mahler / Steinbach am Attersee."

407 *To Justine*

Postcard[1]
[Postmark: Leipzig, 11.12.96]
[Arrival postmark: Hamburg, 12.12.96]

Arrived happily (or actually, unhappily from boredom).[2]

Noisy room. Today I will move into another. Everything is announced already. I have to go to Krause's right away.[3]

Hopefully I will find a letter soon.

Best wishes
Gustav

Shelfmark: E14-MJp-552
Notes
[1] Addressed to "Fräulein Justine Mahler / Hamburg Hoheluft / Bismarkstr. 86."

[2] Mahler was in Leipzig rehearsing for the Lisztverein concert on 14 December. The first two movements of the Second Symphony were on the program.

[3] Leipzig pianist and teacher Martin Krause (1853–1918) was one of the founders of the Lisztverein.

408 *To Justine*

HÔTEL DE PRUSSE / LEIPZIG

[Leipzig, 11 December 1896]

My dears!
I already have 24 visits from nothing but critics here.—I appear to be assured of a brilliant reception.—The orchestra is grandiosely composed, and tomorrow I have the first rehearsal (9 o'clock). I am curious! I will have a really good sleep tonight, and then tomorrow will be quite fresh again.

I eat very moderately and carefully! And the powders seem to work splendidly for me. Write!

Best wishes to all of you,
Your
Gustav

Shelfmark: E14-MJ-553

409 *To Justine*

Postcard[1]
[Postmark: Leipzig, 12.12.96]
[Arrival postmark: Hamburg, 13.12.96]

The first rehearsal is over! It went the way I am accustomed to! At first, complete stupidity and gruffness—at the end, *applause*. Was invited to Krause's yesterday (among others, *Menter* was there, a splendid person).[2]

Kraus [*sic*] behaves *splendidly*. My Leipzig campaign will be a great help for the future. Next year they want to perform the whole *symphony*! Horrors! Tomorrow I am invited to *Flechtig's*.[3] C.W.'s letter is very welcome to me.[4]—My digestion is splendid again today. I am taking magnificent care of myself as well. I slept too!

Affectionately, G.

Shelfmark: E14-MJp-554
Notes

[1] Addressed to "Fräulein Justine Mahler / Hamburg, Hoheluft / Bismarkstrasse 86."

[2] German pianist and composer Sophie Menter (1846–1918).

[3] Unknown.

[4] Mahler mentions receiving a letter from Cosima Wagner in an unpublished letter to Mildenburg (11 or 12 December). Mildenburg had been in Bayreuth at the beginning of December rehearsing Kundry.

410 *To Justine*

HÔTEL DE PRUSSE/LEIPZIG

[Leipzig, 13 December 1896]

My dears!

Well, 2nd rehearsal today! This one, however, went very badly. I was in an enormous rage. Most of all I would have liked to fling my baton in their roguish faces. Inn band [*Wirthshausorchester*], tired and unwilling.

But it doesn't matter! I'll press on with it.

Leipzig will be very useful to me. It will be reviewed everywhere.

Today I was invited to Flechtigs (with Kraus [*sic*]). It was funny yesterday: I dined at midday with Carreño—she grumbled about d'Albert and marriage.[1] In the evening with Menter—she grumbled about Popper and marriage.[2] I really had to smile! The latter, however, is without a doubt the more significant.—In the evening I was also at Frau Nikisch's. A publisher has announced himself; I asked him to come tomorrow.—Damn it, don't just write postcards.—And you really can be somewhat more detailed!

Frau Markus's [*sic*] invitation is awkward for me. Just see to it that Birrenkoven comes as well, so that more people are there!

I will not write again. So, Tuesday night, as indicated, I am coming.

Affectionately
Gustav

My digestion is again quite good! But I've also taken excellent care of myself.

Shelfmark: E14-MJ-555

Notes

[1] Pianist Theresa Carreño (1853–1917) had divorced Eugen d'Albert (1864–1932), pianist and composer, in 1895. (He was the third of her four husbands, and she was the first of his six wives.)

[2] Austrian cellist David Popper (1843–1913) was married to Menter between 1872 and 1886.

411 *To Justine*

Postcard[1]
[Postmark: Dresden, 15.1.97]
[Arrival postmark: Hamburg, 16.1.97]

Not a moment of time. Excellent health. Dress rehearsal turned out splendidly. II. Symphony No. 2 and 3 and Urlicht. *Not* the Blumenstück.[2] Schott will be at the concert today. The performance will be very good. Freund was at the dress rehearsal and sends his greetings.

Affectionately, G.

Shelfmark: E14-MJp-556

NOTES
[1] Addressed to "Fräulein Justine Mahler / Hamburg, Hoheluft / Bismarkstr. 86."
[2] The concert took place the same day.

412 *To Justine*

SENDIG'S HOTEL EUROPAEISCHER HOF / DRESDEN

[Dresden, 15 or 16 January 1897]

Dearest!
Everything turned out excellently. Everyone was enchanted.—Count Seebach came directly to me and announced that the King and Prince Georg were enchanted and didn't find me "crazy" at all.—Couldn't find out very much about Vienna; at any rate, I am not without prospects for Dresden.—I will probably come Sunday evening.

Affectionately,
Gustav

SHELFMARK: E10-MJ-449

413 *To Justine*

HOTEL CONTINENTAL / MOSCOU

[Moscow, 12 March 1897][1]

Dearest!
Finally arrived. Unfortunately, faithfully accompanied by my inseparable friend, a migraine.—Now I am starting to feel better.—Moscow is making a wonderful impression on me, which I suppose will increase even more when I am completely rid of my malady. I was met at the train station by a valet from the orchestra, who recognised me by means of my photograph, which was in his hand. He spoke only *Russian*—I, Bohemian [*böhmisch*]—finally it worked. How lucky that I have my fur and galoshes with me. There are only open sleighs and the trip here was ice cold. But how wonderful—this quiet! No rattle of wagons. Marvellous air. Rehearsal already tomorrow at 9 o'clock. I'll write again soon.

Say hello to Frau Marcus and Tönchen. Go to *Berkanns* [sic] and *Behns*!

Affectionately, your
Gustav

SHELFMARK: E14-MJ-557
NOTE
[1] Mahler was in Moscow 12–16 March and conducted a concert of the Kaiserlich-Russische Musikalische Gesellschaft on 15 March.

414 *To Justine*

HOTEL CONTINENTAL / MOSCOU

[Moscow, 13 March 1897]

My dears!
I am quite enchanted by Moscow. Today I had rehearsal. The orchestra behaved splendidly and does its things very well.—Life here is marvellous. For 30 pennies one can get anywhere by sleigh.—There is a samovar in my room, from which I drink tea incessantly. An engagement here would be something wonderful. My room is extraordinarily quiet.

The people here are extremely kind and helpful. Too bad that I am not conducting all of both concerts. Life here is decidedly cheap and as good as I have ever found in England.

Best wishes to you all from
your
Gustav

Saturday

SHELFMARK: E14-MJ-558

415 *To Justine*

HOTEL CONTINENTAL / MOSCOU

[Moscow, 14 March 1897]

Dearest!
I still have no news! This is the 3rd letter from here that I have written. Today I had a "Russian" breakfast; I am curious how it will agree with me! The weather is continuously clear and calm. Unfortunately not very cold—it is almost thawing—and the sleigh riding is very bumpy.—The city is marvellous, and I stroll around a lot. But it really is very disagreeable not to understand *a word* of what people are saying.

I am anxious for the news that I will receive from you all.

Concerts only begin here at *9 o'clock* and last until 11:30.

People here all seem so familiar.—One recognises them out of Tolstoy and Dostoyevsky.—If one sees the confusion of sleighs and pedestrians, one understands that strolling is pursued in a big way here. It is really extremely amusing to observe the passers-by. Every 3rd building is a church with 20 domes. Each passer-by crosses himself 20 times in front of each dome—now you can imagine the wobbling.

—I just got your letter, dear Justi—So it is raining there? Here the weather is constantly marvellous.—You all would enjoy it tremendously.

Hiesiger is collecting me at 4 o'clock in order to show me the city.[1] Up to now, on my own, I happily avoided all guides, who presented themselves in abundance. But now I *have to go*.

So—more soon!

Affectionately, your
Gustav

Sunday

SHELFMARK: E21-MJ-669
NOTE
[1] Unknown.

416 *To Justine*

[Moscow, 15 March 1897]

My dears!
Thank God, the day of departure is nearing! It is wonderfully beautiful here, in fact—but one must understand the language. To stroll around the whole day this way, without speaking a word, is not for me. The dress rehearsal turned out very well and the concert is in a few hours.—Tomorrow I am leaving and on Thursday afternoon am in Berlin, where I hope to find news of you all. At any rate, Justi, in case you haven't already done so, send the indicated music (*Mazeppa* and the orchestral parts for the Fantastique and Coriolan) to Munich right away.[1] I am curious how the public will behave. The orchestra is very nice and accommodating towards me—but it is very undisciplined and overtaxed, and every moment I have to "turn a blind eye." However, more and more I see now what I could achieve with a good orchestra, if I had time to teach them.

Now I will undertake a proper sleigh ride in order to take a bit of oxygen into my blood. Up to now I have had about 10 degrees cold and marvellous sunshine constantly.

I am curious if they will engage me again for next season.

Best wishes to all of you from
your
Gustav

Best greetings to Frau Marcus and the Her[t]zes

SHELFMARK: E6-MJ-292
NOTE
[1] For the concert of the Kaim Orchestra conducted by Mahler on 24 March.

417 *To Justine*

[Moscow, 15 March 1897]

My dears!
Thank God! The concert begins in an hour. I have an engagement afterwards with Nikisch, with whom I was just speaking at the hotel, and who is coming to the concert (so at least one pair of ears that can hear). The food is really very bad here. Only the caviar is wonderful; I live almost solely on it!

It really would be terrible if one were damned to pass one's life here (i.e., not because of *the food*).

Tomorrow I will steam away from here with a hurrah! By the way, the steam is very fine here: they heat here only with wood, since coal is much too expensive and the forests are so large they can't be destroyed.

Imagine, I don't even find the tea much better than ours!

The only thing that might interest somebody—the populace—one cannot understand.

The apples, however, are excellent! And that is the main thing, after all! I will take a basketful on the trip.—I will try to travel 2nd class. It is a difference of perhaps *60 marks* and I absolutely must bring something back. From Berlin (where I will spend the night) I will send you right away everything that I can spare. Then at least it is safe! Life in the hotel is very expensive for someone like me who understands *hardly anything*.

So, best wishes! I will write again from Berlin.—It will take at least 3–4 days until I am on the spot.

Your
Gustav

SHELFMARK: E14-MJ-559

418 *To Justine*

Letter card[1]
[Postmark: Berlin, 18.3.97]
[Arrival postmark: Hamburg, 19.3.97]

Dearest!
From the train compartment, just before arriving in Berlin, only the report that yesterday in fact I had a bit of migraine—better today, however, and am arriving in Berlin with a gigantic appetite. I am continuing on to Munich, again overnight. I arranged to travel 2nd class as far as Warsaw, then—and it went quite well.

I actually regret that I didn't take the whole round trip ticket *2nd* [class]. This afternoon I will send you all the money that I brought with me, and leave myself 150 *marks* for the rest of the trip. I think that it will be roughly 900 marks, after defraying the secondary expenses.

Write me in Munich right away. Hopefully the music has already been sent off?

Affectionately,
Gustav

Thursday, 11 o'clock

SHELFMARK: E14-MJ-560
NOTE
[1] Addressed to "Fräulein Justine Mahler / Hamburg / Hoheluft / Bismarckstr. 86."

419 *To Justine*

[Berlin, 18 March 1897]
10 o'clock at night

Dearest!
10 o'clock at night, before my departure for Munich! I was together with Marschalk, with whom I had an appointment at 2:00, and who "confessed"

to me.—You either seem to have taken the business more tragically than I assumed, or you even imagine that I might be in a remorseful mood. So I just want to reassure you that *I* am absolutely unmoved by all the nonsense. Please—it could hardly have been otherwise. Just think: all the participants were enthusiastic (i.e., those who were most thoroughly occupied with the work).—All those listeners who were sticking their noses in for the first time were stirred by shock.—Friends shaken and enemies agitated! So that it is quite splendid! I see these 3 movements as the vanguard, and will follow up in the fall or so with the *whole work*![1] Then you will experience something.—By the way, it is *good* the way it turned out. Why I say this (and I speak in *all seriousness*) would lead me too far astray. You all must know only this—by this failure I have obtained my *liberty* and now I am delivered *to myself* again, whereas otherwise I might have succumbed to the weakness of living for the public's thanks.—But also for other reasons: these, in person. So don't make anything of it! Apparently you have not sent me the reviews in order to "spare" me.—

Well, I am not even curious and am really no longer interested in them. I read 2: *Lakowitz* at the train station before the trip, and the *Tagblatt* in Warsaw on the return trip! The others will be just the same. So, forget it! I just cut out the enclosed (not into the bark of all trees)[2] but from the *Münchener* Zeitung in the coffee house. I am sending it to you in case you don't have it.

I am very happy to hear German spoken again at last. I have to draw off 10 percent (130 marks) for Wolff. Today I sent you *900* marks. Now, I will be very thrifty, and you can still count on at least *500* marks that I will bring with me.—Write me in Munich if this is enough—or rather, if you counted on more!

My digestion is splendid—and I am taking very good care of myself! I am eating apples en masse. The Russian ones were wonderful. In 14 days I will be with you again! Perhaps by then something will already have been decided about our future . . . ! That really would be the best. And then they can all get lost! And if not—they can do it anyway!

Just think how amusing all of this will look in my biography someday. Perhaps not even Wagner had such a collection of stylistic fantasies [*Stylblütchen*] to show.—Well this is quite certain: either I am a talentless and shameless dilettante, or such an original mind that for the time being people cannot tell back from front.—What can I do about the fact that people are so frightened of me, and would prefer the opposite.—Just run your gauntlet unflinchingly in Hamburg.—By the way, it is funny that Marschalk more or less admitted to me that he was so strongly influenced by his neighbours that he was actually completely incapable of judgement.—He went away from me entirely *changed in his views*, which just shows how weak average people really are in the end. But he behaved very nicely and told me that it went just the same for *Hauptmann* with Florian Geyer.[3]—Friends and enemies were against him, and abandoned him! So, best wishes!

Gustav

The music has gone already?

SHELFMARK: E18-MJ-641

Notes

[1] Mahler is referring to the Berlin performance of the second, third, and sixth movements of the Third Symphony, which took place on 9 March; Justine was present.

[2] Apparently an allusion to the first line of "Ungeduld" (Schubert, *Die schöne Müllerin*): *Ich schnitt es gern in alle Rinden ein* ("I would gladly carve [cut] it into the bark of all trees").

[3] Gerhart Hauptmann (1862–1946), German author and playwright, known particularly for his naturalistic dramas. *Florian Geyer* (premiere 4 January 1896) was a failure with both audiences and critics.

420 *To Justine*

[Munich, 19 March 1897]

Dearest Justi!
Arrived here safely and found the *parcel* with the *Fantastique* and *Coriolan*. But *Blumenstück* was *not there*, as you told me in your last letter.

So send it *immediately* in any case!

My health is excellent throughout, as seldom is the case.

My address is *Hotel Marienbad*!

I leave here on the *25th*. I was just together with Heinrich [Krzyzanowski], and he enthused terribly about you.

Tomorrow I will start to make my visits.—The orchestra is said to be very good; that really is the main thing.

Affectionately,
Your
Gustav

Say hello to Frau Marcus and Frau Her[t]z.

Shelfmark: E14-MJ-561

421 *To Justine*

Postcard[1]
[Postmark: Munich, 21. Mar 97][2]
[Arrival postmark: Hamburg, 22.(3.97)]

D.J. Early this morning the orchestral parts of the Blumenstück came too. But now the *score* is missing. Take it out of your desk and send it directly for me to *Singer* in Budapest, well registered.

I was already together with Strauss. The rehearsals start tomorrow. Today I am making visits.

The weather is terrible! My health and mood splendid.

Best wishes to everybody
G.

Shelfmark: E14-MJp-564

Notes

[1] Addressed to "Fräulein Justine Mahler / Hamburg / Hoheluft, Bismarkstr. 86."

[2] From the contents, it is likely that this was written on 20 March.

422 *To Justine*

[Munich, 21 March 1897]

Dearest Justi!

Just think, the Phantastique [*sic*] is now indeed not possible, unfortunately—not enough rehearsals and extra instruments.—I am compelled to perform Beethoven's C-minor [Symphony]. As an introduction for me, the enclosed correspondence from Berlin appeared today in the Münchener Allgemeine Zeitung, a paper with a very wide circulation. I was greatly amused. This is quite splendid. This smoothes the way for me more than you could have imagined. Strauss, with whom I was together yesterday, and to whom I played the last movement of my II. [Symphony] (he was downright *enthusiastic*), also thinks that I am already on the right path, and that my triumph is now only a question of a very short time.—I already had a rehearsal with the orchestra. It is *very good* and behaves charmingly. I am curious what sort of stir I will cause with my view of the C-minor. I have already arranged to have all the reviews sent directly to you. I am stopping two days in Vienna and will put up in the *Hotel Höller* on *Burggasse*. Direct your next letter there. In Budapest I will stay in the *Königin von England*.

My health, still excellent. Travel seems to suit me very well.

Best wishes from your
Gustav

Shelfmark: E14-MJ-562

423 *To Justine*

Postcard[1]
[Postmark: Munich, 22 Mar 97]
[Arrival postmark: Hamburg, 23.3.97]

D.J. Received your letter!

Am hugely busy and today only send greetings. Send the score of the Blumenstück to Budapest right away, addressed to Singer.

Health, excellent.

Had great success in Moscow—but all of the details are too uninteresting to speak of. Public too Asian!

Affectionately, G.

Shelfmark: E14-MJp-563

Note

[1] Addressed to "Fräulein Justine Mahler / Hamburg / Hoheluft Bismarkstr. 86."

424 *To Justine*

[Munich, 24 March 1897]

Dearest Justi!
Today's dress rehearsal came off brilliantly and was mightily *applauded* by the orchestra. They are all now once again on *my* side! Even Dr. Keim [*sic*, Kaim] is as though transformed, and courts me enormously. It is to be hoped that something or other will come of this in the future. Write to the Hotel *Königin von England* in Budapest, where I will be staying.

In Munich I found some "*fans*" who also sing and play my *songs* (N.B. and *bought* them). Tomorrow I leave for Vienna, where Natalie will meet me at the train station and will have already worked out a program of visits etc. with Papier. At it turns out, Berlin has really *not* harmed me, but has only stirred the emotions and focused attention on me.—The concert begins in an hour. I won't write tomorrow.

Just write about yourself in more detail—damn it, for heaven's sake—and not always simply news about the weather.

How is it going at the theatre—or rather, does one notice a little difference, as it is called?

I am together with Heinrich (who, by the way, is now okay financially) a lot and enjoy his company. He hasn't changed.

Today I am conducting *my* C-minor (Beethoven) again and am really curious whether I again will fall victim to the critics, my old, true friends. The orchestra is *splendid*—nothing but young, enthusiastic people with *good* instruments. I would really like this position.

Best wishes to you all
from Gustav

SOURCE: Photocopy of autograph letter sold by Alfred Rosé; now in Bayerische Staatsbibliothek, Munich (partial facsimile published in *Gustav Mahler Briefe und Musikautographen aus den Moldenhauer-Archiven in der Bayerischen Staatsbibliothek* [Munich: KulturStiftung der Länder/Bayerische Staatsbibliothek, 2003], p. 12). Text previously published in *Gustav Mahler Unbekannte Briefe*, ed. Herta Blaukopf (Vienna: Paul Zsolnay, 1983), pp. 113–14.

425 *To Justine*

Postcard[1]
[Postmark: Munich, 25. Mar 97]
[Arrival postmark: Hamburg, 26.3.97]

Very great success (disputed in the usual beloved manner by certain parties)—I hope for favourable consequences—perhaps. Am just departing.

I will write again from Vienna. *Levi* was at the concert too. The orchestra *welcomed* me, which never happens here, and took part in the applause. Everyone was astonished by it. Well, they indeed know why.

Affectionately G.

SHELFMARK: E14-MJp-565
NOTE
[1] Addressed to "Fräulein Justine Mahler / Hamburg / Hoheluft, Bismarkstr. 86."

426 *To Justine*

[Vienna, 26 March 1897]

Dearest Justi!
For an hour I have been cooling my heels in the outer office of Besetzny [*sic*, Bezecny],[1] who is having "office hours." I am using the time to write you a few lines.—Yesterday I was met at the station by Natalie and—Frau Papier, with whom I then dined. My prospects here don't seem to be too bad at all.

This morning I was with Jahn, who was very nice to me, and assured me that if he stays director, he will think of me first and foremost.—At the same time, however, he assured me that the decision couldn't happen before *September* when an operation is expected to occur.

I will now talk to Wlassa[c]k and Besetzny [*sic*]. This afternoon I will visit critics. I was just at Brüll's.[2]—Tonight I am at "Nanna's" and Fritz is coming too.—Did you already receive the reviews from Munich? I still don't know about them. If they are *very* good, then send them to *Chevalley* on *my* behalf for possible publication.[3]

Affectionately,
Gustav

SHELFMARK: E8-MJ-384
NOTES
[1] See appendix.
[2] Ignaz Brüll (1846–1907), Austrian pianist and composer.
[3] Heinrich Chevalley (1870–?), Hamburg music critic; from 1897 music critic of the *Fremdenblatt*.

427 *To Justine*

[Budapest, 28 or 29 March 1897][1]

Dearest Justi!
I must make the most of every moment.

The business in Vienna is going excellently.

Here, naturally lots of hoopla.

My health is marvellous.

You both could send Birrenkoven a few flowers from you.

I am coming around the *3rd or 4th*.

On the return trip I have to stop in Vienna.

Affectionately
G.

Singers have already gone to a lot of trouble.

Shelfmark: E8-MJ-381
Note
[1] The letter is written on the back of a Hungarian telegraph form. Mahler left Vienna on 28 March for Budapest, where on 31 March he conducted a concert for the benefit of the Pester Journalistenvereinigung (the concert included Beethoven's Fifth and the second movement of Mahler's Third Symphony).

428 *To Justine*

HÔTEL À LA REINE D'ANGLETERRE / BUDAPEST

[Budapest, 30 March 1897]

Dearest Justi!
You will already have the Munich reviews. I enclose an extract from a letter from Heinrich Krz[yzanowski] from which you will see that Weingartner is sticking at it. Tomorrow night there will be lots of hoopla here. On 2 April I will be in Vienna, where much will be decided. At the last moment, I let all the mines be tripped, and apparently everything stands very well. Best wishes to all of you.

In haste.
Your
Gustav

Shelfmark: E8-MJ-387

429 *To Justine*

Postcard[1]
[Postmark: Budapest 97 Apr. 1]
[Arrival postmark: Hamburg, 2.4.97]

D.J. So, last night turned out brilliantly. Banquet and speeches afterwards! Today, to Vienna and to Hamburg not before *the day after tomorrow*. I will let you know my arrival!

Best wishes to everyone,
G.

Shelfmark: E14-MJp-566
Note
[1] Addressed to "Fräulein Justine Mahler / Hamburg / Hoheluft Bismarkstr. 86."

Undated Letters from Hamburg

430 *To Justine*

[Hamburg][1]

Dearest Justi,
Since I have been without any news of you all for so long, I am starting to get uneasy. Please let me know the reason for your silence *immediately*. One of you can certainly write a few lines.—It is not very considerate to leave me without any sign of life, especially now when after all I have to gather my thoughts. So, send news *immediately*.

Best wishes from
Gustav

SHELFMARK: E10-MJ-464
NOTE
[1] The paper matches that used in letters of 1891 and 1892.

431 *To Justine*

[Hamburg, before September 1894][1]

Dearest Justi,
I am enclosing Emma's school report that was sent to me; this time, unfortunately, it did *not* turn out to be a good one. It would seem that your absence did have an effect on her diligence after all. Please give her a thorough talking to, and make it completely clear to her that I have duly noted that she has done so much more poorly.—

How did the conversation turn out? Very dampened spirits, no doubt?

I assume that you received my letter with the enclosures?

Write soon, and very best wishes!

Ever your
Gustav

I'll send the report back to her by registered mail.

SHELFMARK: E6-MJ-299
NOTE
[1] Owing to the mention of Justine's absence, this was likely written between December 1892 and April 1893 when she was with Alois in Merano, or between December 1893 and May 1894, when she was in Italy.

432 *To Emma*

[Hamburg, before September 1894][1]

Dear Emma!
Here I am sending you, as you wished, your report [*Ausweis*]; I cannot conceal from you that I am not exactly very pleased to find that you have done worse in

so many subjects.—After the very promising beginning, I had expected something else from you.—I will send the money to Nina in the next few days.—

With best wishes,
your brother,
Gustav

The mark in French language study is completely *incomprehensible* to me!

SOURCE: Typewritten transcription in the Bibliothèque Musicale Gustav Mahler

NOTE

[1] This letter may relate to the previous one.

433 *To Justine*

[Hamburg, before February 1895][1]
[missing beginning; Mahler wrote p. 2 at the top of the page]

If only Otto would hold out! It really would be a stroke of fortune! Support him in this through all possible means.

I am in a truly furious [*furiosen*] mood—i.e., *internally*. Externally quite *calm*! Everything is going against me!

That's why I need some consideration from you all. Life is truly no joke for a man like me, who has to scrape and tussle through life and, wounded, conquer every foot of ground.

Next time you will receive my photographs, which this time at last actually turned out exceedingly well.

Best wishes from your
Gustav

Let me know in time how much I have to send you on the *1st*.

SHELFMARK: E21-MJ-670

NOTES

[1] It is possible that this fragment forms the conclusion of an unsigned letter (such as letter 324 or letter 353), although the paper does not match. The creases in it indicate that it could have been folded to fit with a smaller letter. The contents do not allow one to draw a firm conclusion, however. The reference to Otto could refer to the difficulties he was having in Bremen during the fall of 1894. Photographs are mentioned in letters of November and December 1892, as well as early 1893.

Vienna
April 1897–November 1907

Chronology

1897 *8 April*: announcement of GM's engagement as conductor at the Vienna Hofoper.
15 April: GM signs his contract at the Hofoper.
25 April: GM leaves Hamburg for Vienna; Justine and Emma remain.
11 May: Debut at the Vienna Hofoper with *Lohengrin*.
Summer: Kitzbühel, Steinbach and Gries am Brenner, Vahrn.
13 July: GM named deputy (*Stellvertretender*) director of the Hofoper.
August: Justine and Emma move to Vienna to live with GM.
8 October: GM becomes director of the Hofoper.

1898 *Summer*: Vahrn; GM composes "Lied des Verfolgten im Turm" and "Wo die schönen Trompeten blasen."
25 August: Emma Mahler marries Eduard Rosé.
24 September: GM named conductor of the Vienna Philharmonic concerts.

1899 *22 January*: GM in Liège to conduct his Second Symphony.
9 April: GM conducts Second Symphony in Vienna.
Summer: Bad Aussee; GM composes "Revelge" and begins the Fourth Symphony.

1900 *15–22 June*: GM travels to the Paris Exhibition with the Vienna Philharmonic.
Summer: Maiernigg am Wörthersee; GM completes Fourth Symphony.
20 October: Second Symphony performed by the Wolf Verein in Munich.
18 November: GM conducts his First Symphony at the second Philharmonic concert.

1901 *17 February*: premiere of *Das klagende Lied* in Vienna (without *Waldmärchen*).
24 February: GM almost dies of a severe haemorrhage.
April: GM resigns as conductor of the Philharmonic.
Summer: Maiernigg am Wörthersee; GM composes three of the *Kindertotenlieder* and four Rückert songs and begins the Fifth Symphony.

September: GM engages Bruno Walter for the Hofoper (debut: *Aida*, 27 September); conflict with Natalie Bauer-Lechner.
7 November: GM dines at Berta Zuckerkandl's and becomes interested in Alma Schindler.
25 November: premiere of the Fourth Symphony in Munich.
16 December: premiere of the Fourth Symphony in Berlin.
20 December: GM attends performance of the Second Symphony in Dresden conducted by Ernst von Schuch.
27 December: official announcement of GM's engagement to Alma Schindler.

1902 *12 January*: premiere of the Fourth Symphony in Vienna.
9 March: marriage of GM and Alma Schindler.
10 March: marriage of Justine Mahler and Arnold Rosé.
11–30 March: GM and Alma travel to St. Petersburg, where GM conducts three concerts.
9 June: premiere of the Third Symphony in Krefeld at the Allgemeine Deutsche Musikverein festival.
Summer: Maiernigg am Wörthersee; GM completes Fifth Symphony and composes "Liebst du um Schönheit."
3 November: birth of Maria Anna (Putzi).
11 December: birth of Alfred Rosé.

1903 *23 January*: premiere of Fourth Symphony in Wiesbaden.
2 April: GM conducts First Symphony in Lemberg (Lwów).
15 June: GM conducts Second Symphony in Basel at the Allgemeine Deutsche Musikverein festival.
Summer: Maiernigg am Wörthersee; GM composes first three movements of the Sixth Symphony.
18–26 October: first trip to Holland. Performances of the First and Third Symphonies. Friendship with Willem Mengelberg.

1904 *15 June*: birth of Anna Justine (Gucki).
Summer: Maiernigg am Wörthersee; GM composes the last two songs of *Kindertotenlieder*, completes Sixth Symphony, and begins the Seventh.
18 October: premiere of Fifth Symphony in Cologne.
20–28 October: second trip to Holland. Double performance of the Fourth Symphony.

1905 *Summer*: Maiernigg am Wörthersee; GM completes the Seventh Symphony.

1906 *7–12 March*: third trip to Holland. Fourth Symphony and *Kindertotenlieder* in Amsterdam.
27 May: premiere of the Sixth Symphony in Essen at the Allgemeine Deutsche Musikverein festival.
Summer: Maiernigg am Wörthersee; GM composes the Eighth Symphony.
3 November: birth of Alma Rosé.

1907 *1 January*: beginning of press campaign against Mahler.

Summer: Maiernigg am Wörthersee.
12 July: death of Maria Anna; shortly afterwards, GM's heart disease is diagnosed.
5 October: GM released from his duties at the Hofoper, effective 31 December.
24 November: GM's farewell concert in Vienna (Second Symphony).
9 December: GM and Alma leave Vienna.

Letters

434 *To Justine*

[Vienna, 28 April 1897]

Dearest Justi!
After all the rabble-rousing, and before a dinner that [Rosa] Papier is giving for me, for the moment I can somewhat reassure you about the state of things. As I expected, they don't stand as badly as they looked from a distance. I was just with Besetzny [*sic*, Bezecny] and Wlassa[c]k. Jahn comes May 2nd, people are gradually settling down, *Liechtenstein* is supposed to be favourably disposed towards me;[1] in the next few days I will have an audience with him. I was also at Brülls. I will take the apartment. Elise shall attend to me there. And in any case you have a room there too. The people are terribly nice. So both of you can come in May, if you like. Somehow or other something will be provided for Emma.

Write me about everything right away; in particular, let me know about Mildenburg—all the details too. She certainly should not sing Prophet and Figaro right after one another.

The trip was very unpleasant—a Herr *Grünfeld* from Iglau (school colleague and a very good-natured, well-meaning fellow) was there too.[2]

I have been interviewed also.

Best wishes to everyone
from
Gustav

Best greetings to Frau Marcus.

Shelfmark:E8-MJ-383
Notes
[1] See appendix.
[2] Unknown.

435 *To Justine*

Correspondence card[1]

HOTEL BRISTOL, VIENNA

[Postmark: Vienna, 28.4.97]
[Arrival postmark: Hamburg: 30.4.97]

Dearest Justi!
Everything is going really well! I have thought over the business with Brüll, however, and will ***not*** move there. If you both come, a solution will have to be found another way. Mind you, I loathe inn life [*Wirthshausleben*] exceedingly.

Do write me in detail! As soon as something happens, I will let you know, won't I. For the time being, I have to wait for *Jahn's* arrival.

Best wishes to all of you
Gustav

Follow the business of how the Wagner performances turned out.

SHELFMARK: E12-MJp-500
NOTE
[1] Addressed to "Fräulein Justine Mahler / Hamburg / Hoheluft / Bismarkstr. 86."

436 *To Emma*

Postcard[1]

HOTEL BRISTOL, VIENNA

[Postmark: Vienna, 1.5.97]
[Arrival postmark: Hamburg, 3.5.97]

Dear Emma!
Thank you for your letter! You could do this more often. I have a tremendous amount to do! Everything is going better than one feared. I probably will *not* go to Brüll's—the reasons for it in person (namely because of [other] people; they themselves are as *charming* as ever). Pollini is also staying in the Bristol, so we will be meeting again! I will indicate soon when you both should come! Please, write in detail.

Affectionately,
Gustav

Best wishes to the Behns.

SOURCE: Typewritten transcription in the Bibliothèque Musicale Gustav Mahler
NOTE
[1] Addressed to "Fräulein Emma Mahler, bei Dr. H. Behn / Harvesthude / Hamburg / Oberstrasse 83."

437 *To Justine*

HOTEL BRISTOL / VIENNA

[Vienna, 2 May 1897]
Sunday

Dearest Justi!
Elise was just here! Everything seems to be going splendidly. Without exception, the critics are capitulating (Hansli[c]k in the lead)—At 10:30 I am with Jahn! On Tuesday at 12:30 I am summoned to see *Liechtenstein.*—I will see if I can find something for the two of us. Possibly you could stay with Schlesingers and Emma with Albi. Just wait a few more days! We will discuss in person what we'll do for vacation. I will not go to Brüll's because of the anti-semites etc.

Warmest greetings to everyone
Gustav

SHELFMARK:E8-MJ-377

438 *To Justine*

Correspondence card[1]

HOTEL BRISTOL, VIENNA

[Postmark: Vienna, 3.5.97]
[Arrival postmark: Hamburg, 4.5.97]

Dearest Justi!
I write daily, don't I?—Tomorrow I am going to Venice for 2 days on behalf of the Intendant.[2] Tuesday, 11th is my debut: Tannhäuser![3]—For the time being, indulge yourselves in Hamburg until the clouds here have dispersed a little bit.—By the way, everything is going well!

Affectionately, and *hurriedly*
Gustav

[across the top of the letter:] Yesterday I encountered Pollini! It was touching!

SHELFMARK:E12-MJp-501
NOTES

[1] Addressed to "Fräulein Justine Mahler / bei Frau Marcus / Hamburg / Heimhuderstrasse 50 [*sic*]." (Marcus lived at number 60.)

[2] Mahler went to Venice to attend the world premiere of Leoncavallo's *La Bohème*, which Jahn had agreed to perform at the Hofoper.

[3] Later switched to *Lohengrin*.

439 *To Justine*

Correspondence card[1]

HOTEL BRISTOL, VIENNA

[Postmark: Vienna, 4.5.97]
[Arrival postmark: Hamburg, 5.5.97]

Dearest Justi!
So, midday to the *Lord High Steward* [*Obersthofmeister*] and tonight to Venice. When I return, I begin with *Tannhäuser* and *Don Giovanni*. For the time being, write to the *Hofoperntheater*. I won't be back before Sunday, however. In *Venice* I am staying at the Hotel *Britannia*.

Best wishes to everyone
from Gustav

Up to now I have *written daily*!

SHELFMARK:E12-MJp-502
NOTE
[1] Addressed to "Fräulein Justine Mahler bei Frau Marcus / Hamburg / Heimhuderstrasse 60."

440 *To Justine*

HOTEL BRISTOL, VIENNA

[Vienna, 4 May 1897]

Dearest Justi!
I've just come from Liechtenstein! He was *extremely charming*—I was with him for a half hour.—He will resolve the whole question in 2–3 months. It really seems that he has chosen me for *Director*.[1] At any rate, it is of the utmost significance that I get along with him so well. This evening I leave for Venice and will probably stay there until *Saturday*, so you can write me at the *Hotel Britannia* at least *once*. Altogether, things are going *very well*. Jahn is very nice and everyone is accommodating me splendidly. Affectionately,

Gustav

SHELFMARK:E8-MJ-378
NOTE
[1] On 4 April, Mahler had signed a one-year contract as *Kapellmeister* for 5,000 florins a year, but there was open speculation in the press that he was destined for higher office. Indeed, Mahler himself wrote to Wlassack on 9 April to thank him for his help in obtaining his "initial [*anfänglichen*] position" (GMB[2] 229) making it clear that Papier and Wlassack had him in mind for the directorship from the beginning.

441 *To Justine*

Postcard: Un Saluto di Venezia[1]
[Postmark: Venice, 5.5.97]
[Arrival postmark: Hamburg, 7.5.97]

Kindest regards from here![2] Wonderful spring weather. My duties at the Vienna Hofoperntheater please me much more than those at the Hamburg Stadttheater! For the time being, stay quietly in Hamburg and walk in the open air!

Gustav

[across other side:] Next letters again to Vienna, Hofoper

SHELFMARK:S2-MJp-767

NOTES

[1] Addressed to "Signorina Giustina Malheurina / bei Frau *Adele Marcus* / Germania / Hamburg / Heimhuderstrasse 60."

[2] Mahler draws an arrow to the Palazzo Ducale depicted on the postcard.

442 *To Justine*

[Vienna, 10 May 1897]

Dearest Justi!
I've now survived the first orchestral rehearsal as well! Everything turned out splendidly. I have won over the orchestra, and the others were already on my side.—

So, tomorrow *Lohengrin* as my debut, and—just think—next week *Walküre and Siegfried*, as was just indicated to me. This is wonderful isn't it?—I already have the singers.—I am now well ensconced everywhere.

But I am tired! At any rate, I will telegraph you all the day after tomorrow.

Right! I am having Elise come, since there is a bright kitchen at her disposal in which she can sleep.—I will then eat at home.—I am thinking that you [should] come already in *June* and stay with *Schlesingers*—or rather, Albi.

Affectionately, your
Gustav

SHELFMARK:E8-MJ-375

443 *To Justine*

THE I. AND R. DIRECTORATE OF THE I.R. COURT OPERA

[Vienna, 12 or 13 May 1897]

Dearest Justi!
Enclosed, the most important reviews—especially *Speidel*, who sets the standard here, and who judges *very* sharply.[1] The anti-semitic papers are partly silent and partly laudatory. Personnel, orchestra etc. etc. entirely for me!

Your question why I write so laconically is comical! So what do you imagine? That I have time to write letters now? I really don't understand you!

I have had Elise come to me because my [domestic] service was too bad.—I would very much like to have you here yourself, but I am afraid that the *money* won't suffice. Anyway, I spend an awful lot! I think that you [should] come in *June* and then we'll go to the country together!

When *would you like* to come? Then just come, dolt, and we'll set ourselves up already! I think, however, that this rest will do you a lot of good and, anyway, you cannot really help me! I will buy you both bicycles before you come!

Affectionately your
Gustav

(out of breath, as always, but very cheerful)

SHELFMARK:E8-MJ-385
NOTE
[1] At the time, Ludwig Speidel (1830–1906) was the critic of the *Fremden-Blatt*. His review praised Mahler extensively.

444 *To Justine*

[Vienna, mid-May 1897]

Dearest Justi!
Once again, I am writing this card in the court theatre offices [*Generalintendanz*] in between times! Everything is going splendidly. My second debut is Walküre, Wednesday 26th., which I am rehearsing with the singers entirely from scratch.[1] Hopefully this time it will go even better. Before the holidays begin, I hope to have gained a *completely firm* foothold.

We are now all looking for apartments. As soon as I find one that is suitable, I will just rent it for 1 August. When *do you want to come here*? Might it interest you to be here already on the *26th*? I will leave this completely up to you. Perhaps you could head to the Tyrol with Natalie sooner in order to find something suitable for us.—

I have received a number of fan letters here. I will send you one that particularly pleased me.—

Send Elise Böhme's invoice.—Why haven't you sent me the Neue Hamb. Zeitung as arranged?

Imagine, since my arrival in Vienna right up to this very day I have not yet had a hint of a migraine; in addition, my digestion is splendid too! So the Viennese climate seems to be very good for me!

Best wishes to you all,
your Gustav

How is Frau Marcus? When is she coming here?

SOURCE: Typewritten transcription in the Bibliothèque Musicale Gustav Mahler. Original letter was sold by Alfred Rosé; present whereabouts unknown. (An obvious transcription error has been silently corrected.)
NOTE
[1] This performance was cancelled at the last minute, owing to the illness of Luise von Ehrenstein; see below, letter 446.

445 *To Justine*

THE DIRECTORATE OF THE I.R. COURT OPERA

[Vienna, May 1897]

Dear Justi!
Natalie is a dolt, and so are you! I would *hardly dream of it*! I have advised her [Mildenburg] against America because she could easily lose her voice.[1] Under no circumstances is she coming *here*. These are nothing but *conjectures* by Papier, Natalie etc.[2] I really have had enough of this gossip factory and at present have entirely other worries.

And I am so sensible too! Idiots! Your trust will come back again when you just get out of that damned nest.—Please do not allow yourself to spread gossip. Natalie watches me here with Argus eyes.[3] If it were up to her, I would only socialise with women over 50. In Venice she apparently fell in with Papier.

I knew nothing of all that. So don't annoy me any more with these *ancient* stories.

Affectionately yours
Gustav

SHELFMARK: E8-MJ-386
NOTES

[1] The possibility of Mildenburg going to the United States is mentioned in four of Mahler's letters to her during this time (GMB[2] 241 is the only one published). In two of these, Mahler indicates his fear that it could damage her voice.

[2] In the end, Mildenburg appeared as a guest in December 1897 and was engaged permanently as of 1 June 1898. The character of Mahler's letters to her changes soon after his arrival in Vienna, as Mahler attempts to end their liaison. For a discussion, see HLGE II, pp. 37–41, 79–81.

[3] In Greek mythology, a giant with a hundred eyes.

446 *To Justine*

[Vienna, 25 May 1897]

Dear Justi!
I have just gotten out of bed and am lying on the chesterfield and scribbling this card in Natalie's fashion (by the way, she was an excellent nurse and did not leave my bedside for 4 days).[1] Hopefully you have already recovered from your motion sickness [*Drehkrankheit*] (the principal malady of sheep [*Schafe*]), just as I have from my inflamed throat. Tomorrow afternoon I have already put myself down for a rehearsal (Zauberflöte).[2] Die Walküre, which ought to have been tomorrow, was unfortunately cancelled by the Sieglinde.[3]

When you have lived here a while with me, you all will appreciate how much more humanely one is treated here.

Why do you hardly ever write? After all, I thought that you were coming already after June 6? At any rate, you must see that you hear a performance here under me. So—now I am "spent" already.

Affectionately yours
Gustav

SHELFMARK:E12-MJ-506
NOTES

[1] Mahler had been suffering from a bad cold and an inflamed throat, which turned into an abscess. After conducting *Die Zauberflöte* on 29 May, a second abscess developed, which was lanced by the doctor on 31 May; see NBL, pp. 91–92.

[2] In the end, this rehearsal did not take place until 28 May.

[3] See above, letter 444.

447 *To Justine*

THE I. AND R. DIRECTORATE OF THE IMP. ROY.
COURT OPERA IN VIENNA

[Vienna, end May 1897]

Dearest Justi!
Was just back at the theatre again!

Conferred with Jahn. If I am not letting the wool be completely pulled over my eyes, he will deal with me completely *honestly*; (apparently he sees me as the only means to still hang on, which in fact is true). Under these circumstances, I wouldn't mind staying here as *Kapellmeister.* A good salary, a long-standing contract, and the Gesellschafts-Konzerte[1] with it is quite decent.

I am now quite back to normal again!

Sunday I have to go to *Munich* to hear Ingwelde.[2] Tuesday, *Figaro, Thursday* Flieg. Holländer *Saturday* Lohengrin.[3]

See to it that you can hear the Lohengrin here under my direction.

Write again soon.

Affectionately yours
Gustav

Hopefully you have already driven the story about M[ildenburg] from your mind?

SHELFMARK:E8-MJ-379
NOTES

[1] Concert series of the Gesellschaft der Musikfreunde established in 1815. Previous directors included Brahms and Hans Richter. In 1897, the Gesellschafts-Konzerte were under the direction of the second-rate conductor Richard von Perger. The Musikverein formally invited Mahler to take over the series in March 1904, but he refused.

[2] Mahler's plan to hear Max von Schilling's opera (which had received its premiere in Munich on 8 May) on 30 May came to naught, owing to his abscessed throat: Mahler was overly optimistic that he was back to normal (see the note to the previous letter).

[3] *Le nozze di Figaro* on 1 June was conducted by Fuchs. By the weekend, Mahler was recovered sufficiently to conduct *Der fliegende Holländer* (5 June) and *Lohengrin* (6 June); Justine was present at the latter performance.

448 *To Justine*

[End July 1897][1]

Dearest Justi,
I am just about to go on a walking trip in the mountains—and hope to be in Vienna in 4–5 days at the most.

My *portfolio* and a package of *music* I am sending directly to you—please, take delivery of it, and guard it for me carefully.

I am going with a knapsack with [only] the necessities.

Tomorrow I will be at the Achensee.

Very best wishes
from Gustav

SHELFMARK: E11-MJ-476
NOTE

[1] Proximity makes it likely that this dates from the summer of 1897, which Mahler spent at Steinbach am Brenner and Vahrn. It is possible, however, that it comes from the following summer when Mahler was staying in Vahrn. (See the following letter for Mahler's travel in late July 1897.)

449 *To Justine*

Correspondence card[1]
[Postmark: Trofaiach, 29.7.97]
[Arrival postmarks: Brixen, 30.7.97, and Vahrn, 30.7.97]

Thursday
Arrived in Trofaiach only yesterday—hospitably received at Villa Jahn—slept and dined splendidly. Am leaving today and arrive at 10 o'clock tonight. At any rate, I will still spend the first few days in a hotel. I was in Ischl at *Wl*[assack]*'s* urging, but in vain since I did not run into Hansli[c]k. I will write again from Vienna and hope to find news of you all too.[2]

Affectionately,
Gustav

SHELFMARK: E12-MJp-503
NOTES

[1] Addressed to "Fräulein Justine Mahler / Vahrn, Südtirol / Villa Mair."

[2] On 13 July, the *Intendant*, Bezecny, distributed a circular letter to the Opera personnel announcing that Mahler would be the deputy (*Stellvertretender*) director while Jahn recovered from his operation. Mahler first learned the news toward the end of the month when he returned from a long bicycle trip. Wlassack wrote shortly afterward and asked Mahler to go to see Jahn for instructions.

450 *To Justine*

[Vienna, 30 July 1897]

Dearest Justi!
I have now arrived in Vienna and just now am sitting on my director's seat (I have been allocated my own office) and the door does not stop opening

and closing. I put up in a hotel since I only arrived at 10 o'clock; probably I will head out to Perchtoldsdorf tonight. Here it has been raining constantly for 4 days.

I have been installed marvellously. It is going splendidly with Jahn; until his arrival I am an *entirely independent* leader.—The enclosed letter from Herr Landau,[1] which I just received, I cannot keep from you all.

The bill from Gross (10 fl.) arrived; I will pay it from here.

I just received 500 fl. from Budapest. *How much should I send you*?

Best wishes to all of you.
Your
Gustav

SHELFMARK:E8-MJ-380
NOTE
[1] Unknown.

451 *To Justine*

[Vienna,] 31 July 1897

Dearest Justi!
Difficulty upon difficulty already. Because of the flooding, all the railways were closed and the personnel couldn't arrive.[1]

The opening performance of Lohengrin—tomorrow—is still questionable. I am now in the city in the Stadiongasse since the weather, and above all the company, in Pötzlensdorf (Friedrike, Herr Hause Ludwig [*sic*] and wife) is not bearable.[2]

I feel splendid. Write daily; I'll have Freund send you 300 fl. just in case.

Best wishes to all of you
Gustav

SOURCE: Typewritten transcription in the Bibliothèque Musicale Gustav Mahler. The original letter was sold by Alfred Rosé; present whereabouts unknown. (An obvious transcription error has been silently corrected.)
NOTES
[1] According to HLGE II, p. 45, Hans Richter was stranded by floods at Hainfeld in Niederösterreich.
[2] It is possible that the Ludwig here is the same one mentioned in Ludwig Karpath, *Begegnung mit dem Genius* (Vienna: Fiba, 1934), p. 62: a former classmate of Mahler's at the Conservatory who once won a *Lied* composition prize over Mahler. Ludwig was then a piano teacher at the Conservatory (his odd first name is likely a transcription problem, but Karpath does not give the correct first name).

452 *To Justine*

[Vienna, c. 4 August 1897]

[in pencil:] Dearest Justi!
It is now gradually starting to settle down. I have already had a cancellation too—instead of *Tell*, Faust, which I took over without a rehearsal. *Very* good

performance.[1] By the way, I have got a very good "official box" (2nd circle) which for the moment is being frequented assiduously by Emma and Albi. By the way, I have been without news of you for 2 days.
[in ink:] That was in the Intendant's office. Now I am writing again in my office (Opera).—I've seen the apartment; it's truly altogether splendid. If only we were back to the status quo. Today the weather is beautiful again and I have some breathing room again and will go out a bit.

When is Frau Marcus coming to Vienna?

Best wishes to all of you.
Your
Gustav

SHELFMARK: E12-MJ-507
NOTE
[1] 3 August 1897.

453 *To Justine*

Postcard: Gruss vom Kahlenberge[1]
[Postmark: Vienna, (illegible).8.97]
[Arrival postmark: Vahrn (illegible)]

The first free afternoon.
I am sitting here on the terrace with Fritz and enjoying myself!

Affectionately
Gustav

SHELFMARK: E6-MJp-316
NOTE
[1] Addressed to "Fräulein Justine Mahler / Vahrn / Villa Mair / Südtirol." The card was written on the same day as the next letter.

454 *To Justine*

[Vienna, early August 1897]

Dearest Justi!
I have a lot to do and to work on right now, mind you; up to now I have conducted all the operas. Richter has come by already and he has come to terms with things in a friendly manner. He is handing Rheingold and Walküre over to me. Both these operas are set for the end of August, so you will arrive just in time.[1] Too bad that Frau Marcus and Tönchen won't be there too. Or might they? I hope to move into the apartment on Sunday and am very much looking forward to it.[2]

Today I was with Fritz on the Kahlenberg, from whence I sent you a picture postcard.[3]

I miss you very much, but I am glad that you are still enjoying beautiful Vahrn and this time won't have to go through the damned business of setting up the apartment. You will also very much enjoy being with Frau Marcus—and she will too.

This month I will also conduct *Figaro, Freischütz, Don Juan* (which Richter handed over to me); *Verkaufte Braut, Hans Heiling, Profet* etc. as well; in a word: almost every day and always *without rehearsal*.[4] Everything is working well with the orchestra; it is a real pleasure [working] with these people.

I am writing in the greatest haste and send greetings to you and Frau Marcus and Tönchen.

Affectionately your
Gustav

SOURCE: Photocopy of autograph letter sold by Alfred Rosé; present whereabouts unknown. Text previously published in *Gustav Mahler Unbekannte Briefe*, ed. Herta Blaukopf (Vienna: Paul Zsolnay, 1983), p. 115.

NOTES

[1] Performed on 25 and 26 August as part of a full *Ring* cycle conducted by Mahler.

[2] Probably Sunday, 8 August.

[3] See the previous letter. Unfortunately, neither postmark is legible.

[4] As Mahler casts this sentence in the future tense, the letter must have been written during the first week of August, before he conducted any of the works mentioned: *Le nozze di Figaro* (14 August); *Der Freischütz* (17 August); *Don Giovanni* (22 August); *Verkaufte Braut* (11 August); *Le Prophète* (15 August). *Hans Heiling* was not performed until February 1898 (and was not conducted by Mahler). In addition, Mahler conducted *Der fliegende Holländer* on 7 August.

455 *To Justine*

[Vienna, 6 August 1897]

Dearest Justi!

Today I was again "summoned" to see *Liechtenstein*. He was even more charming than the 1st time. I was with him for over half an hour. It appears that events are moving *surprisingly quickly*.—I am in *fact* the all-powerful director.

Richter was here too and asked for 6-weeks leave, which I willingly granted him, whereupon everything developed in a comfy, cosy way.[1] It seems to me that I have already told you that he has unloaded *Rheing*. and Walküre on me. I was just at the apartment; it will really be quite charming and will suit marvellously. Frau Marcus and Tönchen can stay with us very nicely. I think that I will move in on Sunday. It now must actually be *6 months* since I have been able to sit within my own 4 walls (since 1 March) and I now have a terrible need to be *at home* once again.

This living in furnished rooms [*Chambregarniethum*] is really not to be endured any longer.

So, people are waiting outside my door again, and I must close.

Have lots of fun in pretty Vahrn.

Affectionately yours,
Gustav

SHELFMARK:E8-MJ-376
NOTE

[1] Correspondence around this leave is found in the Hofoper and General-Intendanz archives: Oper 136 U.Z. 72/1897 and Gen. Int.167 Z. 1099. The first memorandum is dated 9 August, which was a Monday. Given Mahler's comment about moving into his apartment on Sunday (in fact, he did not do so until late Tuesday, 10 August), Richter most likely met with Mahler the previous Friday, 6 August. He was granted leave 20 September–2 November (the draft letter to him in the file is dated 14 August).

456 *To Justine*[1]

[Vienna, 11 August 1897]
Bartensteinstr. early Wednesday 8:00

Dearest Justi!
Just the brief report that I (thank God) moved in here last night, slept splendidly, and just had breakfast. Send your letters here from now on.[2] *Liechtenstein* has instructed Besezny [*sic*] to "grant" Jahn his resignation before his return. Thus the journey to Calvary (the director's chair) has reached its final station.—I have already borne the entire cross of the directorship—at any rate, I won't have to wear myself out as much as in Budapest. My position is still indisputable, and once I have my decree in my pocket, I am ready to resign at any moment.[3] For the time being, naturally, I don't have the slightest reason for this. Even Richter has already acknowledged my authority; ever since I obtained a 6-week leave for him, he has regarded me as an entirely suitable holder of the director's title. Write soon.

Best wishes to you from
Gustav

Frau Marcus should not be a dolt and should arrange her return trip via Vienna. Who knows how everything will be in the winter. Now she can still *bask* a little bit in my new eminence.

Marsop was at Bülow's funeral in Hamburg, where I myself met him and had to go to the greatest pains to avoid him.[4]

The news about my appointment must still remain *the strictest secret*. (Also, don't say a word about Marsop.)

SHELFMARK:E8-MJ-388
NOTES

[1] Justine copied a fourteen-line Italian poem ("Ogni sera di sotto il mio balcone") on the back of the letter.

[2] Bartensteinstrasse 3. Mahler and his sisters lived there until early August 1898.

[3] See Karpath, *Begegnung mit dem Genius*, pp. 58–59. Owing to Jahn's desire to be named as "k.k. Hofrat" (imperial and royal counsellor) and the kaiser's reluctance to do so, the decree was not signed until 8 October 1897 (in the end, he was made a commander of the Order of Franz-Joseph).

[4] Munich music critic Paul Marsop (1856–1925).

457 *To Justine*

Correspondence card[1]
[Postmark: Semmering, 22.12.97]
[Arrival postmark: Vienna, 23.12.97]

D.J!
It is wonderful here! Very cold! Dress yourselves warmly; boots and knitted gloves are necessary. A room is reserved for you. I will certainly meet you. Let me know your arrival!

Best wishes from
Gustav

Shelfmark:E12-MJp-504
Note
[1] Addressed to "Fräulein Justine Mahler / Wien / I. Bartensteingasse 3."

458 *To Arnold Rosé*

THE I. AND R. DIRECTORATE OF THE IMP. ROY.
COURT OPERA IN VIENNA

[Postmark: Vienna, 24.1.98][1]
[Arrival postmark: Meran, 26.1.98]

My dear Rosé!
In great haste!
Lipiner, who turned to Herr Dr. Hausmann[2] for information, brought me his answer today. From this I see, thank God, that your prognosis is quite hopeful, but also that *under no circumstances* should you come back until *he* pronounces you to be completely healed.—I hope that you will follow his orders *meticulously*, since for you (for the whole future) it is a question of *life* and *career*; I ask this most fervently.—

For your further assurance, I have the following to tell you today. I. Today Hellmesberger and his quartet *started their holidays* today, so in this respect you have nothing to worry about.[3]

II. I am granting you an unrestricted leave until you are entirely healed. Your duties will be managed by a substitute paid by the Court Opera.[4]

III. *2000 fl.* have been placed entirely at your disposal by a party unknown to you. You take on absolutely no moral obligations. The people *were able to do it* and disappeared completely once it was done.

Please let me know right away what I ought to do with the money; or rather, whether I should send all of it to you right away, or in instalments. Of course it is primarily intended to cover the costs of your stay in Merano and the cure itself.

Dear Rosé, be sensible and do *everything* to get over this stupid thing. When you are healthy again, we will once again harness you up quite properly.

Best wishes to you from
your
Mahler

Can you read this writing?

SHELFMARK: E8-MAr-389
NOTES

[1] Taken from the envelope, addressed "Herrn Concertmeister Arnold Rosé / Meran / Kaiserhof."

[2] Unknown, but also mentioned in a letter from Justine to Ernestine (13 July 1898).

[3] Joseph "Pepi" Hellmesberger (1855–1907), Viennese violinist, conductor, and leader of the Hellmesberger String Quartet from 1891 (the quartet was founded by his father, Joseph [1828–1893]).

[4] Correspondence in the archives of the Hofoper (Z. 34/1898) and the General-Intendanz (Gen. Int. 79/1898) indicates that Rosé had recently recovered from a "serious illness" (*schwere Krankheit*) but in order to completely regain his health was obliged to go to a "southern climate." On 14 January, Bezecny indicated to the Opera directorate that Rosé's leave was approved until 12 March.

459 *To Emma*

Picture postcard: Gruß vom Semmering / Südbahn-Hôtel[1]
[Postmark: Semmering, 15.10.98]
[Arrival postmark: Boston, Oct 28 1898]

We are thinking of you here, dear Emma, and of your approaching birthday this year and send warm wishes to you, far away—also to Eduard.[2]

Gustav

Warmest birthday greetings from me too. Your J.

SOURCE: Typewritten transcription and photocopy in Bibliothèque Musicale Gustav Mahler
NOTES

[1] Addressed to "Amerika / Mrs. Emma Rosé / Boston—Mass. / Dartmouth Str. [Justine:] 27."

[2] Emma's birthday was 19 October. She and cellist Eduard Rosé (1859–1943) were married on 25 August 1898.

460 *To Emma*

Postcard[1]
[Postmark:Vienna, 20.10.1898][2]
[Arrival postmark: Boston Oct 30 1898]

Dear Emma!
The assembly, well known to you—which has meanwhile moved from Pschorr to another inn—sends you warmest wishes and greetings for your birthday today—also to your husband.

Gustav

All the best on your birthday from me too. I am glad to hear so many good things. Things here are beyond belief [Hier ist's zum Schlagtreffen], *so forgive my stupidity. Your Natalie.*

Warmest congratulations and greetings. Dr. Boer[3]

Your Pepi greets you from the heart.[4]

On this occasion you're getting our seating order at the same time. Best wishes to both of you. Justine.

Source: Typewritten transcription and photocopy in Bibliothèque Musicale Gustav Mahler
Notes
[1] Addressed to "Mrs. Emma Rosé / Boston—Mass. / 27 Dartmouth Street."
[2] Written the day before, on Emma's birthday.
[3] See appendix.
[4] Unknown.

461 *To Justine*

Postcard[1]
[Postmark: Liège, 19. Janv. 1899][2]
[Arrival postmark: Vienna, 20.1.99]

Dearest!
After a pleasant journey and a good night's sleep, I am sitting in the restaurant car having breakfast (*excellent* tea). Hopefully you've already received the newspapers. In a quarter hour I'll be in Lüttich [Liège]. I am properly ahead of you again (about 1 hour). Please write daily and telegraph.

Best wishes to you and Arnold.
Your Gustav

Shelfmark: E14-MJp-567
Notes
[1] Addressed to "Fräulein Justine Mahler / Wien / Auenbruggerstrasse 2 / 3. Stock."
[2] Mahler was in Liège to conduct his Second Symphony with the Philharmonisches Orchester on 22 January.

462 *To Justine*

~~HÔTEL-RESTAURANT / ARNOLD MOHREN / RUE PONT-D'AVROY, *31*... LIÈGE~~

Address: Sylvain Dupuis
Rue du Saint-Esprit
104
[Liège, c. 21 January 1899]

Dearest Justi!

I have been received exceedingly hospitably at the Dupuis'[1]—a very nice couple with delightful young children. They do everything that they can think of for me and—tire me right out with all sorts of attentiveness.—I already have extra rehearsals with everyone. The orchestra is very rough—despite all the complaining when I am in Vienna, compared to the Philharmonic, every other [orchestra] seems bad.[2]—

Also, not all of the instruments that I wanted are represented, so: I have to "laboriously make shift"—The choir is very good and very willing, but sings out of tune (naturally I have again caused a furore amongst the ladies). Soloists—typically French.[3] But—something will come of it. The city is not particularly exciting—the impression it makes is like Hamburg in the areas near Fuhlentwiete, Neuer Wall, etc.

So many times have I regretted getting myself into such ventures; particularly during the orchestral rehearsal I became quite miserable about it.—The misery of life, which I have portrayed in the first movements, just does not stop at all.—At any rate, from now on I will no longer betake myself of a private dwelling if the people aren't *very* good and *old* friends. One gets tired of nothing but mutual considerations.

I still don't have any sign of life from you, but today I finally hope for a letter.

Jenny is coming this afternoon![4] Vederemo!

Best wishes to you—and great haste. Despite the long time, every moment is fully occupied because of the way everything is continually broken up.

Your
Gustav

Write and telegraph!

SHELFMARK: S1-MJ-752

NOTES

[1] Belgian conductor and composer Sylvain Dupuis (1856–1931). On 6 March 1898, he performed Mahler's Second Symphony to great acclaim in his Nouveaux Concerts series. It was the first time one of Mahler's symphonies was performed outside of Germany.

[2] As of the 1898–1899 season, Mahler succeeded Hans Richter as the conductor of the Vienna Philharmonic concerts. He resigned at the end of the 1900–1901 season, partly in the wake of his serious haemorrhage in February 1901, but largely owing to the hostility of the orchestra and the press.

[3] The Société Royale La Légia was the choir, and the soloists were Martha Lignière and Mme. Caro-Lucas.

[4] Jenny Perrin-Feld was living in Belgium at the time; see the note to letter 10.

463 *To Justine*

Correspondence card[1]
[Postmark: Prague 3.6.99]
[Arrival postmark: Vienna, 4.6.99]

D.J. I froze a lot on the journey, so in the future, be careful about travelling at night in the summer. Here I have already rehearsed assiduously. The performance "commensurate with their abilities" will hopefully be quite good.[2]—Went walking this morning. Tomorrow will do so again. I feel very well. *Choral society* surprisingly good and very enthusiastic.[3] I will be in Vienna early Monday if nothing intervenes.

Best wishes to you all
G.

SHELFMARK: E14-MJp-568
NOTES

[1] Addressed to "Fräulein Justine Mahler / Wien / III. Auenbruggerstrasse 2 / (Rennweg 5)."

[2] Mahler was in Prague to conduct Beethoven's Ninth Symphony with the orchestra of the Königliches Deutschen Landes-Theater on 4 June 1899.

[3] The chorus was composed of members of the Deutsche Singverein, the Deutsche Männergesangverein, and the Singverein "Tauwitz."

464 *To Emma*

Postcard: Altaussee[1]
[Postmark: Aussee in Steiermark, 11.7.99]
[Arrival postmark: Pörtschach am See, 12.7.99]

A contribution to the collection!

Best wishes to you and to those who remember me.
Arnold.

Best wishes from your Justine
The same, as always
—Natalie

Ditto as well
Gustav

SOURCE: Typewritten transcription in Bibliothèque Musicale Gustav Mahler
NOTE

[1] Addressed to "Frau Emma Rosé / Pörtschach am See / Etablissement Wahlis."

465 *To Justine*

Correspondence card[1]
[Postmark: Ischl, 29.7.99]
[Arrival postmark: Aussee in Steiermark, 30.7.99]

Arrived safely. A[rnold]'s mood has improved significantly.—Café Walter at 12:45. No trace of Lipiner. But very pleasant spa music!—Lipiner just came. Li[e]chtenstein is here already too. Money talks. At 3 o'clock we are leaving for Wolfgang.[2]—

Best wishes
G.

SHELFMARK:E12-MJp-505
NOTES
[1] Addressed to "Fräulein Justine / Mahler R.R. etc. / Markt-Aussee / Villa Seri."
[2] Either the Wolfgangsee or St. Wolfgang im Salzkammergut (on the Wolfgangsee), about eighteen kilometres from Bad Ischl.

466 *To Justine*

[Vienna, 7 August 1899][1]

Dearest Justi!
Hopefully your mood has improved somewhat; the first morning must really have been terrible.—Just go into the water, and everything will get better.—It is very hot here, but at least one can sleep well outside.—Dr. Boër has already arrived.—I am awfully curious what you all will find. I am writing these lines in the apartment after a gourmet dinner; however I found neither envelope nor writing paper. I am using the bottom of your letter and hope that God will help me find an envelope after I finish this letter. The theatre is almost entirely empty.[2]

Bathe assiduously! And do not miss the opportunity through impatience; God knows how long it will be before it is presented to you again so favourably. Hopefully Natalie will bring you to your senses as well, or at least to a proper flotation device.—The enclosed letter is for you to answer! Tomorrow Arnold and I are probably going up the Schneeberg and staying over night there! Best wishes to you all

from your
Gustav

My digestion leaves nothing to be desired.

SHELFMARK:E10-MJ-446
NOTES
[1] Dated on the basis of the following card.
[2] Mahler had returned to Vienna on 1 August for the reopening of the Hofoper.

467 *To Justine*

Correspondence card: Hotel Hochschneeberg[1]
[Postmark: Hochschneeberg, 8.8.99]
[Arrival postmark: Pörtschach am See, 9.8.99]

Just got here. We are staying 2 days! Magnificent air and views! When you come back, we must come up here together again! Hopefully the Oh Oh, Ohs have changed into Ah! Ah! Ahs?

Best wishes to you all! This is my room![2] Gustav

[Arnold Rosé:] Best wishes to you, Em[ma] and Ed[uard].
Your Arnold

SHELFMARK:E6-MJp-317
NOTES
[1] Addressed to "Fräulein Justine Mahler / Pörtschach am See / Wahliss." Justine must have been visiting Emma and Eduard, as this is the same address as letter 464, above.
[2] Mahler draws an arrow to a window on the photograph of the hotel.

468 *To Justine*

[Vienna, c. 10 August 1899]

Dearest Justi!
It really annoys me that Natalie left you waiting so long! I am convinced that otherwise you wouldn't have been thrown into this terrible mood.—We left Schneeberg yesterday because it began to rain.—Today Vienna has cooled down quite a bit.—Arnold dines with me daily, as usual in the apartment. Yesterday Elise had 3 teeth pulled while under laughing gas and because of that she has a migraine today, so we will eat at the pub.—As far as dwellings are concerned, just do everything that you can; whether we can find something in the *open* is very questionable. I am convinced that we should *build* there.[1] And thereby the whole winter would be ruined for us. I enclose the letter about the villa in *Bruck* for you just in case.—However, I think that the South Tyrol is the right place.—Someone who comes from there told me that he *didn't have a single* day of rain.

Now, just grin and bear it. These few weeks too will pass. You'll come back quite penniless and healthy, and we—hopefully will have a beautiful villa for many years.

I am excellent. I enjoy the heat and we are also bathing assiduously. Now I am curious about your next letter.

Tell Natalie that quite probably I will *not* take on the *Phil. Concerts*, thus she shouldn't say anything yet to [Marie] Soldat.[2]

Best wishes to you, dear Justi, and keep your chin up.

Your
Gustav

SHELFMARK:E10-MJ-447
NOTES
[1] For Justine and Natalie's house-hunting trip by bicycle and discovery of Maiernigg on the Wörthersee, see NBL, pp. 140–41.
[2] Mahler did in fact conduct the Philharmonic for two more seasons. Marie Soldat-Roeger (1863–1955) was first violinist of the women's string quartet named after her in which Natalie played viola. She also had something of a career as a soloist. She performed the Brahms Violin Concerto with Mahler and the Philharmonic on 17 December 1899.

469 *From Justine to Emma*[1]

Vienna, 25 Oct. 99

Dearest Emma, I tell you that I was very angry about you not writing and two days ago already I considered telegraphing. You should have at least sent a card with a couple of lines on it immediately upon your arrival. You can just imagine that we were very worried here. I am just happy that you are well. It galls me that I economised on the trip to Hamburg, but it cannot be changed any longer. However, I will shorten my stay there considerably, so that I will be in Vienna again on 14 November. I'll go to Berkan right away on the first morning. I think that it's splendid how he behaved. We will reciprocate in January when he and his wife come to Vienna. I am tremendously happy that you didn't have to pay any duty. Hopefully now I can send you everything that you need. Eduard should find out about this in detail immediately upon his first trip to New York. It must be another few months before you get the things, right? Didn't you ascertain whether someone from Hamburg could have brought them along? Please clarify the following matter for me: I am supposed to still owe Eduard 10 fl. from Vahrn—when and why did he lend this to me at that time? Yesterday I gave Arnold your cushion. I left the choice to him, and he chose the one which you had intended for Gustav; he thanks you very much. The day before yesterday was the première of *Dämon*.[2] Mildenburg was in excellent voice—just as in old times. I now see her much less since Behn is in the picture.[3] What do you think of the fact that I am on "Du" terms with Behn? Herr Schlesinger has sent a letter again. I think that he would now like to be engaged here.[4] But Rottenberg's engagement is as much as certain; he is now here for six weeks.[5] He is a very good musician, and a nice fellow as well, but by no means as good a conductor as Schlesinger, although the orchestra likes him. I am very happy about his engagement: at least he is someone who will not scheme. The Philharmonic concerts are already sold out—in fact, not a single ticket was available and many reservations were in vain. Probably a second series of concerts will take place, such is the demand. I believe I have already told you that nothing has happened with either Russia or Paris. They will not pay as much as Gustav has asked; I am not unhappy about it—it would have been a tremendous exertion for Gustav. We now regularly walk for an hour each afternoon in the Prater, and this does Gustav such good that he is really much healthier this year than usual—even his digestion. I have finally put myself in Hammerschlag's care;[6] however, even though I do scarcely anything about it, I too am again much better. I am already anxious for your address and your detailed news. This letter is additional; I will write again Saturday.

Heartfelt greetings to Eduard, and hugs from your J.

SHELFMARK: S2-ME-769a

NOTES

[1] Written on note paper printed with a silhouette of Mahler (piercing eyes) by Otto Böhler.

[2] Rubinstein's *Der Dämon* was first performed at the Hofoper on 23 October.

[3] At the time, Mildenburg was having an affair with Mahler's friend Hermann Behn.

[4] In October–November 1899, Mahler again tried to convince Bruno Walter to come to Vienna, but in the end Walter's negotiations with the Berlin Opera were too far advanced.

[5] Ludwig Rottenberg (1864–1932), from the Frankfurt Opera, was engaged as a guest conductor in the wake of Johann Nepomuk Fuchs's death on 4 October.

[6] Albert Hammerschlag (1863–1935), a Viennese doctor and, with his brother Paul (1860–1933), a friend of Mahler's.

470 *From Justine to Emma*[1]

Vienna, 5 Nov. [1899]

Dearest Emma,

So, your letter didn't arrive this week either—tomorrow I am travelling to Hamburg, but I will be back already next Tuesday for Arnold's first quartet concert.[2] I would have gladly given up this trip, but I couldn't free myself of it anymore without offending the entire family. That would have been quite the little scene with Toni. She is still writing me idiotic love letters. This time the crowd for the Philharmonic concert was so unbelievably large that a repetition of the first concert will take place on Wednesday and actually in the evening: such a demand is unprecedented.[3] Gustav had no luck with *Der Dämon*. I think that the last performance will take place next week. Mildenburg was fantastic, almost like her best times in Hamburg. Last night we were with her and Behn together at Theuer's;[4] she is always so nice, and I always enjoy being with her. In fact, we don't see each other often—at most, twice a week. Behn has now taken a small apartment here (room, small room, antechamber, kitchen) (400 fl.) and is setting it up. Mildenburg's mother is also getting an extra apartment because the sister (also trained for the stage) is coming to stay with her. This week I had Fritz, Uda, Bertha, Grethl, Behn, and Rottenberg all at once; I entertained the company morbidly. So today is the first concert and tonight we are at Nina's.—Why do you never write about yourself in more detail? Anyway, I have never seen someone write as inexplicitly as you do—it is then very difficult for me to write, because you do not give me a stimulus in your letters. You can certainly describe your apartment to me sometime, report in really detailed fashion about all the furniture, maids, etc., as I write. Naturally my last letters to you are only echoes of your letters, but look at my past letters sometime, and improve yourself!

Best wishes to Eduard, and kisses from your J.

SHELFMARK: S2-JE-769b

NOTES

[1] Written on note paper printed with a silhouette of Mahler (gesturing to the right) by Otto Böhler.

[2] The first concert of the Rosé Quartet's 1899–1900 season took place in the Kleiner Musikvereinsaal on Tuesday, 14 November.

[3] The first Vienna Philharmonic subscription concert of the season was that afternoon (Weber, *Euryanthe* Overture; Mozart, Symphony No. 41; and Beethoven, Symphony No. 5).

[4] Alfred Theuer, the architect of Mahler's villa and *Häuschen* in Maiernigg.

471 *To Justine*

[Vienna, 10 or 11 November 1899][1]

Dearest Justi!

Just a few lines and a thousand greetings! I don't know whether I'm coming or going! You certainly know how it is going! My health is splendid! The weather is still beautiful and [there is] company daily at mealtime.—The 2nd concert was even better than the first. I have had Hassinger send you all of the significant reviews.[2]—I imagine that you are also in a rush [*Sturm*], but your daily harbour [*Ankerplatz*] is with Frau Marcus—give her my warmest greetings! I really would like to see her again sometime!

So, a thousand greetings, and don't forget that you have to be here on Tuesday.

Your
Gustav

SHELFMARK:E10-MJ-463
NOTES

[1] As the previous letter reveals, Justine was visiting in Hamburg between 6 and 13 or 14 November. Since Mahler mentions the repetition of the first Philharmonic concert on 8 November, this letter must date from shortly afterwards.

[2] Carl Hassinger was a *Kanzleidiener* (factotum) at the Hofoper.

472 *From Justine to Emma*[1]

Vienna, 16 November [1899]

Dearest Emma, I have been back from Hamburg for two days and have received your letter, which was delayed a whole week. There was such a tumult in Hamburg that I did not write Gustav once. At the last moment I had to take over two roles for Frau Lurik. I didn't participate in the main rehearsal [*Hauptprobe*], then however there was a protest so that Frau Lurik had to play her roles after all. I was glad when I was on the way back to Vienna. I couldn't bear it there anymore. Frau Marcus was nice as always, but Toni has lost her only good trait, her kindness. What remains, you can imagine roughly for yourself. The only thing that she has continued from before is the kissing, which in fact is worthless; I found her to be simply unpleasant, and I had difficulty being nice to her. I was to Anna's once for breakfast. She was very nice and showed me Toni's wedding present, a sofa cushion, quite in your style, simply audacious. I would have to write you for hours if I wanted to tell you about all the hassles, but I know one thing: she will never again be my guest, and she won't get another line more from me. I will send you a copy of the play that was performed with the next newspapers. Dodi as the Grandmother and Richard as old Hertz were simply perfect in their costumes and acting. I found Dodi quite changed, in fact she is once again in her third month and right from the first moment she made a terrible fuss and only wants a girl. Anna too, who just had a miscarriage and lost 10 kg. because of it. She just looks distastefully thin. I went to dinner with Max Mumssen. In every respect he has changed for the better. On the surface as well as in essence I conversed marvellously with him. On the other side, I sat beside old Hertz, who insisted on sitting beside me, and behaved, as usual, like a pig. I was glad when I got off at the station in Vienna. By the way, I was to dinner at Berkans once with Birrenkoven and his wife and Zinne,[2] and once to breakfast at Frau Behn's, who droned on out of politeness. Enough of boring old Hamburg. It will interest you to hear that Arnold's quartet is very well attended this year, and that Hanslick himself was at the first quartet [concert]. I already told you that I sent Siegfried [Lipiner] to Hanslick on this account. Arnold must of course never discover this, as he would be furious, but I am still pleased that it succeeded; he seems to be very delighted. Next week he moves into his new apartment. You can be very pleased that you didn't take Marie's sister with you, she has been back home for a long time, she couldn't stand it anywhere, she is not used to work and is also supposed to be very cheeky. I hope that, in time, you will find a capable person. I am enormously happy that all the ladies are so friendly to you. Please just do everything to keep it that way. Gustav's letter to Kneisel also seems to have helped a lot.[3] Gustav said that he has never written such a good letter; did Eduard use it financially too? Naturally that would be what one would very much wish. We still have not heard from Langer. Herr Ründinger[4] appears to have absolutely no intentions of going before God himself calls him into a better world. Since I got back from Hamburg, I have not seen anybody except for Albi, who ate with us yesterday. She is very annoyed that you still have written her absolutely nothing. I never see Karpath either,[5] because we never go to the restaurant now, but always eat at home. Should an opportunity arise, I will naturally take it. I have already written about the concerts. Behn has now taken a small apartment here, and showers Mildenburg with presents. Enough for now. A thousand greetings to you and E[duard] from your J.

[written upside-down across top of outside page of letter:] Next time please let me know your precise address again, Roseburg or Tuin place?

Shelfmark:S2-JE-769c

Notes

[1] Written on note paper printed with a silhouette of Mahler (gesturing to the left, with his hand to his mouth) by Otto Böhler. Many of the Hamburg friends and acquaintances mentioned by Justine are unknown.

[2] Wilhelm Zinne (1858–1934), Hamburg teacher and music critic. His friendship with Mahler was based on their mutual love of Bruckner and bicycling.

[3] On 1 October, Mahler had written to Franz Kneisel (1865–1926), then concert master of the Boston Symphony Orchestra, asking for "goodwill and forbearance" with his brother-in-law, who apparently was having some difficulty in the orchestra at the time (Bibliothèque Musicale Gustav Mahler).

[4] The name may not be correct, as it is difficult to read.

[5] Ludwig Karpath (1866–1936), Viennese music critic. He was a friend and supporter of Mahler's. When his *Begegnung mit dem Genius* was published in 1934, he sent copy number 5 to Justine.

473 *To Justine*

Postcard: Exposition de 1900: Palais de l'electricité[1]
[Postmark: Paris, 15. Juin 00][2]
[Arrival postmark: Klagenfurt, 18.6.00]

I just met the *Kilians* from Iglau in the midst of incredible pandemonium in the "Café de la Paix," where I was waiting for Arnold.—

I am in proper accommodations at the Austrian Embassy, where I have 2 wonderfully quiet and isolated rooms. Vienna compared to Paris is more or less like Iglau to Vienna! I am curious what you will write me from Maiernigg. The trip was good. I met *Singer* in the car; he is the brother of Siegmund Singer from Budapest. Best wishes to you and to Natalie and the Theuers.

From your
Gustav

[across top:] *Just arrived. Best wishes, Arnold.*

SHELFMARK: E6-MJp-318

NOTES

[1] Addressed to "*Autriche* / Mlle. Justine Mahler / Maiernigg am Wörthersee / bei Klagenfurt."

[2] Mahler and the Vienna Philharmonic were in Paris performing at the World Exhibition. This was the first foreign tour of the Vienna Philharmonic in its history.

474 *To Justine*

[Paris, 16 or 17 June 1900]

Dearest Justi!

Everything was going well until a speech from me yesterday (actually a reply to a welcoming speech), in which I made a terrible fool of myself. Once again, I definitely don't seem to be made for such things.

I just came from breakfast at the embassy (that is, at my place) where I met this Italian Countess Esterhazy, who asked about you right away.—Kielmannsegg from Vienna were there too.[1]

I slept *wonderfully* in my rooms! Not a sound for miles around!

Best wishes to you and Natalie,
your
Gustav

SHELFMARK: E14-MJ-569

NOTE

[1] Erich, Graf Kielmannsegg (1847–1923), minister of the interior and *Statthalter* (governor) of Niederösterreich.

475 *To Justine*

[Paris, 18 June 1900]

Dearest!

Just received your letter! Here everything is going splendidly. My apartment is superb! Today I am breakfasting at home again! Until now I have spent every afternoon in the country, always in *Mandl's* company. He is a very nice and extremely obliging man, whom I esteem greatly.—The day before I was at St. Germain; Arnold was there too. Yesterday at Versailles and from there, we went on foot to Marly, through the most beautiful woods and meadows (2½ hours). At Mandl's that evening; you know his wife too, she was with him that time at *Steegers*.[1] A splendid person, who pleases me a lot. That night to the World Exhibition—such illumination decisively recalls 1000 and 1 nights.—Today is the first concert![2] Vederemo! I am absolutely not nervous. *Friday* night departure from here—Arnold and I. We will use every connection in order to get to Klagenfurt as soon as possible.—Under the most favourable circumstances, we hope to be with you already Sunday morning![3] At any rate, however, afternoon. I will write once more and in any case will still telegraph my exact arrival.—Best wishes to the two of you.

Your
Gustav

The weather here is continually beautiful and we are hardly suffering from the heat! Only our friend Arnold is very thick-blooded—his face could be of sandstone!

[on back, in Natalie's hand:]
Rosé Paris Hotel Schenker
Rue l'universitée
Please telegr. detailed news about Gustav
Address Mahler Maiernigg
Klagenfurt

Shelfmark:E14-MJ-570
Notes

[1] Viennese composer Richard Mandl (1859–1918).

[2] The first concert was at 2:30 p.m. on 18 June at the Théâtre Municipal du Châtelet (*Meistersinger* Vorspiel; Mozart's Symphony No. 40; *Oberon* Overture; Beethoven's *Leonore* No. 3 and Fifth Symphony).

[3] On Saturday, 23 June, Justine wrote Ernestine that Gustav and Arnold were expected that night, or the next day at the latest; see also letter 477, below.

476 *To Justine*

Postcard: Trocadéro[1]
[Postmark: Paris, 18. (June 1900)]
[Arrival postmark: Klagenfurt, 21.6.00]

Just after the 1st concert! The success was as usual, even extraordinary! You already know that! I was interviewed considerably after the concert and was very uncouth [*Grob*].

Affectionately, Gustav

Despite everything, you are to be envied! Best wishes

Arnold

Shelfmark:E6-MJp-319
Note

[1] Addressed to "Autriche / Fräulein Justine Mahler / Maiernigg am Wörtersee / bei Klagenfurt."

477 *From Justine to Emma*[1]

Maiernigg am Wörthersee [third week June 1900]
Villa Antonia

Dearest Emma, Eduard's card of the 8th just came. I suspect from it that you indeed won't have left on 1 July, so perhaps this letter will still reach you. You can imagine that all my enjoyment of writing has gone, to wit, of writing to America. I think night and day that you both will soon be on the waves.[2] You must certainly be absolutely amazed about the financial arrangements. I imagine that at any rate you will come over in July. I am terribly pleased about the photographs; I find the one where you are holding him on your arm especially sweet. If only you already had the child over here safely. But no one whom I have asked about the crossing thinks that it is at all risky to travel with such a small child. I am very anxious to hear what you are doing with the furniture, etc. Here we are still speaking of nothing else. Gustav is in Paris, and I have been in Maiernigg for five days.[3] I feel very well here. Gustav's hut [*Häuschen*] in the woods is as if from a fairy-tale, just like someone had put it there by magic, and the structure of the villa promises to be exceptionally beautiful. My thoughts are now always in Weimar—I will come visit in September or October. As I am settled in Vienna, we will stay here until the end of August. Unfortunately we are awfully cramped here in the Villa Antonia. My room is also the dining room, and there are no shaded spots, unfortunately. I can't wait any longer for your letter. In Vienna, we were in terrible agitation for days before the final decision came. Give me your precise next address, and have the money come to you wherever you like; I won't send anything to Berkan, then. A thousand heartfelt greetings to you, Eduard, and the baby from your J.

I am writing by return post to Eduard's card.

SHELFMARK: S2-JE-769d

NOTES

[1] Written on note paper printed with a silhouette of Mahler (leaning to the right and gesturing with his left hand) by Otto Böhler.

[2] Eduard, Emma, and their American-born son, Ernst (1900–1987), moved back to Europe that summer, as Emma was not happy in the United States. That spring, Mahler wrote to both Rudolf Krzyzanowski (now in Weimar) and the *Intendant*, Hippolyt von Vignau (1843–1926), recommending his brother-in-law for the vacant position of *Konzertmeister* and cello soloist in Weimar. Vignau engaged him solely on Mahler's recommendation. (The word "concert master" is clear in all of the correspondence, although it is odd to use it for the principal cellist position.)

[3] Mahler left for Paris on the evening of 15 June and returned on the evening of the 23d or on the 24th.

478 *From Justine to Emma*[1]

Maiernigg 23.6 [1900]

Dearest Emma, since you will be waiting for the money from Freund at any rate, I assume that this letter will still reach you. It is terribly difficult for me to give you any advice. Don't you think that it is impractical to take your furniture with you from Boston to Europe; you could have sold it there at any price, for on account of it you're further tied up in the process of settling in—who knows when it will come. My opinion, which I told you already in my very first letter, is that you should go directly to Weimar. (Certainly you will stop for a few days in Hamburg.) It will then take 4 weeks before you have found and set up an apartment. Eduard will certainly want to practice hard before he starts his engagement. The household will just have gotten going when Eduard's engagement begins. I can't come before the end of September or the beginning of October. I will be glad to see your apartment all set up then. I only wish that you were already safely over here with the child. Hopefully he will tolerate the different food well. It's lucky that the crossing falls during the best season. I'll have money sent directly to you by Freund. As well, I have not neglected to send the 500 fl. to Berkan for you both. Use it, of course, as you need to. It simply isn't possible to arrange anything from here. I'm convinced you'll save something in the inexpensive living conditions of Weimar. Eduard will certainly get 4500 marks. Right now I too have to economise enormously—you have no idea how far I have to stretch a heller. Now we have started to have the villa built, and now there is no turning back. I haven't done anything about clothes this summer; I haven't even bought work blouses, let alone a silk blouse. Now this will be the last big expense that you will have. Eduard will certainly do everything to have his contract extended to a lifelong one as of 1 March. Until then, mind you, I will be very restless; he should just practice diligently and the time in August in Weimar will do him good. Weimar is supposed to be a garden, like a summer place. Don't imagine that everything fell into place so suddenly. I kept all of the correspondence, since Frankfurter, once the matter had already been introduced by Gustav, suddenly turned to Alexander in order for him to intervene with the Intendant. One naturally couldn't give him an answer, but, under the circumstances, he could make inquiries. Bearing this in mind, I enclosed Rudolf Krzyzanowski's letters so you will see. We are certainly much indebted to him in this affair![2]—You know, it wouldn't be all that smart for you and the baby to go to Vienna and Eduard to Weimar. In the first place, it would cost a terrible lot of money. No one is in Vienna now, other than your in-laws, and such rushing about isn't the right thing for the child. You must see to it that you and the little fellow find peace as soon as possible. You can image how much I want to see the little bundle, but just because of that I am not going to rush into it; I would rather come for a few days to see your household at the same time. I will then bring you part of your things at the same time, and Arnold will bring part this winter. Gustav very much intends to speak personally with Vignau on Eduard's behalf this winter. I will send some things with him then, and Berthold too, who is going to Berlin, will take part with him.[3] I am now speaking of silver. Everything else I will pack up this fall into a chest and ship it to you. Believe you me, I trembled all day from agitation before the news came from Weimar. Moreover, I also need my relaxation this year: I have not felt entirely well all winter, and even took to my bed for a few days before I went to the country. But the climate here suits me splendidly, Gustav's hut [*Häuschen*] in the woods is charming—and marvellously quiet, as if in the wilderness—and the structure of the country house promises to be exceptionally beautiful. I tell you, I am happy that this writing into the clouds to America has stopped, since this is absolutely the last letter that I will send you over there. I am very anxious to hear how you will do with the furniture; just write me about it in detail. Gustav is probably coming tonight. He appears to have had a terrible migraine at the second concert.[4] I will be glad when he is here. Enough for now. Each day the photographs please me more and more.

Heartfelt kisses to you for the last time on American soil
Aunt Justi

SHELFMARK:S2-JE-769e

NOTES

[1] Written on note paper printed with silhouettes of Mahler (leaning to the right and gesturing with his left hand; p. 2, Mahler looking to the right and indicating *pianissimo* to the unseen orchestra), both by Otto Böhler.

[2] It is not clear who Frankfurter or Alexander might be. Alexander Rosé (1858–1904), Eduard and Arnold's brother, was a concert agent in Vienna, but Justine seems to imply that this event took place in Weimar.

[3] Probably Berthold Rosé (1870–1925), the fourth Rosé brother, an actor.

[4] See HLGE II, p. 262.

479 *To Justine*

Correspondence card[1]
[Postmark: Schulderbach, 17.7.(00)]
[Arrival postmark: Klagenfurt, 18.7.00]
Monday [16 July]

So, dearest! Morning spent in the train compartment, with a one-hour delay. Then I had an awful meal in Toblach. 3 o'clock to Schluderbach by bicycle, where I spent the entire afternoon gloriously outdoors. Now I am quite content. Tomorrow, to the Misurinasee, where I will spend the day and stay overnight. Down to Cortina the day after tomorrow, then back again to Schluderbach where I probably will stay overnight again. The next day, to *Lienz* via Toblach, where I will stay over again, and then by steamer and bicycle to Maiernigg. Unfortunately I met Nathaniel Rot[h]schild's assistant here, whom I now have to visit in Toblach.[2]

Affectionately G.

SHELFMARK:E13-MJp-537

NOTES

[1] Addressed to "Fräulein Justine Mahler / Maiernigg / am Wörthersee / Villa Angelika."
[2] Nathaniel Rothschild (1836–1905), a scion of the famous banking family.

480 *From Justine to Emma*[1]

Maiernigg am Wörthersee 18.7.[1900]

Dearest Emma, so today the journey starts. Hopefully you will have a good crossing and the baby will get accustomed easily to the different milk. I will breathe a sigh of relief when you have arrived on the spot. Don't worry yourself unnecessarily about setting up the apartment and looking for a maid. It will all be easier than you imagine. You must now stand entirely on your own two feet, and that will not be difficult for you. Eduard will help you with everything. Naturally, from here I can hardly give you any advice, or send you somebody—I don't at all know whom. It would be very expensive, which I cannot bear anymore than you can. I will come at the end of September or the beginning of October. It really was good that you sold your furniture. In any case, it would have been silly to drag these things with you from America. I am certain that the Berkans will be very helpful to you with everything. You both must certainly be absolutely amazed about the contract. Now Eduard should just pull himself together until the half year is up, and then you'll be free of all worries. Arnold is afraid that he will do too much of a good thing, and will overplay and be nervous. Just see to it that you go for regular walks. Isn't it splendid that you have another month ahead of you. Gustav is in Toblach for a couple of days; we couldn't both "manage it" this year. I really have to rest my nerves, which are in all sorts of pieces. We are also living very poorly. At night my room is so terribly hot that I can't sleep, and during the day the landlord's children disturb me so much that it makes me go wild. Arnold is terribly unhappy with his cook in Pörtschach too. Everyone there has naturally asked after you, including your maid from last year. There are supposed to be wonderful gardens in Weimar, and the cost of living there is so cheap that Alice Mumssen, who couldn't make it in Hamburg, moved there. Albi is in the Tyrol and really needs it—she looked absolutely awful. [Fräulein] Dittelbach will already have left Vienna for the country in September. She will have the delivery in the country at an acquaintance's and then board the child with Agnes. This is the first letter I've written in 14 days, since I was so ill that I couldn't hold a pen, but I didn't want to leave you without a sign of life. I will probably send my next letter to Hamburg, but at any rate I will wait for news from you. You could send a few lines from Plymouth about how everything has gone to that point. So, a thousand warm, welcoming greetings to the three of you from your J.

SHELFMARK: S2-JE-769f

NOTE

[1] Written on note paper printed with a silhouette of Mahler (gesturing with his right hand) by Otto Böhler.

481 *To Emma*

[Maiernigg, Summer 1900]

Also from me, dear Emma, in haste (on the verge of going out), best wishes to you and your husband. I am glad always to be able to conclude from your letters that you are both well and are getting along with each other well. We are thinking of you, and of your return to Europe, which at last will not be far away. Gustav.

[other side:] *Many, many warm wishes to you from your Arnold.*

SHELFMARK:S2-ME-770

482 *To Emma*

Postcard: Vestibul, Café Luitpold München
[Munich, c. 19 October 1900][1]

Dearest Emma, warmest congratulations for your birthday. Your J.
From me as well [four illegible words]. Gustav

All the best wishes and greetings too from your old Natalie.

SOURCE: Photocopy of one side only in the Bibliothèque Musicale Gustav Mahler
NOTE
[1] Gustav, Justine, and Natalie were in Munich for a performance of his Second Symphony by the Hugo Wolf Verein on 20 October 1900; Emma's birthday was 19 October.

483 *To Justine*

III. AUENBRUGGERSTRASSE 2

[Vienna, 24 October 1900]

Dearest Justi!
Natalie told you about the journey.[1]—I am already in the thick of things. Cosi fan tutte sold well (around 4200 kr.)—Today Tristan is sold out![2] I will send you the Munich reviews as soon as I have them with me.—The gentlemen are already singing another tune. All the same, the *Allgem. Zeitung* is still thoroughly impudent.[3] The others, however, are good—partly *very* good. Here in Vienna everyone is full of my success.—For two days the weather was very beautiful, but today it is cold and raining. The electric lights are finished, but they don't seem to have been installed practically and I have called Schmitt in order to speak all of this over with him.

I am now curious what you will have to tell me about Weimar. Probably the young international citizen [*Weltbürger*] already plays the piano and eats wholemeal bread with kefir for good digestion.[4]

Best wishes to everyone and write soon.

Your
Gustav

I've already spoken with Ehrbar—it's being *done*.[5]

SHELFMARK:E10-MJ-450
NOTES

[1] It seems that Justine went directly from Munich to Weimar to visit Emma and Eduard.

[2] The only performance of *Tristan und Isolde* that fall took place on 24 October. Mahler conducted *Cosí fan tutte* four times that month (4, 7, 10, 13 October), and Franz Schalk conducted it once, while Mahler was in Munich (20 October).

[3] Karl Pottgiesser's review in the *Allgemeine Musik-Zeitung* is discussed in HLGE II, p. 306.

[4] Ernst Rosé, born in America and thus a citizen. Kefir is a milk product similar to yoghurt, of Turkish origin.

[5] Either Friedrich Ehrbar (1827–1905), Viennese piano manufacturer, or his son Friedrich, director of the Singakademie.

484 *To Justine*

Correspondence card[1]
[Vienna, 27 October 1900][2]
[Arrival postmark: Weimar, 28.10.00]

D.J.
I am finding that you are rather sparse in your communications—actually I learn nothing at all!—The train compartment is ordered and the receipt will be sent to you this very day. Here everything is going marvellously. The theatre is sold out almost daily. Yesterday Troubadour was a great success.[3] In the course of the Munich season my C-minor [Symphony] will attain its *2nd* performance! That *is* a success.[4]

Best wishes to all of you from
Gustav

SHELFMARK:E10-MJp-448
NOTES

[1] Addressed to "Fräulein Justine [Mahler] / bei Concertmeister [Eduard Rosé] / We[imar] / Schröterstr . . ." The card was sent registered.

[2] The right-hand side of the card is cut away in a half circle, thus removing the postmark and half of the address. There does not appear to be any text missing.

[3] *Il trovatore* was performed on 26 October.

[4] It was performed at the Allerheiligen Konzert of the Münchener Musikalische Akademie on 8 November, conducted by Bernard Stavenhagen (1862–1914).

485 *To Justine*

THE DIRECTOR OF THE I. R. COURT OPERA

[Vienna, early June 1901]

Dearest!
It is very nice and hot here! I am quite happy that you are already happily strolling around in your castle.—

I am in agreement with everything that you and Theuer arrange with Vogel. As we decided, I am coming there early *Wednesday* as long as nothing at the last moment intervenes (in which case, I will telegraph).[1] Hopefully your dressing customs allow you and Natalie to meet me at the door, clad in virginal white with all-white kefir and crusty white bread. Just don't work too hard! And I *absolutely forbid* you to go and meet me in Klagenfurt.

Affectionately your
Gustav

Today the *Emperor* is actually coming to the theatre.

[across top of first side:] Best greetings to Natalie, and thanks for the letter.

SHELFMARK: E19-MJ-646
NOTE

[1] Mahler conducted for the last time that season on Monday, 3 June (*Carmen*) and left for Maiernigg on Wednesday, 5 June.

486 *To Justine*

Cartolina Postale Italiana[1]
[Postmark: Misurina, 21.7.01]
[Arrival postmark: Klagenfurt, 23.7.01]

D.J! Arrived in Misurina according to schedule![2] At any rate, a beautiful stay, if one is to improve [oneself]. Only one gets too riled about the bovine guests [*Kuhgäste*].[3] A bunch of very level or gently ascending trails. Hotel *first class*. Accommodation and food equally good. Just right for lazing about. Yesterday in Schluderbach I fell into Fr. G. right away.[4] Then a thunderstorm and constant passing showers. I had to stay in the house, where there was a zither concert. The company apparently loves the arts, and was so stimulated by their enjoyment that their conversation, together with loud noises, lasted until 11:30—I had to close several windows in the little room. I still don't know where I am going today. I am just heading off to an excellently arranged dinner—to conclude, soufflé à la Arnold.

Affectionately,
G.

SHELFMARK: E19-MJp-645
NOTES

[1] Addressed to "Fräulein / Justine Mahler / (bei Klagenfurt) / Maiernigg / am Wörthersee."

[2] Mahler was on a short cycling trip.

[3] Mahler plays on *Kurgäste*, spa guests.

[4] Unknown.

487 *To Justine*

[Maiernigg, early August 1901][1]

Dearest Justi!
Thank God that your card arrived this morning; I had been quite worried. So you got through everything well and will meet me as a goddess of health and freshness. Meanwhile, here I am living the universally known life of the gods (life of the ghetto). In the kitchen, the 3 Graces look after the godly provisions; at the godly repast, Hebe proffers the goblet; afterwards one's digestion is seen to by rowing and climbing late into the night, so that already early in the morning, with a light mind, I settle down into Natalie-like calmness, and on it goes like that.

Sunday, Monday at the latest, I will come to Rupertsheim [*sic*, Rupertihaus].[2] Arnold won't still be there? Hopefully Dr. Boër and Albi will be.

Best wishes to all from
G.

Shelfmark:E9-MJ-406
Notes

[1] This and the following letter are dated in pencil in Justine's hand (20 and 22 July), but these dates cannot be right, as on 21 July, Justine was still in Maiernigg (see the previous letter). An unpublished passage from Natalie's memoirs indicates that Justine's cure took place in August:

> In early August 1901, Justi and Rosé went to Heiligenblut in order for Justi to recover; Albi Adler and Dr. Boer joined them. The two of us, G. and I, remained back in Maiernigg and endlessly enjoyed the calm days, of which the poor fellow—as much as he wants and needs and often stubbornly and boisterously demands them—so rarely partakes: this is owing to the complexity of the siblings' living together, which, albeit ever so intimate, never proceeds altogether naturally and simply, and its core and life-centre must always extend beyond the sphere of both of them.

[2] See below, letter 488. Rupertihaus appears to be the spa where Justine took her cure.

488 *To Justine*

[Maiernigg, early August 1901][1]

Dearest Justi!
Natalie of course is informing you daily about the very monotonous course of our existence. I am working—and cannot get done.—I do not think that I will be able to come before Sunday. Mainly it's also because I still don't want to overtire myself and so always stop at 12:30 and dedicate the afternoon solely to rest. So, please be patient and understanding even from afar. The main thing is that I find you refreshed and strengthened when I arrive. That will contribute the most to my rest (which, after all, I don't need at all, since the climate here is having such a wonderful effect right now).

I was not at all happy with your card from Rupertihaus. First, I was fairly worried because you didn't express yourself very clearly. What happened with you in Dölsach before the Dr. and Albi came? Did you have another nervous heart episode? And under these circumstances, I was doubly worried to know that you had hardly arrived before you had to go up to the shelter. Well, did it have to be immediately? Today too I have had no news at all and there are 4 of you there. Certainly *one* of you could write a daily postcard! Get to it, Albi! Arnold! Interrupt your tiring daily work in order to finally conjure up a few lines for me. I will do without beautiful style and sage thoughts and only want to know how Justi is doing.

Best wishes to all of you, and be good—above all with postcards.

Your
Gustav

Also best wishes too and a dressing down [*einen herzlichen Gruß mit Donnerwetter*] to Dr. Boer.

SHELFMARK:E19-MJ-647
NOTE
[1] See note 1 to the previous letter.

489 *To Justine*

[Vienna, c. 25 August 1901][1]

Dearest Justi!
So, the first day is over. The night of travel just about bearable. Very hot, but a good train compartment. Arrived here—after a delay of 3/4 hour, Marie met me with a reproachful, stupid smile: "so late? I have been waiting since 6 o'clock." I recommended to her that next time she should be waiting since 4, and went off to bathe [and have] breakfast.—Afterwards, I wanted a cigar. *Nowhere* to be found. I finally suspected that they were in the desk. *No key*! Please explain these two things to me.—

Afterwards, to the theatre, where everything is calmly following its course. If Montenuovo weren't there already, I could have easily stayed with you until 1 September.[2]

Later, at Hassingers, young Herr Walter Klenner[3] appeared, extremely well fed and cheerful—almost elegant. As I subsequently heard, every day he gets 2 seats at the theatre, and sometimes 4.—I will put a stop to this, and from now on I will forbid the appearance of all Elises, Maries, and their ilk in the vicinity of my office. Please make this clear to the ladies.—Later, Arnold came. He looks excellent, and is currently going through a mild little treatment which he responds to marvellously. We both think that it would be wonderfully effective on you as well.—

Your room is really delightful—in somewhat of a Secession style, but with wonderfully comfortable furniture, shelves etc. Everything is to be used; nothing merely hangs on the wall. Your bathing room has become a boudoir—no one will believe that you are not "von." The apartment is in the best state, all that is lacking are pictures in the dining room and in your room.—In my study, neither the window nor the doors were painted. Should I have something done?

For lunch, [Café] *Imperial* with Arnold. Boër arrived there proudly, as if nothing had ever happened. He had things to do in Pressbaum and since we wanted to go on an outing anyway, we both accompanied him out there and agreed on a rendezvous with him on the "Kollenberg," or whatever it is called. We went to the place he indicated and almost made it to the Troppberg. Wonderful hike. Rather all over the place, since we didn't really know our way around, and didn't pay attention to the signs. 3 1/4 hours passed before we happened upon a Stadtbahn station. There, quickly had coffee, travelled back, dined in gourmet style at the Imperial, and went to bed (9 o'clock). This was the first outing together with Boër, of whom we—thank God—saw no trace apart from the midday meal and the journey out in the railway carriage.—God knows, he may still be looking for us. The weather is splendid—the cloudy sky that I told you about was only an illusion. Mornings and evenings cool!

I arranged definitively with Arnold that he will visit you on 5 September—either in Misurina or Maiernigg, wherever you should be. I hope to be able to get 10 days of vacation for him. Let him know exactly where you want to meet him. Best wishes to Natalie and Ernestine, and warm hugs

from your
Gustav

SHELFMARK:E19-MJ-648
NOTES

[1] Dated by Justine 26 August 1901. La Grange, relying on a letter to Richard Strauss (MSB, pp. 70–71), gives 26 August as the date that Mahler returned to Vienna (HLGE II, p. 376), yet on 20 August, Mahler also told Nina Spiegler, "Friday or Saturday [i.e., 23 or 24 August] I am going to Vienna" (postcard in the Pierpont Morgan Library). Given Mahler's letters to Justine, the early date is more likely.

All of the letters of this period have dates written across the top by Justine. Sometimes her date can be determined to be the date that the letter was written (i.e., because Mahler mentions a performance or some other verifiable event); at other times, the date seems to be the date the letter was received. (See also note 1 to letter 487, above.)

[2] The Hofoper reopened on 11 August, although Mahler did not conduct until 3 September (with rehearsals beginning 29 August).

[3] Unknown.

490 *To Justine*

THE DIRECTOR OF THE I.R. COURT OPERA

[Vienna, c. 25 August 1901][1]

Dearest Justi!

Just to let you know that I found the cigars and the key to the desk. A letter from Schlesinger just came that [indicates] that the resignation is already with the emperor and now is surely to be expected.[2] He will arrive 20 September, once he has completed his cold water cure.—Please send me Lipiner and Mildenburg's address.[3]—Today it is raining. We are very happy!

Hopefully you still have good weather! Are you all bathing diligently according to the Gustav method? Everyone here is amazed about my appearance! Your room looks better and better, the more one looks at it! It seems to me that you will never ever want to leave it!

Lots of greetings and kisses
from your
Gustav

N.B. Written after the letter.

SHELFMARK:E19-MJ-649
NOTES

[1] See note 1 to the previous letter.

[2] Bruno Walter had finally accepted Mahler's invitation to leave the Munich Hofoper to come to Vienna, but, as an appointee of the German emperor, he required his permission to resign. Mahler had written Walter in mid-August to reassure him that he could wait months if necessary for Walter to be free (unpublished letter in the Bruno Walter Papers at the New York Public Library for the Performing Arts). See also Walter's letter of 15 August to his parents: BWB, pp. 42–43.

[3] Mildenburg was now having an affair with Mahler's friend Siegfried Lipiner.

491 *To Justine*

[Vienna, 27 August 1901][1]

Dearest Justi!

It has been raining since yesterday! Because of that, Lohengrin today was very well attended. The most interesting news is that Förster-Lauterer sang for me today and, vocally, she is her old self again.[2] Unfortunately, for years in Hamburg she wasn't in full possession of her resources. It wasn't getting worse, but not better [either]. But *item*—I will let her appear as a guest in the 2nd half of September and vederemo. I eat daily with Arnold and Boer at the Imperial. Freund always comes waddling along too.

Hopefully you've already received my letter of yesterday.

The streets here are more torn up than ever before. Be glad that you still are not here.

The business with the bats really is too silly! Have you really had the curtain removed for *ever*?

By the way, tonight I am going to the performance for the first time (Fleischer-Edel).[3] And the *Viehharmoniker* deputation has announced themselves for early tomorrow.[4] I am already rejoicing unendingly to be able to confer with Herr Simandl again. Poor Hellmesberger is still waiting for the outward honour.[5] Now I am going to have tea!

Now you can all be quite calm about this "inn life." I go home at *10* o'clock daily and sleep wonderfully.

The apartment makes such a curiously quiet, tidy, and comfortable impression that I think that once you arrive we won't go to the inn any more than absolutely necessary. You will be entirely thrilled.

I send you many kisses, dear Justi. Enjoy your quiet and comfort and *don't be annoyed*.

Your
Gustav

SHELFMARK: S1-MJ-753
NOTES

[1] Dated by Justine 27 August 1901. This is a good example of how questionable these dates can be: from the contents, this letter *was* written on 27 August (*Lohengrin* was performed that day, conducted by Schalk).

[2] Berta Foerster-Lauterer (Lautererová) (1869–1936), soprano, married to composer Josef Bohuslav Foerster. She appeared to great acclaim as Sieglinde (11 September) and Mignon (17 September) and was engaged as of 1 October.

[3] Katharina Fleischer-Edel (1875–1928), dramatic soprano. (HLGE II, pp. 376–77, is mistaken in suggesting that the performance was *Faust*.)

[4] Untranslatable pun on *Philharmoniker*: *Vieh* are livestock (or, more generally, beasts).

[5] Franz Simandl (1840–1912) was a contrabassist in the Hofoper orchestra and the president of the Philharmonic Committee, 1899–1903. Although Hellmesberger was elected conductor of the Philharmonic for the 1901–1902 season on 28 May 1901, it seems that the decision was not yet final, and the Philharmonic delegation hoped to woo Mahler back to conduct that season (he had resigned at the end of the previous season). In the end, Hellmesberger was confirmed as the conductor in an open meeting that fall.

492 *To Justine*

[Vienna, c. 28 August 1901][1]

Dearest!
Natalie just wrote me that tonight she will come looking for me here from Gloggnitz. Did something happen to her mother?[2] Schlesinger telegraphed me yesterday that his release was granted and that he is at my disposal in the middle of September.

Today I received the enclosed letter from Berliner.[3] Please send me his address right away so that I can answer his letter.

I engaged Förster Lauterer, and she is staying here straight away. That will interest *you*, won't it?

Natalie mentioned to me that you want to come here soon. I beg you, dear Justi, under no circumstances do this. You do know how much I miss you; and nevertheless, under no circumstances do I want you to come here a day earlier than necessary. The 14 days that still remain will certainly pass quickly, and if you spend them in the country the gain will be immense. (Even if it tends to be really boring.)[4]—I would prefer that you went to Schulderbach right away. Arnold will follow on the 5th! You both can stay there for a few days and then go together to Maiernigg. Then a few more days there, and then together to Vienna. That seems to me to be the most reasonable thing, and Arnold rather needs it too. So, be reasonable and come only on 15 September!

Lots of greetings and kisses from
your
Gustav

Your letter just came. Naturally it is quite all right with me if you stay in Maiernigg. It is best that you act according to Dr. Blumenthal's wishes. The basket for dirty laundry is really *not* there *either*!

SHELFMARK:E19-MJ-650
NOTES

[1] Dated by Justine 28 August 1901.

[2] See the discussion of Natalie's relationship with Mahler in the introduction.

[3] Does not survive.

[4] Mahler mentions this in an unpublished postcard to Nina Spiegler (postmarked 20.8.01) in the Pierpont Morgan Library: "Justi is staying for about another 3 weeks. The poor thing unfortunately needs it very much and must be looked after in Vienna this year. For the moment she has managed to pull herself together again."

493 *To Justine*

[Vienna, c. 29 August 1901][1]

Dearest Justi!
Here there has been real April weather for the past few days.—

To know that you are alone out there with Ernestine in such a state of affairs is certainly quite unpleasant.

I think that if perchance the weather were continually bad, then it would certainly be better for you to come to Vienna. But, I beg you, don't be foolish, and if you can withstand it out there, it will surely be extraordinarily good for you. I want to say this to you in any case.

Here, it's terrible.

Marie is behaving just like a grown up; very ambitious. The coffee is sometimes very good, sometimes awful. But everything is very tidy and nice, and the apartment is now all fixed up and waiting for you! So, just let everything be dependent on the *weather* and your health, and certainly not on your mood. Ernestine will act as a shining example of objectivity!

Affectionately yours
Gustav

SHELFMARK:E9-MJ-407
NOTE

[1] Dated by Justine 29 August 1901.

494 *To Justine*

[Vienna, 3 September 1901][1]

Dearest Justi!
I am immensely happy that you feel so well and will hold out steadfastly until the 15th. Arnold is coming Thursday afternoon, as he probably told you. My greatest regret is that I can't superintend. I'm already wrapped up fully here. We will have a very eventful season. I am already stirring up the waves and the kettle is already cooking and sizzling.

This time you are both being unjust to Natalie. She has not even been together with him [Arnold] very much. Even before her arrival, when I told him that she would be coming, he already made that certain face. If he told you something else, he apparently only wished to gloss over it, as he likes to do. It is also entirely clear that Arnold is very opportune for her, and that she patronised him in my presence and yours, as no one else does. It thus suits her very well, and that you at all suppose that it is she who is distancing you from me—I really must smile. Think about it! Do you really think that *she* is in a position to drive you from me? Still, I advise you not to tell him anything of my comments, and certainly don't let him read this letter. Otherwise, you'll only make him all the more disconcerted.

I feel splendid, and Marie is doing a very good job. I go walking diligently, Kahlenberg, Klosterneuberg etc. Alone and with Natalie. The fact that I am not asking Arnold's permission is something that you'll probably not have any trouble understanding.—That people gossip about it, as they talk about everything, is immaterial to me. One cannot avoid it; after all, it's better than if it were [Rita] Michalek or [Selma] Kurz.[2] By the way, do you imagine that they don't talk about both of you?[3] Naturally, you are the last to discover it; that's always the way. Since we have all already reached adulthood, we can carry on as usual. Moreover, I have so many other worries right now that, honestly, I cannot find any opportunity at all to worry about it.

Walter is coming in mid-September. I am already rejoicing greatly. Woess's piano transcription [*Clavierauszug*] is very good and is already being printed.[4] Yesterday the little Brecher was with Natalie and me in the coffee-house, where we ate our evening meal.[5] I got quite an agreeable impression of him. There will be jealousy on all sides again once Walter is there. Hopefully they will spare me. There's no way that I wouldn't dare to associate with anyone as a friend. I am enclosing W's last letter. Let me know right away everything that A. should bring with him for you. Will the spring be made useable yet this year? One of these days I'll visit Theuer in Baden. Are you still splashing about in the morning[?] Today, Carmen—I am conducting for the first time.[6] The 1st act is newly staged. I will permit no others in the box. The only exception we will make is for Nanna.

With heartfelt greetings and kisses,
your Gustav

Please, dearest, and look after yourself for me and do not overtire yourself!

Shelfmark:E9-MJ-408
Notes

[1] Dated by Justine 4 September 1901, but from the contents written on 3 September.

[2] Rita Michalek-Merlitschek (1875–1944) and Selma Kurz (1874–1933), sopranos at the Hofoper, were both linked romantically to Mahler.

[3] See the introduction for a discussion of Justine and Arnold's relationship.

[4] Of the Fourth Symphony. Josef Venantius von Wöss (1863–1943), a Viennese harmony teacher and composer, made piano transcriptions of Mahler's Third, Fourth, Eighth, and Ninth symphonies and *Das Lied von der Erde*.

[5] Conductor and composer Gustav Brecher (1879–1940), a protégé of Richard Strauss. He conducted four performances of *Martha* at the Hofoper in 1901: three in May and one on 18 September.

[6] On 3 September.

495 *To Justine*

[Vienna, 4 September 1901][1]

Dearest Justi!
I noticed that I forgot to enclose Walter's letter; I'll do it today.[2]

It is raining here today, hopefully not where you are.—Up to now I have seen nothing of Toni Franke.[3] You did write me that he would be here already?! Yesterday I conducted for the first time—without the slightest strain, despite manifold vexations. Schoder was marvellous.[4]—So you will travel over night, then? Why did you change your mind? At any rate, I will order a half compartment in the *sleeping car* for you and Ernestine. Many greetings to Ernestine. Thank her for her letter, which she should repeat.

I am having myself shaved away from home in a shop that is very convenient for me on the way to the Opera. The older barber wasn't there, as he told me.—I sometimes still have cold baths—in Sofienbad. But the Wörthersee is grander. I diligently correspond with Montenuovo. He is hungry for news, and always writes very nicely.

Now I am going to have myself shaved, and then to the Opera.

Lots of greetings and kisses,
your
Gustav

SHELFMARK: E19-MJ-651

NOTES

[1] Dated by Justine 5 September 1901.

[2] Does not survive.

[3] Unknown.

[4] *Carmen*, on 3 September, with soprano Marie Gutheil-Schoder (1874–1935).

496 *To Justine*

[Vienna, 4 September 1901][1]

Dearest Justi!
I forgot to write down Walter's address; please send it to me right away. Here the weather is also terrible—it annoys me because I assume the same in Maiernigg.—Arnold has a light catarrh [head cold] (hoarseness) but it is already better today. He refused a little bit (perhaps only pro forma) to depart tomorrow, but I persuaded him heartily, and so tomorrow night he will hopefully arrive in Maiernigg. It will certainly do him good too.[2] If I don't write, you don't need to worry about anything. I have so exceedingly much administration to do right now that I really have time for nothing else.

I met Dr. Singer on the street today; he found my appearance splendid.[3] Tomorrow night he will visit me. Mildenburg finally arrived today too. (I already had [received] 3 letters from her, surely dictated by Lipiner)—we knocked heads together quite a bit, and I flatly requested that she not use a go-between for anything that she wants of me. I suspect that the correspondence from now on will be related to Lipiner. I will remain cool, however.

I had to laugh about a letter that arrived this morning from Schoder, and which I am also enclosing for your enjoyment—an amusing woman of the rarest composition.[4]

When I arrived home today, a feeling of odd warmth came over me: hanging in the hall were your clothes, hats etc. etc., apparently sent by you and unpacked by Marie with her customary promptness.

At first, I thought that you were here already, but soon I realised what was happening.—Marie behaves extremely steadfastly; I am convinced that her little finger is worth more than all of Elise—who should be gotten rid of sooner rather than later. Well—I won't interfere in these matters. So tomorrow evening you both won't be bored any longer, and, with company, will put up with bad weather and the malice of the heavens cheerfully.

Warm wishes to you from your faithful
Gustav

Source: Photocopy in the Mahler-Rosé Collection; original letter sold by Alfred Rosé

Notes

[1] Dated by Justine 5 September 1901. From the contents, 4 September is likely.

[2] In the end, Rosé did not go; see below, letter 499.

[3] Gustav Singer (1867–1944), Mahler's physician.

[4] Does not survive.

497 *To Justine*

[Vienna, 5 September 1901][1]

Dearest Justi!

I have been thinking whether because of the continuously bad weather and your inclination to rheumatism it might be more advisable to break off your stay in Maiernigg earlier. Do what you think best.

I only just discovered that after my departure you suffered from your nervous condition again. It seems, apparently, that you have to keep yourself away from all excitement and strain, at least for a time. If you can, we will endeavour to eat only at home. And under no circumstances may you go to bed late. This year, I will hold myself back from conducting anyway, once I have Schlesinger.—It is really lucky for both of us that you feel so well in our villa. It would be quite strange if you did not finally become entirely healthy and fresh; only you must have the strength to go out there alone in the spring. I see, anyway, how well the solitude suits you.—But it is very wrong that you never tell me the unvarnished truth about your health—because of that *I am never entirely easy, despite all assur-*

ances.—By the way, I was afraid with this dampness that you would succumb to arthritis again.—

Here you will also feel very well, since the apartment is now as comfortable and quiet as you could wish.—Fritz came today; I want to go out with him to Heiligenstadt tomorrow. Tonight I am conducting Tannhäuser (it is already sold out).[2] Write me when you are coming.

Concerning Natalie, Arnold told me today what she and he had agreed to in the summer.—It is comical how people decide about me over my head.

If you both put up with it—well—then you are certainly right. It is really too bad that cats always land on their feet: whenever I'm surest of matters with N[atalie], the old sore always opens somewhere. In the long run it will prove unbearable to me.—How often do I stand completely alone in consequence of the peculiar chain of circumstances! That N[atalie] could ever completely satisfy me, even you yourselves don't believe; I'm already tired of using this old refrain when it comes to this matter.—However—and this is the reason that I speak of it again today—if you were *more open*, this wouldn't have to happen!—Had I known, for example, how Natalie arranged these walks, I would simply not have put up with it, and an estrangement like this past summer's would have never happened.—I am always the "innocent lamb," and—preoccupied by my troubles and fantasies—unsuspectingly submit to everything and take it.

So, dearest, let this again at least be a lesson to you: least of all would Natalie be able to "drive you from me," and, at any rate, you know that no one yet has succeeded in doing this, and also that no one will succeed.[3]—All this is now *unimportant* and *insignificant* in comparison to thoughts about your health and your *well-being*.

Deeply, your old
G.

SHELFMARK: E9-MJ-409
NOTES
[1] Dated by Justine 6 September 1901.
[2] 5 September 1901.
[3] See introduction.

498 *To Justine*

THE DIRECTOR OF THE I.R. COURT OPERA

[Vienna, c. 6 September 1901][1]

Dearest!
Owing to the telephone, I completely forgot! I do think that *the whole thing is not necessary*. Let me know how much it will cost, and then I will write you my opinion about it.—If only your weather would get a bit better!

Deeply, your
G.

SHELFMARK: E19-MJ-652
NOTE
[1] Dated by Justine 6 September 1901.

499 *To Justine*

[Vienna, c. 7 September 1901][1]

Dearest Justi!
The enclosed arrived today.

Actually, I have been rather restless since your last letter. There is such a strange tone in it, one that I am not used to from you. I have the feeling that something is not quite in order. Either you are unwell or something or other is bothering you. To Arnold, of course, you wrote that you would not stay much longer; to me, you mentioned nothing about it. I think myself that with the incessantly bad weather you should come back sooner. I am quite fine. I, too, no longer get "annoyed," and try to keep things away from my soul. A's face has already got its normal chubbiness back, and everything is in order.[2] You don't need to give it another thought. Please, dear, just say what's on your mind—this sort of resignation that emerges from your letter is without "moral worth" for the Mahler race. I don't know where in the world you could find a better friend and comrade, to whom you could say everything so frankly and freely, than me.

I am thinking of going out Sunday and Monday, since I don't have anything to do.[3] How would it be if you went to Semmering and stayed there for a few days in order to still enjoy some mountain air? Perhaps we, A. and I, could meet you there and then lead you home in triumph.

But, naturally, if you are enjoying it there, then continue to stay for a long time. The main thing is that you get really strengthened for the winter. Many kisses.

Your
Gustav

Shelfmark: E9-MJ-410
Notes

[1] Dated by Justine 7 September 1901.

[2] It appears from this, and subsequent letters, that Arnold did not join Justine in Maiernigg as had been planned.

[3] The Hofoper was closed on Monday, 9 September.

500 *To Justine*

THE DIRECTOR OF THE I.R. COURT OPERA

[Vienna, 8 September 1901][1]

Dearest Justi!
Your last letters, and also Ernestine's (for which I hereby thank her warmly), have quite reassured me—so much so that I would almost like to suggest that you stay there for a few more days, since it finally must have gotten nice and then you could enjoy it to the full. Furthermore, I am afraid that you will not be able to get a train compartment on the *14th and 15th*, which is the busiest travel

time, and besides I would be very worried. Please, definitely *do not travel on these two days* when there is so much traffic. Shouldn't I do something about the railcar?—Today I got the statement from Schott: again *21* marks! I'll put them aside for you again.—Natalie told me today that she intends to go to Maiernigg on Tuesday and stay with you. *Is that all right with you*? She does not know that I am asking you. If I should prevent this (naturally, without telling her about it), telegraph me. Probably since she can't benefit from being here, she is reaching for the flesh pots of Egypt.[2]—Lipiner comes tonight and has already given me a rendezvous. I think that terrible wrath will descend because of Mildenburg. Montenuovo comes tomorrow. Many kisses, dearest, and I remain

Your
Gustav

Warmest wishes to Ernestine from me. I am very glad that she is also so pleased. Next year as well she absolutely must come with us to the Wörthersee.

Shelfmark:E9-MJ-411
Notes
[1] Dated by Justine 10 September 1901, but Mahler's mention of Natalie's planned trip to Maiernigg on Tuesday, 10 September, makes this impossible. Mahler reports on his rendezvous with Lipiner in the next letter, firmly dated 9 September.
[2] Allusion to Exodus 16:3: "And the children of Israel said unto them, Would to God we had died by the hand of the Lord in the land of Egypt, when we sat by the flesh pots, and when we did eat bread to the full; for ye have brought us forth into this wilderness, to kill this whole assembly with hunger."

501 *To Justine*

[Vienna, 9 September 1901][1]

Dearest!
So, I was with Lipiner last evening, and to my amazement nothing was said about Mildenburg; the tone was congenial and dignified, as it always used to be—only tonight he is going to Hietzing.—It would be hard for her to talk him out of the box, so I'll probably have to make an exception for him. This afternoon he wants to go up the Kahlenberg with me. From there, I have discovered completely new and marvellous walks. I am curious if you will be able to go up there with me, or if you would rather stay quietly at home. Natalie wants to come to Maiernigg tomorrow (Tuesday) in the evening. If you telegraph me to tell her not to come, I will advise her to visit Mankiewicz in Gmunden.[2] I think that right now she would only disturb the two of you from your cosy quiet.—She always does it that way: driven by her intensity, she falls to the ground between two stools. I told her my view in very plain terms, and I warned her. Maybe she will finally accept what she has been told. At present, she keeps reasonably quiet. Bertram has again vowed everlasting improvement and will stay for the time being—but I think that this will only last for a short time.[3]

Going on walks after eating does me a tremendous amount of good.—It doesn't seem right at all to me that you want to go to Hammerschlag. He is certainly not the right one either. We must look for another doctor for us. When you come, we will talk about everything.

How long do you want to stay there? If you feel so well there, then you should put off your return as long as possible.

What you have told me about the garden's progress etc. makes me quite envious that you all can inspect all this. How gladly would I come visit for a few days, instead of Natalie! Unfortunately, however, such a thing is impossible. I don't think we'll be tied up at Easter, so we will go to Maiernigg for a week if the weather cooperates.—

Your letter just came. Just what I feared—that you still are not entirely on top of things [healthwise]! You must use the entire winter this year to rest, and do not let anything tempt you "to join in"! I will look after everything, by the way, and permit you nothing at all! It would be really something if a Mahler were not able to manage to get up again if he had the serious will to do so. You must not let yourself be depressed by it. Naturally, do not write me if it tires you. I would be very grateful to Ernestine if she took it over. I ask for *honesty*, however!

So, Saturday night! Wonderful! I will meet you at the station. *8:50* in the evening. I will bring Arnold with me.[4]

For now, best wishes. I have to go to the office.

Your
Gustav

If no telegram should come today, I will hold Natalie back, that is, send her to Gmunden. I firmly think that that is better for you.

SHELFMARK: E9-MJ-412
NOTES

[1] Dated by Justine 10 September 1901, but Mahler mentions Natalie's visit "tomorrow (Tuesday)," which makes the date of this letter 9 September.

[2] Henriette Mankiewicz (1854–1906), Austrian painter and artist.

[3] Theodor Bertram (1869–1907), Austrian baritone. He was engaged briefly by the Hofoper (1–19 September), but Mahler found his performance in the title role of *Der fliegende Holländer* disappointing; see HLGE II, pp. 377–78.

[4] It seems that Justine returned to Vienna on Saturday, 14 September.

502 *To Justine*

[Vienna, between 8 and 10 September 1901][1]

Dearest Justi!
So: the *Viehharmoniker* gentlemen were here. We arranged to perform my Fourth during November in an evening concert.[2] That is preferable to me, too. You will want to attend all the rehearsals and (as I know you), the performance

as well. But, I tell you, I will only allow it if you keep your word and come back as a "completely healthy" Justi.

Today it is nice weather again—hopefully also over there with you, and you will stay for a good long time.

I am going to Hesch's in St. Veit, where the *baptism* of his new-born offspring is taking place.[3]—Nina Hof[f]mann babbled away in such a childish, naive and confused fashion, just as she always does when she's visiting me. But I was very "nice," and she was quite content. I gave her a box for Tannhäuser.

Natalie's mother is rather well again. Arnold, however, does not seem to entirely agree with my contact with her [Natalie] because since then he has wrapped himself in that certain extremely curt silence, mimicking the stone guest. He looks excellently, however, and feels better than ever. We have been walking diligently.

The Munich premiere under Weingartner is set for 18 November,[4] and in Frankfurt, the 3 Pintos will be performed, to which I was invited. Possibly you and Natalie could go there in order to see it yourself.

I am looking forward to seeing the blinds; they will really finish off my room.

I am already curious what you will look like when you arrive, and how you will like everything here.

Edel is already *done* and is travelling back to Hamburg today. To this day I like Förster 10 times better than her. I am having her appear for the first time as Sieglinde.

Yesterday Bertram promised me definite improvement and eternal loyalty. Now he is having terrific success.

Warmest greetings and kisses, my dear
Your Gustav

Many greetings to Ernestine. She should send me a few lines sometime.

SHELFMARK: E19-MJ-654

NOTES

[1] It is difficult to date this letter any more precisely. Natalie's ill mother is mentioned in letter 492 (c. 28 August), and the only *Tannhäuser* performance between August and mid-October was on 5 September. Katharina Fleischer-Edel (see letter 491) was appearing as a guest in *Lohengrin* (15 and 27 August, 7 September); since she was finished, this letter must have been written after 7 September, but before 11 September (when Foerster-Lauterer appeared for the first time as Sieglinde; see letter 491).

[2] The Vienna premiere of the Fourth Symphony did not occur until 12 January 1902.

[3] Wilhelm Hesch (1860–1908), bass, engaged at the Hofoper between August 1896 and January 1908.

[4] The world premiere of the Fourth Symphony took place in Munich on 25 November 1901 with the Kaim Orchestra. In the end, Mahler conducted.

503 *To Justine*

THE DIRECTOR OF THE I.R. COURT OPERA

[Vienna, c. 10 or 11 September 1901][1]

Dearest Justi!
It's pretty chaotic here. Above all, yesterday Hesch succumbed again to his old illness, and Reichenberg has apparently become an imbecile.[2]—I had already stopped Natalie even before your letter came, correctly estimating your current state of mind. I only ask of you, dearest Justi, that you won't allow such a mood to grow in you; apart from everything else, you must also be able to put yourself in her position. Fortunately she knows like no one else just how to come out on top of everything, and today [she] is completely *normal.*—(I told her absolutely everything on my mind—even that I'm no "monster," but that she simply does not attract me—and now I believe that she'll finally leave me in peace.) Don't forget because of all this what a valuable human being she is; after all, that she loves me above all else and would rather let herself be struck by me than stroked by another is hardly a crime.

If I were to "look for someone else" it is very much to be doubted whether this would be preferable to you or would please you more.—So—don't let it fester! We must pull ourselves together (—me too!) in order to remain fair to one another. Don't let on that I've told you all this.—She still has no idea that we are so close to each other, and she would find it an insulting indiscretion.[3]—I am often together with Lipiner. Thank God, it is taking a normal course! I am very happy that I can associate with a man—I have much need of it!

By the way, I myself think that it is time that you came back, because there in your solitude many of your "points of view" are becoming confused. Here you will hopefully quickly come back again to a natural, normal relationship with the outer world.—

I will look after you now, and be very strict, and never let you get carried away (e.g., as with the theatre and inn, etc.).

I am very happy about Ernestine; she should visit us more often.

At my direction, Fritz is having himself operated on today in the Rudolphinium. I have also taken on the follow-up treatment.

So, finally Saturday. A thousand greetings

from your
Gustav

I hope that you and Ernestine will find an *entire* reserved train compartment; I already arranged it. Just ask the conductor about it right away. Where should we have dinner? Should I have something prepared at home?

SHELFMARK: E19-MJ-659
NOTES

[1] Dated by Justine 13 September 1901.

[2] Franz von Reichenberg (1855–1905), bass. Engaged by the Hofoper between June 1884 and April 1904.

[3] See the introduction.

504 *To Justine*

THE DIRECTOR OF THE I.R. COURT OPERA

[Vienna, 12 September 1901]

Dearest Justi!
First of all, I'll tell you what will certainly make you happy: *Förster* had a really splendid, indisputable success. She was wonderful, and in *very* good voice. Her engagement is now assured, and she will continue to stay with us.[1] The *entire* train compartment is already reserved for Saturday, so hopefully you will have a good trip.—Hopefully you will let me know where you want to eat dinner.

The weather here is really very bad. But the apartment is charming and I think that you will find yourself very much at home in it. Right from the beginning we will arrange that we dine at home—*even* if it's something *cold*, which I now do very often and very gladly.—So, now I will leave everything until we see each other—which I am already looking forward to "terribly."

Your
Gustav.

Shelfmark: E19-MJ-657
Note
[1] As Sieglinde on 11 September. She was engaged as of 1 October and remained with the Hofoper until 30 September 1913.

505 *To Justine*

THE DIRECTOR OF THE I.R. COURT OPERA

[Vienna, early September 1901][1]

Dearest!
Yesterday only a postcard and again no letter today! Hopefully you are not unwell. Naturally, I am now wondering again—Ah! Your letter just came, so I will read it first.

—Well, thank God, now I am calm again.—The latest is that I have *Slezak* right away;[2] he will perform next week already—in exchange for which I've got to throw Bertram out.[3] It shouldn't be hard for me to keep you away from Walter and every Tom, Dick, and Harry [*Krethi and Plethi*].[4]—That you behaved so bravely about the little mouse deserves an extra honorarium!

It's starting again with Natalie. It hurts me terribly, but now I must tell her the unvarnished truth and, of course, shatter her. But hopefully she'll soon be helped back on her feet again.

Fritz was here with me and we hiked from the Kahlenberg [to] Klosterneuberg on a splendid trail; I'll have to take you along it. Today he is going to Gersum's. I feel splendid!

Affectionate kisses from your
Gustav

Shelfmark: E19-MJ-658

Notes

[1] Likely written shortly before Justine's return on 14 September.

[2] Leo Slezak (1873–1946) had first appeared as a guest in January 1901. His huge success in *Guillaume Tell* led Mahler to begin negotiations with the Königliche Opernhaus, Berlin, to free Slezak from his contract. By early September 1901, Mahler had succeeded, and Slezak was engaged as of 15 September.

[3] Bertram's contract was terminated on 19 September.

[4] Mahler's meaning is not precisely clear, as Bruno Walter remained a lifelong friend of Justine's; see the introduction, however, for a discussion of certain tensions in the relationship.

506 *To Justine*

[Berlin,] Wednesday [11 December 1901][1]

Dearest Justi!

Many thanks for your letter. Rehearsal today! Everything is going splendidly. I will conduct the *performance* myself, as I arranged with Strauss today. The solo is sung *splendidly* by Frl. Plaichinger.[2]—This very afternoon I am going to see Emma (whom I have already telegraphed) and am back again tomorrow when I hope to find more news of you. It was marvellous in Dresden with Schuch; I've already rehearsed everything with the soloists.[3]

Schuch is dead keen (as usual), but I do think that it will be very good there too. Along with your letter, I received a very nice but somewhat immature letter from Alma. She writes that when I come back, I must take you [*sic*, her] "to your dear sister." She longs to be with you. Perhaps she's forgotten that you are supposed to be together today (Wednesday)?[4]

Now, off to the Anhalt station. From there, I will write you in detail. On Friday morning I have my next rehearsal. It's a good life here with Berliner. He will write you himself. Terrible pen, this!

Affectionately yours,
Gustav

Source: Photocopy of autograph letter sold by Alfred Rosé; present whereabouts unknown. Text previously published in *Gustav Mahler Unbekannte Briefe*, ed. Herta Blaukopf (Vienna: Paul Zsolnay, 1983), p. 116.

Notes

[1] Dated by Justine 11 December 1901. As with the August–September letters, Justine's dates are not always reliable.

[2] The Berlin premiere of the Fourth Symphony, with the Tonkünstler Orchestra, took place at the third subscription concert of the season, 16 December. The soprano soloist was Thila Plaichinger (1868–1939). (The Novitäten-Konzerte were directed by Richard Strauss.)

[3] The Second Symphony was conducted by Ernst von Schuch in Dresden on 20 December. The soloists were soprano Erika Wedekind (1868–1944) and alto Irene von Chavanne (1868–1938).

[4] At a gathering at Berta Zuckerkandl's; see below. Berta Zuckerkandl, née Szeps (1864–1945), was a Viennese friend of Mahler's; her sister was Sophie Clemenceau. It was at a dinner at Berta's home on 7 November 1901 that Mahler first became interested in Alma Schindler.

507 *From Justine to Gustav*[1]

[Vienna,] Thursday [12 December 1901]

Dearest Gustav, today I received your first lines. They sound very cheerful and content, and I was naturally very glad about the whole tone of the letter.

Well, yesterday at Z[uckerkandl's] I also met the *mother*, but I was so *entranced* by the daughter that I hardly had eye or ear for her. It seemed so convenient for her [Alma] to leave with me, and you can imagine how she behaved towards me (at the beginning, understandably somewhat awkwardly; me likewise) that I requested her to visit me; she seemed very pleased by my invitation, and we arranged that she will come alone on Saturday afternoon. Unfortunately, I am no longer impartial because I am too taken by her. I liked her *quite* a bit, and I am immensely looking forward to Saturday. I feel much more drawn to her than to her mother; by your descriptions I had expected the opposite. She was as pretty as a picture and was wearing the same blouse again, but it still looked like new. Even before I had invited A, her mother very cordially invited me to come with you for sure next time you visit. I realised that it was a great sacrifice that she came to Z[uckerkandl]'s because the visit caused such a sensation and it was criticised that she had never been to a reception [*Jour*] before. Yesterday I bought a splendid silver belt buckle. It cost 23 kr., but I think that the buckle will be to her taste. Last night Arnold and I were at Albi's for dinner.

I am already very curious what you arranged in Weimar.[2] If only this worry were already passed. I am terribly happy that you are conducting in Berlin yourself. Please ask Berliner, or Strauss himself, to telegraph after the performance for sure.

Tomorrow I will write again—and, on Saturday evening, in detail about everything.

Heartfeltly,
Your J.

SHELFMARK:E8-JM-399
NOTES

[1] We are indeed fortunate that four letters from Justine to Gustav survive from this crucial period in Mahler's life. When read in conjunction with Gustav's letters to Alma and Alma's entries in her diary, they allow a reasonably accurate reconstruction of events; see the introduction.

[2] See the next letter.

508 *To Justine*

[Berlin,] Thursday Evening [12 December 1901][1]

Dearest Justi!
I just came back from Weimar. I found both of them in the best of health and spirits.[2] They met me at the station with Krzyzanowski and were together with me at the hotel until 12 o'clock. Krz. showed his old warmth and naturalness, which I was very happy about.[3] Krz. assured me (also in Vignau's name) on a walk to Belvedere this morning that E[duard]'s business is going splendidly, and

his definite employment is only a matter of 2–3 weeks.[4] [Vignau] is travelling, left his apologies for me, and, splendidly, gave me a rendezvous for tomorrow in Berlin.

Funnily enough, while we sat in the pub, *Krasselt's* quartet recital was just across the street. Around 10:30 the doors swung open—both Krasselts and their company. The cellist, who was with me the day before yesterday in Vienna, was in visible distress—at the next table, we took no notice of either of them! Our neighbours' moods were obviously somewhat disturbed, but we did not let ourselves be put off and were very merry.—I gather from Krz.'s account that Krasselt (the violinist) behaved stupidly and vulgarly, and E. bears no fault at all.[5]

Today I dined at E's with the whole Kr.[zyzanowski] family.—There is a very warm relationship between them and E., and I think that we can look forward to their future without worry.

I am already very eager for what you will write me about Wednesday.

As far as *I* am concerned, that you are so stirred up and already looking for apartments etc. is still very premature! Please, dearest, don't rush things—just keep your spirits up! I must still consider very carefully! The dear girl is herself now badly stirred up, and finds herself in such an uncustomed situation, one in which I must keep my eyes open for us both. She would still need to mature a great deal—as I have just clearly seen once more—before a step of such great consequence could be seriously faced on my part.—You, on the other hand, naturally, are entirely the ruler of your own decisions. And whatever happens, the two of us will remain bound for life; I want to see you happy, and help you with everything that you need for your settling and contentment.

Don't worry at all about apartments and such details! We have a lot of time! I can see that I now have to keep calm for everybody.—I have just decided that you should already arrive here for the concert *Monday* morning; perhaps you will have fun here.[6] The orchestra is behaving excellently. We will then travel together to Dresden on Tuesday, and will be alone together for a few days. Do you want to do that? Then telegraph me your answer right away. I beg of you, really look at Alma with your cooler, feminine eyes; I am basing quite a lot on your judgement.

Lots of greetings and kisses
from your
Gustav

SHELFMARK: OS-MD-683 (copy). Alfred Rosé left the original letter to Henry-Louis de La Grange in his will.

NOTES

[1] Dated by Justine 10 December 1901.

[2] Mahler had gone to Weimar to visit Emma and Eduard Rosé.

[3] Mahler's old friend Rudolf Krzyzanowski was the conductor of the Weimar Hoftheater from 1898 to 1907. In September 1896, he had joined Mahler in Hamburg as *Kapellmeister*, where—according to Justine's letters to Ernestine—relations between them were strained.

[4] At Mahler's urging, Eduard Rosé had been engaged as concert master and solo cellist in September 1900. On the business in question, see Bernhard Post, "Eduard Rosé: Ein Musik-

erschicksal im Spannungsfeld zwischen europäischer Kultur und deutscher Provinz," *Mainzer Zeitschrift* 96–97 (2001–2002): 417–35, particularly 421–23.

[5] Violinist Alfred Krasselt (1872–1908) was the concert master of the Weimar court orchestra and leader of the eponymous string quartet. His brother, Rudolf (1879–1954), was a cellist.

The Mahler-Rosé Collection contains a draft letter, in Mahler's hand, for Arnold Rosé to send to Rudolf Krasselt (S2-MArD-775). This draft belonged to Ernst Rosé (son of Emma and Eduard) and was purchased by the University of Western Ontario Music Library at the Sotheby's auction of his collection in December 1984. It was likely written in late 1901 or early 1902:

> [Mahler:] Just now I have discovered how uncollegially and unfairly your brother, Kasselt, the Weimar Concertmaster, has behaved towards my brother, and, in the event that you would be hired here by director Mahler, further information about him would be fabricated. I hardly need to say how painfully upset I am about all this—as is Director Mahler. In any case, I regard it as my duty to inform you that, as of today, I am—under these circumstances—not in a position to accept you into my quartet, as was originally intended. I hasten to give you this news as quickly as possible, as I know the importance you have attached to this portion of your future occupation when making your decision.
>
> If you wished on your part to draw conclusions of this state of affairs, I would be prepared to recommend this to Mahler.
>
> [Justine:] In haste, the gist of G[ustav]'s letter to Krasselt (for A[rnold]).
>
> Most affectionately. Yours.

[6] The Berlin performance of the Fourth on 16 December.

509 *To Justine*

PALAST HOTEL / BERLIN W.

[Berlin, 13 December 1901][1]

Dearest Justi!

You can imagine how I smiled and laughed about your lines of today. I imagined that it would be just so, and have felt such warmth and gaiety in your few intimations. How nice it would be if everything for you and me would turn out as it appears to be going right now.[2]—I beg of you, really and truly fall in love with Alma and I will be twice as happy. But—she is still *so* young and I lose my courage every time I think about the age difference.—If you can, stay calm and consider, or rather, help me consider. It is no small matter, and the wish should not be father to the thought.—I am still without news from her. What you will tell me about Saturday afternoon will be doubly important to me.

Perhaps you should leave early Sunday, so that you can have another good sleep before the concert. And it would be very nice if we were alone again for a few days.—Today Schuch wrote me that the King of Saxony wants to come to the concert on Friday. I want to send him [Schuch], in confidence, a short program that Graf Seebach will give to the King on Monday, since he is very interested in my work.

I have put together a few hints, which I present to you in sketch form—that is, what one correctly calls *ad usum Delphinis*. Of course, it is only intended for someone naive who doesn't discern things all that deeply. If you want, give it to Alma to read so that she will get at least a little glimpse into the outer framework.[3] All of this is still so new to her, and you must be my intermediary—in this, as in everything of significance to my life and being. I am writing in great haste so that the letter will go off on the night train again.

Today, Vignau visited me here. He spoke very nicely about Eduard, and also assured me that everything is now *almost* in order.

Many greetings and kisses.

Your Gustav

Telegraph your arrival.

SHELFMARK: E3-MJ-139

NOTES

[1] Dated by Justine 12 December 1901. As Mahler mentions meeting with Vignau in Berlin (mentioned in the previous letter [12 December] as arranged for "tomorrow"), this letter must date from the 13th. This is confirmed by Alma's diary entry for 14 December, which mentions the arrival of this letter during her visit with Justine (Alma Mahler-Werfel, *Tagebuch-Suiten 1898–1902*, ed. Antony Beaumont and Susanne Rode-Breymann [Frankfurt-am-Main: Fischer, 1997], p. 741).

[2] Mahler is alluding to Justine's relationship with Arnold Rosé; see introduction.

[3] This program, written for King Albert I of Saxony (1828–1902; reigned 1873–1902), has been frequently published; for the original German (with a facsimile of p. 1), see BGA, pp. 87–89. An English translation appears at the end of Edward R. Reilly, "*Todtenfeier* and the Second Symphony," in *The Mahler Companion*, ed. Donald Mitchell and Andrew Nicholson (Oxford: Oxford University Press, 1999), pp. 124–25. (Mahler had already met the king in Leipzig at a performance of *Die drei Pintos* in 1888; see letter 50.)

510 *From Justine to Gustav*

[Vienna,] Friday Evening [13 December 1901]

Dearest Gustav, I just got your letter of Thursday. After Berliner's latest news that you yourself are conducting, you can imagine how much I thought about coming to Berlin on Monday, but after careful consideration, I decided against it. If I were not driven by the desire to be alone with you, I would actually also give up Dresden because of the cost. It is simply necessary, *absolutely* necessary, to consider every kr. before spending it. Today, Lipiner firmly hammered away at me to give up the trip. It is an outrageous luxury of me, if I don't. I had thought that if I came early Thursday, it wouldn't cost so much, but I would really like your *well-considered advice*. I am quite ready to give it up—so let me know!

I am indeed very curious about tomorrow when Alma will be alone with me. For me, it comes down to a few things that I can only repeat again and again: that she is good, and that she loves you, for then you can mould [*erziehen*] her as you have already moulded me. If she loves you, she will make you happy. It is fortunate that you can already see with unbiased eyes. Tomorrow, naturally,

I will see another side of her and she can behave more freely than the other day in front of her mother. I am entirely happy about your behaviour towards me and my affair, [and] that you also feel that we could never become lost to one another and will always remain the truest of friends. For your happiness, your peace, I could sacrifice everything. If you can but rejoice in my happiness, my contentment, just like I do for you out of the deepest depths of my heart, then I thank God on my knees and feel the wish of mother on her deathbed—her last words were: *child, you must be happy*—and only when you are happy as well will it have been fulfilled, and only then. You know that I must marry, I consider this an absolute necessity for us both. You will also marry, and that will be the solution for everything. Your wife will not be able to help but love you passionately; you already compel everyone to do so, man and woman. I maintain that my Arnold loves you more than me. Tomorrow night I am at Lipiners, and Sunday night with Nana.

I think about you all day long.

Heartfelt kisses from your
J.

How I really feel, I am not able to write after all.

SHELFMARK:E8-JM-400

511 *To Justine*

PALAST HOTEL / BERLIN W.

[Berlin,] *Sunday* 15 Dec. [1901][1]

Dearest Justi!
Don't worry about the costs of your trip. Think: it is a birthday present for you. It is already too late to give you my advice now, because either you are already on your way here, or this letter will be in your hands the day after tomorrow, when I will already be on my way to Dresden. So I will expect you there for *sure*. Address: Hotel Bellevue, Dresden. I am sending the enclosed letters—the one from the teenage girl will amuse you again.

What will you tell me about Alma! Yesterday I had a very nice letter from her, which relieved me of all doubt about her warm-heartedness and intellectual rectitude [*geistige Gradheit*]. I think that *there* everything is in order.—Only: whether a man on the verge of getting old has the right to chain so much youth and freshness of life to his over ripeness—chaining spring to autumn, forcing it to skip over summer—that frightens me. I do know that I have a lot to offer—but the claim of *youth* may not be bought for anything. If Beethoven, Wagner, and Goethe arose today, the heart of the young would bend down before them and pray, but—but flowers can only grow and blossom in the spring—for me this is the great question!—Naturally, for a while everything will still be fine, but what then, when my fruitful autumn gives way to winter? Do you understand this?

I was very happy about what and how she wrote about you! She calls you "sister," and is as delighted by you, as you are by her. She sees my characteristics in you too, and when you speak, she thinks that she is hearing me. You can imagine what a bond that forms.

This could not have worked out better, since it guarantees all of us a secure future!

Frau Schlesinger just came to speak to me about her son.[2]

Many greetings and kisses,
your
Gustav

Best wishes to Arnold too.

SHELFMARK:E19-MJ-653
NOTES

[1] It is not clear whether the day and date were written by Gustav or by Justine (it differs from her other dates). It is, nevertheless, correct.

[2] Presumably, Bruno Walter's mother.

512 *From Justine to Gustav*

[Vienna,] Sunday 5 *o'clock* [15 December 1901]

Dearest Gustav, this is the first moment that I've had to write since Alma left here yesterday, as I accompanied her to the Währingerstrasse, then went to the Lipiners for the evening. This morning, since I got up, there has been one visitor after another. Tomorrow I get my certificate and Tuesday I leave early in the morning and am in Dresden at 7 p.m. I am terribly looking forward to it. I didn't go to Berlin for many reasons that I will tell you in person. My impression of A. requires a longer conversation: she seems *very* young to me, though, and as of now still has very little idea about you. Mind you, she would still have to grow up a lot before she could be your wife, [although] real, true love could hasten the matter a lot. Right now she seems to me not much more than a very pretty, nice girl. I am very curious about her letters [to you] in Berlin. She was very natural and looked at everything. Her primary interests were the library and the scores. Well, I'll tell you everything in detail, Gustav. I cannot tell you *how* I long to see you happy and made happy, and I am afraid that any woman whom I could think of as *your* wife would never, never suffice for me. Again, again and again, the main thing must be that she loves you, and totally subjects herself to you. You must be very open towards her, and immediately tell her what doesn't please you, or seems odd to you; you must watch for even the tiniest details, for they reveal the person. Hopefully Berliner will not forget to telegraph me Monday night. I am waiting for the telegram to arrive with much anticipation.

A thousand heartfelt greetings and kisses from

your
J.

SHELFMARK:E8-JM-401

513 *From Alma to Justine*

[Vienna, 15 December 1901]

Dearest Fräulein,
Many heartfelt thanks for the use of the letter.—You gave me great enjoyment by doing so.

I copied it for myself and am sending you back the manuscript.[1]

Please do not be angry that I took up so much of your time last evening—it was so tremendously lovely.

I was unable to tear myself away.

I am *hugely* envious of your impending little trip.

Heartfelt greetings from your
devoted
Alma

Shelfmark:E8-AJ-403
Note

[1] Alma copied the program of the Second Symphony into her diary.

514 *From Justine to Gustav*

[Vienna,] Monday [16 December 1901]

Dearest Gustav! Your letter of Sunday just arrived. I can really sympathise that you are anxious about the great difference in age, but believe me, men like you are not to be measured like others. It does not worry me at all. You will remain young in every respect longer than she will. You must remember that a woman becomes a mother, and these duties even everything out as long as she learns to understand you completely. Today I wrote her a few lines in response to her letter, which I enclose for you. I will tell you entirely honestly why I didn't go to Berlin—namely I had a little nervous condition again, heart trouble, and that made me so terribly depressed and worried that I didn't dare travel alone. Last night was the first night that I slept since you left.

If you are at the opera tomorrow when I arrive, leave instructions at the hotel where I should go, or if I should wait for you at the hotel—after all, Feuersnot isn't very long.[1] Lipiner is furious that I am going to Dresden; he finds it irresponsibly foolish. But I am accepting it as a birthday present from you.—I am curious how Alma will behave at the upcoming rehearsals for the Fourth—she is already really looking forward to them. Yesterday I had lots of presents and got wonderful flowers, but had such a bad day that I would have rather just taken a sleeping pill.[2] I was at Nana's in the evening. Arnold picked me up after Rheingold.[3] I am looking forward to Dresden tremendously.

Many heartfelt greetings and kisses from
your Justi

Shelfmark:E8-JM-402
Notes

[1] Strauss's second opera, *Feuersnot*, had its world premiere in Dresden on 21 November 1901. Mahler attended a performance on 17 December.

[2] Justine's birthday was 15 December.

[3] The previous evening.

515 *To Justine*

HÔTEL BELLEVUE, DRESDEN-A.

[Dresden, 17 December 1901]

Dearest Justi!
I couldn't meet you at the station because I had to go to Feuersnot, which was put on specially for me. I am very distracted and worried because of your letter today.

In any case, I am leaving you the ticket. If you like, come over to the theatre—it is beside the hotel. If you would rather have a rest, then stay in your room (the larger of the two) and I will come over directly after the opera. If you are going to stay in, send a servant over to the theatre to my box to tell me how you are.

Affectionately, G.

SHELFMARK:E18-MJ-642

516 *From Alma to Justine*

[Vienna, December 1901]

Dearest Justi!
Don't be angry if I address you so familiarly—but I always do just what I feel.

Your dear, dear letter made me very happy.

So much lies unspoken between us.

It was really and truly good to become closer, just like friends. The next time we see each other, many barriers will fall.

_____________ All of them! ______________

Very best wishes,
Alma

I almost went to you yesterday!

SHELFMARK:E8-AJ-404

517 *To Justine*

HÔTEL D'ANGLETERRE, ST. PETERSBURG

[St. Petersburg, c. 14 March 1902][1]

Dearest Justi!
We both arrived here very merry and have a charming little apartment, which will provide quite good accommodation for 2 weeks.—Unfortunately, in the course of the first night (which bestowed upon us only a train compartment where the heat couldn't be turned off) I was running up and down with a

migraine, and Alma was pretty tired since she didn't close her eyes either. So the first day of our married life passed quite dismally; to make up, the 2nd was all the more entertaining. Frank—who is a very fine fellow (his wife is a simpler, but apparently fine person, and 4 children like organ pipes)—is very attentive and very charmed by Alma; we had lunch with them yesterday.[2]—Naturally, as matters stand, my digestion was entirely interrupted; but as of this morning I can report that I am already in presentable shape again, without taking any medicine.

Unfortunately, with Alma it entirely failed, and although yesterday I gave her Singer powder [*Singerpulver*], it has not yet worked. I have to draw on all of my experience now.—This morning we were at the *Hermitage* and saw some superb Rembrandts.—Next time, dearest, you will certainly be here; I miss you very much and look forward to our Easter Sunday noon dinner.

Alma is as wonderful as ever.—Please, let us hear something about you, both of you, soon, and in detail.—By the way, Alma doesn't want to buy any fur, and in its place got a fine pineapple from me.—So I hope to bring back to Vienna at least 2500 [kronen], then.—Affectionate greetings and kisses, dearest Justi. I don't notice any difference at all between now and before! Isn't that remarkable? Hopefully, you feel this too. Best wishes to Arnold

from your old
Gustav

Please see to it right away that *Stritzko* and *Woëss* [*sic*] are sent wedding notices.[3]

SHELFMARK: E1-MJ-1

NOTES

[1] Gustav and Alma were married in the Karlskirche on 9 March; Justine and Arnold were married the following day in the Evangelische Kirche on the Dorotheergasse. Gustav and Alma must have left for St. Petersburg on the evening of 10 March or on the 11th, arriving in St. Petersburg around the 13th.

[2] Mahler's cousin Gustav Frank, with whom he had shared a room in Vienna; see letter 1.

[3] Josef Stritzko (1861–1908), director of Waldheim-Eberle & Co., publisher of Mahler's first four symphonies; Josef Venantius von Wöss (see note to letter 494).

518 *To Justine*

HÔTEL D'ANGLETERRE, ST. PETERSBURG

[St. Petersburg, 17 March 1902]

Dearest Justi!

Today your 2nd letter came, which pleased me very much. I can tell you the very nicest things about Alma. You will be happy with her, everything has taken root inside her so much. She always speaks very kindly and often of you and Arnold. When we are back, you will see that we have all only become richer.

Unfortunately, she is not very well. She suffers a lot from nausea,[1] and recently she has come down with a cough, which bothers her very much.

Today is the first concert.[2] The highest society will be there. Even at the dress rehearsal there was a grand duchess (Constantina), who addressed Alma and me warmly. The orchestra is behaving splendidly, is very good and willing, and gives me ovations at every opportunity. If the public tonight is as warm, there should be a lot more trips to Petersburg in the future.

We already have a lot of invitations. My health is splendid—marriage seems to suit me very well.—By the way, Alma has written you twice already. Please answer her directly sometime soon. I hoped to get a few lines from Arnold—and news about the performances. Hopefully he will overcome his laziness in writing [*Schreibfaulheit*] (here I am even lazier in writing than usual) and will let us hear something about him.—Yesterday I was at a reception where I had a long conversation with a Duke von Mecklenburg (a member of the imperial family); he has an amateur quartet himself, and is an avid musician. He spoke very enthusiastically about the Rosé Quartet (without knowing that Arnold is my brother-in-law) and declared that currently it is the best quartet in the world. He said that we ought already to have heard it frequently here, but something always seems to intervene. Everyone would be very interested to have Arnold here with his quartet sometime; perhaps I can arrange something for next year.—It is *not* cold here. We are getting along very nicely with our clothes.—Frank, with whom we are together daily (he spends every free moment with us), is behaving tremendously warmly and is certainly a splendid fellow. We have already eaten with him twice. His wife is homely, but very nice and good. He has 4 children, all very nice, and a little bit reminiscent of the Herrmann family.

I send greetings and kisses to you, dear Justi and Arnold, and remain

your faithful
Gustav

Shelfmark: E1-MJ-2
Notes

[1] In fact, Alma was pregnant. Their first daughter, Maria Anna, was born 3 November.

[2] The first of three concerts with the orchestra of the Mariinsky Theatre was on 17 March (Beethoven, Symphony No. 3; Mozart, Symphony No. 40; *Vorspiel und Liebestod aus "Tristan und Isolde"*).

519 *To Justine*

HÔTEL D'ANGLETERRE, ST. PETERSBURG

[St. Petersburg, 23 and 24 March 1902]

Dearest Justi!

Today is the 2nd concert.[1] It is a terrible struggle. Orchestra rehearsals daily at *9 o'clock*. At the same time, I have caught another terrible cold, with a cough (but without fever). Alma is very miserable. So you can imagine that we will be tremendously happy to be back in Vienna again. I will let you know our exact day of arrival. I am already really looking forward to it. By the way, from your letter to Alma today, I see that, to my disadvantage, I missed the last quartet. By your description, the Schönberg quartet [*sic*] would have interested me very much.[2]—Here I am so strained and tired that I can do absolutely nothing—also [I am] in such a bad mood because of the never-ending catarrh. So you really must not be surprised that I don't write very much. We decline almost all invitations. Frank is with us daily, and is the only person that one wants to see.

So! Now I have gotten up. Last night was the concert—and I had a migraine. Today I feel full of spirit [*candelaber*] once again. The success remains just as great, although I cannot judge it.—

Unfortunately, the return journey is very stupid. I can leave here only on Friday and arrive at the Vienna Nordbahnhof on *Sunday* around 3:30—so, so much for the celebratory dinner. Shall we postpone it until Monday? Of course, whatever you arrange is fine with me. Perhaps you'll both meet us at the station? Imagine, I am really bringing about 2800 fl. with me. We have been good, haven't we?—Today there is a breakfast for me at the Austrian ambassador's. Up to now, Alma has had to decline everything. Today I hope that she actually can come with me. Tonight we are having wiener schnitzel at Frank's. I can't stand the food here, just like I can't stand anything else. Imagine, Alma suffers *terribly* from constipation, while my digestion has been consistently marvellous. I am very curious what you will have to tell me about yours. At any rate, let's both walk together for an hour on Sunday. Alma is still in bed and sends her greetings to both of you ("a whole lot!," she just called). I think that she's also looking forward to coming back to Vienna.

Many greetings and kisses—say hello to dear Arnold for me, too.

Always your
Gustav

SHELFMARK: E3-MJ-3

NOTES

[1] Tchaikovsky, *Manfred* Symphony; Beethoven, *Egmont* Overture; Sauer, Piano Concerto No. 1 (Emil Sauer, piano); Wagner, *Eine Faust Ouverture*.

[2] On 18 March, the Rosé Quartet (assisted by Franz Jelinek, 2nd viola, and Franz Schmidt, 2nd violoncello) gave the world premiere of Schönberg's string sextet *Verklärte Nacht*. It has long been assumed that Mahler and Schönberg probably first met at a rehearsal of this work, but Mahler's reference to it as a "quartet" suggests that he was completely unfamiliar with the piece.

520 *To Justine*

Picture postcard[1]
[St. Petersburg, 27 March 1902 (Postmark: 14.III.1902)][2]
[Arrival postmark: Vienna, 29.3.02]

Dear Arnold!

We know that you are a collector of picture postcards. [Alma writes: (?)]. What do you think of this beauty? By all appearances, it seems to be the 18th century![3]—But even if not, she is charming, isn't she! And she herself is not able to keep me here! *I am leaving*! Thank God! Sunday afternoon we are in Vienna. Hopefully you've kept the evening free.

Best wishes to you and Justi.

Your Gustav

Since Gustav has already exhausted our joke, all there is left is for me to send you my best wishes. Your Alma.

This card was written under Alma's supervision, grown out of her droppings, so to speak!

SHELFMARK: E1-MArp10

NOTES

[1] Addressed to "Abcmpia [Austria] / Herrn Concertmeister Arnold Rosé / Wien / III. Metternichgasse 5."

[2] The postmark gives the date in the Julian calendar, still in use in Russia.

[3] The card depicts a woman in a *décolleté* dress and wig, in eighteenth-century French style.

521 *To Justine*

HÔTEL DISCH, COLOGNE

[Cologne, 3 June 1902]

Dearest Justi!

Had the first rehearsal today—1st movement, later 4th and 5th (thus haven't heard everything yet).[1] The effect is surprisingly magnificent. I have not had to make a single change and am very satisfied.—Alma is very weak and ill. I am very cheerful and my digestion is splendid.

Say hello to Arnold—we'll see each other in Crefeld, then.—*Certainly don't* miss coming.

Affectionately yours,
Gustav

SHELFMARK: E1-MJ-4

NOTE

[1] Initial rehearsals for the Crefeld premiere of the Third Symphony at the annual Tonkünstlerfest of the Allgemeine Deutsche Musikverein (9 June) took place in Cologne. (Mahler's letter to Strauss of May 1902 [*MSB*, pp. 83–85] gives the first rehearsal as 3 June.)

522 *To Emma and Eduard Rosé*

Postcard: Gruss aus Crefeld[1]

[Postmark: Crefeld, 10.6.02]
[Arrival postmark: Weimar, 11.6.02]

My dears! I announce the victory of my third offspring and congratulate you belatedly on the arrival of your second.[2]

[Justine:] Many greetings—letter from Vienna. Justi [different hand:] a[nd] Pepi.

[Alma, across top:] Best wishes—Alma

SHELFMARK:S2-MEp-768
NOTES
[1] Addressed to "Frau Concertmeister Rosé / Weimar / Kurthstrasse 14."
[2] Mahler is referring to the success of his Third Symphony the day before. Emma and Eduard's second son, Wolfgang (1902–1977), was born 10 April 1902.

523 *To Justine*

[Maiernigg, July 1902]

Dearest Justi!
That was really bad news! How these future world citizens [*Weltbürger*] do inconvenience one. Even before they see the light of the world, they forbid or order what they want.[1] How lucky, by the way, that you noticed in time! Let it be a warning to you then. Perhaps you could still come here in August with Arnold?

Albi and (perhaps Ernestine too?) will hopefully look after you and afford you a little company above all. Hopefully Arnold will be able to get away for a while, though, and *at least* go to his beloved Wörthersee where it always suits him so well! His old room is ready for him. We *quite certainly* expect him!

The enclosed review was sent to me. Otherwise nothing. It is beautiful here now—(very hot, which I do like a lot; Alma less) and I am very unhappy that you are not here too, and that we cannot go on our old, lovely walks together.—Alma cannot bear these either, and I go mostly alone.—

Why have you both spoiled the holidays, both of you? Ha! Let us hear something from you soon, above all, how you are feeling!

Affectionately yours
Gustav

SHELFMARK:E1-MJ-6
NOTE
[1] Justine was pregnant with her first child, Alfred, born 11 December 1902.

524 *To Justine*

[Maiernigg, July 1902]

Dearest Justi!
You can blame my work (I am up to my ears in it at the moment) for the fact that I haven't yet written and thanked you for your birthday greetings.[1]—All the more often I have thought of you and Arnold, and I assure you you are really missed here. It is too terrible that, poor thing, you have to give up everything this year in service to the future generation, about whose gratitude one

doesn't know anything yet.—I very much miss detailed news! How much longer will this house arrest last, then?

You will certainly have learned that Lipiner was here and, after a short stay in Klagenfurt, has left again without having a look at my house.—I visited him at the café and found him looking marvellous and very creative. One could just wish that he would get down to work sometime.

When is Arnold leaving? And where to? I *absolutely* expect him here in *Maiernigg* for a few days!

Hopefully you both will be here again next year, and we'll be together as was our wont. I am counting on it and with it!

Best wishes to both of you from

Your old
Gustav

Reviews and invitations to conduct my works are flowing from all sides.

It will probably start next winter.

Alma is reconciling herself well to our solitary life and is quite cheerful.

SHELFMARK:E1-MJ-5

NOTE

[1] That summer, Mahler completed his Fifth Symphony and composed "Liebst du um Schönheit," plus portions of the Sixth Symphony. (His birthday was 7 July.)

525 *To Arnold*

MAIERNIGG AM WÖRTHERSEE

[Maiernigg, Summer 1902]

Dear Arnold!

[ink:] We are having constantly beautiful weather here [pencil:]! (I can't write with this damned pen!) For heaven's sake, just come!—Don't let the rainy Viennese weather [*Patschwetter*] stop you.—It must be beautiful now in Schluderbach too! It really would be stupid to spend the holidays in Vienna, when a change of air would do you both so much good. So: leave Vienna anyway! Maybe this time it will suit Justi here so well that you will just stay here. Or if you need some mountain air first, then just go [to] Schluderbach for a while and then come back here!

Write in any case.

Affectionately,
your
Gustav

SHELFMARK:E1-MAr-11

526 *To Justine*

Correspondence card: Reifnitz am Wörthersee (photo)[1]
[Postmark: Klagenfurt, 22.8.02]
[Arrival postmark: Edlach, 23.(8.02)]

Dearest!
So, the 5th is here! Tomorrow and the next day, I will rest (by the way, I am *quite fresh* despite *continual* work). I will travel Monday night and will be with you early Tuesday. I am very much looking forward to it.

Affectionately, G.

SHELFMARK: E19-MJp-655
NOTE
[1] Addressed to "Frau Justine Rosé / Edlach / bei Payerbach a.d.S. / Edlacher Hof."

527 *To Arnold*

DER DIRECTOR DES K. K. HOF-OPERNTHEATERS

[Vienna, August 1902]

Dear Arnold!
Why don't you write a card? You do know how much I would like to know how your consultation struck you. Hopefully Justi is feeling better and better! The heat here is dreadful, we couldn't sleep all night. I am really glad that you are staying in Edlach for a while longer.—

Enclosed, a letter from G. Adler; I think that you really should thank him with a few lines.[1]

Best wishes to you both. Write me a postcard from time to time.

Affectionately, your
Gustav

SHELFMARK: E19-MAr-662
NOTES
[1] A letter from Justine to Guido Adler, dated 27 August, may have been prompted by Mahler's suggestion. She begins by thanking him for writing and indicates that she and Arnold had been in Edlach for 14 days (so, since about 13 August). Justine continues:

> Mind you, my husband had to take a 4-week rest leave: the many irritations of the summer took so much out of him that he now has to undergo a slight cold-water cure. Gustav was here for the day yesterday on his way to Vienna—with the completed Fifth, [and so] consequently in a very good mood. (Guido Adler Papers, MS 769, box 31, folder 12, Hargrett Library, University of Georgia)

528 *To Justine*

[Vienna, 1 January 1903]

Dearest Justi!

Since I may not get around to it again today to come over (I'm now working on the clean copy of my 5th and am up at the Hohenwarte for lunch),[1] I say *Happy New Year* to you and yours and hope that you and Alma will be able to spend this year merrily with us, instead of in bed.

In haste, affectionately
your Gustav

Say hello to Arnold a[nd] Emma

SHELFMARK: E1-MJ-8

NOTE

[1] His parents-in-law, Carl and Maria Moll, lived on the Hohe Warte.

529 *To Justine*

VICTORIA HOTEL & BADEHAUS / WIESBADEN

[Wiesbaden, 21 or 22 January 1903]

Dearest Justi!

As is my wont, I send you greetings from abroad, and a short, telegraphic note that I arrived in Frankfurt with a migraine and today I am terribly bored here in Wiesbaden.[1] The orchestra is quite presentable, but the public—as I see already today—is terrible, à la Marienbad. How did I get into this mess?[2]—

Now, however, I must give you a little piece of my mind. For some time I have seen that "something" has been bothering you—I don't know whether it is touchiness towards Alma, or towards me as well.—I think that I can sense the same thing from Arnold too—probably you stir each other up into such moods.

First, I tell you that it is *stupid*, and second, that it is *bad*! This sensitivity, I would think, you really could leave to those with a "Jewish nature"—and if there were actual, legitimate grounds, just keep in mind that everyone has his own load to bear, and that one must not make it more difficult for oneself, or for others! Really, etc.!

Finally, you surely have not forgotten that nothing has ever been as hateful to me as these personal grudges, and I don't want to assume that you are now indifferent to it, as to a certain degree it appears to me. I am not speaking here of Arnold at all. From him, I have always been accustomed to it—but in the end, he has always regained the right tone and set our relationship right. So—don't throw out the baby with the bathwater, and don't stir each other up!—

But I didn't write you *for that*. When I began, I really intended only to drop you a line. It only occurred to me right in the middle of it.

Best wishes to you both, and to Emma, if she is still there.

Affectionately, your old
Gustav

SHELFMARK: S1-MJ-754

Notes

[1] Mahler arrived in Wiesbaden on 21 January to conduct his Fourth Symphony at the Kurhaus on the 23d.

[2] According to Henry-Louis de La Grange, Mahler's words *Wer hat mich gebracht in diesem Land* are a paraphrase of a famous line from Molière's *Fourberies de Scapin*: *Mais qu'allait-il donc faire dans cette galère?* ("But how did he come to be on this prison galley?" i.e., how did he get himself into this mess?); HLGE II, p. 556, n. 89. (Mahler used it again in a letter to Alma of 10 September 1908.)

530 *To Justine*

HOTEL GEORGE / LWÓW

[Lwów, early April 1903][1]

Dearest Justi!

Many thanks for your dear lines![2] Why do you apologise first? I certainly would have been glad to see you, but everyone does have enough to do himself and really doesn't need to "show" first that he is deeply sympathetic to another.—It is going really well here with the orchestra—everything else is much of a muchness. Too bad that Arnold didn't come through here earlier! How is your little boy? Why don't you write whether he has already completely recovered from his last attack?—It really is funny that I now, like Arnold, always travel so miserably; this time I really had to endure my regular migraine again. Hopefully you—you and Alma—are together quite a lot? With best wishes

Your old
Gustav

Shelfmark: E18-MJ-634

Notes

[1] Mahler conducted two concerts, both of which included his First Symphony, in Lemberg (Lwów) on 2 and 4 April. He arrived on the morning of 31 March.

[2] Mahler enclosed a card from Justine in his letter to Alma of 1 April, and a letter from Justine in his letter to Alma of 3 April.

531 *To Justine*

HÔTEL DES TROIS ROIS À BÂLE

[Basel, 14 June 1903]

Dearest Justi!

The 3 rehearsals are over, then. Everything is excellently prepared, the chorus is *wonderful*—I am hoping for a satisfactory performance.[1]—The church is wonderfully atmospheric. Today we are going to look around the city a little bit for the first time. (Böcklin, Holbein etc.)[2] Up until now we have wandered around only a little. Kittel just arrived and sings "Urlicht" splendidly. I still don't know how the soprano is.[3] Too bad that you both are not here. Arnold would have had a much better impression than in Munich.[4] The orchestra is decidedly better and really pulls itself together, although they are still somewhat condescending. No one we know is here yet. Alma feels all right, but always has trouble with her stomach.

On 2 December my 3rd is being performed in Frankfurt under my direction.[5]—

Best wishes to you both. What does Arnold think about Goritz? Everyone is scolding him so strongly!

Your
Gustav

Alma, who is just getting dressed, sends her greetings.

SHELFMARK:E19-MJ-663
NOTES

[1] Mahler conducted his Second Symphony at the annual Tonkünstlerfest of the Allgemeine Deutsche Musikverein.

[2] Mahler obviously planned to visit the Museum an der Augustinergasse. He was by this time an admirer of Böcklin; see NBL, p. 182.

[3] Hermine Kittel (1879–1948). The soprano was Maria Knüpfer-Egli (1872–1924).

[4] In October 1900.

[5] The performance was given by the Opera orchestra and chorus with Clara Weber, contralto.

532 *To Justine*

Correspondence card: Klagenfurt: Villacherstrasse[1]
[Postmark: Klagenfurt, (30.6.03)]
[Arrival postmark: Kumpendorf, 1.7.03]

D.J! A[lma] has been on her back for 2 days—again her tiresome inflamed throat.[2] Because of that, we are under house arrest, and since I am familiar with your anxiety, I didn't come over alone as I first wanted to.—As soon as she is recovered again, Anton[3] will appear in a green apron as ambassador.

Affectionately, G.

SHELFMARK:E18-MJp-633
NOTES

[1] Addressed to "Frau Justine Rosé / derzeit / Krumpendorf / Villa Schöller."

[2] Mahler writes "angina," meaning pharyngitis (inflammation of throat), not the more familiar chest pains (angina pectoris).

[3] Servant in Maiernigg.

533 *To Arnold*

THE DIRECTOR OF THE I.R. COURT OPERA

[Postmark: Klagenfurt, 9.7.04][1]
[Arrival postmark: Goisern, 10.7.04]

Dear Arnold!
I only just learned (from Frau Theuer) that poor Alexander was released from his suffering.[2]—Unfortunately I know absolutely nothing more of the circum-

stances. I am living here quite alone, without coming into contact with the outer world (Alma and the children are still in Vienna). I will spare you empty platitudes of condolence—of course, one can just thank God that the suffering of a man, who certainly had no more use for the world, was shortened.—Could I perhaps do something to be helpful to you around Klagenfurt? Stand in for you somewhere? Please, just send the word. Say hello to Justi, and be yourself, dear Arnold, affectionately greeted by

your
Gustav

SHELFMARK: E8-MAr-390
NOTES
[1] Taken from the envelope, addressed "Herrn Concertmeister / Arnold Rosé aus Wien / derzeit in Goisern bei Ischl."
[2] Arnold's brother Alexander Rosé.

534 *To Emma*

[Cologne, 19 October 1904]

DOM HOTEL / KÖLN

Dear Emma!
You will certainly have already heard that Alma is not here. The doctor forbade her the trip.

Because of that, I will bring the two petticoats with me via Amsterdam, for which I am just about to leave. Last evening turned out quite well. The public was disconcerted at the beginning—but came along in the end.[1] Best wishes to you and Eduard

from your brother
Gustav

SOURCE: Transcription in the Bibliothèque Musicale Gustav Mahler
NOTE
[1] Mahler was in Cologne to conduct the world premiere of his Fifth Symphony with the Gürzenich Orchestra on 18 October. He then travelled to Amsterdam for three concerts with the Concertgebouw Orchestra, in which he conducted both his Second and Fourth symphonies.

535 *To Arnold*

Postcard[1]
[Postmark: Amsterdam, 24. Oct. 04]
[No delivery postmark]

Dear Arnold!
The 5th appears not to have found very much understanding.[2] To date, I haven't been able to obtain any reviews here, mind you—one can't find German newspapers here at all.—

Yesterday the 4th was played *twice* in a row in a *single concert.*[3] With *mounting* enthusiasm! Who would have thought it!

Best wishes to you both. Travelling is terribly tiring for me! I am in Vienna again on Saturday.

Your
Gustav

SHELFMARK:E11-MArp-481
NOTES

[1] Addressed to "Österreich / Herrn Concertmeister / Arnold Rosé / Wien / Hofoper."

[2] For a discussion of the failure of the Fifth with the critics, see HLGE II, pp. 29–32.

[3] The first Concertgebouw concert (23 October) was the Fourth Symphony, with Alida Oldenboom-Lutkemann (1869–1932), soprano. An intermission separated the two performances of the symphony.

536 *To Justine*

VAN EEGHENSTRAAT 107 / AMSTERDAM

[Postmark: Amsterdam, 27. Oct. 04][1]
[Arrival postmark: Vienna, 28.10.04]

Dearest Justi!
Since I received this review, translated by admirers here, twice, and since a statement about the reception of the 4th especially may interest you, I am sending you one of them.

Strange: the 4th was much more successful here than the 3rd, and by all appearances captured the public in one go.[2]—So here, too, you see—other countries, other customs.—

For today, only best wishes to you both—and I'll see you soon!

Your
Gustav

SHELFMARK:E6-MJ-293
NOTES

[1] Taken from the envelope, addressed to "Frau Concertmeister / Justine Rosé / in Wien / k.k. Hofoper." (The envelope is catalogued separately [E7-MD-345], but must belong to this letter.)

[2] Mahler conducted the Third Symphony in Amsterdam on 22 and 23 October 1903.

537 *To Justine and Arnold*

Postcard: Strassburg Münster, Plattform[1]
[Postmark: Strasbourg, 18.5.05][2]
[Arrival postmark: Vienna, 20.5.05]

Warmest wishes to you both.
Gustav
Alma

[another hand:] All best, Dr. Pollack.[3]

SHELFMARK:E12-AJp-511

NOTES

[1] Addressed (by Alma) to "Nieder-Oest. / Frau Justine Rosé / Wien IV. / Taubstummeng. 4."

[2] Mahler conducted the Fifth Symphony in Strasbourg on 21 May and a Beethoven concert on the 22d. (The concert on the 21st also included Strauss's *Sinfonia Domestica*.)

[3] Theobald Pollack (1855–1912), civil servant in the railway ministry and old family friend of Alma's.

538 *To Justine*

Picture postcard: Essen ["Musikhalle" handwritten by Alma][1]
[Postmark: Essen, 27.5.06][2]

[Alma:] Double isn't enough (especially with such an address)[3]
Anna[4]
[Mahler:] Greetings from Gustav
Carl[5] Soph.
Clemenceau[6]
Oskar Fried[7]

SHELFMARK:E12-AJp-512

NOTES

[1] Addressed "Wien / IV. Taubstummengasse 4 / Herrn und Frau / Arnold Rosé."

[2] The world premiere of the Sixth Symphony took place under Mahler's baton at the Tonkünstlerfest of the Allgemeiner Deutscher Musikverein in Essen on 27 May.

[3] Reference to *doppelt gemoppelt hält besser* ("do it twice to be on the safe side"), and apparently also to "IV . . . 4" in the Rosés' address.

[4] Anna Moll, Alma's mother.

[5] Carl Moll, Alma's stepfather.

[6] Sophie Clemenceau, née Szeps (1859–1937), was a Viennese friend of Mahler's. She was the daughter of journalist Moriz Szeps; her sister was Berta Zuckerkandl. She was married to Paul Clemenceau (1854–1944), the brother of politician Georges Clemenceau.

[7] Conductor Oskar Fried (1871–1941).

539 *To Arnold*

Correspondence card[1]
[Postmark: Klagenfurt, 14.8.06]
[Arrival postmark: Aussee in Steiermark, 15.8.06]

Dear Arnold!
In haste, I acknowledge receipt of your letter. Mind you, it is an unpleasant surprise. Hopefully you made sure that Prill is on the spot.[2]—Maybe it wasn't necessary at all. *Who* made the "ultimatum," then? Hopefully you both are well. I have been very industrious. What is Justi up to? Why didn't you mention it?

Best wishes to all,
your
Gustav

SHELFMARK:E12-MArp-508

NOTES

[1] Addressed "Herrn Conzertmeister / Arnold Rosé / Reitern Aussee / Steiermark."

[2] Paul Prill (1860–1930) had been one of Mahler's assistants in Hamburg before moving to Nuremberg. Nothing can be traced of this incident.

540 *From Alma to Justine*

Postcard: [ruins][1]
[Postmark: Rome, 23.3.07][2]
[No arrival postmark]

Dearest Justi. Heartfelt thanks for your dear card. Once again "[illegible]." We are having a lot of bad luck trying to get our luggage back. We may absolutely never travel again. Alma

[Mahler:] Affectionately, Gustav

[Alma, written across the top of the photograph:] All the best to Arnold.

SHELFMARK: E12-AJp-513

NOTES

[1] Addressed to "Vienna / Austria / IV. Taubstummeng. 4 / Frau Justi Rosé."

[2] Gustav and Alma were in Rome for two concerts with the Accademia di Santa Cecilia (25 March and 1 April; at the latter concert, the Adagietto from the Fifth was on the program). Although they arrived in Rome on 19 March, their luggage did not turn up until the end of the month.

541 *To Emma*

[Postmark: (Place illegible) 15.6.07][1]

Dear Emma!

Set your mind at ease! I will continue to send you the 50 fl. in the next months.[2] Also, without your letter I could only think that the sudden absence of the usual instalment would plunge you into too embarrassing a financial situation.—Just arrange for it in the long term.

How my circumstances will now turn out, I still can't see clearly yet.—All the same, however, I must reckon that, for the rest of my life, I can no longer count on a basic salary, and so must bring the essential order into my affairs through stringent economy.

Best wishes, and let yourself be heard from sometime—also, how your cure turned out.

Your
Gustav

SOURCE: Photocopy from the Internationale Gustav Mahler Gesellschaft, Wien (Mahler, E.11/122)

NOTES

[1] Addressed to "Frau Concertmeister / Emma Rosé aus Weimar / in Bayern / Bad Steben / Villa Anna."

[2] According to La Grange, Mahler had borrowed money from Justine and Emma's shares of their parents' estate to build the Maiernigg villa; see HLGE II, pp. 495–96 and n. 78, and HLGE III, p. 662, n. 158. (Oddly, Mahler often continued to use the old-currency name, florins (or gulden), instead of kronen.)

542 *To Justine*

Picture postcard: Drei Zinnen: Hütte bei Sexten[1]
[Postmark: Innichen, 13.8.07]
[No arrival postmark (Aussee)]

Very best greetings from here. Write me soon. Alma

Dearest Justi! I would really like to hear something of you. We are staying here until the end of August. Very best wishes. Jenny[2]

Affectionately, Gustav

(On *20.* Aug. I will be in Vienna)
[draws a picture of a labyrinth] *Direct and indirect greetings to Herr and Frau Rosé, respectively, from Pianola Perrin*

SHELFMARK:E12-AJp-514
NOTES
[1] Addressed to "Aussee / Steiermark / Reitern 22 / Frau Jus. Rosé."
[2] Jenny Perrin-Feld and her husband were visiting.

543 *To Justine*

HÔTEL D'ANGLETERRE, ST. PETERSBOURG

[St. Petersburg, 7 November 1907 (Postmark: 27.10.07)][1]
[Arrival postmark: Vienna 9.XI.07]

Dearest Justi!
It was very nice that you roused yourself to write. I have thought about you a lot too—and would have written as well, if I were not so incredibly strained and already so very busy corresponding with Alma.[2]—I don't think that we will leave Vienna permanently under any circumstances. Even if we left, I am convinced that we would perhaps be able to be together more often than now.—This is the sort of thing that always happens: no visitor comes to Vienna without visiting the museums once. And there are maybe a million Viennese who have never been there. I myself haven't seen them for decades—and here in Petersburg I've already been to the Hermitage twice.

I thought of Arnold in Helsingfors and marvelled at his digestion, since he praised the hotel there so much.—I couldn't bear the heavy, greasy food. The racket in the hotel was dreadful too. Otherwise, though, it is a beautiful city—in particular, the sea cuts such a beautiful line into it. In comparison, Petersburg pleases me extraordinarily, and I wouldn't have anything against living here, in the country. The Russians grasp the value of this, and English do all the more. In comparison, the Viennese really are *misera plebs* [miserable plebeians]—it is horrible to think of those blocks of rental apartments, the close smell of goulash in the streets, and the dreadful wind that always blows.—

By the way, the orchestra here is really splendid, and reminds me of the Viennese [one]—also in its playing pranks![3] But I have them firmly twisted around my little finger, and they would happily like to engage me for 2 of their own concerts. I seem to be valued more by them than by our dear *Viehharmoniker*.[4]

Next Tuesday I return to Vienna and hope to see you and Arnold soon—he will be back soon too, I suppose. I would like good *zakuska*,[5] however, since I am now very pernickety in such things.

Cheers until we meet again.
Your
Gustav

SHELFMARK: E6-MJ-294
NOTES

[1] Taken from the envelope, addressed to "Abcmpia [Austria] / Frau Concertmeister / Justine Rosé / Wien / IV. Taubstummengasse Nro. 4." The postmark gives the date in the Julian calendar, still in use in Russia.

[2] Mahler was away from Vienna between 19 October and 12 November conducting two concerts in St. Petersburg (26 October and 9 November) and one in Helsinki (1 November). The second St. Petersburg concert included his Fifth Symphony.

[3] As during his 1902 visit, the orchestra was that of the Mariinsky Theatre.

[4] See note 4 to letter 491, above.

[5] *Zakuska* are appetisers or little snacks, generally eaten with vodka.

544 *To Justine*

Picture postcard: Paris: La Gare de l'Est[1]

[Postmark: Paris, 12.12.07]
[No arrival postmark]

[Mahler:] Today we board ship.[2] Offer rosaries and the like! Best wishes to you both. Your

Gustav

[Alma:] Cheers, old friends—you'll get a long letter from me from ship. Best wishes to Arnold and you. Alma

What do you think of the fact that my coat inspired the hack at the N. Fr. Presse to coin a phrase!!!

SHELFMARK: E12-AJp-515
NOTES

[1] Addressed to "Madame / Justine Rosé / Vienne / IV. Taubstummengasse 4."

[2] For New York, where Mahler had been engaged by the Metropolitan Opera.

Undated Letters from Vienna

545 *To Justine*

[Between 1902 and 1904][1]

Dearest Justi!
On behalf of Alma, who, for a change, feels sick again just now, I'm letting you know that we expect you tonight. Alma says "we want to provide milk too."

So, it is wise that you are coming.

See you soon!

Your
G.

At *8*?

SHELFMARK: E1-MJ-7
NOTE
[1] Probably written during one of Alma's pregnancies (Maria Anna was born 3 November 1902, and Anna Justine was born 15 June 1904).

546 *To Justine*

THE DIRECTOR OF THE I.R. COURT OPERA

[Maiernigg, summer between 1903 and 1906][1]

Dearest Justi!
The news you gave me about all of you was very welcome. Your pouring rain must be very unpleasant—but my usual country rain isn't pleasant either. And for somebody who relies on hiking all by himself to have to stay close to his room and entertain himself must almost be considered a catastrophe. But the main thing, after all, is that one comes face to face with oneself, which humans often don't experience in a lifetime. Every year a person should be retired to an Alpine pasture for 14 days (naturally with a dairymaid à la Elise), *then* he would surely give peace and receive peace. Too bad that the Tauern rail line is still not finished—I would have come over for a few days. My only excitement is Anton, who, while we are rowing, told me all the calamities that have occurred in Carinthia during the course of the last year. Don't be put off by this, and send me a little card from time to time (without waiting for an answer)—above all, about how you all are. The little lad is well, though, despite the rain?

Affectionate greetings to both of you
Your
Gustav

SHELFMARK: E18-MJ-635
NOTE
[1] As Mahler only mentions Alfred Rosé, the card was likely written before the birth of Alma Rosé, 3 November 1906. (Mahler mentions the Tauern line as being open in July 1909; see letter 562.)

547 *To Emma*

Visiting card: Kapellmeister Gustav Mahler

Dear Emma! Come to the Opera around 8:30 (perhaps with Albi) and wait for me in the *Arcades* as usual.

Best, Gustav

Source: Transcription in Bibliothèque Musicale Gustav Mahler

548 *To Justine*

Dearest Justi!
Don't be angry, dear people—tomorrow at *9 o'clock* I have to rehearse and probe (probably Arnold), and so that is why [I'm off] to bed at 10:30, probably—that is why we will postpone the house ball [*thé dansant*] until Arnold can [be there], and that is why we expect you, straw widow, here alone tomorrow night.

Affectionately,
your
Gustav

Shelfmark: E1-MJ-9

549 *To Justine*

Dearest Justi!
Alma invites you and Arnold to eat with us tomorrow at noon. Mama and Gretl will be there too.[1]—She thanks you very much—I don't know what for, she murmurs it from the half sleep into which she has just fallen.

Affectionately
G.

By the way, I am coming over in around a half hour.

Shelfmark: E19-MJ-661
Note

[1] Alma's half sister, Margarethe (Grete or Gretl) Legler-Schindler (1880–1942). Her mental problems emerged with a suicide attempt in 1911 and, from then on, she spent the rest of her life (with one brief period as an exception) in mental institutions in Germany and Austria. Her death was as a result of the Nazi euthanasia policy for mentally ill patients. (I am grateful to Dr. Janet Wasserman, New York City, for this information.)

550 *To Justine*

THE DIRECTOR OF THE I.R. COURT OPERA

Dearest Justi!
It is such a bother to drag the money around with me. I would rather send it right to you.—Here is Alma's reckoning.

Remainder for you	720 Kronen
for Emma	
for 2 Months	280 "
Total	1000 Kronen

Is that right?

Please telephone me at the Hohe Warte that you have received the money all right.[1]

Affectionately yours,
Gustav

SHELFMARK:E6-MJ-300

NOTE

[1] La Grange suggests that this card must have been written in 1907 or later, as Mahler was staying at the Hohe Warte; see HLGE III, p. 662, n.158. As it was written on Hofoper stationery, it is doubtful that it was written after 1907. See above, letter 542. According to BGA, p. 414, Gustav and Alma did not give up the Auenbruggerstrasse apartment until the fall of 1909.

551 *To Justine*

THE DIRECTOR OF THE I.R. COURT OPERA

Dearest Justi!

I was supposed to bring the enclosed letter over to you this afternoon.

Owing to an unforeseen event, I am prevented from coming over; since I don't know what is in the letter, I would rather send it. I hope to see you tomorrow and satisfy myself of the results of your number one son's [*Deinem Herrn Sohn*] education. Anna just went into great raptures about him.

Best wishes to you and Emma.

Your
G.

SHELFMARK:E18-MJ-636

552 *To Arnold*

THE DIRECTOR OF THE I.R. COURT OPERA

Dear Arnold!

I just found the enclosed part with fingerings. Are these *yours*?

More precisely, should I leave them? It is to be printed accordingly.

How are you?

Affectionately,
G.

[pencil:] The servant will take your answer with him right away.

SHELFMARK:E8-MAr-391

553 *To Justine*

Friday, please

5:30

Your G.

Please send me the score of the 7th. I need it.[1]

G.

SHELFMARK:E18-MF-637

NOTE

[1] It seems likely that Mahler is referring to his own Seventh Symphony, composed 1904–1905 and first performed in Prague, 19 September 1908.

The Last Years
New York, Toblach, Vienna

Chronology

1907 *12 December*: GM and Alma depart for New York.
1908 *1 January*: GM's debut at the Metropolitan Opera (*Tristan*).
2 May: GM and Alma arrive back in Europe.
Summer: Toblach; GM composes *Das Lied von der Erde*.
19 September: premiere of Seventh Symphony in Prague.
11 November: GM and Alma depart for New York.
1909 *19–30 April*: GM and Alma in Paris; GM sculpted by Rodin.
Summer: Toblach; GM composes Ninth Symphony.
26 September–7 October: fourth trip to Holland.
13 October: departure for New York.
Fall: GM conductor of the New York Philharmonic.
1910 *11 April*: GM and Alma arrive back in Europe.
Summer: Toblach; GM begins Tenth Symphony.
June–July: Alma goes for cure at Tobelbad and begins an affair with Walter Gropius.
End July–August: Alma back in Toblach; visit of Gropius and marital crisis.
25–28 August: GM travels to Leiden to consult Sigmund Freud (*26 August*).
12 September: premiere of Eighth Symphony in Munich.
18 October: GM and Alma depart for New York.
1911 *21 February*: GM conducts for the last time.
24 February: GM falls ill.
8 April: GM and Alma depart for Europe.
16 April: GM and Alma arrive in Paris.
11–12 May: GM and Alma travel to Vienna.
18 May: GM dies in Vienna.
22 May: GM buried in Grinzing.

Posthumous Events

1911 *20 November*: Bruno Walter conducts premiere of *Das Lied von der Erde* in Munich.

1912	*26 June*: Bruno Walter conducts premiere of Ninth Symphony in Vienna.
1924	*12 October*: Franz Schalk conducts premiere of two movements of the Tenth Symphony in Vienna.
1931	*14 April*: Alois Mahler dies in Chicago.
1933	*15 May*: Emma Rosé dies in Weimar.
1938	*22 August*: Justine Rosé dies in Vienna.
1964	*11 December*: Alma Mahler-Werfel dies in New York.
1975	*7 May*: Alfred Rosé dies in London, Ontario, Canada.
1999	*3 May*: Maria Rosé dies in London, Ontario, Canada.

Letters

554 *To Justine and Arnold*

HOTEL MAJESTIC / NEW YORK

[New York, mid-February 1908][1]

Dearest Justi and Arnold!

You know my old habit of entrusting "external" affairs to the Ministry [for External Affairs], and here especially, where I am surrendering myself to laziness and gluttony, I never get around to anything at all. Also the feeling that when the addressee gets the letter in hand nothing in it is true anymore, paralyses all desire to write. So, e.g., when you get this letter, in the meantime I will have had a real scribbling fever and the postman will bring you 25 letters from me and then you will think that I have cracked up.

I have nothing essential to report. Life goes along monotonously as never before. I endeavour to earn my salary with the least amount of work possible, and have been counting the days until I can board ship.[2] But the country is incredibly interesting, and will provide lots to talk about.

I have no news from Vienna about the Opera. I counted on you for it. But—you both seem to have left everything to the Ministry for External Affairs too. The Neue Freie Presse appears irregularly and incomplete—the most interesting issues apparently remain lying in some ship's hold.

That you both are well I have learned from Mama, who is the only diligent correspondent among all of us.

Best wishes to both of you from your
old
Gustav

and send off a really gossipy letter sometime. Best wishes to Albi too. I received the Vischer book—thank her most kindly for me.[3]

Shelfmark: E20-MJ-664

Notes

[1] Justine has written across the top "25. Feber 1908," likely the date when the letter was received.

[2] Gustav and Alma left New York on 23 April on the *Kaiserin Auguste Viktoria*, arriving at Cuxhaven on 2 May.

[3] A book by Friedrich Vischer (*Auch Einer!*) is also mentioned earlier, in letter 347.

555 *To Justine*

[Postmark: Toblach, 17.6.08][1]
[No arrival postmark]

Please, dearest Justi, go to my apartment and get my *snow boots* from the middle (smaller) chest in my bedroom and send them to me as soon as possible—I am freezing like a badger (for I believe that they freeze—it could be another animal too.) Hopefully I'll see you soon. In haste.

Your
Gustav

Shelfmark: E20-MJ-667

Note

[1] Taken from envelope, addressed to "Frau Justine Rosé / in / Wien / IV. Taubstummengasse / Nro. 4."

556 *To Arnold*

[Toblach, end August or early September 1908]

Dear Arnold
I am passing through Vienna on the *5th* (Saturday) (en route to Prague) and will expect you, if you are free, at midday, 1 o'clock on the first floor of the Hotel Meissl und Schade[n].[1]

Affectionately, your
Gustav

Shelfmark: E11-MAr-482

Note

[1] Mahler was en route to the Prague premiere of the Seventh Symphony, 19 September 1908. He left Toblach on Friday evening, 4 September, and was in Vienna on Saturday the 5th (where he did meet Rosé; see BGA 252).

557 *To Justine*

HOTEL ESPLANADE—HAMBURG, AM DAMMTHOR BAHNHOF

[Postmark: Hamburg, 9.11.08][1]
[Arrival postmark: Vienna, 10.XI.08]

Dearest Justi!
In haste, only so that you won't think any foolish thoughts, I thank you for what you sent and declare most solemnly and –ly [*sic*] that it really never would enter my head to be angry with you. So: let's forget it and be the same old [friends] (unfortunately soon also in the true sense of the word!). But I really was amazed when I opened the package—I cannot conceal it.—It is not the Rübezahl at all, but something *quite* different—namely, from the Argonauten and purely lyrical! Did you give it to Roller, then? He did speak of Rübezahl! I remember this book very well too—it is smaller. So, where is it then? I don't understand![2]

For today, only warmest greetings to you and Arnold from you[r] very rushed

Gustav

I am off right now to Frau Markus's [*sic*] for dinner.

SHELFMARK: E20-MJ-665
NOTES
[1] Taken from envelope, addressed to "Frau Concertmeister / Justine Rosé / in Wien / IV. Taubstummengasse 4." Verso: "Absender / Mahler."
[2] See BGA 265. Alma Mahler's version of the incident makes it sound more serious than Gustav does in this letter; see her *Gustav Mahler: Memories and Letters*, ed. Donald Mitchell and Knud Martner, trans. Basil Creighton, 4th ed. (London: Cardinal, 1990), pp. 143–44. Although she claimed that Mahler tossed the manuscript overboard on the way to New York, the *Rübezahl* libretto remained in her possession (and is now in the Yale University Library). This was likely the fate of the *Argonauten* libretto (1879–1880), however, as it does not survive.

558 *To Justine and Arnold*

Postcard: "An Bord der 'America'"[1]
[Postmark: Deutsch-Amerik. Seepost, Hamburg–New York, 13.11.08]
[No arrival postmark]

[Mahler:] How do you like this?—where we have just tramped around.
Affectionately Gustav
[Alma:] 1000 greetings to you both. Alma.
Write us *right* way and lots. Cheers.

SHELFMARK: E12-AJp-516
NOTE
[1] Addressed to "Wien–Oe / IV. Taubstummeng. 4 / Arnold & Justine Rosé."

559 *To Alfred Rosé*

Picture postcard: Greater New York: Flatiron Building[1]
[Postmark: New York, Dec 22 1908]
[No arrival postmark]

Many greetings and kisses from Aunt Alma.
[Anna:] Guki
[Gustav:] Uncle Gustav
[Miss Turner:][2] Guckie
[Miss Turner:] Miss Turner

SHELFMARK: E8-MAAl-405
NOTES
[1] Addressed to "Mr. Alfi Rosé / Vienna Austria / IV. Taubstummeng. 4."
[2] Anna's governess.

560 *To Justine from Alma*

[New York, Spring 1909][1]

Dearest Justl
How I now understand your infamous laziness in writing. I almost have to force myself to take a pen in hand. Above all—to know—that it takes *so* long until you have it—oh—it is *too* boring. I am sending you a few reviews *only* because I promised. Basically, it really doesn't matter what these idiotic people write.

Gustav is at the Opera right now—he conducts very little and also doesn't trouble himself very much with rehearsals.—The 3 concerts were wonderful. The ones for next year are not absolutely certain yet.—A lot of work has been done for them, but Gustav will only do it if they fulfil all his wishes. Justl, don't be annoyed!—My head is spinning. I *can't* write.—

Once more, hugs. Alma

[Gustav, written across top of page]: Very best wishes (with this terrible pen!) A month has slid by! This time Weingartner is doing nothing for my amusement either.[2] We are slowly starting to get ready for the return trip—I just bought Almschi a suitcase and 2 travelling bags (incredibly cheap and practical).[3] I'll write once more before then. A thousand greetings. Send off a really gossipy letter sometime. Gustav

SHELFMARK: E3-AJ-148
NOTES
[1] From the contents, it appears that this letter must date from Mahler's second season in New York. (After the 1908–1909 season, Mahler conducted only once more at the Metropolitan Opera: four performances of Tchaikovsky's *Queen of Spades* in March 1910.)

[2] Mahler may be referring to the twin scandals that marked the beginning of Weingartner's tenure at the Hofoper during the first half of 1908: his dismantling of the famous Mahler/Roller *Fidelio* and his restoration of the traditional cuts in *Die Walküre*. For further details, see HLG III, pp. 263–64, 329–31.

[3] They left for Europe on the *Kaiser Wilhelm II* on 9 April, arriving in Cherbourg on the 18th.

561 *From Alma to Justine*

[Paris,] 28 April [1909]

Dearest Justi!
I have just received your letter and will simply tell you right away that it is also *my deepest* wish that we all be on the *very best* of terms when we arrive home—for that reason I wrote the letter—to clear out all of the obstacles lying in *my* way.—Think of Berlin, and you will know what I meant—or perhaps you don't remember anymore and have forgotten.—But, let us speak no more of it—I have written *my* anger out of my soul. I admit that this was handled very egotistically by me, but in my friendships I cannot go around roadblocks—I must clear them away!—Sunday night we are in Vienna!—

Every day I am with him at Rodin's—for *me*, that is the most important thing about this Paris trip!![1]—Admittedly, Gustav is not used to it *at all*—standing still 1 1/4–1/2 hours daily. It is tiring him *a lot*. If only it *turns out really well*.

Cheers, and best wishes to you both.

Alma

[from Gustav, written across the top of the letter:] Until we see each other soon, dearest Justi and Arnold. "Standing" in Paris is terribly tiring. Best wishes. Your Gustav.

Shelfmark: E3-AJ-147
Note

[1] Carl Moll had arranged for Auguste Rodin (1840–1917) to sculpt a bust of Mahler. At this initial meeting, Rodin made seven different models, and Moll went to Paris in November to choose which one was to be cast in bronze. In fact, two different versions were made; see HLG III, pp. 1047–49. Justine and Arnold's bust is now part of the Mahler-Rosé Collection. On the Rodin busts, see Danièle Gutmann, "Die Mahler-Büsten von Auguste Rodin," *Nachrichten zur Mahler-Forschung* 8 (1981): 4–9.

562 *To Arnold and Justine*

[Toblach, June 1909][1]

My dear Arnold!
With warmest thanks I got what you sent. Please, let me know when you have to have it back, or possibly if it's enough that I bring it with me to Vienna this fall.

It is really wonderful here and this year you ought not to miss visiting us. The Tauern rail line will already be open in July, so it is really not difficult for you. Just don't neglect to carefully arrange your visit with Alma so that, in the end, you don't find the house full if you come unexpectedly.

Dearest Justi, since at our departure you dropped a few hints about correspondence, you could send off a few lines to me sometime too, in which you describe a little bit about your (inner and outer) lives.—Especially right now, since I am absolutely alone and more receptive to news than usual, it would do me good.[2]—For years, I have shaken the habit of corresponding completely, since I have always had a correspondent in the house. First you, dear Justi, and now Alma looks after this. One really gets used to it and dictates letters in one's mind. This is the main reason that you rarely get anything written from me. So: let's all better ourselves. For today, best wishes from your

Gustav.

SHELFMARK: S1-MAr-762
NOTES
[1] Dated across top by Justine "Juni 1909."
[2] Alma was at a cure in Levico between 9 June and mid-July.

563 *To Justine*

NAAMLOOZE VENNOOTSCHAP
"HET CONCERTGEBOUW"—AMSTERDAM

[Postmark: Amsterdam, 6.10.09][1]
[Arrival postmark: Vienna, 8.10.09]

Dearest Justi!
Warmest thanks for your letter (which I will destroy right away).—Hopefully you have gained the feeling that I have not changed (not at all) in my attitude to you. On the contrary, you have become accustomed to regarding me, wandering restlessly—as always—over the waves of life, as a fighter against the winds and the waves, who mostly has to use all the power of his spirit and his body to keep his head above water.—To be sure, it is a different matter whether one now also sits in the boat and shares the dangers too, along with the trip, storms, and sunshine, or whether one looks on from afar on the shore and sometimes loses sight of the boat and the sailor.—Hopefully there will yet be a time for me someday when I can come into the harbour and begin to live and breathe, and when we will all be on better terms with each other. And above all when we can send the stupid misunderstandings, lack of understanding, and the whole mess of sensitivity and jealousy packing. It really doesn't make sense to spoil the few minutes that one spends tearing by on this little star with the "cussedness of things"; the cussedness of the object already absorbs enough room, light, and air. Here, I am tiring myself out now again—to what end, I don't know myself.

If I land again sometime, I also intend not to worry any more about my compositions, but mostly to make more and play them for myself one day. One must have some enjoyment.—The news about Epstein is very important![2] *How unfortunate* that your source was so unpardonably foolish and superficial.—Poor Epstein might have been able to have a pleasant, carefree summer. Who knows how many more he has left! If only people weren't so *oblivious*!

Just write me a lot in New York, and if you don't get any reply, just think about the wind and the waves.

If necessary use the address:

New York
Carnegie Hall
Philharmonic Society

I will gladly send Emma a picture postcard.

About Paris, up to today I still haven't had any news from Arnold—that is why I am going to the Bellevue again this time.

Really best wishes to both of you from me. Say hello to Albi too.

Your old
Gustav

SHELFMARK: E20-MJ-666

NOTES

[1] Taken from envelope, addressed to "Frau Concertmeister / Justine Rosé / in Wien / Favoritenstrasse 20." Mahler was in Holland to conduct three performances of the Seventh Symphony with the Concertgebouw, one in Den Haag (2 October) and two in Amsterdam (3 and 7 October). Gustav then met Alma and Anna in Paris on 8 October. On the 13th, they departed for New York from Cherbourg on board the *Kaiser Wilhelm II*.

[2] Julius Epstein (1832–1926), pianist and Mahler's former teacher at the Conservatory.

564 *To Justine*

Picture postcard: La Transatlantique allemande
"Kaiser Wilhelm II" de la Nord Lloyd[1]
[On board, 17 October 1909]
[Postmark: Deutsch-Amerikanische Seepost,
Bremen–New York, 19.10.1909]
[No arrival postmark]

[Alma, above the photograph:] *Sunday*

[Alma:] Dearest Justi! Since you didn't telegraph us in Cherbourg this time, it has gone badly for us. There was a big storm and we all were sick. Today, fog! Cheers—Alma

[Gustav:] Greetings. Yuck! Gustav

SHELFMARK: E12-AJp-517

NOTE

[1] Addressed to "Mrs. Arnold Rosé / Vienna–Austria / IV. Favoritenstr. 20." The card was postmarked the day of their arrival in New York.

565 *To Justine and Arnold*

Telegram[1]

Toblach, 28 July [1908 or 1909][2]

do you both, arnold & justi want to come here for a few days now we are all alone and all four would get a lot out of it affectionately gustav and alma

SHELFMARK: E3-AJt-149

NOTES

[1] Addressed to "herrn u frau rose / reitern 22 aussee."

[2] Owing to the events of the summer of 1910, this telegram is unlikely to be from then.

566 *To Justine*

[Postmark: New York, Mar 18 / 1910][1]
[Arrival postmark illegible]

Dearest Justi!
It is entirely out of the question that anybody could object if you came to Paris.[2] Rest assured that any intrigues against it are out of the question. You must be aware that, personally, I would be very happy to see you 2 weeks earlier. It is also obvious that I will be very tied down and busy during this time. So it really just depends on you being reasonable about whatever might happen, and not insensitive. I *must* [be spared] conflict or sensitivity, which really rob me of light and air.

I felt remarkably well this year and myself am surprised at how well I overcome all strains.—I am decidedly more able to work, and happier, than I've been in 10 years.—

Whether there's any chance of my 2nd taking place in Paris, I can only say when I get there; the particular difficulties in performing this work are too diverse and unique. And less than entirely adequate performance I will not allow.—

I learned from Lallemand that this year Arnold had a tremendous success, despite the drought, and wins ground from year to year.[3]—I am already looking forward to Vienna enormously. Children, try to get along with each other, and keep the peace. This constant gossip is really too stupid.

In haste.

Affectionately,
your old (unfortunately)
Gustav

Shelfmark: E19-MJ-656
Notes

[1] Taken from envelope, addressed to "Austria / Frau Concertmeister / Arnold Rosé / IV. Favoritenstrasse 20."

[2] Mahler conducted the French premiere of the Second Symphony on 17 April at the Théâtre du Châtelet (Concerts Colonne).

[3] Guillaume, Baron de Lallemand du Marais (1860–1931), was part of Mahler's Paris circle, which included the Clemenceaus, Georges Picquart (1854–1914), and Paul Painlevé (1863–1933).

567 *To Justine*

[Postmark: Toblach, 15.7.10][1]
[No arrival postmark]

Dearest Justi!
Above all, I have to thank you for your present, which really couldn't have been better chosen.[2] Your fingers must have really flown. You already know that I'm becoming a more and more useless correspondent.—Especially right now, however, I have to become silent to the outside.[3] The various well-wishers who

have appeared over the last few days will have become conscious of this too. But after all, for a start, I have declared the summer to be my time.—One cannot find peace in the world, anyway, and "there's always something."—I arranged with Gutmann that Arnold is playing the concert in Munich.[4] Has he not said anything to him yet? I am counting on it very much and it will be very nice to work with each other again for a few days. I'll certainly see you there too. I don't know yet if Gucki will be sent to you now, or is coming here soon with Alma—the news from Tobelbad flows meagrely.[5]—In Tobelbad the fun didn't do the little one any good. You did hear that already, right?

Now, again warmest thanks, dearest Justi, and best wishes to both of you

from your
Gustav

I didn't get the letter from Ledetsch. I take notice of your report and will do something after Alma arrives.

Shelfmark: E20-MJ-668

Notes

[1] Addressed to "Frau Concertmeister / Justine Rosé / Steiermark Aussee / Reitern 22."

[2] Gustav's fiftieth birthday was 7 July.

[3] That summer, Mahler was working on the Tenth Symphony.

[4] Mahler hoped that Arnold Rosé could be the concertmaster for the world premiere of the Eighth Symphony on 12 September 1910 (repeated 13 September). Owing to a misunderstanding between the impresario Emil Gutmann (1877–c. 1920) and Mahler, Rosé did arrive for rehearsals only to discover that the orchestra knew nothing of his participation; he generously withdrew. (See GMB[2] 454; HLG III, pp. 789–90; and Alma Mahler, *Memories and Letters*, pp. 181–82.)

[5] Unsurprisingly, as Alma had started her affair with architect Walter Gropius (1883–1969) while they were both taking a cure at Tobelbad.

568 *From Alma to Justine*

Postcard[1]
[Postmark: Neuilly, 8.5.11]
[No arrival postmark]
Monday

Pulse[2]	120
Temp.	37.3
Appearance	good
Appetite	good—? satisfactory
Mood	better
Night	bad—fever
Sleep	no sleep
	Medicine—no effect[3]

Shelfmark: S3-AJp-779

NOTES

[1] Addressed to "Justine Rosé / Wien XIX. / Pyrkergasse 23."

[2] The italicised text is written in another hand, possibly that of Anna Moll. The rest is written by Alma in her characteristic purple ink.

[3] After landing in Cherbourg on 16 April, Mahler, quite ill, spent several days in Paris before being taken to a clinic in Neuilly on 21 April for treatment. Finally, on 11 May, Alma and Gustav left for Vienna, where he died in the Sanatorium Loew on 18 May 1911.

APPENDIX
Biographical Notes

Bauer-Lechner, Natalie (1858–1921), violinist and diarist. Although she first met Mahler at the Vienna Conservatory when he was a student and she an alumna, their close relationship began when she visited him in Budapest in the fall of 1890. From 1893 to 1901, she spent every summer but one with Mahler (but see letter 380) and faithfully recorded their conversations in a diary ("Mahleriana"). A good friend of Justine's as well, she appears frequently in the family letters. Much to her chagrin, her relationship with Mahler seems to have been solely platonic and ended with Mahler's engagement to Alma Schindler in 1901. Natalie's *Erinnerungen an Gustav Mahler* first appeared in 1923; an enlarged edition was published by her great-nephew in 1984, but portions still remain unpublished.

Behn, Hermann (1859–1927), friend of Mahler's from Hamburg. Behn studied law in Heidelberg, but was more drawn to music. He studied with Anton Bruckner in Vienna and Joseph Rheinberger in Munich, and composed songs and a piano sonata. His principal activity was as a transcriber and arranger of others' works. In this capacity, he arranged Mahler's Second Symphony for two pianos, four hands. Behn, with another Hamburg friend, Wilhelm Berkhan, paid the costs of printing his arrangement as well as the full score of the work; the two supporters also paid the costs of the Berlin premiere of the Second Symphony in December 1895.

Beniczky, Ferenc (Franz) von (1833–1905), *Intendant* of the Budapest Opera during most of Mahler's tenure there.

Bertha. *See* Löhr

Bezecny, Josef Freiherr von (1829–1904), *Generalintendant* of the Viennese theatres from 1 November 1885 to 14 February 1898.

Boër, Ludwig (1863–1942?), Viennese doctor and friend of Mahler's. In addition to being Mahler's personal physician, he frequently treated singers from the Hofoper (although he is not mentioned in official Hofoper personnel lists).

Bülow, Hans von (1830–1894), German conductor, pianist, and composer. While he had no time for Mahler's music, Bülow greatly respected him as a conductor.

Ernestine. *See* Löhr

Frank, Gustav (1859–1923), Mahler's cousin. He was the son of Marie Mahler's younger sister, Anna, and Ignaz Frank. An engraver, he lived in St. Petersburg between 1890 and 1911 and was a member of the Imperial Russian Academy of Arts.

Freund, Emil (1859–1928), Viennese lawyer. One of Mahler's closest friends since their childhood in Iglau, he looked after Mahler's legal affairs.

Fritz. *See* Löhr, Friedrich

Hoffmann-Matscheko, Nina (1844–1914), author, was married to the Viennese painter and stage designer Joseph Hoffmann (1831–1904). She was a particular friend of the Mahlers, many of whom lived with her at various times. In 1895, Otto Mahler committed suicide in her apartment in Vienna.

Jahn, Wilhelm (1835–1900), conductor and director of the Vienna Hofoper, 1881–1897.

Kössler, Hans (1853–1926), German composer and professor at the Budapest Conservatory.

Krzyzanowski, Heinrich (1855–1933), Austrian writer. A close friend of Mahler's in his youth, he studied German philology at the Universität Wien before moving to Starnberg, near Munich, in 1883. His brother was Rudolf Krzyzanowski.

Krzyzanowski, Rudolf (1859–1911), Austrian conductor. Like his brother, Heinrich, he was a close friend of Mahler's in his youth. In 1896 he and his wife, soprano Ida Doxat (1867–?), joined Mahler in Hamburg, where—according to Justine's letters to Ernestine Löhr—considerable tension arose between them. In 1898 he became conductor of the Weimar Hoftheater, serving 1898–1907. (NBL incorrectly gives his date of birth as 1862, but see Löhr's note 8 in GMB², p. 432.)

Liechtenstein, Rudolf Fürst von und zu (1838–1908), *Erster Obersthofmeister* of Kaiser Franz-Joseph, 1896–1908. As such, he was the *Oberster Hoftheater-Direktor*; in practice, he left most administrative duties to his assistant Montenuovo (q.v.).

Lipiner, Siegfried (1856–1911), Austrian writer and poet, librarian of the Austrian Reichsrat. He and Mahler became close friends during Mahler's early years in Vienna. Wagner and Nietzsche were impressed by his first volume of poetry, *Der entfesselte Prometheus* (1876). In 1887, he published the first volume of his translation of Polish poet Adam Mickiewicz, *Todtenfeier*, which may have had an influence on Mahler's eponymous symphonic poem (later, the first movement of the Second Symphony). Lipiner was first married to Nina Hoffmann, who later married Albert Spiegler (q.v.). His second wife was Spiegler's sister, Clementine.

Löhr,[1] Bertha (1867–1933), sister of Friedrich (born Löwi; name change 18 February 1895). She studied piano with Hans Rott and Mahler. Later owned a paper shop.

Löhr, Ernestine (1863–1942?), sister of Friedrich (born Löwi; name change 15 June 1892). She was a particularly close friend of Justine Mahler's. On 10 July 1942, she was deported to Theresienstadt.

Löhr, Friedrich "Fritz" (1859–1924), archaeologist and philologist (born Löwi; name change 26 January 1887). A close friend of Mahler's since their days at the Universität Wien, Löhr worked as a private teacher in Vienna, where his pupils included Otto and Emma Mahler. He became the secretary of the Vienna Archaeological Institute at its founding in 1898.

Löhr, Louise (1862–1938), painter (born Löwi; name change 18 February 1895). Sister of Friedrich.

Löhr, Ludovica "Uda" (1854–1936), née Czilchert. Married Friedrich in 1887.

Löhr, Margarethe "Gretel" (1878–1934), sister of Friedrich (born Löwi; name change 30 September 1901).

1. Information about the Löwi/Löwy/Löhr family, which is not readily available, is taken from Uwe Harten, ed., *Hans Rott (1858–1884): Biographie, Briefe, Aufzeichnungen und Dokumente aus dem Nachlaß von Maja Loehr (1888–1964)* (Vienna: Verlag der Österreichischen Akademie der Wissenschaften, 2000).

Löwi, Hermann "Papa Löwy" (1827–1913), father of Friedrich, Louise, Bertha, Ernestine, and Margarethe; also of another son, John Leo (1856–1883). Married to Anna Bunzl (1831–1885). Löwi was a tradesman and a businessman in Vienna. (Between 1887 and 1901, all of his surviving children changed their surnames to Löhr. Throughout the notes in this volume, "Löhr" is used for all of his children, regardless of the date of the letter. The text of the letters themselves has not been changed.)

Löwi/Löwy. *See* Löhr

Marcus, Adele (1854–1917), a widow living in Hamburg. She and her daughter Toni (1876–1942) were particularly close friends of the Mahlers. Her mother, Helene Hertz, is also mentioned in the letters.

Marschalk, Max (1863–1940), German composer, music critic, and publisher. First acquainted with Mahler after publishing a favourable review of the Second Symphony, Marschalk remained friends with him until his death.

Mihalovich, Ődőn (Edmund) von (1842–1929), Hungarian composer, educator, and head of the Academy of Music in Budapest, 1887–1919.

Mildenburg, Anna von (1872–1947), Austrian soprano. A student of Rosa Papier's in Vienna, she made her debut in Hamburg in 1895. Mahler admired her greatly, both artistically and personally, and began an affair that dominated his final years in Hamburg. Although he broke off the affair when he moved to Vienna, she followed Mahler in 1898 and remained with the Hofoper until 1916. She was particularly known for the great Wagner roles, Leonore (*Fidelio*), and Donna Anna (*Don Giovanni*). During her early years in Vienna, she had affairs with Hermann Behn (q.v.) and Siegfried Lipiner (q.v.). In 1909, she married the Austrian writer Hermann Bahr.

Montenuovo, Alfred Fürst (1854–1927), *Zweiter Obersthofmeister* of Kaiser Franz-Joseph during Mahler's tenure at the Hofoper. Although the *Erster Obersthofmeister* was officially responsible for the court theatres, he delegated day-to-day responsibility to Montenuovo. Montenuovo later succeeded Liechtenstein (q.v.) as *Erster Obersthofmeister*, 1909–1917.

Natalie. *See* Bauer-Lechner, Natalie

Neumann, Angelo (1838–1910), Austrian impresario. Initially a singer, Neumann became a well-known director and the first to stage the complete *Der Ring des Nibelungen* outside of Bayreuth. From 1885, director of the Deutsches Theatre in Prague.

Nikisch, Arthur (1855–1922), Austro-Hungarian conductor. He was principal conductor in Leipzig when Mahler arrived there in 1886, and later became Mahler's successor in Budapest. From 1895 until his death, he was conductor of the Leipzig Gewandhaus Orchestra and the Berlin Philharmonic.

Nina. *See* Hoffmann-Matscheko, Nina

Papa Löwi. *See* Löwi, Hermann

Papier, Rosa (1858–1932), Viennese soprano and well-known voice teacher; Anna von Mildenburg was her student. She was a strong supporter of Mahler, and, as her lover was Eduard Wlassack, the chancellery director [Kanzleidirektor] of the Hoftheater-Intendanz, she was not without influence at the Hofoper.

Pollini, Bernhard (1838–1897), director of the Hamburg Stadttheater from 1874 to 1897.

Quittner, Ludwig (1858–1922), husband of Leopoldine Mahler (1863–1889). In a letter to Ernestine Löhr of May 1895, Justine indicates that Quittner was about to remarry.

Rosé, Arnold (1863–1946), Austrian violinist. Long-time concertmaster of the Vienna Hofoper orchestra and the Vienna Philharmonic, Rosé founded his eponymous string quartet in 1883. In 1902, he married Mahler's sister Justine. Their children, Alfred (1902–1975) and Alma (1906–1944), also became musicians.

Sax, Hans Emmanuel (1858–1896), Viennese national economist. Close friend of Mahler's and Friedrich Löhr's (q.v.). In the late 1880s, he was stricken with terminal *Lungenkrankheit* (tuberculosis) and moved to Merano, where he married and enjoyed some years of relative happiness before his death.

Schlesinger, Bruno. *See* Walter, Bruno

Schuch, Ernst Edler von (1846–1914), Austrian conductor. From 1872, he was active in Dresden, where, in 1882, he became director of the Hofoper (later *Generalmusikdirektor*).

Seidl, Anton (1850–1898), Austrian conductor, active in Prague during Mahler's tenure there. After 1885, he was based in New York.

Singer, Zsigmond (Siegmund) (1850–1913), Budapest correspondent of the (Vienna) *Neue Freie Presse* and a close friend of Mahler's during the Budapest years. In 1905 he succeeded Miksa (Max) Falk as the editor of the *Pester Lloyd*.

Spiegler, Albert (1856–1940), Austrian doctor (by training) and research chemist. He was a close friend of Mahler's from the early Vienna years.

Spiegler, Clementine (1864–1926?), Albert's sister, later married to Siegfried Lipiner (q.v.).

Spiegler, Nina "Nanna" (1855–1937), née Hoffmann. First married to Siegfried Lipiner (q.v.); in August 1891 she married Albert Spiegler (q.v.).

Staegemann, Max (1843–1905), German actor and singer. From 1882, he was director of the Leipzig Neue Stadttheater.

Strauss, Richard (1864–1949), German composer and conductor. He and Mahler first met in 1887, and, although their relationship was often troubled by misunderstanding and jealousy on both sides, they remained strong supporters of each other's compositions.

Toni. *See* Marcus, Adele

Uda. *See* Löhr, Ludovica

Walter, Bruno (1876–1962), né Schlesinger, German pianist, composer, and conductor. Between 1894 and 1896, Walter was engaged at the Hamburg Stadttheater, first as chorus director, then as *Kapellmeister*. His relationship with Mahler was characterised by mutual admiration, friendship, and support (although they always addressed each other with *Sie*). In 1901 he joined Mahler at the Vienna Hofoper. After Mahler's death, Walter gave the first performances of *Das Lied von der Erde* and the Ninth Symphony. He published a book on Mahler in 1936 and an autobiography, *Thema und Variationen*, in 1947. From their first acquaintance in Hamburg until the end of his life, Walter remained close to Justine and Emma and their families (using the familiar *Du* in correspondence).

Weber, Karl von (1849–1897), Saxon army officer and grandson of composer Carl Maria von Weber. Mahler was friendly with him and his wife, Marion (1856–1931), in Leipzig (in fact, Mahler and Marion von Weber had an affair). Through Weber, Mahler obtained the sketches and drafts of Carl Maria von Weber's unfinished opera *Die drei Pintos*. Mahler's completion of the work, with Weber's revision of the libretto, was a huge success at its Leipzig premiere in January 1888.

Wlassack, Eduard (1841–1905), *Kanzleidirektor* of the *Generalintendanz* of the Vienna court theatres, 1881–1893 and 1895–1903. He was a strong supporter of Mahler and, with his lover Rosa Papier, was instrumental in bringing him to Vienna.

Zichy, Géza Graf von (1849–1924), Hungarian composer, pianist, and *Intendant* of the Budapest Opera, March 1891–1894.

Index